SOCIAL RESEARCH METHODS

 SOCIOLOGY IN
ACTION

To all instructors and students who put sociology into action.

Sara Miller McCune founded SAGE Publishing in 1965 to support the dissemination of usable knowledge and educate a global community. SAGE publishes more than 1,000 journals and over 600 new books each year, spanning a wide range of subject areas. Our growing selection of library products includes archives, data, case studies, and video. SAGE remains majority owned by our founder and after her lifetime will become owned by a charitable trust that secures the company's continued independence.

Los Angeles | London | New Delhi | Singapore | Washington DC | Melbourne

SOCIAL
RESEARCH
METHODS

→ SOCIOLOGY IN
ACTION

KRISTIN KENNEAVY
Ramapo College of New Jersey

CATHERINE E. HARNOIS
Wake Forest University

MAXINE P. ATKINSON
North Carolina State University

KATHLEEN ODELL KORGEN
William Paterson University

Los Angeles | London | New Delhi
Singapore | Washington DC | Melbourne

FOR INFORMATION

SAGE Publications, Inc.
2455 Teller Road
Thousand Oaks, California 91320
E-mail: order@sagepub.com

SAGE Publications Ltd.
1 Oliver's Yard
55 City Road
London, EC1Y 1SP
United Kingdom

SAGE Publications India Pvt. Ltd.
B 1/I 1 Mohan Cooperative Industrial Area
Mathura Road, New Delhi 110 044
India

SAGE Publications Asia-Pacific Pte. Ltd.
18 Cross Street #10-10/11/12
China Square Central
Singapore 048423

Printed in the United States of America

Library of Congress Control Number: 2021924013

ISBN (pbk) 978-1-5443-7393-5

ISBN (loose) 978-1-0718-7596-4

Acquisitions Editor: Jeff Lasser

Content Development Editor: Tara Slagle

Production Editor: Rebecca Lee

Copy Editor: Talia Greenberg

Typesetter: diacriTech

Cover Designer: Gail Buschman

Marketing Manager: Victoria Velasquez

This book is printed on acid-free paper.

22 23 24 25 26 10 9 8 7 6 5 4 3 2 1

BRIEF CONTENTS

DETAILED CONTENTS

LEARNING ACTIVITIES

PREFACE

Welcome to *Social Research Methods: Sociology in Action*. We are proud to be part of the *Sociology in Action* family of texts and hope that you will enjoy using this book as much as we enjoyed creating it. Having taught research methods classes ourselves, we understand how crucial it is for students not just to read the textbook, but to engage with the material in a hands-on and creative way so that they can expand their knowledge and develop their burgeoning skills. As we collaborated in creating this text, we felt confident that a book that included such opportunities would be well-received. Hands-on learning is especially important in a social research course, as there is no substitute for actually doing the tasks that build to a completed research project.

Social Research Methods: Sociology in Action includes the tools and techniques that will allow instructors to put together an active learning course that promotes student learning, retention, and engagement. Without the right tools, incorporating active learning into the curriculum can be onerous and time-consuming. This text eases the burden for instructors by incorporating numerous dynamic activities that allow students to more fully interact with and comprehend the material. Instructors in all course sizes, those teaching online and those teaching in-person, will be able to use and adapt these activities to fit the specifications of their classroom experiences. The exercises include creative, hands-on, data analytic, and community learning activities.

The contributors to this text are avid users of active learning techniques themselves, and their expertise shines through. Each chapter features social research content, discussion questions, active learning exercises, and real-world profiles of Sociologists in Action. These profiles showcase the varied types of research and career positions that sociologists pursue and help students to envision their own sociological journeys. Together, we have created a book that requires students to do sociology as they learn it and creates a bridge between the classroom and the larger social world.

Organization and Features

The clear organizational style of each chapter helps students follow the logic of the text and concentrate on the main ideas presented. Each chapter opens with focal learning questions, and each major section ends with review questions to remind students of the emphasis in the presented material. The chapters contain definitions of key concepts and approaches, descriptions of the broad and varied approaches sociologists take to their research, as well as copious examples. Chapters close with a conclusion, and end-of-chapter resources include a list of key terms and a summary that addresses the focal learning questions. The active learning activities and Consider This marginal questions throughout each chapter help create a student-centered class that engages student interest.

The book's rich pedagogy supports active learning and engagement throughout each chapter.

- Learning Questions start off every chapter, introducing students to the focus of the chapter and preparing them for the material it covers. These questions are tied to the learning objectives provided in the instructor resources. Each learning question addresses a main section of the chapter.

- Check Your Understanding questions appear at the end of every major section in a chapter, providing students with an opportunity to pause in their reading and ensure that they comprehend and retain what they've just read.

- Doing Sociology activities appear multiple times in each chapter. These active learning exercises enable students to apply the sociological concepts, and methods covered in the text. Each chapter contains a variety of exercises so that instructors can use them in class, online, or as assignments conducted outside of class.

- Consider This questions are designed to spark deep thinking as well as classroom discussions.

- Sociologists in Action boxes feature a student or professional "sociologist in action" doing public sociology related to the material covered in the chapter. This feature provides examples of how sociology can be used to make a positive impact on society.

- Key Terms appear in bold where they are substantially discussed for the first time and are compiled in a list with page numbers at the end of their respective chapters. Corresponding definitions can be found in the Glossary.

- Every chapter concludes with a Chapter Summary that restates the learning questions presented at the start of the chapter and provides answers to them. This provides an important way for students to refresh their understanding of the material and retain what they've learned.

In addition, as appropriate, chapters include information on careers that relate to the chapter content. This allows students to recognize, even during their first sociology course, the wide variety of career options a sociology degree provides.

ACKNOWLEDGMENTS

We would like to acknowledge the many people who worked with us on *Social Research Methods: Sociology in Action*. Our thanks, first and foremost, go to the contributors who wrote the chapters and helped us to create an active learning introductory sociology course in one text. Their exceptional ability to use active learning in the classroom has impressed and inspired us. We appreciate their willingness to share what they do so well and to collaborate with us on *Social Research Methods: Sociology in Action*.

We would also like to extend our gratitude to Maxine Atkinson and Kathleen Korgen, the editors of the original *Sociology in Action* text, and the editors for the series. Their commitment to and knowledge of engaged learning, and to the discipline of sociology, are at the core of this text. Our thanks also go to the wonderful people at SAGE for their tremendous work on this project. Acquisitions editor Jeff Lasser believed in the need for this text, brought us together, and is the chief reason why this book (and the entire *Sociology in Action* series) became a reality. Tara Slagle, our content development editor, provided her great expertise in helping us to shape this book, and supported us through its production (and through a pandemic). Rebecca Lee engineered the transformation of the manuscript into real book pages.

We are also deeply indebted to the following reviewers who offered their keen insights and suggestions:

Nizia Alam, University of Georgia

Chris F. Biga, University of Alabama at Birmingham

Deirdre Caputo-Levine, Idaho State University

Walter F. Carroll, Bridgewater State University

Courtney A. Crittenden, University of Tennessee at Chattanooga

Jillian Crocker, SUNY College at Old Westbury

Jessica Crowe, Southern Illinois University, Carbondale

Shannon N. Davis, George Mason University

Tyler Dupont, State University of New York at Oneonta

Vicky L. Elias, Texas A&M University–San Antonio

David Frantzreb, University of North Carolina at Charlotte

Bonnie E. French, Caldwell University

Scott E. George, Wilmington University

William Haller, Clemson University

Samuel D. Hakim The University of Alabama

Christine Hegel, Western Connecticut State University

Curtis Holland, SUNY College at Old Westbury

Manuela Jimenez, Arizona State University

Jeehoon Kim, Idaho State University

Frank P. Lambert. Middle Tennessee State University

Lynette Martin, Ohio State University

David B. Monaghan, Shippensburg University of Pennsylvania

Christine Monnier, College of DuPage

Etta F. Morgan, Jackson State University

Kendra Murphy, The University of Memphis

Madeleine Novich, Manhattan College

Boniface Noyongoyo, Marshall University

Jamie L Palmer, University of Nevada—Reno

Kate Parks, Loras College

Heather Parrott, Long Island University–Post

Arthur Redman, Chicago State University

Charles G. Ripley, Arizona State University

Anya Galli Robertson, University of Dayton

Vaughn Schmutz, University of North Carolina at Charlotte

Beth P Skott, University of Bridgeport

Daniel Stockemer, University of Ottawa

Jennifer A. Strangfeld, California State University, Stanislaus

Kimberly Tauches, Centenary University

Mark D. Thomas, Albany State University

Matthew Weinshenker, Fordham University

ABOUT THE AUTHORS

Kristin Kenneavy, PhD, is an associate professor of sociology and convenes the Civic and Community Leadership minor at Ramapo College of New Jersey. Her research interests center on bystander intervention to prevent interpersonal violence, gender, media, and young adults. She teaches courses such as social research, data analysis, public sociologies, crime & media, environmental sociology, and sociology of media and pop culture. She is the recipient of Ramapo College's Henry Bischoff Award for Excellence in Teaching.

Catherine E. Harnois is professor and chair of sociology at Wake Forest University. She is the author of two books: *Feminist Measures in Survey Research* (SAGE, 2013) and *Analyzing Inequalities: An Introduction to Race, Class, Gender & Sexuality Using the U.S. General Social Survey* (SAGE, 2018). Her research focuses on intersectionality, particularly as it relates to research methods, political consciousness, identity, and discrimination. Her work has appeared in the journals *Gender & Society, Ethnic and Racial Studies, Social Psychology Quarterly, Journal of Health and Social Behavior, Social Science & Medicine, Sociological Methods and Research,* and other scholarly outlets.

ABOUT THE SERIES EDITORS

Kathleen Odell Korgen, PhD, is a professor of sociology at William Paterson University in Wayne, New Jersey. Her primary areas of specialization are teaching sociology, racial identity, and race relations. She has received William Paterson University's awards for Excellence in Scholarship/Creative Expression and for Excellence in Teaching.

Maxine P. Atkinson, PhD, is a professor of sociology at North Carolina State University in Raleigh. Her primary area of specialization is the scholarship of teaching and learning. She has received the American Sociological Association's Distinguished Contributions to Teaching Award and the University of North Carolina Board of Governors' Award for Excellence in Teaching.

ABOUT THE CONTRIBUTORS

R. Saylor Breckenridge, PhD, is an associate professor of sociology at Wake Forest University. His areas of expertise include social statistics, research methodology, and organizational sociology. He has served as the director of both the Sociology Program and the Methodology, Measurement and Statistics Program at the National Science Foundation. His research has focused on organizational, labor, and cultural components of industries such as wine production, vinyl records, and Major League Baseball. He regularly teaches courses on social statistics and research methods, along with introductory sociology, business and society, and the organizational structures and social context of the movie industry.

Steve Gunkel is a full teaching professor in the Sociology Department at Wake Forest University. He earned his BA and MA in sociology at Washington State University and his PhD in sociology at Indiana University. He teaches courses in research methods, criminology, social statistics, white-collar crime, social problems, deviance, principles of sociology, corrections, and family Vvolence. He has served as the president of the North Carolina Sociological Association. His research has appeared in

Social Problems, Journal of Criminal Justice, Social Science Research, Sociological Spectrum, Great Plains Research, Sociology Compass, and *Sociation Today.*

Sara Haviland is a research scientist at Educational Testing Service in the Center for Education and Career Development, where she studies the social, policy, organizational, and individual factors that affect work and careers, with a focus on education and training. Prior to ETS she was a senior researcher at the Education & Employment Research Center at Rutgers University. She has experience in a variety of grant-funded research programs, including research evaluation. She holds a BA in social theory and ethics from Oglethorpe University, and an MA and PhD in sociology from the University of North Carolina at Chapel Hill.

Allyson L. Holbrook, PhD, is a professor of public administration and psychology at the University of Illinois at Chicago in Chicago, Illinois. Dr. Holbrook's research and teaching primarily focus on survey methods as well as understanding how public attitudes are developed, change, and affect behavior. She is a coeditor of *Public Opinion* Quarterly, an interdisciplinary journal that publishes empirical research focused on measuring and understanding public opinion.

Mellisa Holtzman, PhD, is a professor of sociology at Ball State University in Muncie, Indiana. Since joining the faculty in 2002, she has established herself as both a teacher and a scholar. Dr. Holtzman has won five university and regional teaching awards; secured several teaching and research fellowships, including a grant from the National Science Foundation; and used her pedagogical expertise to codesign a novel sexual assault protection program called *Elemental*. Her research on sexual violence prevention is published in numerous outlets, including *Journal of Interpersonal Violence, Journal of American College Health, Sociological Focus,* and *Sociological Inquiry.* Dr. Holtzman enjoys teaching at both the undergraduate and graduate level and currently offers classes in theory, family, law, introduction to sociology, and sociological thinking.

Anne Kristen Hunter works at the University of West Georgia library, where she is interested in social movements and the sociology of culture, and in making research methods accessible to audiences of nonexperts. She studied sociology as an undergraduate at Ohio State University and earned her masters at the University of North Carolina. She is currently pursuing a Masters of Library Science at the University of Alabama. She has previously worked at the Odum Institute for Research in Social Science at UNC, and as a sociology instructor at UWG.

Edward L. Kain is professor emeritus of sociology at Southwestern University in Georgetown, Texas. Throughout his career he regularly taught introductory sociology, demography, research methods, and family sociology. His publications include two books on families, a number of edited volumes on teaching, and dozens of articles and chapters on gender, family, and the scholarship of teaching and learning. Research in this last area includes work on patterns and change in the sociology curriculum and doing research with undergraduates. He has received a number of local, regional, and national awards, including the Distinguished Contributions to Teaching Award of the American Sociological Association.

Maura Kelly is an associate professor in the Sociology Department at Portland State University. Her areas of expertise include work, gender, sexualities, popular culture, and research methods. As a public sociologist, she researches inequalities in the construction trades and advocates to increase opportunities for women and people of color in the trades.

Heather A. McKay is the director of the Education and Employment Research Center at the School of Management and Labor Relations. In this capacity, she conducts research and evaluations on community college programs, state and federal workforce development systems, and education and workforce policies. She completed her bachelor's degree at Bryn Mawr College. She has a master's degree in history as well a master's degree in global affairs from Rutgers University. In addition, she is a PhD candidate in global affairs at Rutgers University.

Emily McKendry-Smith is an associate professor of sociology at the University of West Georgia, where she is cocoordinator of the interdisciplinary Asian Studies minor. She teaches courses on theory, religion, family, and research methods. Dr. McKendry-Smith uses ethnographic field methods to study new religious movements, focusing on the case of the Brahma Kumaris in Nepal. Her research examines the intersection of religious beliefs and other belief systems, such as ideas about modernity, notions of place, and national identity. She earned her undergraduate degree at Knox College and her PhD at the University of North Carolina.

Krista McQueeney is associate professor in the Department of Sociology, Criminology, and Anthropology at the University of Wisconsin–Whitewater. She received her PhD in sociology from the University of North Carolina at Chapel Hill. Her research focuses on mass media, intersectionality, and violence. In 2018, Dr. McQueeney coedited the volume *Girls, Aggression, and Intersectionality: Transforming the Discourse of Mean Girls in the United States* with Routledge Press. Her articles have appeared in *Social Problems, Journal of Contemporary Ethnography, Journal of Prison Education and Reentry*, and *Violence Against Women*, among other peer-reviewed venues. She is currently writing a book about white women's racial violence in the United States.

Kathleen C. Oberlin is a mixed methods researcher based in Chicago, and currently works at Facebook. She explores ways to improve users' experiences with technology and works with a multidisciplinary team of designers, engineers, and other researchers to bring new concepts to life. Formerly, she was assistant professor in the Department of Sociology at Grinnell College.

Heather Parrott received her PhD from the University of Georgia, where she also completed graduate certificates in nonprofit management and women's studies. She has worked at Long Island University for 12 years, teaching a variety of courses (research methods, statistics, gendered violence, poverty, and social problems) and helping community organizations with their data and research needs. Dr. Parrott recently left her tenured position at Long Island University to join a local nonprofit. She is the new director of Development and Education at VIBS, a Family Violence and Rape Crisis Center, where she uses her academic skills for data management, grant-writing, and community education.

Adam Saltsman is an assistant professor and director of the Urban Action Institute in the Department of Urban Studies at Worcester State University in Worcester, Massachusetts. His institute is focused on connecting students to community partners for social justice work in Worcester. A political sociologist, his research and teaching focus on the politics of belonging and urban exclusion among refugees and others who are on the move or displaced. In addition to focusing on these issues in the context of the United States, Dr. Saltsman has done research for many years in Southeast Asia. His book *Border Humanitarians: Insecurity and Order on the Thai–Burmese Frontier* is forthcoming with Syracuse University Press.

William J. Scarborough is an assistant professor of sociology at the University of North Texas. His research examines the cultural and economic determinants of gender and race inequality across the United States. His work has been covered widely in media outlets such as the *Washington Post,* the *New York Times,* and CBS, as well as cited in the U.S. House of Representatives. Dr. Scarborough's recent research appears in the journals *Gender & Society, Demography, Social Science Research,* and the *Journal of Business Research.* He is also coeditor of the *Handbook of the Sociology of Gender* (Springer Press, 2018).

Jennifer A. Strangfeld, PhD, is an associate professor at California State University, Stanislaus. She teaches sociological research and capstone courses, as well as sociology of food and food labor, and sociology of the body. Her current research is centered in critical race theory, focusing on the educational experiences of Latinx first-generation college students. Dr. Strangfeld received the CSU Stanislaus Elizabeth Anne B. Papageorge Faculty Development Award, which recognizes outstanding achievement in probationary faculty. She is also the first woman in her family to earn a bachelor's degree and the first ever in her family to earn a graduate degree.

Kimberly Tauches received her PhD in sociology from the State University of New York at Albany with specializations in gender and sexuality studies. She has taught at Skidmore College, Kean University, Centenary University, and currently teaches at Harford Community College. Her research focuses on how people perform gender in everyday life.

1 MAKING THE CASE FOR SOCIOLOGICAL KNOWLEDGE

Kristin Kenneavy

STUDENT LEARNING QUESTIONS

1.1 What is sociology? What is social science?

1.2 How do sociological research and the scientific method help us to overcome everyday misperceptions?

1.3 What are ways in which social science research is valuable as a life skill?

1.4 How does social science research benefit society?

HOW I GOT ACTIVE IN SOCIOLOGY

Kristin Kenneavy

I grew up in a very small town in northeastern Wisconsin. When I was in high school, my English teacher assigned us a research paper. We had to go to the school library and find news articles, books, and other types of primary sources about a topic. I chose women's rights. I don't know why I picked that topic, but it turned out that I really enjoyed learning about it. At that time, in the early 1990s, the modern Women's Movement had been active for decades, and during the 1980s, had already survived what Susan Faludi (1991) had called *Backlash*. Her book, subtitled *The Undeclared War Against American Women*, was about this phenomenon and one of the sources I utilized for the paper I had to write. I subsequently went to college at the University of Oklahoma, and there I continued to explore the topic of women's rights when I took a course called "Sociology of Gender." It was one of the most fascinating classes I had ever taken, and so I decided to declare a minor in sociology. I was already learning a lot about differences in male and female patterns of speech in my major, which was communication. Through graduate school and beyond, most of my work has had a theme of gender running through it. I have studied how gender role attitudes affect whether Americans support civil liberties for gays and lesbians; how media consumption affects gendered dating attitudes among adolescents; and, most recently, how men and women differ in their approaches to acting as active bystanders to prevent interpersonal violence. Hopefully you will find some aspect of sociology that you love, and will continue to learn about it for years to come!

Have you ever wandered around a public place, like a mall or an airport, and spent time people-watching? Perhaps you noticed people of two different ages sitting together and wondered why. Are they a parent and adult child? Are they coworkers? Maybe they are in a cross-generational friendship or romance. You might consider clues that could lead you to favor one of those conclusions over another. How close together are they seated? Are they holding hands? Do they have laptops out in front of them? Most likely you find the process of people-watching to be sort of fun; after all, you get to make observations, and craft a little story (let's call it a hypothesis) about what you think is happening. If you watch further, you may even be able to gather some evidence that supports your interpretation of the relationship.

If you have engaged in people-watching, then you are already acting like a sociologist who is doing a research project. Although the process of doing research can be complex, and at times even intimidating, try to remember this example. Without even trying, you already know how to do many of the types of techniques on which sociologists rely when they engage in social science research. The big difference is that sociologists do research systematically and scientifically. What does this mean? Let's find out.

SOCIOLOGY AND SOCIAL SCIENCE

Before we go further into the chapter, it is important to define some key terms, like sociology and social science. In a nutshell, sociology is one type of science that falls under the umbrella of a group of related sciences that are collectively known as "social science." The next sections will go into more detail about the similarities and differences between these two terms.

What Is Sociology?

Sociology is the scientific study of society, including how society shapes individual people and groups, as well as how individual people and groups shape society (Korgen & Atkinson, 2019). Consider the example of Greta Thunberg, a Swedish teenager who, at age 15, spearheaded a movement of young people to protest global warming. She began by standing outside of Swedish parliament and eventually organized a school climate strike called *Fridays for Future* that became a worldwide phenomenon.

What are some of the ways in which society has shaped Greta's activism? First, she is a young person living in an era whenj threats to the world environment are considered a very serious issue. As a result, Greta became aware of such environmental problems at a relatively early age. Second, she lives in a democratic nation in which her freedom of speech is protected. In some parts of the world, Greta would not have been able to stage a strike among her fellow students to skip school to protest climate change without serious repercussions or even threats of violence. Finally, Greta lives in a modern era when it is relatively easy to communicate information and spread ideas. As a result, other people in Sweden and around the world joined her in her efforts to bring the dangers of climate change to the attention of world leaders. Without these circumstances, her story would have been very different.

The technological and political landscape, Swedish history and culture, as well as the changing climate all play a role in shaping Greta's life, but Greta has also shaped many aspects of society. She started out as a single young girl with a sign, but caught the public's attention through her determination and persistence. She is now the recipient of numerous awards and honors for her work related to challenging inaction regarding global warming and other environmental concerns. She has addressed the United Nations and the World Economic Forum, and her speeches have been widely covered in news media reports. By thinking about Greta Thunberg, her global influence, as well as the circumstances that led her to call attention to climate change, and the factors that contributed to her successes, we can begin to understand the complex relationship between individuals and society. Greta's case represents just one example, however. And we don't need to focus on world-famous people in order to examine the interplay of individuals and society. In fact, sociologists research all sorts of people, doing all sorts of things, in all sorts of contexts, in order to understand the relationship between individuals and society (Mills, 1959).

Greta Thunberg has been instrumental in bringing more attention to the issue of climate change in recent years. She is seen here alongside President of the European Commission Ursula von der Leyen at a meeting of the European Union Commission on March 4, 2020.

©Thierry Monasse/Stringer/Getty Images

What Is Social Science?

Sociology is part of a larger body of theory, knowledge, and research techniques know as social science. Before we can discuss social science, it is probably a good idea to identify some of the characteristics of science more generally. Science is an approach to knowledge generation that focuses on collecting data—or observations—using our senses, from the world around us. Scientists use theoretical explanations about such observations as a way to make sense of possible patterns in data. Those patterns can lead scientists to generate **hypotheses**, or testable statements that make predictions about how the world works. Those hypotheses are then tested using more observations, and the cycle begins again. Social science functions in this manner, but instead of making observations about fish, or volcanoes, or diseases, social scientists observe social life.

All social sciences examine aspects of social life, but they do so in different ways. They also tend to ask different types of questions. The social sciences include anthropology, economics, political science, psychology, and social geography, to name a few.

You might ask yourself, what do these fields have in common, and how do they differ? One helpful contrast is to think about sociology is different from fields like psychology, political science, or economics. Most likely, a psychologist would approach the issue of a climate change a bit differently from how a sociologist would approach it. Psychologists tend to focus more on individual people and less on the broader society. A psychologist might want to know how people assess the risks associated with climate change or how people think about issues such as recycling. How do attitudes about recycling relate to the identities people hold and ultimately to their behavior? Sociologists who study climate change tend to research it as a general pattern, or social phenomenon. As a result, they may be more likely to examine broad trends in beliefs about science and climate change. They might analyze rates of recycling, how they differ across age groups, municipal areas, or national contexts, and how they may have changed over time, perhaps with respect to historical shifts in a particular society. Political scientists might focus on how flooding due to climate change could be an issue in state elections, and might suggest policy solutions that would address how to coordinate efforts to address an issue like farm waste pollution. Economists might attempt to estimate the costs associated with reducing carbon footprints by consumers cutting down on meals that include meat. Although these examples show that various social sciences have different emphases, the point to remember is that they are all grounded in scientific discovery, about which there will be more discussion in the next section.

CONSIDER THIS...

We often see psychologists portrayed in popular media. Sociologists are less often featured in the media. How would you explain the difference between psychology and sociology to a friend or roommate?

DOING SOCIOLOGY 1.1

Applying Social Science Research

In this activity, you will consider the role of research in making important life decisions.

Think about some of the big decisions you've made in the past, such as your decision to apply to college and your decision about which college to attend. With this in mind, write answers to the following questions:

1. What types of resources did you consult when applying for college?

2. What types of criteria did you consider?

3. How did consulting data help you with your college selection process?

Think about some of the big choices that you may need to make in the future, such as selecting a graduate school, a company or organization for which to work, a town in which to live, or how to invest for retirement.

1. How might knowledge of how to find and assess quality research be helpful in one of these decisions?

Check Your Understanding

1. How does Greta Thunberg's story illustrate how sociologists think about the world?
2. How is sociology similar to, and different from, other social sciences?

SOCIAL SCIENCE RESEARCH

Why should we do social science research? Taking a casual, people-watching approach is a great start, but social scientists are generally trying to arrive at some sort of objective "truth." Truth? If you are already thinking, "What is truth?," Whose truth?," and "How do we decide how to arrive at the truth?," then congratulations—you are thinking critically! Luckily, curious, critical thinkers like yourself have been wrestling with these questions for thousands of years. The way in which social scientists approach generating truthful knowledge is by using the scientific method. The scientific method is most often associated with the natural sciences (like chemistry or physics), so you might be surprised to learn that sociologists use it too. We will get into the specifics of the scientific method in just a bit, but first, let's explore why we need help to arrive at the "truth."

Our Tricky Human Brains

Imagine if you had to figure out what you should do when you walk into your classroom afresh every day. You'd walk to the door. Should you knock on it or just go in? Should you say "hi" to everyone as you enter? Should you take a seat, or maybe stand at the front of the room? Should you do some much-needed stretches or take out your textbook? Luckily, you don't have to figure this out every day because you have some previous experience with how to enter a classroom. If you had to re-learn this process every time you came to class, your brain would be too worn out to learn anything new.

Humans live in a complex world. We are surrounded by sensory stimuli at all times. As a result, our brains have adapted by creating some shortcuts so that we can do more than just react to the world around us. There are four primary shortcuts that can lead to erroneous conclusions about social life (Chambliss & Schutt, 2019).

Overgeneralization

Overgeneralization happens when you rely on a few of your own experiences to make broad claims about other situations or other groups. As an example, perhaps you have witnessed aggravating and unsafe behaviors by people who are in their teens. You may begin to think that *all* teens are prone to misbehavior and are generally out to cause trouble. This process is not dissimilar from what we sometimes call stereotyping, or painting a group of people with a description that may not actually apply to everyone within that group. We need to be careful not to apply our limited knowledge to a group of people or observations with which we are unfamiliar because, when we do so, it limits our ability to correctly perceive what is taking place.

Selective or Inaccurate Perception

Selective perception is when we pay attention to those things, people, and experiences with which we are most familiar or that align with things that we already believe to be true. Let's return to the example of teens misbehaving. You have already made an overgeneralization that "all teens are out to cause trouble." How likely are you, then, to notice every time you see a teen behaving badly? Probably more so than you are to notice if adults, elders, or children are behaving badly, right? Part of this process is failing to notice disconfirming evidence (that is, evidence that challenges what you believe). For instance, do you happen to notice all those teens who are well-behaved and maybe even helpful to others? Probably not. Our brains don't necessarily do this on purpose, but when we only pay attention to certain people, behaviors, or items, we run the risk of misperceiving the world around us by only attending to those observations to which we have become accustomed.

CONSIDER THIS. . .

Think about a time when you purchased something new, like a sweet pair of headphones, or maybe your first car. Did it suddenly seem as if that product was everywhere you looked? How might our attention to what is familiar lead us to inaccurate observations about patterns of social behavior?

Illogical Reasoning

When we reason illogically, it means that we have come to conclusions based on a misinterpretation of the evidence at hand, usually because of faulty assumptions about that evidence. You may be aware of a recent group of vocal advocates called "Flat Earthers." Members of this group assume that, since they cannot see the curvature of the Earth from their vantage point, the planet is actually flat. Most of us would agree that the Earth is round (or vaguely egg-shaped) because we assume that the photos taken of it from outer space are a representation of a three-dimensional object. When we utilize incorrect assumptions in trying to explain the social life that we experience every day, this could lead us to incorrect conclusions. To continue our example from above, since you already think that teens are the worst, you may conclude that parents and high schools are doing a poor job of socializing and educating teens. However, you would be making an erroneous assumption because you have conflated the assumed characteristics of teenagers with the assumed characteristics of the institutions that mold them.

Resistance to Change

No one likes to admit they are wrong. But if we never consider new ideas or new information, then we will never learn anything! Imagine you were confronted with some statistics that indicate that most teens actually display behaviors that are very pro-social and positive. Would you want to change your mind about your conclusion that all teenagers are terrible? It is likely that you may actually grumble about this finding because it doesn't square very well with what you believe about teens in general.

In everyday life, we can also overrely on some types of information. For instance, you might fully support a particular politician, but it may not be such a great idea to take everything they say as completely accurate or factual. Similarly, many people rely on information from journalists, religious figures, or even role models, like parents or celebrities, as "truth." When we rely too heavily on authority figures, we may be misled if *their* own conclusions are incorrect. Finally, another type of information that can lead us astray is "common sense." Common sense is not always accurate, though we often take it for granted as fact. It's worth remembering that what is common sense to one person may be utter nonsense to another, so it is an unreliable source of knowledge.

Given that these four types of commonplace misperceptions are quite likely to trip us up as we try to arrive at "the truth," then what steps can we take to try to overcome these problems? Let's return to the idea of the scientific method to help us make accurate claims about social life.

As part of the Fridays for Future movement started by Greta Thunberg, thousands of students staged a protest in Leeds, UK, on November 29, 2019.

©ASSOCIATED PRESS

The Scientific Method

We know that our human brains are easily led astray when we make only casual observations about social life. Luckily, the scientific method uses a relatively strict set of steps that can help us to sort fact from fiction. It generally suggests that you first start with a research problem or a research question (What is going on with that mixed-age couple?). You then propose some sort of explanation of why the phenomenon is happening in the way it is (I think they are coworkers), and then you gather data to test whether your explanation was correct (Oops. Now they are holding hands and kissing—probably not coworkers). So, the scientific method works a lot like people-watching except that it demands that observations are empirical and systematic. Let's unpack those terms.

The scientific method demands that we collect empirical data, which means that the information can be observed using our human senses. By taking an empirical approach, we cease to rely on previously held beliefs, the authority of others, or common sense. We are being very deliberate about the type of evidence we are going to consider. We basically aren't going to take anyone's word for it that something is true. Rather, we may need others to review our work and verify that our conclusions are correct.

Furthermore, the data must be gathered in a *systematic* fashion. To gather data systematically means that you have to make a plan for how you are going to collect data and let that plan dictate which observations are included and which are left out. In systematic data collection, we avoid overgeneralization. Rather than misapplying potentially wrong conclusions based on a handful of observations, we will select observations in a way that will represent a larger population.

Social science should also, ideally, be replicable. By being very explicit and transparent about the way in which we went about gathering the data for a study, other social scientists should be able to redo our study and get the same, or similar results. In real life, it isn't particularly common for a study to be replicated (and some really can't be replicated because they are completed in a specific time and place). However, if another researcher were to try to repeat your study faithfully, and if they got completely different results, then researchers would have to consider why the differences emerged. In fact, social science studies often find dissimilar results; these differences force researchers to consider their theories, methods, and findings more critically in order to account for the discrepancies.

Something important to remember is that no *one* social science study is going to be able to establish "the truth" on its own. Rather, we have to think of empirical research as part of an ongoing conversation in which many people are trying to establish truth collectively. This brings up some terms that you should know. When we think that we can see the world as it is, without bringing to our conclusions all our personal experiences, misperceptions, and prior knowledge, we are claiming that we can be objective. As you may have guessed, it is almost impossible for any human to be entirely objective because *each of our perspectives is influenced to some extent by our own personal experiences, values, misperceptions, and knowledge.* These can't help but affect the types of problems we choose to study, the ways in which we choose to study them, and how we interpret the data we examine.

If we think of social science research as being part of a larger enterprise that is trying to approximate the truth from multiple perspectives, then we do not have to try to reach objectivity. Instead, we can hope to achieve what is called intersubjectivity. Intersubjectivity happens when multiple researchers look at aspects of a research problem, and over time and in collaboration, try to establish some sort of scientific agreement as to what is actually happening with respect to a particular pattern in social life. This may not sound as convincing as having a purely objective stance, but it is certainly much more realistic, and possibly more helpful.

DOING SOCIOLOGY 1.2

Misperceptions and the Media

In this activity, you will apply common misperceptions to critically analyze an example from the media.

We often come across research that is presented via news media. Let's say that you come across a news report that states that eating chocolate will help you lose weight. Write four questions you would want to ask about the report. Use the four types of common misperceptions, and your knowledge of the scientific method, to guide your response.

1. What are four types of thinking that can cloud our ability to correctly perceive social life?
2. What are the benefits of using the scientific method when doing research?
3. What does it mean for research to be empirical, systematic, and replicable?
4. What is the difference between objectivity and intersubjectivity?

SOCIAL RESEARCH AS A LIFE SKILL

At this point, you may be asking yourself, "Sociology and social science research sound sort of interesting, but what's in it for me? What am I going to get out of this experience?" Well, there is a reason why pretty much every sociology program in the United States requires a research class. Learning about how to do social science research offers you an opportunity to develop many different skills. The next section will feature four good reasons why learning this material is useful, as opposed to just interesting.

Making Real-World Decisions

The world around us can be overwhelming. We live in a complex social world that is becoming more globally connected every minute. In the midst of this, we still have to try to make sound life choices. How will understanding social research help with this? Well, one of the critical mindsets that you will develop through this course is healthy skepticism, which will allow you to synthesize information and evaluate competing claims. Think back to Doing Sociology 1.1 earlier in this chapter. You were asked to think about the types of information that you utilized to make decisions about where you would go to college. If you said that you consulted websites that compared colleges and universities based on numerous criteria, then you were utilizing social science research.

A key goal of descriptive social science research is to provide you with facts about a particular entity or phenomenon. What you may not have known is that colleges and universities are often the providers of information to clearinghouse websites. You may now be thinking, "Hey, wait a minute. If the colleges provided those data, then wouldn't they want to give the website numbers that portray them in the best possible light?" Great job—you are using healthy skepticism to inform that question. Yes. Colleges and universities want to recruit as many bright, prepared students as they can in order to collect tuition and enhance their prestige (giving them the ability to recruit even more bright, prepared students in the future). Thankfully, the vast majority of colleges and universities don't just make up their outcomes on the criteria that are of interest to prospective students and their families. Instead, there is usually a unit within the college that is tasked with gathering the types of data for which such websites and review magazines are looking. The people working in what are called institutional research offices are trained professionals who often have degrees in—you guessed it—social science research. They may do research on the proportion of graduates who have a job within 6 months of graduating. They may also need to gather information on the types of majors that are available, whether or not there is an active alumni network, and how many students graduate within 4 years of enrolling. These are all important considerations to which students might attend when deciding where to go to college.

Similarly, there will be many instances in which you will need to make informed decisions based on the available research. Your job in this course over the next few months is to become equipped to evaluate the quality of that research. You should start to develop the habit of asking questions like, "Who gathered these data? Are they trained to do it in an ethical and systematic fashion? Who decided that these are important criteria? Have they left out any other criteria that may have been important to my decision? How have these data been reported? Is everyone's information included, or have some folks' outcomes been left out so that the numbers look better than they really are?" These types of questions reveal critical thinking skills that will be strengthened by learning about the research process. You can apply them to decisions like choosing a financial adviser, selecting a town in which to buy a home, or evaluating the quality of elementary schools within that town—all important adult life decisions.

Being an active user of social media requires media literacy.

©iStockphoto.com/P. Kijsanayothin

Media Literacy

Media are rife with information, and claims about social life abound. You have probably seen thousands of claims like the following: "This toothpaste will freshen your breath *and* whiten your teeth! It's been scientifically proven!" Even just watching depictions of life on popular television shows can lead you to believe that they represent some sort of social reality. The media, be they news or entertainment-based, convey information about social life. However, much of what is presented can be distorted or exaggerated. Having the ability to sort fact from fiction in news accounts, advertisements, and fictional portrayals is called being media literate.

Let's think through an example. Imagine that you regularly get your news from social media feeds such as Facebook, Twitter, or Reddit. You may follow some sources, but you also click through the news stories that your friends post. As a social scientist, you may ask yourself, "Am I really getting balanced news if I primarily rely on my friends to provide me with links?" Chances are, you are probably not going to get a broad cross-section of news that way.

Knowledge of research methods enables you to understand that your friends are not a random sample of the population. In fact, since they are your friends, it is entirely likely that they have many similarities to you. They may come from the same town, they may be more likely to be of the same political orientation, and they may likely also be of the same age or racial/ethnic group. If this is the case, then you might be consuming news media that are only relevant to what your friends think is interesting or important. If you were inclined to have a more broad-based view of what is happening in the world, you may need to do some research. For instance, you might want to find out how news sources have been measured on a political spectrum, and how they are ranked with respect to providing facts versus presenting an agenda or possibly even misleading information. Being able to ask questions about media presentations, and to find your own news, is facilitated by having a good working knowledge of how to evaluate sources for quality.

Citizenship

Learning about social science research can also give you insight into the types of laws, policies, and programs that govern much of our social life. There is a tremendous amount of disagreement in the United States, currently, around a wide variety of social policies. How can research help us to make sense of the many political claims that are so prevalent?

Let's think through an example. A referendum is a vote by citizens in a specific area (like a town, or a whole state) about a single political question. Let's say that there is a referendum in your town about whether or not to build a new community center. Those in favor of the community center claim that it will provide a space for kids, teens, and older adults to utilize for educational and entertainment events. They point to the lack of such a space currently, and argue that the proposed center will foster a deeper sense of community in the town and can also function as a way for key groups to find out about social services and opportunities for involvement in the area. Those opposed to the idea state that the increased tax revenue needed to build, maintain, and staff the facility is greater than the proposed benefits. They also assert that the increased traffic to that part of town is a potential problem and may result in hidden costs, like having to re-time some of the traffic lights. How are you, as a citizen, going to make up your mind about whether the benefits of the community center outweigh the costs?

As someone who knows about social science research, you could start looking into how the pro–community center group came up with their estimates of how many people will use the center. Do their assumptions make logical sense? Have they included a plan for how they will advertise the events that take place in the space? Did they conduct any surveys of residents of the town to see if they would have an interest in using the center in some way? How are the costs and benefits associated with the proposed community center distributed across socioeconomic, racial, and ethnic groups? All of these issues can be answered if you are able to anticipate and consume research-based information.

In addition, you may want to examine the types of evidence being presented by those opposed to the plan. Have they conducted a traffic study that indicates that there actually would be more cars driving in that particular part of town? What about the increased tax revenue? You would want to examine whether the proposed costs for the project seem to outstrip whatever funds the town has put aside for the project, any anticipated revenues for the center that would balance the costs, and any fund-raising or sponsorship by local businesses that may be planned. Citizens are often faced with complicated choices. Being able to sort through various types of research and ask smart questions about assumptions is a key skill needed by an informed citizen.

SOCIOLOGISTS IN ACTION
Erin J. Augis

I study ways people engage religious beliefs and practices to effect self-determined actions for social change. For many years, I studied how contemporary West African Muslim women worked for improved living conditions and independence from older generations' norms through conservative, reformist Sunni organizations. Currently, I continue to pursue my curiosity about ways devout people have worked for progress in my new research program on the history of American Protestants who lived in southern Ohio (along the Ohio River) and worked for the abolition of slavery during the 1830s and 40s. Abolition was the first widespread human rights movement in the United States, and Protestants who participated tended to be conservative in religious beliefs and social practices (opposing the consumption of alcohol and emphasizing the importance of theological studies), but they were rigorously progressive in their advocacy for the freedom of enslaved peoples.

Inspired by the research of Ann Hagedorn, author of *Beyond the River: The Untold Story of the Heroes of the Underground Railroad* (Simon & Schuster, 2004), I focus my studies on the Reverend John Bennington Mahan of Ohio, who died opposing slavery in 1844. *Beyond the River* centers on the abolitionist river town of Ripley, Ohio, and the life of Reverend John Rankin, one of the most active abolitionists in the U.S. leading up to the Civil War. Reverend Mahan was Rankin's close associate, and he aided hundreds of enslaved people in their escapes, also traveling regularly to preach against America's peculiar institution. He went to trial twice and was imprisoned once because he was accused of "stealing" enslaved peoples and disrupting the peace. Although he was acquitted, he became ill in jail and died of tuberculosis that he had likely contracted there. At his arrest, he was denied a writ of *habeus corpus* by the lawyer Thomas Hamer, who was an anti-abolitionist. While today Hamer is nationally lauded as a hero of the Mexican War, Reverend Mahan is largely unknown.

Reverend Mahan's gravestone is small but historically momentous. Although he and his family were bankrupted by the legal costs for his defense, they remained defiant even in his death. His epitaph reads, "Victim of the slave power." "The slave power" was the abolitionists' derisive term for politicians and elite plantation owners who benefited from and defended the predominance of slavery in the American economy. I am working with the National Park Service and local residents to protect Reverend Mahan's grave, and collaborate with area librarians, archivists, and Reverend Mahan's great-great-great-granddaughter to identify and safeguard the written antislavery sermons, letters, legal depositions, and accounts records that he left behind, which are in various locations in Ohio and Kentucky. I am not only writing sociological analyses of Reverend Mahan's religious and social activism; I am working to preserve the physical artifacts of his human rights legacy for future generations to appreciate.

Erin J. Augis is a professor of sociology at Ramapo College of New Jersey, where she specializes in the sociology of religion.

Discussion Questions

1. What methods of data collection do you think Professor Augis uses to uncover sociological insight into Protestant abolitionists?
2. In what ways has Professor Augis made her academic work public?

Working in a Career

Finally, one of the key reasons why you are probably reading this book at all is that you are in college, in the hopes of eventually graduating and finding employment, or even opening your own business. You may not know yet what you want to do when you graduate, or maybe you do have an idea and you don't think that it will involve having to do your own research. Perhaps it won't. However, in many types of jobs that sociology students enter, even if you don't end up conducting research, odds are that you will be the *consumer* or *communicator* of some types of research. In addition, being able to indicate on a résumé that you have had some coursework in how to do research may actually help you to land a job in the first place.

Many professions rely upon social research, and students with degrees in sociology go on to work in a wide variety of fields. For instance, police officers may not be at the top of your list in terms of professions that use research, but all police departments actually do gather data. Officers need to keep track of the number of incidents to which they are called, whether there was an arrest, and what type of offense was committed. These statistics are compiled and reported to the Federal Bureau of Investigation (FBI) as part of the Uniform Crime Reporting Program (Federal Bureau of Investigation, n.d.). In turn, this program publishes research reports that keep track of crime trends for the entire United States. Knowledge of crime trends is then utilized by police chiefs to make decisions about the types of training that police officers need and how to deploy their departments' resources.

CONSIDER THIS. . .

Take a minute to think about a job that you would really love to do, without worrying about whether it is realistic. In what ways might research knowledge be a useful skill for the job that you envision?

Sociologists work in a wide variety of domains, including social services, government, health care, nonprofit organizations, for-profit businesses, law enforcement and legal services, marketing, international development work, education, and human resources, just to name a few! In all of these fields, being able to locate, understand, critique, and communicate research findings is an important job skill.

DOING SOCIOLOGY 1.3

Questioning News Sources

In this activity, you will critique the way in which social science research is described in a news media article.

In 2020, during the early days of the COVID-19 pandemic, CNBC.com published an article titled "Science says pets can buffer stress, boost productivity and help keep you healthy while you WFH [work from home]" (Stieg, 2020). The article contends that pets help to reduce stress and bolster happiness and work productivity, stating:

A 2012 study from Virginia Commonwealth University found that employees at a retail business who brought their dogs to work had higher job satisfaction than industry norms and had the lowest levels of stress ratings throughout the day. Of those dog owners who came to work with a dog, 50% said that having their pet present was important to their productivity.

The research study to which the CNBC article refers, titled "Preliminary investigation of employee's dog presence on stress and organizational perceptions" (Barker et al., 2012), compares the levels of stress, job satisfaction, and perceptions of the employer of three groups: one in which employees brought their dogs to work, a second in which employees did not bring their dogs to work, and another group of workers who didn't have pets. The research article describes the results as follows:

Combined groups scored significantly higher on multiple job satisfaction subscales than the reference norm group for these scales. No significant differences were found between the groups on physiological stress or perceived organizational support. Although perceived stress was similar at baseline; over the course of the day, stress declined for the DOG group with their dogs present and increased for the NODOG and NOPET groups. The NODOG group had significantly higher stress than the DOG group by the end of the day. A significant difference was found in the stress patterns for the DOG group on days their dogs were present and absent. On dog absent days, owners' stress increased throughout the day, mirroring the pattern of the NODOG group.

Think about the difference between the two descriptions of this research study.

1. Compare and contrast the titles of each piece. Does one suggest more certainty than the other?

2. How would you describe the tone of each piece? Which words or phrases convey the tone?

3. Consider the fact that the original study focused on a workplace of 450 people and the CNBC.com report is focused on the effects of dog ownership while people are working from home. Do you think that dogs have a similar effect on productivity in home and office settings? Why or why not?

4. The original study examines dog ownership, but the headline of the CNBC.com article speaks of "pets" more generally. Do you think that all pets have similar effects on stress and productivity? Why do you think the CNBC article uses the language of pets more broadly?

Check Your Understanding

1. How can you utilize healthy skepticism to question information when making a consequential life decision?
2. How can a good working knowledge of how to evaluate sources help you to become media literate?
3. What research skills are important for informed citizens?
4. In what ways might knowledge of social science research assist you in obtaining or performing a job?

THE BENEFITS OF SOCIAL SCIENCE RESEARCH FOR SOCIETY

We've discussed why understanding how to "do" and critique social science research is useful for you, personally. But how is such research beneficial for society? There are numerous ways in which social research can make the world a better place. Let's examine some of the primary societal benefits of social research.

Document Social Inequalities, Societal Transformations, and Emerging Issues

Society often changes very rapidly. Social science research allows us to document changing social relations. In 2020, people around the world were thrown into a crisis as a result of the spread of the COVID-19 pandemic. Families were forced to quarantine at home. Some workers were able to work remotely, but millions of workers were laid off from their jobs, as shown via data regarding unemployment provided by the Bureau of Labor Statistics. In the United States alone, well over 100,000 people lost their lives to the virus.

In the midst of the crisis, issues of inequality emerged and were covered in the mainstream press. After politicians and journalists started to call for data on infections and deaths to be released organized by racial and ethnic categories, it became clear that there were disparities in terms of which groups were being infected and dying at higher rates. The Centers for Disease Control and Prevention (CDC) began to release data in April of 2020 that indicated that Black and Latinx Americans were disproportionately affected by the virus, with respect to infections and deaths. Early statistics indicated that Black people represented 34% of infections, but only made up 13% of the overall population of the United States (Artiga et al., 2020). Not only were communities of color being hit harder by the virus's effects, but these communities were also more likely to experience some of the secondary problems caused by COVID-19, such as job loss and food insecurity (Ro, 2020).

People of color have been disproportionately impacted by COVID-19, as this protester conveys.

©iStockphoto.com/LeoPatrizi

The COVID-19 pandemic illustrates the importance of social science data and the organizations tasked with supplying such data. Without the CDC, Bureau of Labor Statistics, and World Health Organization, we would not be able to identify the uneven toll that the COVID-19 pandemic took across racial and ethnic groups. The data they provide are pivotal for documenting and understanding the social determinants of health inequities.

Challenging Stereotypes and Misinformation

Another benefit that social research has for society is that it enables us to challenge misinformation and stereotypes. You have likely heard our current era described as the "information age." We are flooded by information on social media, on 24-hour news networks, the radio, and other places, but as discussed previously, the information broadcasted is not always true. Politicians, celebrities, and influencers make claims about the world that are often "liked" or otherwise supported by thousands of people, giving credibility to these claims even if they are baseless.

Consider when, in 2015, Donald Trump announced his presidential campaign and, in his speech, characterized Mexican immigrants as drug dealers, criminals, and rapists. He said, "They're sending people that have lots of problems, and they're bringing those problems with us. They're bringing drugs. They're bringing crime. They're rapists. And some, I assume, are good people" (Lee, 2015). Journalists, social scientists, and everyday people turned immediately to social science research, which overwhelmingly showed this stereotype to be untrue. As the National Academies Press (2016) and several others summarized, social science research shows that immigrants have significantly lower crime rates than native-born populations, and communities with a high proportion of immigrants have lower crime rates compared to those with lower proportions of immigration. Social science research was pivotal to addressing this misinformation.

Social science research can not only provide evidence that a claim is incorrect, but it can also complicate statements that are overly general. You may have heard, for example, about the gender wage gap in the United States: the fact that, among full-time, year-round workers in the United States, men continue to earn significantly more than women. But did you know that among workers with a bachelor's degree or higher, the gender wage gap is significantly worse?

Figure 1.1 shows data collected and analyzed by researchers at the U.S. Census Bureau in 2017. It shows how differences in wages vary for workers of different education levels, and also different ages. Among workers with a bachelor's degree or higher difference in the "median" or typical wage for men and women workers is about $21,000. For men and women without a bachelor's degree, the difference is a little less than $10,000. But note that men and women without a bachelor's degree typically make substantially less than men and women with a bachelor's degree. And, of course, these earning figures are further complicated when race, ethnicity, and occupation are included as well. Knowledge of sociological research methods can help us, as a society, to challenge misinformation and oversimplistic claims.

CONSIDER THIS. . .

Why do you think the gender wage gap is bigger among workers with higher levels of education compared to those with lower levels of education?

FIGURE 1.1   ■   Median Earnings for Full-Time, Year-Round Workers by Education Attainment for Men and Women

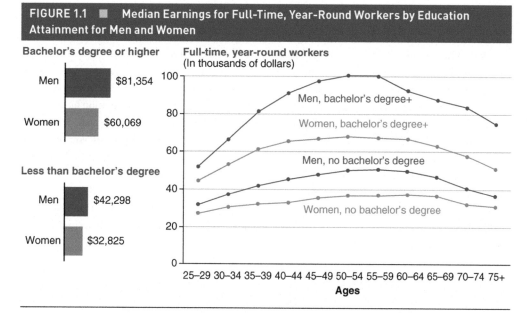

Source: U.S. Census Bureau, 2017 American Community Survey.

Inform Public Policies and Programs

Another way in which social science research benefits society as a whole is by its use in policy and program evaluation. Around the world, federal, state, and local governments, international organizations, nonprofit organizations, and for-profit companies collectively invest billions of dollars to address social problems and to create a better world. How do we know if the programs, policies, initiatives, and products they create are actually achieving their desired goals? Social science research, grounded in solid research methods, is key.

Consider the issue of government funding for early childhood education. Head Start and Early Head Start are federally funded programs that promote "the school readiness of children from birth to age five from low-income families by enhancing their cognitive, social, and emotional development." The programs also offer some services to low-income women who are pregnant (Benefits.gov, n.d.). According to a 2018 report from the Congressional Budget Office, the program served approximately 900,000 children in 2017 and cost taxpayers approximately $9 billion (averaging approximately $10,000 per child). These are big numbers. Is the program worth it? Social science research can't tell us if the program is worth it from a moral or ethical point of view, but it can help to clarify the social and economic impact of the program. In fact, analyses of Head Start's return on investment show that the program actually *saves* taxpayers money in the long term—and lots of it! Early education programs help young people to do better in school, graduate from high school, and earn higher wages. By promoting education, investments in early childhood education are also investments in health, well-being, and economic growth. And these outcomes are shown again and again in social science research (Heckman, 2017; https://www.acf.hhs.gov/sites/default/files/opre/hs_impact_study _final.pdf).

Let's consider a very different example. Your campus almost certainly has policies in place to prohibit unwanted sexual conduct between students. Under the Obama administration, the U.S. Department of Education changed these policies, and under the Trump administration, the policies changed again. Many people speculated about the impact these changes would have on students, colleges, and universities. Social science research tracking the extent of sexual violence on campus, feelings of comfort and discomfort for students of all genders, instances of interpersonal sexism, changes to institutional support for gender-related issues, and institutional funding patterns more generally, can help us turn speculation into empirical research. The findings from this research can help us to ground the debate about campus sexual harassment and gendered violence in real-world evidence, which in turn can help us to design and sustain policies and programs in line with our values and goals.

Strengthening Democracy

Public knowledge of social science is also critical for a healthy democracy. In order for a democracy to function well, citizens need to be informed as to issues that are taking place within their town, state, country, and even globally. As discussed previously, much of this information is generated from social science research— research describing patterns and trends in social life, health, and well-being. For democracy to live up to its ideal, members of society need not only to have this information but must also be able to make sense of this information, discuss it, and respond to it in a meaningful way. By learning the ins and outs of sociological research, critically evaluating the claims and information you encounter, and sharing what you know with others, you are actually helping to strengthen our democratic society.

Perhaps even more importantly, learning about sociological research methods sets you up to make a meaningful contribution to collective knowledge—a chance for you to ask and find answers to the questions that are most important for you and your community. As we will discuss throughout this book, putting sociology into action can empower you and your community, and help to build a more socially just world.

DOING SOCIOLOGY 1.4

Checking Your Own Misconceptions

In this exercise, you will compare your own perceptions of U.S. society to real-world data.

The U.S. Census Bureau collects data on the characteristics of the U.S. population. Take a moment to consider how you would respond to these questions:

- About how many people are there in the United States?
- About what percentage of people living in the United States are foreign-born?
- About what percentage of people living in the United States are veterans?
- About what percentage of people living in the United States describe themselves as having some sort of disability?
- About what is the typical household income?
- About what percentage of children under the age of 18 are living in poverty?

Now consider the actual data. According to the U.S. Census Bureau:

- The total U.S. population is 328,239,523.
- 13.7% of the people living in the United States are foreign-born.
- 6.9% of people living in the United States are veterans.
- 12.7% of people living in the United States describe themselves as having a disability.
- The median household income is $65,712.
- 16.8% of children under the age of 18 are living in poverty.

Write your answers to the following questions:

1. How greatly did your perceptions vary from the actual data?
2. Are you surprised by any of these findings? Why or why not?
3. Choose one fact that stands out to you as particularly interesting or important. What makes this information especially interesting or important?

Check Your Understanding

1. How does social science research help us to understand social inequalities?
2. How can social science research help us to combat stereotypes and misinformation?
3. How might social science research inform policies and programs that affect our lives?
4. In what ways can social science research help us to strengthen democracy?

CONCLUSION

You should now have a greater understanding of what social science entails, how it has the potential to benefit you, and how it has the potential to benefit society as a whole. It is important to keep in mind that humans cannot always perceive the world accurately due to misperceptions. As a result, we can utilize the scientific method, which allows us to gather empirical observations about the world around us. This systematic approach to accumulating accurate information is indispensable. By increasing our knowledge of how to conduct and evaluate social science research, we are strengthening our own skills: our ability to use research to make decisions, to navigate a complex media landscape, to understand job prospects, and to become better citizens. Finally, it is important to recognize the many ways in which social science research can make the world a better place. Some of these ways include documenting social inequalities, disputing harmful stereotypes, informing policies and programs, and strengthening democracy. In the next chapter, you will begin your journey into learning about sociological research by starting to understand the role of theory, or explanations about patterns in social life.

REVIEW

1.1 What is sociology? What is social science?

Sociology is the scientific study of society, including how society shapes individual people and groups, as well as how individual people and groups shape society. Sociologists research all sorts of people, doing all sorts of things, in all sorts of contexts, in order to understand the relationship between individuals and society. Sociology is part of a larger body of theory, knowledge, and research techniques known as social science. Social science is a form of science that investigates the social world. As a science, social science is an approach to knowledge generation that focuses on collecting data—or observations—using our senses, from the world around us. Scientists use theoretical explanations about such observations as a way to make sense of possible patterns in data. Those patterns can lead scientists to generate hypotheses, or testable statements that make predictions about how the world works. Those hypotheses are then tested using more observations, and the cycle begins again.

1.2 How do sociological research and the scientific method help us to overcome everyday misperceptions?

There are at least four types of everyday misperceptions: Overgeneralization occurs when you rely on a few of your own experiences to make broad claims about other situations or other groups. Selective perception is when we pay attention to those things, people, and experiences with which we are most familiar or that align with things that we already believe to be true. Reasoning illogically means that we have come to conclusions based on a misinterpretation of the evidence at hand, usually because of faulty assumptions about that evidence. And being resistant to change is when we fail to change our minds in light of new evidence. The scientific method helps us to overcome these misperceptions by guiding us to make systematic observations about the social world, to argue logically about the explanations for the patterns that we detect, and to be open to new information that could result in a different explanation for a pattern.

1.3 What are ways in which social science research is valuable as a life skill?

With respect to making sound life decisions, a critical mindset that you will develop through learning about sociological research is healthy skepticism, which will allow you to synthesize information and evaluate competing claims. Another important life skill is media literacy. Much of what is presented can be distorted or exaggerated. Having the ability to sort fact from fiction in news accounts, advertisements, and fictional portrayals is called being media literate. A third way in which social science knowledge is valuable is in the context of working in a career. Many career paths utilize sociological research. Even if you don't envision yourself doing research someday, it's quite possible that you might need to consume or explain social research to others in the course of your job. Finally, learning about social science research can also give you insight into the types of laws, policies, and programs that govern much of our social life. There is currently a tremendous amount of disagreement in the United States around a wide variety of social policies. Understanding social research that examines such policies can make you a better citizen.

1.4 How does social science research benefit society?

Social science research helps us to document social inequalities, societal transformations, and emerging issues. Society often changes very rapidly. Social science research allows us to understand changing social relations. Another benefit that social research has for society is that it enables us to challenge misinformation and stereotypes. Research can be gathered to dispute claims that might malign a particular group of individuals. A third way in which social science research benefits society as a whole is by its use in policy and program evaluation. How do we know if the programs, policies, initiatives, and products they create are actually achieving their desired goals? Social science research, grounded in solid research methods, is key. Finally, for democracy to live up to its ideal, members of society need not only to have information, but must also be able to make sense of this information, discuss it, and respond to it in a meaningful way. By learning the ins and outs of sociological research, critically evaluating the claims and information you encounter, and sharing what you know with others, you are actually helping to strengthen our democratic society.

KEY TERMS

empirical data (p. 8)

hypotheses (p. 5)

intersubjectivity (p. 8)

media literate (p. 10)

objective (p. 8)

referendum (p. 10)

replicable (p. 8)

scientific method (p. 8)

sociology (p. 4)

systematic data collection (p. 8)

2 POSING QUESTIONS, CRAFTING EXPLANATIONS, AND COMMUNICATING RESULTS

Mellisa Holtzman

STUDENT LEARNING QUESTIONS

2.1 What are the three major sociological theoretical perspectives, and why is theory important?

2.2 How do sociologists generate research questions?

2.3 What are key aspects of the sociological research process?

2.4 How do sociologists communicate their research results, and what are the major parts of a research article?

In Chapter 1, you learned about the importance of social science research and the basic forms it takes. With that background information in mind, you are now ready to learn about the research process. Of course, this entire text is devoted to that topic, but this chapter will provide you with an overview of the process in its entirety. Later chapters will address specific aspects of the research process in more detail.

As the chapter title suggests, you can think of research as a process where sociologists (1) pose questions, (2) craft explanations, and then (3) communicate results. While true, there is actually a step that precedes these. Sociologists must start the research process by first consulting theory.

HOW I GOT ACTIVE IN SOCIOLOGY

Mellisa Holtzman

I started college as a psychology major. I knew I wanted to work with people and make a difference in the world. Psychology seemed like a good fit.

All was well until my sophomore year, when I took a class called "Perception." I naively believed this class would be about ESP, intuition, and other "fun" aspects of perception. I quickly discovered the class was about how the brain processes the information we perceive with our senses. I felt like I was in a biology class, and I hated it.

This class helped me realize that I did not enjoy psychology's focus on the internal processes of humans. Instead, I was far more interested in how society influences individuals. In other words, I was curious about factors that are external to humans. So, I switched my major to sociology and invested myself in understanding how culture affects people and how people, in turn, can shape and change culture. Eventually this gave rise to my interest in sexual-assault prevention.

WHAT IS THEORY AND WHY DOES IT MATTER?

Theory refers to the general or abstract principles associated with a particular discipline—in this case, sociology. Sociological theory, then, represents a set of background perspectives about how the social world operates. These background perspectives are important because they shape not only the kinds of questions sociologists ask, but also how they interpret the data they collect. In effect, theory serves as a lens through which we view the social world. As such, it is an important first step in sociological research.

Theories

Within sociology, there are three primary theoretical perspectives that inform our understandings of the social world. Functionalism is the perspective most closely associated with Émile Durkheim. Durkheim was a French intellectual writing in the late 1800s and early 1900s. He is widely considered the father of sociology because he was one of the first scholars to advocate for sociology as a distinct discipline. He argued that individuals' behaviors are shaped by the society in which they live and that a full understanding of human behavior must account for the impact of these outside influences (which he called social facts). Sociology, he asserted, was the discipline best suited to that task (Pampel, 2007).

Durkheim was interested in how large collections of individuals—all of whom have their own interests and needs—could work together in a coordinated way. Functionalist theory thus argues that society is composed of interrelated systems that shape and constrain individuals, and in so doing, help create, maintain, and stabilize that society (Durkheim, 1893/1984). For instance, societies rely on a number of institutions, including the political system, legal system, and educational system, to meet citizens' needs. But these institutions do more than just deliver goods and services to the populace. They also constrain the behaviors of the people who come in contact with them. For instance, the political system regulates how people interact with the government, the legal system regulates how people interact with one another, and the education system regulates how people interact with and access information. All of this regulation ensures some level of uniformity and order within society, thereby making large-scale cooperation possible. In short, functionalist theory proposes that every institution in society has an important part to play in the maintenance and stabilization of society. From this we can see that functionalist theory focuses on the *benefits* of institutions and social patterns for society.

Conflict theory, in contrast, tends to focus on the strife that institutions and social patterns create in society. Conflict theory is most closely associated with Karl Marx and Max Weber. Marx and Weber both argued that institutions produce inequalities of power and resources in society. Marx, who was writing during the height of the industrial revolution in Europe, focused on social inequality related to ownership and wealth. Marx saw society as divided into two main groups: the wealthy capitalists (also called bourgeoisie) who own the technology and resources to make things and the workers who struggle day to day to make ends meet (also called the proletariat) (Marx, 1867/1977). Marx was highly critical of the long work hours, dangerous working conditions, and dismal wages 19th-century workers faced, especially since those same conditions were creating tremendous wealth for capitalists. He also argued that capitalists purposely used society's institutions, like religion, media, and politics, to keep workers divided from one another and thus unable to protest effectively against their unfair treatment. Marx saw power struggles between the capitalists and workers as *the* defining feature of the social world—all human experiences, he argued, are fundamentally shaped by our place within this particular power struggle.

The status of essential workers, such as warehouse workers, changed as a result of COVID-19, as the importance of the role they play was fully recognized.

iStock.com/vichie81

Writing more than 50 years after Marx, Weber saw power in more complex terms. Weber challenged Marx's argument that power and inequalities can be understood solely in terms of economic position. Weber argued that power stems not only from people's economic situation, which he called their class position, but from two additional sources. Status positions give people unequal access to prestige and social honor and party position gives people unequal access to special interest groups, such as unions, lobbies, and political associations (Weber, 1925/1978). For instance, in our society most people believe that teachers fulfill a very important and highly valued role; thus, they are held in relatively high esteem. Yet, despite having an esteemed status position, they often receive fairly low pay. As a consequence, their class position is lower than their status position. Importantly, one way for teachers to try to increase their class position is by participating in a union—it is through this party position that they can gain some additional power and push for higher pay and better benefits. Thus, while Marx focused only on power differentials based on wealth, Weber emphasized the more nuanced ways that power can operate in a society. In so doing, he gave us a powerful set of conceptual tools.

Although there are significant differences between the perspectives of Marx and Weber they share a focus on power and inequality, and that is what sets conflict theory apart from functionalism. Conflict theory tends to focus on the struggles that individuals and groups engage in as they vie for power. Rather than seeing institutions as entities that benefit society, conflict theorists view institutions as sites that often maintain inequalities, creating further conflict and strife. Many modern conflict theorists, including W.E.B. Du Bois and Patricia Hill Collins, have illustrated the degree to which these inequalities are also grounded in race, gender, and sexuality.

Symbolic interactionism (sometimes abbreviated as SI theory) is the last of the three major theoretical perspectives in sociology. This theory is most closely associated with the work of George Herbert Mead, a scholar who was intensely interested in social reform and helping oppressed individuals (Pampel, 2007). In fact, his interest in helping others is one of the primary reasons why SI theory is so very different from functionalism and conflict theory.

Mead was concerned with how a person's social interactions—with their parents, friends, and teachers, for example—would influence the development of their sense of self and their life experiences (Mead, 1934/1962). Thus, unlike conflict theory and functionalism, both of which use a macro approach for understanding the social world, symbolic interactionism uses a micro approach. A macro approach is one that focuses on large-scale entities and institutions, like the economy, politics, law, and education. A micro approach is one that emphasizes individual-level and group-level interactions.

Mead's focus on social interactions is an important aspect of SI theory because he argued that social interactions create, sustain, and transform the social world. He—and many of his students—argued that the social world was produced *entirely* through social interactions. From this perspective, things like race, gender, marriage, and even religion do not have a pre-determined, inherent meaning. Rather, repeated social interactions produce the meanings and hierarchies associated with socially constructed characteristics, events, and identities. For instance, although there is no biological evidence for the belief that some races are superior to others, humans have, for a variety of historical reasons, created this idea. As our interactions continue over time, this idea is continually reinforced and maintained—so much so, that we eventually forget we created it in the first place and we assume it is based on some kind of natural truth. This perspective on the creation and maintenance of social meaning is often referred to as "the social construction of reality," and it is a direct outgrowth of SI theory.

CONSIDER THIS. . .

Which theory resonates most with your world view? Why do you think you prefer this theory?

Sociological Theory

In this exercise, you will test your knowledge of sociological theory.

1. What is functionalism?
   a. A theory that suggests power dynamics are the most important variable for understanding society's functioning
   b. A theory that suggests all parts of a society are important for that society's functioning
   c. A theory that suggests social realities are created during and through human interactions
   d. A theory that focuses on how intersecting identities affect an individual's life experiences

2. What is conflict theory?
   a. A theory that is based, in part, on Durkheim's work
   b. A theory that focuses on power
   c. A theory that focuses on the interrelated parts of a society
   d. A theory that focuses on women's subordinate position in society

3. What is symbolic interactionism?
   a. A theory that suggests humans have the capacity to interpret symbols during interactions
   b. A theory that suggests power dynamics are the most important variable for understanding society's functioning
   c. A theory that suggests social realities are created by societal structures
   d. A theory based in part on Marx's work

4. Why is Weber characterized as a conflict theorist?

Why Theory Matters

What does all of this theory have to do with the research process? Theory shapes the way sociologists ask questions, interpret data, and come to understand the social world. Let's consider the issue of inequality to further illustrate this point. A functionalist analyzing inequality might first note that most societies—if not all—have some degree of inequality. They might then consider the possible benefits that inequality brings to society. For example, a functionalist would argue that inequality in wages and wealth promotes hard work. By rewarding socially important positions with higher pay and status, inequality encourages talented and hard-working people to aim for these important positions. Notice that our perspective here is shaped in two important ways by our reliance on functionalism: (1) we are focusing on the possible positive contributions of inequality, and (2) we are using a macro orientation to ask how inequality benefits society rather than how it harms individuals.

Now let's consider how a conflict perspective makes sense of inequality. This perspective focuses on the ways that inequality *harms* groups of people. A conflict theorist would likely ask questions like: How do powerful groups of people (business owners, politicians, boards of directors, etc.) maintain their power and keep more subordinate groups of people (laborers, citizens, consumers, etc.) from threatening it? This is a very different way of looking at inequality! We are no longer trying to examine the benefits of inequality; instead, our focus is on the conflict and strife it causes between groups. Notice, however, that our focus is similar to functionalism in one way: We are still operating at the macro level, and that is because conflict theory focuses on how groups of people vie for power and how societal structures and institutions keep power in the hands of some and out of the hands of others.

Lastly, what would a symbolic interactionist perspective on inequality look like? Because SI theory operates at the micro level, our focus will be on how an individual's interactions with the world promote and maintain inequality. An SI theorist might ask how interactions within poor neighborhoods, schools, and family environments shape the way economically disadvantaged children come to understand their place in the world. Using an SI theory framework, we are less inclined to ask what the benefits or harms of inequality are; instead, we are likely to ask what inequality *means* for the people who experience it and how that meaning then shapes their future. Table 2.1 provides an overview of how each of these three major theories view different systems.

TABLE 2.1 ■ Variations in Perspective Based on Theory			
	Functionalism	**Conflict Theory**	**Symbolic Interactionism**
Family	Provides economic support	Promotes gender inequality	Shapes a person's identity
Religion	Promotes a moral code	Separates people by beliefs	Promotes ritualized behaviors
Inequality	Motivates hard work	Creates divisions by class	Affects childhood socialization
Crime	Creates jobs (police, etc.)	Results in unfair profiling	Creates a culture of fear

As you can see, theory is important in shaping how sociologists understand the social world. Theory is foundational to all that we do. Now that we understand the connection between theory and the research process, we can start to examine the other steps in the research process.

Check Your Understanding

1. What is theory, and why is it important in the research process?
2. What are the primary differences among functionalism, conflict theory, and symbolic interactionism?
3. How do these differences impact the way sociologists ask questions about and come to understand the social world?

POSING QUESTIONS

Why are divorced mothers more likely to have custody of their children than are divorced fathers? How do Black and Latinx individuals respond to and cope with housing discrimination? What types of community characteristics promote good health and wellbeing? These are just a few examples of sociological questions—questions that seek to understand the complex relationships between people and society.

Sociologists regularly pose questions about the social world. In doing so, though, they must be mindful of the difference between empirical and non-empirical questions, and inductive and deductive questions.

Empirical and Non-empirical Questions

Empirical questions are those you can answer with scientific data. In other words, you can use the steps of the research process to arrive at an answer to the question. Each of the three questions listed in the preceding section is an empirical question. We can use science to determine the processes that make it more likely that women have custody of their children than men, to identify how Black and Latinx individuals respond when they experience housing discrimination, and to identify the characteristics of communities that are associated with positive health outcomes.

Non-empirical questions, in contrast, are those that cannot be answered scientifically. They tend to be more opinion based—for instance, are mothers better parents than fathers, are white Americans better home-buyers than Black and Latinx Americans, and what are the qualities of good communities? These questions cannot be definitively answered using scientific methods, in part because what makes someone a "better" parent, home-buyer, or something a "better" community cannot be conclusively defined. Instead, it is a matter of opinion.

As sociologists, we need to ask empirical questions. Sociology is an empirical discipline and sociologists are scientists. This is an important point because sometimes people fail to recognize sociological questions as scientific questions. People often assume that science deals with the natural world or chemical reactions, but social issues can be subject to scientific scrutiny as well.

CONSIDER THIS. . .

Why do you think some questions are easily recognized as scientific issues while others often are not?

DOING SOCIOLOGY 2.2

Creating Empirical Questions

In this exercise, you will practice developing empirical questions.

Questions about emotions, feelings, and subjective perceptions can be asked in a way that is empirical. Using what you've learned about empirical questions, answer the following questions:

1. Develop an empirical question about happiness.
2. Develop an empirical question about perceptions of friendly behavior.
3. Develop an empirical question about shyness.
4. Develop an empirical question about a concept of your choice.

Inductive and Deductive Questions

Inductive reasoning involves moving from the specific to the general. Inductive questions, then, are those that result from specific observations of facts that a researcher thinks might point to a general tendency. Imagine that a researcher knows of 50 divorced couples with children, and in 48 cases the mothers have custody of their children. They may wonder whether this fact illustrates a broader pattern whereby mothers are given custody of their children more often than fathers. They might then generate broader research questions: Do divorced mothers generally get custody of their children more often than divorced fathers? If so, why?

Deductive reasoning, on the other hand, starts from general theory and moves toward specific examples. Deductive questions start with a theoretical premise that a researcher hopes to verify by examining specific observations in the social world. For instance, gender socialization theory suggests that females are taught to be caregivers, nurturers, and primary parents to children while males are taught to be breadwinners, protectors, and secondary parents to children. Given this theoretical understanding of gender roles, a researcher could set out to determine how these cultural ideas influence child custody decisions. They might ask: Do societal gender role expectations affect custody placements at divorce? And if so, how?

Sociologists ask inductive questions in some cases, and deductive questions in others. The distinction between the two types of questions is important, though, because they start and end in different places. Inductive questions start with specific patterns in social life and end by generating a general explanation for those patterns—in other words, they end by generating theory. Deductive questions are the exact opposite—they start with an existing theoretical premise and seek to test the validity of that premise by examining specific patterns in social life. In fact, here's a quick way to help you remember the difference between inductive and deductive questions. *Inductive* is associated with specific *observations* and both of these words begin with vowels, while *deductive* is associated with general *theory* and both of these words begin with consonants.

Check Your Understanding

1. What is the difference between empirical and non-empirical questions?
2. What are inductive and deductive questions?
3. Why are these distinctions important?

CRAFTING EXPLANATIONS

Once we have posed a research question, we want to try to answer it. The process of crafting explanations starts by reviewing what other researchers have written on the topic. This is called a literature review. Sociologists read the existing research, articles, and books that address the issue they are studying. Through this process, they see which theoretical perspectives other researchers have used to understand the issue. They also develop a solid understanding of what is known about the issue and what remains to be learned.

A literature review is an important step in the research process for three reasons. First, it saves researchers from "reinventing the wheel"—investigating a question that has a well-established answer, or conducting a study that has already been conducted multiple times. Second, reviewing the existing research on a topic can help researchers refine their research question. By knowing what others have already discovered about this topic, we can sharpen and narrow our own research questions. Third, and most important, science is most useful when it builds off of itself. As sociologists, we want to ensure that we are helping move our discipline forward. The best way to do that is to be certain we are always engaged in a dialogue with one another. Understanding the work that precedes our own is the best way to engage in that dialogue and continue to enhance our collective understanding of the social world.

Developing a Research Design

The next step in the process of crafting explanations is to develop a research design. This is when sociologists articulate their hypotheses and identify their independent and dependent variables.

A hypothesis is an unverified but testable statement that a researcher believes represents a potential answer to their research question. In other words, it is an educated guess—and that guess is based, in part, on sociological theory and the previously completed literature review. For instance, imagine that a sociologist wants to understand why poverty rates in the United States are significantly higher than poverty rates in other wealthy Western nations. After reading the existing literature on poverty and considering both functionalism and conflict theory, they might offer the following two hypotheses as potential answers to the research question:

1. Poverty rates are higher in the United States than in most other wealthy Western nations because a higher proportion of U.S. citizens choose not to pursue the education and training necessary to secure high-paying jobs.

2. Poverty rates are higher in the United States than in most other wealthy Western nations because U.S. tax laws perpetuate income and wealth disparities.

Notice the specificity of these hypotheses. Although they are both "educated guesses," the guesses are informed by the existing research literature and theoretical perspectives in the field. The background information that this prior research and theory provide is precisely what allows for the formulation of detailed hypotheses. That, in turn, is what keeps advancing scientific knowledge.

DOING SOCIOLOGY 2.3

Creating a Hypothesis

In this exercise, you will formulate a sociological research question.

1. Select something in the social world that intrigues you (e.g., social media, dating patterns, homelessness, economic inequality, day care for children, etc.), then list what you know about this issue.

2. Why do you think your chosen issue is important in life? How do you think it might be related to other social issues like gender, age, race, religion, etc.?

3. Write a research question based on your chosen social issue.

4. Write at least one hypothesis for your research question. Be sure to be specific—your hypothesis should not be answerable by a simple yes or no.

After formulating their hypotheses, sociologists must identify their independent and dependent variables. Variables are elements of the social world that can have more than one value. For instance, in the hypotheses about poverty rates, a country's poverty rate is a variable, the tax laws are a variable, and the educational motivation of citizens is a variable. Independent variables (IV) are those variables that sociologists believe will impact some aspect of the social world. In the example given, the researcher believes tax laws and/or motivation levels may influence poverty rates. These concepts represent the independent variables—those are the things expected to cause a change in something else. Dependent variables (DV), then, are those variables that sociologists expect to be changed by something else. In this case, the level of poverty within a country is the dependent variable because the researcher believes it will be impacted by tax laws and the citizenry's motivations.

CONSIDER THIS...

What are the IV and DV for this hypothesis? "Children who spend their leisure time playing outdoors have better health outcomes than children who spend their time watching television."

Collecting Data

So how do sociologists answer their research questions and test their hypotheses? They collect and analyze data from the social world. Collecting data involves gathering information about the social world. Analyzing data refers to making sense of the information that has been gathered.

Let's consider surveys as an example. Surveys involve asking research subjects (the people being studied) to respond to a series of questions that are purposely designed to elicit information about the researcher's topic of interest. For instance, imagine a sociologist wants to understand minority group members' perceptions of local police officers. They may generate a set of survey questions that ask minority respondents to report on how much they trust, admire, dislike, are comfortable with, and/or are suspicious of local police officers. These questions will typically be asked on paper or through an online system. Collecting data in this way is both efficient and cost-effective. It allows the researcher to gather a great deal of relatively uniform data from a large number of people.

Surveys are only one example of how sociologists can collect data. They can also use interviews, participant observation, existing documents, and experiments. Upcoming chapters will discuss various data collection methods in more detail.

Analyzing Data and Drawing Conclusions

Regardless of the data collection method sociologists use, once they have gathered their data, they must make sense of them. Data analysis can take many forms. For instance, survey data are often analyzed using quantitative methods—this means researchers transform respondents' answers into numbers, enter those numbers into spreadsheets, and then use statistical programs such as Excel, SPSS, or R to help them test their hypotheses. Alternatively, data can also be analyzed using qualitative methods. In this case, data are left in textual form and sociologists look for common words and phrases used by the respondents. Patterns in the way these words and phrases are used are then grouped by theme (similarities in the messages they portray) and those themes help sociologists tell the story revealed in the data.

When using qualitative methods, sociologists look for patterns in the words and phrases of respondents in order to find larger themes in their research.

Silvia Li Volsi/EyeEm/Getty Images

The differences between quantitative and qualitative analyses are important and will be discussed at length in later chapters. For now, let's return to our earlier discussion of theory because it also plays an important role in the analysis process. Because theory is the lens through which sociologists make sense of the social world, it is critical for helping sociologists contextualize their research findings. For instance, imagine you are a sociologist with an interest in crime. You have gathered data on crime rates for your city and asked city residents, politicians, and employees (police officers, court officials, etc.) to discuss how crime has or has not impacted their lives. If you analyze your data using a functionalist perspective, you will likely be attuned to the possible benefits of crime for your respondents (it creates jobs for police officers and court officials). If you use a conflict perspective, you will likely focus on the various ways power differentials impact people's perceptions of crime (individuals with arrest records likely view the legal process with more suspicion and doubt than do victims, politicians, and police officers). And, if you use a symbolic interactionist perspective, you will likely emphasize what crime means to various individuals (victims of crime may feel violated while perpetrators of crime may feel they had few other choices available to them).

In short, a sociologist's theoretical approach informs not only which research questions they ask, but also the lens through which they collect and interpret their data. This is very important. Sometimes students ask: Isn't it problematic that the answers to research questions change based on the theory a sociologist uses? Doesn't that introduce potential bias? Shouldn't research questions have only one right answer? These are certainly meaningful and even understandable questions, but the answer to each of them is "not necessarily." The social world is incredibly complex. Human lives and the structures we create are messy. Consequently, there is often more than one way to define a situation. This means we frequently need multiple perspectives on the same issue. One sociologist can use one theoretical perspective to understand a particular facet of an issue. A second sociologist can then use a different theory to understand some other facet of that same issue. Why? Because research questions do not always have a single right answer. Making sense of the world we live in requires that we consider our data through a number of theoretical perspectives. When we do that, we have the best chance of understanding and shaping our social lives.

SOCIOLOGISTS IN ACTION
Chadwick Menning

Several years ago, Chadwick Menning developed an interest in sexual assault prevention on college campuses. Advocates, the media, and politicians were frequently noting that one in five college women experience a completed or attempted assault during their college career. As a result, he began to wonder what existing prevention efforts looked like on college campuses. He also wondered if those efforts could be improved. Eventually, he and colleague Mellisa Holtzman turned this curiosity into a sociological research question: What programming features increase the effectiveness of campus sexual assault prevention programs?

A review of the existing research literature made it clear that there are two broad types of prevention programs in existence:

1. Primary prevention programs provide educational information on consent, party culture, and the role of alcohol in assault. Their goal is to change the way people think about sex and assault in an effort to change our cultural understandings of these issues.
2. Risk reduction programs provide self-defense training to potential victims. Their goal is to equip individuals with the tools needed to protect themselves if they are in a dangerous situation.

The literature review also revealed that most campuses favor primary prevention programs over risk reduction programs. This means students are rarely exposed to both curriculums.

Based on this literature, they developed a hypothesis:

● College sexual assault prevention programs that address both primary prevention and risk reduction will be more effective at lowering assault rates than programs that focus on only one type of programming.

Testing this hypothesis required several steps. First, they *designed* a program that combined primary prevention and risk reduction. To do that they enlisted the help of 15 college students who spent an entire semester working alongside them to create and refine a new type of sexual assault protection program (Holtzman & Menning, 2015). This program is called Elemental.

Second, they collected survey data on students who took the program *and* on those who did not take it. They did this because they wanted to determine if Elemental participants exhibited lower assault risk than students who had not participated in the program.

Third, they used quantitative analyses to examine students' experiences with assault. They found that Elemental students experience a 66% reduction in their risk of assault compared to students who have not taken the program (Holtzman & Menning, 2019; Menning & Holtzman, 2015). And, most important, their analyses suggested this effect is due, in part, to the fact the program offers training in both primary prevention and risk reduction (Menning & Holtzman, 2020). In short, their hypothesis was supported.

Chadwick Menning is a professor of sociology at Ball State University and a co-creator of Elemental.

Discussion Question

Which steps of the research process do you see in the discussion of Elemental?

Check Your Understanding

1. Why is reviewing the literature an important step in the research process?
2. What are hypotheses, and how does theory impact their formulation?
3. What are independent and dependent variables?
4. How does theory factor into the data analysis process?

COMMUNICATING RESULTS

The final step in the research process is communicating the results—but that can mean a variety of things, including communicating findings to other scientists, to policy makers, and to the public. Importantly, the type of audience with whom a sociologist hopes to communicate will affect the strategies they use for disseminating their findings.

Academic journals are an important vessel for disseminating research findings to others in the academic community.

Zoonar GmbH/Alamy Stock Photo

Conveying Findings

Many sociologists—especially those who work at universities or research institutes—put considerable effort into communicating their results to other scientists. This is important because peer-to-peer communication is how a discipline grows. Scientists read each other's work and build off it (recall the literature review process discussed earlier in this chapter). There are two primary venues used for this kind of communication. First, sociologists publish their work in academic journals. These publications feature scientific articles describing their research question, hypotheses, methods, analyses, and findings. Getting one's work published in a journal, however, is not an easy process. Authors must first submit their work to the journal editor for consideration. If the editor sees promise, they will send a blinded (anonymous) copy out to two or three other scientists in this field. The job of these scientists is to conduct a thorough peer review. They scrutinize the author's research methods and findings, point out weaknesses, and make suggestions for improvements. They also offer a recommendation to the editor regarding whether or not the paper should be accepted for publication, rejected (declined), or given a "revise and resubmit" (a chance to make changes and try again). Often papers go through a series of peer reviews before being accepted for publication. It is not uncommon for an article to spend a year or more in the review and publication process. This helps ensure published work is rigorous, meaningful, and as unbiased as possible.

Because science relies so heavily on peer dialogue, another way for sociologists to disseminate their findings is through academic conference presentations. In this instance, they present their findings to a live audience during a formal presentation. Often, they are presenting work when it is in its early stages—perhaps preliminary findings—and asking the audience for feedback. This allows sociologists to refine their studies before submitting the final work to a journal for consideration.

Sociologists do not always want to convey their findings to strictly scientific audiences, though. In fact, applied sociologists—sometimes called public sociologists—are often more concerned with disseminating their findings to policy makers, community organizations, and local citizens. They target these audiences in an effort to produce change at the local level. Rather than confining their work to academic journals read primarily by other scientists, public sociologists bring their research to everyday people by writing articles for newspapers and magazines, doing interviews with television and radio, participating in local outreach efforts, and attending community meetings.

Regardless of the type of outlet used to disseminate sociological research, communicating findings to a larger audience is an important step in the research process. It ensures continuous dialogue and growth within the field, raises community awareness on social issues, and contributes to cultural change. For all these reasons, sociological research plays a critical role in shaping our social world.

Figure 2.1 provides an overview of the steps we have discussed throughout this chapter, from developing research questions to presenting the results of that research.

FIGURE 2.1 ■ The Sociological Research Process

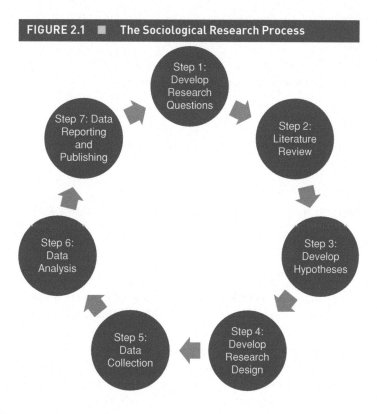

CONSIDER THIS...

Newspapers, television, and social media sites can be important sources of sociological knowledge. Can you recall a media story that explicitly mentions sociology? Do you think it is important for media reports to explicitly discuss sociology?

DOING SOCIOLOGY 2.4

Understanding an Academic Abstract

In this activity, you will learn how to derive information about a sociological study from an abstract.

When researchers publish a sociological study, they almost always include what is called an "abstract," or a very brief summary of the research that is usually only a few hundred words long but conveys quite a bit about the research that has been completed.

Read the following abstract for a sociological journal article:

> This study explores if bystanders to sexual violence are assigned blame when they fail to intervene. During 2017, 31 female and 20 male U.S. college students were asked to read three of six randomly assigned sexual assault vignettes and participate in an interview about their perceptions of bystander inaction. Qualitative analyses reveal that college students do hold bystanders accountable for inaction, but the assignment of blame depends upon the bystander's knowledge of the perpetrator's intentions, the degree of similarity between respondents and the bystanders in the vignettes, and the degree to which the bystanders could have behaved differently. Bystanders do face moderate blame for their inaction, this is true in a variety of assault situations, and it suggests bystander training increases perceptions of culpability for non-intervention. This information can help campus administrators improve the efficacy of their bystander education programs. (Holtzman, 2020)

Answer the following questions based on the abstract:

1. What sort of theory does the author appear to be using to contextualize the findings?
   a. Functionalism
   b. Conflict
   c. Symbolic interactionism

2. What method of data collection is mentioned in the abstract?
   a. Surveys
   b. Experiments
   c. Interviews

3. Does this appear to be quantitative or qualitative research?
   a. Quantitative
   b. Qualitative
   c. Both quantitative and qualitative

4. What are the key findings of the study? Is there a conclusion? If so, what is it?

Reading Sociological Research

Before we wrap up this chapter, let's take a moment to discuss the parts of an academic journal article. This will help you learn how to read and critique scientific information. Perhaps it will not be surprising to hear that most scientific articles are divided into sections that roughly correspond to the stages of the research process. Articles generally start with a brief Introduction that states the sociologist's research question. This is followed by a review of the literature, a discussion of relevant theory, and often—particularly in deductive work—a statement of the researcher's hypotheses. The Methods section of the paper describes the research subjects, the data collection process, and the kinds of analyses conducted. The Results section outlines the study findings. The Discussion section offers an in-depth discussion of the study's implications, any possible limitations contained in the current research (e.g., the research may not apply to everyone), and future directions for research. If there are alternative interpretations of the researchers' findings, authors often make note of them in the Discussion section, and discuss how future research might clarify which interpretation makes the most sense.

Reading a journal article for the first time can feel a bit daunting, but there are a few things you can do to make the process a bit easier. First, you should recognize that there are two basic kinds of articles—those that are reporting the findings from a quantitative study and those that are reporting the findings from a qualitative study. Quantitative articles typically have many numbers and tables in them. Qualitative articles are mostly textual and often contain a large number of quotes from interviewees but relatively few (if any) tables.

Once you have identified the kind of article you are reading, you can make some strategic decisions about how you engage with each section of the article. For instance, I tell my students that when they are reading quantitative articles, they should read the Introduction and Literature Review closely because those sections contain important background information that will help them contextualize and understand the study's findings. With respect to the Methods section, however, I often tell my students that if they are new to statistical concepts and techniques, they should take what they can from the Methods section but not panic if they encounter unfamiliar words or confusing notation. Similarly, if they find the tables in the Results section confusing, they should focus their efforts on understanding the written description of the results and the summary that will be contained in the Discussion section. These are not hard and fast rules on reading quantitative journal articles, but these tips can help ease the anxiety students often feel the first time they open a journal article.

For qualitative articles, though, the reading is a little different. In this case, the Methods section is very important because it explains how the researcher made sense of their textual data. Because qualitative research relies so heavily on a scientist's ability to organize data and recognize the patterns it contains—generally without the assistance of statistics and software packages—assessments about the reliability of their results will often hinge on your understanding of the methods that were employed. Thus, it is important to closely read the Methods sections in qualitative research. Likewise, the Results section is critical because it contains the quotes used to illustrate and give meaning to the research findings. Overall, then, qualitative articles are often slightly longer and more time-intensive to read than quantitative articles, but they also provide us with detailed and in-depth knowledge of social processes and patterns.

Check Your Understanding

1. What kinds of outlets do sociologists use to communicate their research findings?
2. What are the parts of a scientific journal article?
3. What are some strategies for reading sociological research?

CONCLUSION

As you can see, sociological research is the result of a number of interrelated processes, from the application of theory and a review of the literature to data collection, analysis, and the communication of results. Research is one of the most important things a sociologist does because it not only helps us understand our social world, it is also instrumental in helping us change it. Effective social change is based on a number of things, including dedicated people who are willing to pursue a cause, but the roles of data and research in facilitating that process cannot be overstated. In short, by learning how to do research you are, in effect, learning how to change the world!

The remaining chapters in this text will break down the research process in more detail and teach you how to engage in each of these steps. Along the way you will also learn about research ethics, mixed methodologies, and using research to promote social justice. Research is an important aspect of sociology, and although you cannot master the process in a single semester, this text will provide you with foundational knowledge that you can build upon as you continue to grow as a sociology student.

2.1   What are the three major sociological theoretical perspectives, and why is theory important?

There are three prominent theoretical paradigms in sociology—functionalism, conflict theory, and symbolic interactionism. Functionalism is a theoretical perspective that argues that society is composed of interrelated systems that shape and constrain individuals, and in so doing, help create, maintain, and stabilize that society. Conflict theory is a theoretical perspective that focuses on the strife that institutions and social patterns create in society. Finally, symbolic interactionism is a theoretical perspective in which repeated social interactions produce the meanings and hierarchies associated with socially constructed characteristics, events, and identities. Theory is important because it shapes the way sociologists ask questions, interpret data, and come to understand the social world.

2.2   How do sociologists generate research questions?

Sociologists pose empirical (as opposed to non-empirical), inductive, and deductive research questions. Empirical questions are those that you can answer with scientific data; you can use the steps of the research process to arrive at an answer to the question. Non-empirical questions cannot be answered scientifically and tend to be more opinion-based. Inductive questions result from specific observations of facts that a researcher thinks might point to a general tendency. Deductive questions start with a theoretical premise that a researcher hopes to verify by examining specific observations in the social world.

2.3   What are key aspects of the sociological research process?

Designing a study that can answer one's research questions is a multistep process. It begins by reviewing what other researchers have written on the topic. This is called a literature review. The next step is to develop a research design. This occurs when sociologists articulate their hypotheses and identify their independent and dependent variables. Sociologists then collect and analyze data from the social world. Collecting data involves gathering information about the social world. Analyzing data refers to making sense of the information that has been gathered. Because theory is the lens through which sociologists make sense of the social world, it is critical for helping sociologists contextualize their research findings.

2.4   How do sociologists communicate their research results, and what are the major parts of a research article?

Sociologists communicate their results to a larger audience through such things as scientific journals, academic conferences, or public engagement via newspaper articles, television interviews, podcasts, blogs, and community outreach events. Most scientific articles are divided into sections that roughly correspond to the stages of the research process. Articles generally start with a brief Introduction that states the sociologist's research question. This is followed by a review of the literature, a discussion of relevant theory, and often—particularly in deductive work—a statement of the researcher's hypotheses. The Methods section of the paper describes the research subjects, the data collection process, and the kinds of analyses conducted. The Results section outlines the study findings. The Discussion section offers an in-depth discussion of the study's implications, any possible limitations contained in the current research (e.g., the research may not apply to everyone), and future directions for research.

KEY TERMS

academic conference presentations (p. 31)

academic journals (p. 30)

analyzing data (p. 28)

applied sociologists (public sociologists) (p. 31)

bourgeoisie (p. 22)

class position (p. 23)

collecting data (p. 28)

conflict theory (p. 22)

deductive questions (p. 26)

dependent variables (p. 28)

empirical questions (p. 25)

functionalism (p. 22)

hypothesis (p. 27)

independent variables (p. 28)

inductive questions (p. 26)

literature review (p. 27)

macro approach (p. 23)

micro approach (p. 23)

non-empirical questions (p. 25)

party position (p. 23)

peer review (p. 31)

proletariat (p. 22)

qualitative methods (p. 28)

quantitative methods (p. 28)

research subjects (p. 28)

social facts (p. 22)

sociological questions (p. 25)

sociological theory (p. 22)

status position (p. 23)

survey (p. 28)

symbolic interactionism (p. 23)

theory (p. 22)

variables (p. 28)

3 CHARACTERIZING THE DIMENSIONS OF SOCIAL RESEARCH

Emily McKendry-Smith and Anne Kristen Hunter

STUDENT LEARNING QUESTIONS

3.1 What are the four goals for sociological research?

3.2 What are the key features of qualitative and quantitative data?

3.3 What does the unit of analysis refer to in sociological research?

3.4 What is the key difference between cross-sectional and longitudinal data?

3.5 What are three audiences that sociologists typically write for, and how does sociological writing differ depending on the audience?

INTRODUCTION

Why do sociologists conduct research? There are a number of reasons. First and foremost, sociologists conduct research because systematic analyses of the social world help us to understand what's going on around us. Sociological research makes sense of the workings of both small groups and communities, countries and companies, organizations of all kinds, all across the globe. Sociologists also conduct research because doing so helps us understand how social change occurs. By connecting the theoretical insights of the sociological imagination with the tools of sociological research methods, our research helps to shed light on the lives of individual people, the overall organization of society, and the relationship between the two.

As you may already have noticed from the examples in Chapters 1 and 2, sociologists investigate an exceptionally wide range of topics, issues, and questions. If you ask a sociologist, "What aspects of social life can sociological research help to explain?" they will likely tell you, "All aspects of social life!" If you ask a sociologist, "Which methodological tools can sociologists use to conduct their research?" they will likely answer, "A very wide range of tools!" Sociological methods range from qualitative analyses of images, to ethnographic studies of organizations, to statistical analyses of large-scale numeric data, to name only a few.

Given the diversity of topics and methods of sociological research, it's sometimes hard for students to get a handle on what exactly sociology is, and what exactly sociological research methods entail. This chapter provides an overview of the basic dimensions of sociological research. It examines three central questions: What are the main goals of sociological research? What are the main types of sociological research? And how are the results of sociological research communicated and shared?

HOW I GOT ACTIVE IN SOCIOLOGY
Emily McKendry-Smith

As a teenager growing up in the 1990s, I lived through several events that illustrated the importance of religion in the social world—from debates about teaching evolution in schools in my home state to the events of September 11, 2001. As a college student, I was looking for a way to study religion that would help me make sense of these kinds of events. Through my coursework, I eventually discovered that what I was looking for was sociology—where religion is studied based on the way it is lived. Coursework on other issues such as families and social movements has helped me learn about other important social institutions, and how they intersect with religion.

Many of my earliest courses on sociology focused on globalization, which taught me to have an international perspective and to think about the world as interconnected. I ended up doing research on religion in Nepal, so sociology has taken me places I never dreamed of when I was starting out. I must also acknowledge the mentoring of my first sociology professor, Chad Broughton, whose "tale of two cities" approach to globalization is available to everyone in the book *Boom, Bust, Exodus*.

GOALS FOR SOCIOLOGICAL RESEARCH

A goal isn't an expectation about a research finding, a predetermined outcome we hope to find, or an agenda we're hoping to advance. Rather, the goal of a research project relates to how the empirical data we collect and analyze will be used. The goal of social research is *the purpose* that research serves *the reason* a sociologist has for conducting it.

Sociologists have four primary goals for conducting research:

- To *explore* a new or previously undocumented social phenomenon;
- To *describe* a social phenomenon;
- To *explain* why two or more concepts are related or unrelated using theoretical perspectives; and
- To *apply* sociological findings to social problems.

Our research goals are shaped, in part, by the intended audience. Is the research project meant to inform an ongoing sociological debate, or is it meant to inform policy makers or organizational leaders? Maybe the project is designed to assess and address a problem in the researcher's local community. Having an initial idea of the audience also helps direct the way we present our research findings.

HOW I GOT ACTIVE IN SOCIOLOGY
Anne Kristen Hunter

My first psychology class claimed that it would help me understand other people better, but it was sociology's insistence that everything is *not* just inside people's heads, that groups matter, that poverty and discrimination are *real* and they *matter*, that really helped me understand the world I saw around me. Sociology answered questions I didn't even know how to ask until I learned it.

We live in an unjust, unequal, and unfair world, and sociology is the only thing that helps me make sense of that. Understanding alone doesn't make things better, but it keeps me from feeling lost or helpless. In particular, Allison Pugh's *Longing and Belonging* and Elizabeth Armstrong and Laura Hamilton's *Paying for the Party* helped me finally understand why I didn't "fit in" as a child or in college. Zygmunt Bauman's *Modernity and the Holocaust* and Randall Collins's *Violence* give me a starting place to address the most upsetting events I see on the news.

Sociology also teaches that societies *can* and *do* change, that what is true here today is not true everywhere always, and shows how people who wanted social change have accomplished it before. People make the world, and we can work to make it different.

Exploration

Sometimes social change happens rapidly. New social issues, identities, or groups can come into being suddenly and in other cases suddenly come to an end. The conservative Tea Party, which emerged suddenly in 2009, is one such example. The 2015 U.S. Supreme Court ruling in the case of *Obergefell v. Hodges*, which put an end to state-level bans on same-sex marriage, is another. All of a sudden same-sex couples across the United States had the right to marry. Our society is always changing, and change creates new issues to explore and new questions to ask.

When researchers examine a previously unexamined issue, ask a previously unasked question, or look at the world in a radically different way, they're conducting exploratory research. Exploratory research is our first approach to a topic that is new, different, unexpected, and unstudied—or at least *under*-studied. Every piece of social research has to start somewhere, and when we're starting something new, our goal is often *exploration*. Because the topic is so new, sometimes we don't even know enough to ask very sophisticated questions about it. We don't yet know what we want to know! Instead, our questions are very basic, and very general, like "What is this?" or "What does this mean?" or "What is this like for the people living it?"

When researchers explore, we often use a diverse set of methodological tools, analyzing many types of data in many different ways. An exploratory analysis of the Tea Party movement might include talking with people who identify as Tea Party members, looking at photos and videos of Tea Party rallies, analyzing the text of speeches made at Tea Party events, and analyzing the demographic characteristics of Tea Party members (such as race, gender, age, socioeconomic status, or region of the country). The methods we chose might change during the course of the study, as we learn more about the issue and the questions that interest us.

New laws can confer new rights or benefits but can also take away old ones. The challenges of a changing climate might make some traditions impossible to maintain and may alter or even bring an end to life in coastal communities. Longer lifespans and lower birth rates have given us a society of people older than ever before. Other changes have given us a population that is more racially diverse, as our country changes from a place where there are more white Americans than every other racial and ethnic group put together, to one where white Americans are still the largest group but no longer the majority. It is not simply change in the world around us, but people's *responses* to a changing world, that produce the need for exploration.

There are two common situations where we might initially think our goal is exploration, but later realize we want to do something else. The first situation is when a social phenomenon is *new to you* even though others have already studied it. The first time you learn about something, it's tempting to think it might be the first time *anyone* has learned about it. Reading what other social scientists have previously written helps us check if we need to explore, or if we should form a descriptive or explanatory goal instead.

The second situation is related, and can happen after we review the literature. We can find ourselves saying something like, "Other scientists have studied Topic A and Topic C, but there's a whole other topic between them, about which nothing has been written!" Sometimes this in-between topic really is so new that it requires true *exploration*, but many other times, knowing something about its neighbors lets us approach Topic B as an expansion of what's already known.

A photo of a Tea Party rally might be analyzed to look at the number of people; apparent age, race, or gender of the protesters; the messages on protesters' signs; or even the design of the protesters' costumes and apparel.

©KAREN BLEIER/Staff/Getty Images

Description

Suppose that after making your New Year's resolutions, you started tracking some of your daily activities. Perhaps you got a fitness tracker bracelet. Perhaps you began keeping a list of everything you spent money on, or you took photos of each of your meals. After a week or a month of doing this, you could look back on the records you'd been keeping to learn about yourself. Sociologists conducting **descriptive research** have goals very similar to what you would have in this situation. Their goals are to document and describe an aspect of society that is of interest to them.

Descriptive information is important because it gives us accurate information about the social world. More so than any other methodological goal, descriptive research seeks to answer questions about "how much?" or "how many?"

If what we want to know is the size of different social groups, then our goal is a descriptive one. We might ask, for example, "How common are same-sex marriages?" or "Is the number of Catholics in America growing or shrinking?" When we try to determine the prevalence of different opinions, when we want to know *how many* people believe different things, then our goal is similarly descriptive. We might ask, "What proportion of Americans support paid parental leave?" or "How much trust do people have in Congress?" In these cases, our goals are descriptive.

In addition to documenting *what* people believe, descriptive research can be used to determine how often people believe information that's factually correct, and how many hold mistaken views or are unsure. This form of descriptive research is less common but can be valuable for determining the effectiveness of education, or the spread of misinformation. For example, researchers at the Pew Research Center published a report describing what Americans know about the Holocaust. Based on a survey of American adults, they tell us what percentage know to what the term *Holocaust* refers, in what time period it took place, and so on (69% correctly answered that the Holocaust took place between 1930–1950; see Figure 3.1).

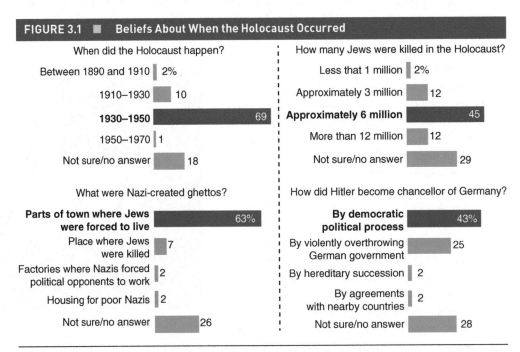

FIGURE 3.1 ■ Beliefs About When the Holocaust Occurred

When did the Holocaust happen?

Between 1890 and 1910	2%
1910–1930	10
1930–1950	**69**
1950–1970	1
Not sure/no answer	18

How many Jews were killed in the Holocaust?

Less that 1 million	2%
Approximately 3 million	12
Approximately 6 million	**45**
More than 12 million	12
Not sure/no answer	29

What were Nazi-created ghettos?

Parts of town where Jews were forced to live	**63%**
Place where Jews were killed	7
Factories where Nazis forced political opponents to work	2
Housing for poor Nazis	2
Not sure/no answer	26

How did Hitler become chancellor of Germany?

By democratic political process	**43%**
By violently overthrowing German government	25
By hereditary succession	2
By agreements with nearby countries	2
Not sure/no answer	28

Source: "What Americans Know About the Holocaust," Pew Research Center, Washington, DC (January 22, 2020), https://www.pewforum.org/2020/01/22/what-americans-know-about-the-holocaust/

Descriptive research can also serve as the inspiration for other types of research. For instance, the Pew Research Center report tells us that college graduates tend to know more about the Holocaust than people who have completed high school but did not attend college. Noticing this difference is the first step to conducting additional research. Someone interested in this topic might wonder what happens in college to explain this difference—is it additional history classes, out-of-class lectures and events, or access to resources in the college library? Another researcher might wonder if specific changes to the high school curriculum could improve student learning. In this way, descriptive research can serve as a springboard into conducting explanatory or applied research, discussed next.

Explanation

When researchers document differences or inequalities among social groups, sociologists investigate the causes of those differences, where they come from, why they exist, and how they affect other social phenomena. These questions are the basis of explanatory research, in which researchers attempt to document and explain social patterns.

Social patterns are complex and, as a result, sociologists often spend their entire careers asking and answering a series of questions about a particular social phenomenon. For example, how do we explain the persistence of racial/ethnic inequality? Why do some people have a high degree of confidence in political institutions, and others not? Why do some entrepreneurial efforts fail and others succeed? What community-level characteristics are associated with greater health and well-being?

When researchers conduct explanatory research, they begin by considering a variety of possible explanations. Suppose, for example, that you studied the academic performance of first-year students in a high school history class. You noticed that students averaged a B in the class, but that students who had attended one middle school mostly got Cs, and students from the other middle school in town mostly got As. You might try to assess the sources of these differences. To do so you would need to gather information about the students and the schools. When you're deciding what kind of information to gather, you're developing hypotheses, ideas about what might be driving the outcome of interest that can be represented as testable statements.

You might wonder things like, is it that the high school has the same start time as the higher-scoring middle school, while the lower-scoring students have all had to start waking up earlier than they're used to? Is the curriculum at the high school a closer match to what was being taught at the one middle school, so that those students came in already knowing what the students at the other school needed to learn for the first time? If we found evidence that supported these hypotheses, we might follow up by exploring ways to better align the curriculum and course schedules and to ensure greater student success.

We might also think about potential hardships that students face or resources they may have. Are students from one middle school more likely to eat breakfast at home? Are students from the other school getting up earlier to catch buses that take longer to arrive? Do students have equal access to tutoring? If our research supported these hypotheses, we might follow up by asking why other social inequalities seemed to be segregating higher- and lower-income families into different middle schools.

If *none* of our hypotheses were supported, we might look deeper into previous research on education and try to identify other possible causes to explain the effect we observed. This is how explanatory research builds up over time. We observe a social pattern, we ask what factors might be contributing to that pattern, and our findings form the basis for a new round of questions. Sometimes we focus on questions like *what is the cause?* Other times we think we know a cause, but not exactly how it works. Then we ask new questions like *by what mechanism does X influence Y?*

Descriptive research and explanatory research both play important roles in developing and testing social theory, in a process called the cycle of research. Description helps to build up a rich picture of an area of social life. Using that information, we're able to develop theories that put it all together and make sense of it. Later, we can look back at our theories and try to think of what else they imply, what else they might predict. Then we can test out our theories as explanations of other social phenomena. That research is likely to uncover additional questions that we need good descriptive research to answer, and so the cycle continues. Initial questions lead to description, description leads to theory, theory leads to explanation, explanation raises new questions.

Application

So far, the goals we've discussed have all been focused on research for the sake of discovery—research that satisfies our own curiosity, or that we can share with other sociologists, or that adds to the sum total of human knowledge. All this information is potentially valuable for understanding and addressing a range of problems. Sociologists sometimes conduct research with a more specific and concrete goal, however. Applied research refers to research conducted with the goal of having practical use regarding problems and issues in society today. Sociologists work in collaboration with (or as members of) government agencies, for-profit industries, activist groups, and local, national, and international nonprofit organizations, where we use our knowledge of sociological theory and methods to answer questions and advance these organizations' goals. The two most common forms of applied sociological research are program evaluation and community-based research.

Program Evaluation

Suppose you are an employee of a nongovernmental organization (NGO) working to improve nutrition in a developing country. Your NGO develops a program to improve maternal and child health by providing food to pregnant women who are suffering from malnutrition. You have been implementing the program for over a year now—but how can you know if it is really working? What sort of information would you need to have to know if this program is achieving your goals?

Evaluation research is a type of applied research, in which sociologists use their methodological skillset to determine how well a program or initiative is achieving its desired goals. Sociologists can use their research skills to assist government agencies, nonprofit and for-profit organizations, and a range of other organizations. In the earlier example, if our goal is to improve maternal and child health, we would want to collect information that tells us something about this. Perhaps we would look at the birth weights of infants whose mothers had participated in the program. We could then compare these with the birth weights of infants whose mothers had not participated, helping us understand if our food program is increasing children's health at birth. We might also want to look at other outcomes, or potential effects of the program, that we think are important. For example, we might also consider other aspects of mothers' and children's well-being to gauge the overall effectiveness of the program.

Program evaluation allows us to assess whether our attempts to change social conditions are having the desired effects as well as any unanticipated consequences. For example, if your NGO found that infant birth weights were not increasing when pregnant women were provided with food, you might think about other ways of improving maternal and child health. Program evaluation is important not only to people who administer programs but also to their funders, who provide the money for these initiatives. After all, who wants to pay for something if it is not working?

Community-Based Research

Community-based research, sometimes referred to as community action research, is another type of applied research. In this type of research, sociologists use their methodological toolkits to address problems or understand issues facing a particular community. A key feature of this type of research is that it is collaborative; both researchers and community members are engaged in all steps of the research process. Researchers view community members as equal partners in the research who provide valuable knowledge and insights about their communities.

Sociologists conducting community-based research work with members of the community to develop their research questions as well as their data collection and analysis plan. They also work to ensure that the findings and information that result from their research are shared with all partners. As described in more depth, how sociologists share the results of their research depends in part on the goal of the research project. In the case of community-based research, sociologists and their community partners often share the results with government agencies, local media, and the local community more generally.

By its very nature, community-based research is applied, as it always relates to problems, issues, or goals that are of interest to and have been identified by a particular community. This research is often intended to result in some sort of action that can be taken to address the research problem or issue. In other words, community-based research does more than just identify problems—it provides empirical evidence to help solve them.

DOING SOCIOLOGY 3.1

Matching Situations to Goals

In this exercise, you will develop your skills in determining which type of sociological research project is suited to particular situations.

Read the following vignettes and identify the research goal (explore, describe, explain, or apply) that corresponds to each of the following situation briefs.

Scenario 1: Jameela works for her college's student newspaper. A recent article about how the school plans to build a new student center near Greek Village resulted in the newspaper's highest-ever number of comments on a single article. The student commenters were very divided. Some favored the new building; others were opposed.

Jameela thinks she can use some of the methods she learned in sociology to help investigate the student reactions to the project. Rather than trying to get an exact count of student opinions, she wants to understand the reasons behind them. Jameela thinks she can start by looking for differences between the positive and negative comments, to identify groups of students who are mostly in favor or mostly opposed. Then, with her editor's approval, she plans to interview students from key groups to learn more about the basis for their opinions.

Scenario 2: Malcolm has a part-time job at his university's bursar's office. Every semester, students are dropped from their classes for not paying their fees at the beginning of the term. Over the fall, the bursar's office began an advertising campaign to remind students to pay their fees before the deadline. This spring, the number of dropped students is down, but not as much as the office had hoped.

Working with a full-time staff member, Malcolm helps identify students who didn't pay their fees on time, and contacts them so they can be interviewed. The interviews reveal that most of the students knew about the fee payment, but hadn't received their student loan checks in time to meet the deadline. Malcolm helps his staff supervisor prepare a report suggesting changing the fee payment to accommodate students who rely on loan checks.

Scenario 3: After reading several personal essays about having a gender-nonbinary identity online, Kayden thinks they might identify as nonbinary as well—*and* thinks that nonbinary identity might be a good topic for their senior thesis.

After getting help from a university librarian to find previous social research, Kayden has several older history articles about "third gender" identities in other countries in the past, and a few articles from a decade ago about a "genderqueer" identity and "ze" pronouns in the United States, but nothing that seems to match the "enby" identity they encountered online.

1. Would you classify Jameela's investigative project (Scenario 1) as exploratory, descriptive, explanatory, or application? Why?

2. Would you describe Malcolm's project (Scenario 2) as exploratory, descriptive, explanatory, or application? Why?

3. Would you classify Kayden's research goals (Scenario 3) as exploratory, descriptive, explanatory, or application? Why?

Check Your Understanding

1. What are the four goals of sociological research?
2. What is the cycle of research?
3. What's the difference between evaluation research and community-based research?

QUALITATIVE AND QUANTITATIVE DATA

After a sociologist has decided on their research question, an important early decision is whether qualitative data or quantitative data arebest suited to answering that question. Qualitative data (with an "L") consist of Language—descriptions, definitions, narratives, images, or histories. They are rich and detailed and can often consist of quite a lot of data. When sociologists collect qualitative data, we typically gather a lot of information from a relatively small number of cases, and we look for deep understanding.

Quantitative data (with an "N") consist of Numbers—counts and amounts, as well as classifications and categories. They are succinct and contained. When we collect quantitative data, we typically have large samples (perhaps hundreds or thousands of observations), and we draw from a broad range of questions. (If it helps, you can also remember that *qual* sounds like *talk* while *quant* sounds like *count*.)

Wherever our data come from, we almost always have a choice to gather qualitative or quantitative data (or both!) from whichever sources we've chosen. When we talk to people directly to ask them questions, we can ask them to select their answers from short lists of possibilities, or we can ask them to speak at length when they answer. When we look at things other people have made, we can choose to focus on interpretation and meaning, or we can assign them to a handful of categories and start counting them. For example, if we want to look at the messages in love songs, we could look at which qualities the singers want from their partners and how they describe their ideal relationships, or we count how often singers use words like *honey* and *baby* or *sleeping* and *kissing*. These decisions arise less from the kinds of things we've chosen to collect, and more from our goals for conducting research. The only "correct" way to analyze your data is the way that best provides the information you need to answer your research question.

Qualitative Data

Qualitative data usually consist of long passages in complete sentences. Whether we're transcribing the answers people give to our questions or taking notes on our own observations, these paragraphs and pages of text make up the body of qualitative data. Probably the most common forms of qualitative data are transcripts from interviews and field notes from direct observation, but there are few true limitations. Qualitative data can come from almost any place we can find text or images, or hear people talking, or watch what they're doing.

When we analyze qualitative data, we look for commonalities or *themes* where multiple passages of text from different sources contain similar perspectives on the same topic. Themes emerge from rereading the data looking for repetitions and similarities. When we find several people saying the same things, or several observations that went the same way, or a pattern of images or behaviors, we have begun to identify a theme.

For example, suppose that you wanted to observe how the students at your university reacted to a snow day. You might watch the quad and see a small group building a snowman, another group engaging in a snowball fight, a few people sledding downhill on cafeteria trays, and others playing a game using their phones together. Inside the library, you might see a group playing a board game, and others watching movies or playing video games in pairs. Although there could be class the next day, you don't see anyone reading a textbook or writing a paper, at least not in public. From these observations, you might identify themes of "games" or "groups of friends." These are themes that help organize common elements of your observations. This could be the start of an exploratory or descriptive project.

We can also use themes to make comparisons, such as when we find multiple contradictory perspectives on the same topic or identify groups of research subjects who seem similar to each other but different from other groups. When we ask people to define what a term means to them, we might hear several definitions that disagree. When we ask people to narrate how an event went for them, we might find that other differences between those people match the differences in their life histories.

For example, imagine that you conducted interviews with recent college graduates to learn how they felt about their decision to earn a degree. "Money" might be a common theme, an issue that many graduates mention. Within that theme, however, you might notice two main ways of talking about money. Some former students might talk about having more money since they graduated from college. They might mention things like "no more ramen" or "more than I used to make" or "able to treat myself!" Other recent graduates might talk about

What theme would you use to classify what this family is doing on a snow day?

©iStockphoto.com/FatCamera

feeling like they don't have *enough* money. They might talk about "student loan payments" or "still need a roommate" or "not able to save anything." Understanding these important qualitative differences could be the basis of an explanatory or applied project.

Quantitative Data

Quantitative data consist of data that are either already numerical or data that can be represented by numbers. When we want to know how many people live in a particular community, we would want numeric information to answer this question. We could either start counting ourselves, or turn to an existing collection of data, such as the U.S. Census, or municipal records. If we were interested not only in the number of people living in a particular community but a more nuanced description of who was living in the community, we could collect additional information from the community residents. We could ask about how much education they received, how much income they receive from their jobs, how many people live in their household, how many hours per day they watch television, or their age. We can collect categorical information to learn if they are employed or unemployed; if they identify as men, women, or nonbinary; if they describe themselves as white, Black, Hispanic/Latinx, Asian, Native American, or another race or ethnicity. We can ask about their religious affiliation, their engagement with social media, or their views on social and political issues. All of these things can be represented numerically, and in fact are commonly used in quantitative analyses.

Once we collect information from a large number of people, or about a large number of observations, we can combine it to identify patterns, trends, differences, and similarities. We can also make claims about the overall group. Analyzing quantitative data allows researchers to report things like the average income for people in a particular community, or the average wages for people who hold particular jobs. Quantitative data also reveal variation. In addition to the average wages, quantitative data can illustrate the range of incomes for people in a community or profession and the degree of similarity or variation. From one person we can learn their individual race or gender, but from many, we can learn what proportion of the population identifies with particular racial or ethnic groups, and what percent describe themselves as men, women, or nonbinary.

Researchers can also use quantitative data to make comparisons. By collecting data at two different time points, we can document and better understand how things change over time. This is how governments track the unemployment rate, for example, or how news organizations track the changing fortunes of political candidates over the course of an election. Over longer time periods, we can track changes to family life or the use of technology. What percent of adults are married? What's the average age of the population? What percent of households have telephone landlines or cable television? To how many streaming services does the average individual subscribe? The answers to these questions today are different than they were 10 or 20 years ago, and they can reveal large-scale changes to society.

We can also compare smaller groups within a population. The very simplest quantitative comparisons involve looking at two groups to see how they differ on a single question. On average, how many hours per week do men and women spend in paid employment? How much time do they have, respectively, for leisure and sleep? How many children do college graduates typically have, and does this compare to the average number of children among those with less than a college degree? How does the rate of teenage pregnancy in the United States compare to that of other wealthy, Western nations? Even simple questions can reveal unexpected and important answers. More complex questions rely on this same logic but include more details to produce richer answers. Quantitative data are a great potential resource for documenting social inequalities and how they change over time. The *causes* of inequality are many, and they overlap and intersect in surprising ways. Finding and investigating these inequalities is a common basis for explanatory and applied projects.

CONSIDER THIS...

How could you study wealth inequality using qualitative data? How could you study wealth inequality using quantitative data?

DOING SOCIOLOGY 3.2

Quantitative or Qualitative Data?

In this activity, you will learn to distinguish between scenarios that require qualitative versus quantitative data collection.

Students in a sociology of religion class are planning to conduct research on the practice of veiling—or wearing *hijabs* or headscarves—by Muslim women in America. For each of their research questions, decide whether qualitative data or quantitative data would be the most appropriate way to answer the question.

Muslim women wearing a *hijab* in the United States may not look exactly like the images of Muslim women in other countries that sometimes appear in American news media.

©Mireya Acierto/Getty Images

1. **Research Question 1:** Is wearing a *hijab* related to women's other characteristics, such as age, economic status, or race/ethnicity?
   a. Quantitative
   b. Qualitative

2. **Research Question 2:** Some Muslim teenage girls say they want to be "fashionable" while wearing a *hijab*. What do they mean when they say this?
   a. Quantitative
   b. Qualitative

3. **Research Question 3:** How are hijab-wearing women portrayed in different types of media, such as current television shows or recent movies?
   a. Quantitative
   b. Qualitative

4. **Research Question 4:** Do Muslim women who wear the *hijab* in America experience more discrimination than Muslim women here who do not?
   a. Quantitative
   b. Qualitative

Check Your Understanding

1. What kinds of information are considered qualitative data (with an L)?
2. What types of information are considered quantitative data (with an N)?
3. How should sociologists decide whether to collect qualitative or quantitative data?

UNITS OF ANALYSIS

A third important decision for researchers thinking about data collection and analysis is the unit of analysis. The unit of analysis is the thing (for example, a person, institution, organization, state, or municipality) about which the researcher collects information. Some of the most common units of observation in sociology are individual people, groups of people, and objects that people have made. The specific people, groups, or objects from which you collect data are called cases, but the general type of research subject is the unit of analysis. If you conducted the same study again in the same way, you would have different cases, but the same unit of analysis.

A single research study might combine the results of multiple analyses on multiple different units, but each analysis can usually only be performed on a single type of unit. You might interview individual artists about their use of social media *and* look at the photos of their art that they post online, for example, but the questions you ask of the artists will be different from the qualities you measure in the photos. These are two separate pieces of research on two different units of analysis that can be combined into the same study.

The Individual Unit

Probably the most common unit of analysis in sociological research is *individuals*. Many sociologists collect data directly from, and about, individual people. Counting, observing, and talking to individual people is often our best way to learn what we want to know, even if what we're really interested in are the systems and institutions in which those people participate.

Of course, after deciding to study individuals, we still have decisions to make about what kind of individuals to study. Even the broadest, most comprehensive studies, the ones that aim for "nationally representative" data, still typically limit themselves to individuals who are adults, who live independently rather than inside an institution (such as prisoners and hospital patients), who live in the same country where the study is being conducted, and who speak one of the two or three most commonly spoken languages in that country. Some of these decisions are made for ethical reasons, some for practical reasons, and some because of the limits of scope inherent in our research question, but it's important to know that we can't study everyone, so we have to specify who we will be studying.

Other Units of Analysis

At other times, researchers might want to collect data where organizations, institutions, or communities might be the unit of observation. Researchers might collect information on community characteristics, like the average educational attainment of community members; average rent costs; the presence or absence of public libraries, sidewalks, or green spaces. Researchers interested in organizations might collect information about the number of employees an organization has, the average wages they pay for employees in particular positions, the rate of employee turnover, as well as any information about tax incentives the organization may have received.

When researchers study artifacts, such as text, tweets, or images, they must make careful choices about the unit of analysis. Sociologists studying pop music, for example, could focus on single tracks or entire albums. When studying television, we could examine scenes, episodes, seasons, or series. If we want to know about web comments, should we look at individual comments, threads, or entire comment sections? When faced with so many possibilities, we make these decisions by remembering our research question and goal, and thinking about what kind of information we want to measure. The correct unit of analysis is the one that allows us to collect the data we need for our specific project.

CONSIDER THIS. . .

Suppose that you wanted to study something to do with magazines as a cultural object. What kinds of information could you collect if your unit of analysis was magazine covers? What about magazine articles? Magazine ads?

DOING SOCIOLOGY 3.3

Picking Units

In this activity, you will practice identifying units of analysis.

1. Refer to Figure 3.2. What different potential units of analysis can you find? Describe at least three.

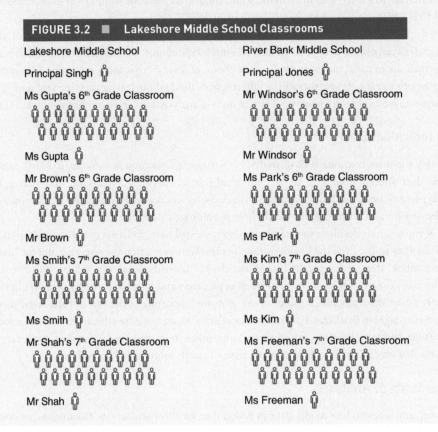

FIGURE 3.2 ■ Lakeshore Middle School Classrooms

Check Your Understanding

1. What does the unit of analysis refer to?
2. What is the most common unit of analysis in sociological research?
3. What are some other examples of units of analysis?

CROSS-SECTIONAL AND LONGITUDINAL DATA

Another question sociologists need to answer involves time. Will they collect data once, from a single point in time, or are they preparing to collect data on an ongoing basis, making repeated observations over the coming years or decades? Cross-sectional research involves collecting from specific research subjects only once. Longitudinal data collection involves collecting data on multiple occasions.

Cross-Sectional Data

Most sociological research is collected cross-sectionally. For instance, a sociologist might design a survey and send it out to a group of individuals once. When the surveys come back, the researcher analyzes the data that result from the survey. This is an example of cross-sectional research because the data are collected at only one time-point. You may ask, but what if it takes months to get all of the surveys back from the respondents? Needing time to gather data doesn't make a study longitudinal. The important take-home point is that the questions are asked only once of the respondents. Cross-sectional research is usually much easier to conduct. The researcher only needs to find their research subjects once, only needs to collect data a single time, and can pursue other research projects after this one is finished.

Cross-sectional research is sometimes called "retrospective" because of the way it looks backward. Individuals answering questions from a cross-sectional survey, for example, might be asked a few questions about their present, and many about their past. Demographic characteristics such as gender and race are typically fixed at birth and usually don't change later in life. A person's *parents'* occupations or highest levels of education might be set even earlier. And we sociologists can directly ask people questions about their childhoods, such as where they lived before age 16, or how often their family ate dinner together while growing up. A sociologist trying to establish cause and effect might attempt to connect the person's distant past to their recent past. But it's important to remember that all this information comes from someone taking part in the study in the present, retroactively recalling their personal history. It's always possible that who we are in the present changes the way we remember who we were in the past. It's also possible that important events happen in a different order for different people, which makes it risky to assume that we know which is "cause" and which is "effect."

Longitudinal Data

Longitudinal research is sometimes called "prospective" because it allows researchers to look forward. A sociologist who studies middle-schoolers and follows them as they attend high school, go to college, get married, and start jobs can learn how these events unfold in real-time. Researchers can watch how success or failure at one life-stage can amplify or be offset by repetitions and second attempts. The order in which events occur during different people's lives can itself become a question to study. People who appear very similar at the beginning of a study might follow very different trajectories forward. People who all experience the same important event (e.g., natural disasters, economic recessions, political revolutions) might react in very different ways. Analysis of longitudinal data allows us to learn things about cause and effect that wouldn't be visible any other way. It is one thing to ask Nobel Prize–winning scientists, successful musicians, or influential activists about their pasts and to try to determine what led to their success. It is something else entirely to follow dozens of young scientists, novice musicians, or leaders of burgeoning social movements and to learn about the causes of success and failure by watching both occur over the course of the study.

So far, the examples we've considered have all involved following *the same individual people* over time. The longitudinal data produced this way are called panel data. If it helps, you can think of the panelists on a game show, who continue to answer questions during each new round of the show. But there are two other ways to collect longitudinal data.

When we examine changes to *the same population* over time, we are collecting trend data. A trend study collects the same information about the same broadly defined group of people but *does not* contact the same individual people within that population. A trend study might be about a single population, for example, looking at Americans' changing opinions about same-sex marriage or interracial marriage over the course of decades, or at their opinions of a presidential candidate over a few months during the campaign. A trend study can also compare populations, for example, by looking at crime rates or homeownership rates in different cities. Trend data are sometimes called "repeated cross-sectional" data, because each time-point is collected just like cross-sectional data; but when the same information is collected about the same population repeatedly, it becomes possible to chart a trend. It's even possible to assemble a trend-line out of multiple studies conducted by different researchers—as long as they ask the same question and draw their sample from the same population.

The final type of longitudinal data are cohort data, and we collect them by studying *the same age group within a population* over time. "Cohort" is another name for "generation," and some cohort studies are designed to look at the major generations with which we all are familiar, for example, comparing the political liberalism and conservatism of Gen X and the Baby Boomers, or looking at household income and college debt among Millennials and Gen Z. (Other cohort studies use smaller "generations" instead.) The reason why sociologists collect cohort data is to try to distinguish between the effect

Members of Gen Z are starting to graduate from high school and college. How would you compare their job prospects to those of earlier generations?

©iStockphoto.com/kali9

of being part of a particular generation, and the effect of being a certain age. For example, suppose we know that Millennials today are less likely to own a home than members of Gen X. But we also know that Millennials are younger than members of Gen X, and might have less money or less family stability simply because they are at an earlier point in their life course. Cohort data would let us tell if Millennials are less likely to own homes than members of Gen X were, *when they were the same age that Millennials are today.* As you might imagine, collecting cohort data requires careful planning. The data need to include the research subjects' ages, and need to be timed correctly so that it's possible to compare each cohort at the same points in their lives. For example, if we wanted to compare the postcollege prospects of young adults who graduated high school in the year 2000 (born in 1982) to those who graduated in 2010 (born 1992), we might conduct one survey in 2006 and a second in 2016. By comparing the two surveys, we could learn how people born 10 years apart were doing around age 24. If we wanted to add another age group, or check in again after the second group turned 34, we could conduct another wave of data collection in 2026!

The practical barriers to longitudinal research are many. The research team needs to have personal commitment, and enough funding, to follow through with a project that might last an entire career. An older researcher who begins such a project might retire before it's finished; a younger researcher might help complete a project that began before they were even in college. Panel data are especially daunting to collect, because the researchers need to keep track of where their research subjects are living and ensure that they have their subjects' consent to continue being studied for the entire duration of the data collection process. The difficulty and expense of a longitudinal project are repaid with rich, accurate information about change over time at which cross-sectional research can only hint.

CONSIDER THIS...

Imagine that you are looking at a photo of your high school class attending graduation. What kinds of things could you learn from this still photo?

DOING SOCIOLOGY 3.4

Decisions, Decisions!

In this exercise, you will practice thinking through the different aspects of sociological data.

The General Social Survey, the National Longitudinal Study of Adolescent Health, and the Global Feminisms Project are important resources for analyzing social life in the contemporary United States and worldwide. Read the descriptions of these that follow, then answer the questions.

Source 1: The General Social Survey (GSS) was first started in 1972, and since 1994 it has been conducted every even-numbered year. The GSS sample is intended to be representative of the adult population of the United States. The survey is administered face to face, using the same list of questions, and the same choices for responses, for each person who participates. The sampling procedure means that surveyors talk to different people every time. It's possible that a handful of people have participated in more than one GSS survey—but if so, there's no way to know it, and no way to connect their responses on one survey to the other. Many of the questions in the GSS ask for opinions, ranging from "strongly disagree" to "strongly agree." Although some questions address topics of special interest that change from year to year, many questions are asked consistently and allow researchers to study changes in Americans' opinions over time.

Source 2: The National Longitudinal Study of Adolescent Health (Add Health) started in 1994, and has had five waves of data collection, the most recent ending in 2018. The Carolina Population Center (CPC) started by creating a list of all the high schools in the country and then taking a representative sample of schools from that list. Then it used each school's student roster to create a sample of students attending each school. The core of the Add Health data is the five waves of surveys that are always administered face to face in the participant's home. As much as possible, the CPC has tried to recontact the same participants every single wave, so that they can track the changes as they grow from adolescence to young adulthood to adulthood.

Source 3. The Global Feminisms Project (GFP) began in 2002 as an archive of oral histories from women scholars and activists from four countries: China, India, Poland, and the United States. Since then the project has expanded to include interviews from Brazil, Nicaragua, and Russia. In total, the archive now includes transcripts of more than 70 interviews, all of which are in English, as well as some videos of activists recounting their experiences.

1. What kind of data are included in the description of each source, qualitative or quantitative?

2. What is the unit of analysis used in the description for each source?

3. Are the data provided by each source cross-sectional or longitudinal?

Check Your Understanding

1. What is the key feature that makes data cross-sectional?
2. How do sociologists collect longitudinal data?
3. What are the three types of longitudinal data?

WRITING RESEARCH FOR DIFFERENT AUDIENCES

Sociologists conduct research for and communicate with many different audiences. As previously noted, the intended audience is itself one of many considerations for researchers when deciding which research question to investigate. The audience also shapes how we communicate about what we've learned from our studies. An audience made up of sociology professors will have different questions, will want different kinds of answers, and will expect a different style and vocabulary than an audience of policy makers or community partners.

Academic Audiences

Sociologists typically write articles for publication in academic journals in order to share their research with other scholars as well as other interested parties, such as students. Publishing academic journal articles allows researchers to engage in a nuanced dialogue with other scholars studying the same topics. When they are writing for an audience of social scientists with expertise in the field, researchers can assume the reader already has some knowledge on the topic. This allows them to devote more space to convey the nuances of particular concepts, arguments, and methodological techniques and to use specialized terms.

Sociological journal articles have a standard format. Researchers begin by summarizing the existing research on a topic, and then describe the particulars of the study they conducted. They detail their methods and their findings, and then discuss the implications of their findings. In addition, academic journal articles typically go through a process known as peer review. Peer review means that before publication, other experts in the field, such as other sociologists who have done research on the topic, critically evaluate the researcher's work. If there are significant problems—with the theoretical framework, the methodological design, or some other aspect of the article—then the publisher will decline to publish the article. Journals in which a sociologist might publish include *American Sociological Review, Social Forces*, and *Sociological Inquiry*. Many of these journals are not publicly accessible and require a subscription, although access is frequently available through college and university libraries. Others, such as *Socius*, can be accessed online without a subscription.

The peer-review process is lengthy, and it can take authors months or even years to publish their work in a journal. As a result, research on an event, such as an election, may not be published until some time after the event has taken place. In addition, because of their complex nature and restricted access, journal articles are often read by relatively few people when compared with other types of writing. However, for researchers who want to engage in conversation with other interested scholars, journal articles are ideal because of their highly detailed and technical nature. In addition, peer review serves as a kind of "quality control" for this type of scholarship.

Audiences of Stakeholders and Policy Makers

Sociological writing for stakeholders and policy makers can take a number of forms. Research reports or policy briefs may be written for the agency or organization that funded the research project or may be written to share findings from research with a broader audience. For example, the Pew Research Center, mentioned earlier in this chapter, publishes reports on a variety of topics, ranging from politics to religion to demographic trends. Journalists often incorporate research findings from Pew into their stories, and in so doing, further disseminate the findings. Sociologists may also write newspaper op-eds, as well as articles in magazines and other publications, to share their research findings with both policy makers and the public.

Writing for policy makers requires authors to write for a broad audience, including for those with little or no familiarity with social science research methods. These reports typically summarize the main findings of the research, may note the limitations of the research, and give policy recommendations based on the research results. Because their readers are typically not experts on the topic, authors avoid using highly specialized terms and technical details. In addition, writing for this type of audience should be engaging, clearly conveying to readers why the topic should be important or interesting to them.

Research reports and policy briefs do not always include all the details about their research methods in the main body of the text. Instead, these documents often include an appendix with this information. Authors might also direct readers to an academic journal article (often via hyperlink) where they can find further information about the research. In addition, this type of writing typically does not engage with sociological theories. If you were writing a research report for your university about drivers running red lights on campus, you would likely not include theories of socialization or social norm violation. A main benefit of this type of writing is that it puts sociological research into the hands of people making decisions. So, if you think drivers running red lights, or anything else, is a problem on your campus, conduct the research and write a report for your university's officials. This is your chance to use the power of sociological research to create changes in society!

Rep. Alexandria Ocasio-Cortez, seen here at a Muslim Get Out the Vote rally in Michigan, is an example of a policy maker.

Audiences of Community Partners

Sociological researchers may write for community partners or community members for a number of reasons. In some cases, researchers design and conduct research in partnership with a community group or organization. In these cases, it is of the utmost importance to convey the findings of the study to these partners. It is important to make sure the results of the research are shared with all partners and to involve community members in the process. Researchers may also want to share the results of their research with members of the local community where the research took place or with the population studied in the research.

As with policy makers, community members may have different levels of familiarity with sociological research. Researchers should take this into consideration when writing for this audience. This writing should be understandable by both experts and non-experts. It should also be engaging, grabbing the reader's interest and attention.

As when writing for policy makers, sociologists writing for community partners typically do not include the methodological details of the study. But even though they may not be discussed explicitly, it is still important for the research methods to be sound. Sociologists are bound by professional ethics to use their best judgment when conducting research, and to communicate their findings, as well as the limitations of their work, in a way that is clear and not misleading. Writing with and for community partners is extremely powerful because it allows researchers to collaborate and share information with people who care about the research topic and are interested and invested in the results. Sometimes projects may feature elements other than writing, such as community discussion forums, slideshows, multimedia presentations, and the like. This is another opportunity for researchers to use their research to create change and impact society.

CONSIDER THIS. . .

On a day-to-day basis, we change our communication styles depending upon with whom we are speaking. What's an example from your own life? Why is it important to adjust our communication styles when communicating with different audiences?

DOING SOCIOLOGY 3.5

Spot the Differences

In this exercise, you will compare writing about research for two different audiences.

The following two paragraphs are both summaries of research on gender differences in Latinx students' experiences in higher education. The first is the abstract from an academic journal article and the second is the executive summary of a policy brief published by a research center. Carefully read both paragraphs, then answer the questions that follow.

Journal Article Abstract: "'They Always Call Me an Investment': Gendered Familism and Latino/a College Pathways," from *Gender & Society*

In the past 20 years, Latinas have begun to outperform Latinos in high school completion and college enrollment, tracking the overall "gender reversal" in college attainment that favors women. Few studies have examined what factors contribute to Latinas' increasing educational success. This article focuses on gender differences in college-going behavior among a cohort of 50 Latino/a college aspirants in the San Francisco East Bay Area. Through 136 longitudinal interviews, I examine trends in Latino/as' postsecondary pathways and life course decisions over a two-year period. Findings suggest evidence for gendered familism, in which gender and racial/ethnic beliefs intersect to differentially shape Latino/as' attitudes, behaviors, and college choices. Gendered familism encouraged Latinas to seek a four-year degree as a means of earning independence, while Latinos expressed a sense of automatic autonomy that was not as strongly tied to educational outcomes.

Executive Summary: "Latino Males: Improving College Access and Degree Completion—A New National Imperative," from *Perspectivas: Issues in Higher Education Policy and Practice*

The educational future for Latino male students is in a state of crisis, a trend that has been especially evident at the secondary and postsecondary levels in recent years. In 2010, three out of every five associate's or bachelor's degrees granted to Latinos were earned by females, and the degree-completion gaps are growing across all critical junctures in higher education. The question of why Latino males are struggling to succeed in America's colleges is complex, and this brief explores some key factors that may be perpetuating this trend at two- and four-year institutions. Specifically, we highlight key findings from our most recent research to inform how institutions can reshape their campus and academic life programming, as well as retool their efforts in outreach and education. We also provide a review of promising institutional practices.

1. What information about the research is included in the journal article abstract? What information about the research is included in the executive summary of the policy brief?

2. Journal articles typically include technical details and use specialized terms. Where do we see this in the journal article abstract?

3. Writing for policy makers is typically engaging, showing the reader that the topic is important. How do we see this in the executive summary?

4. After reading the journal article abstract and the executive summary, what questions do you have, and about what are you curious to know more?

SOCIOLOGISTS IN ACTION

Matthew Braswell

As a sociologist, you have a vast array of methodological tools at your disposal. This means that there will almost always be an opportunity to apply your sociological imagination to a social fact that catches your interest. But it also means that you'll need to think carefully about which tools are the most useful for a particular project.

I'll give you an example. When I was a sociology graduate student at the University of Virginia, I wanted to study medical doctors' culture and learn about how they made sense of what it means to do their job well. I could have written a survey and distributed it to doctors, and I would have learned a great deal from doing so. But I ultimately decided that if I wanted to understand how doctors constructed and lived out their culture on a day-to-day basis, I had to conduct an ethnography—to be there with them as they went about their day at work, watching and listening (but, of course, not interfering!) as they *lived* their efforts to do their jobs as best they could, and as they grappled with the question of just what their best actually meant.

Meanwhile, I spent most of my graduate school tenure working at UVa's Center for Survey Research (CSR), where I learned a great deal about a different form of research. At CSR, we specialized in using mail, telephone, and Internet surveys to help our clients explore issues that interested them. To take one example, we once helped a client carry out a study of whether individuals in our community felt comfortable in their ability to swim, and how the confidence varied among demographic groups. Because we needed to learn about the distribution of attitudes across a wide range of people, we used surveys to do it. This allowed us to perform quantitative analysis to find statistically significant differences in individuals' attitudes about swimming.

I've carried what I learned about research methodology into the working world after completing my doctorate. In my time studying best practices in corporate compliance practices at a consulting firm, I applied the tools and techniques I learned in graduate school and at CSR to my position, helping me to uncover statistical relationships and reveal insights that would have otherwise gone undetected. I continue to call upon my sociological background in my current position as a compliance officer at an insurance company. Sociology prepared me for the opportunities I would pursue in life, even those outside of academia. It gives you tools that you can use to solve problems and discover breakthroughs in virtually any context.

Matthew Braswell earned a PhD in sociology at the University of Virginia and now works in the field of corporate compliance. He enjoys putting sociology into practice to help organizations achieve their goals.

Discussion Question

Why do you think Dr. Braswell used survey research to learn about the distrubution of attitudes related to swimming, but enthongraphy to study how medical doctors construct meaning and live out their culture on a day-to-day basis?

Check Your Understanding

1. What are the reasons why a researcher would write an academic journal article?
2. What does it mean when a journal article has gone through peer review?
3. What should researchers consider when writing for policy makers or community members?

CONCLUSION

In this chapter, we've talked about some of the major decisions sociologists make while designing their research projects in order to collect the appropriate data to fulfill their goals and address their audience. Sociologists need to know *why* they are conducting a study and with *whom* they plan to share their results. They make decisions about the type of data, the timeframe of the study, and the kind of research subjects.

In the next chapter, we'll learn about the decisions sociologists make in order to ensure that their research is performed in an ethical manner. Sociological research can benefit individuals and communities, but it can also be a source of harm. Because our findings are about people, the way we share our results can endanger them. Learning research ethics helps us safeguard our participants. The decisions we make to collect our data ethically are equally as important as the decisions we make to collect them correctly.

REVIEW

3.1 What are the four goals for sociological research?

Sociologists have four primary goals when conducting research: to explore new or unresearched social phenomena, to describe a social phenomenon, to explain how two or more concepts are connected or unconnected, and to apply research to problems and issues in the world today.

3.2 What are the key features of qualitative and quantitative data?

Qualitative data consist of language, often descriptions or narratives. Quantitative data consist of numeric data and categories that can be represented numerically.

3.3 What does unit of analysis refer to?

The general type of research subject, the thing about which the researcher collects information.

3.4 What is the key difference between cross-sectional and longitudinal data?

In cross-sectional data, information is collected from research subjects at only one point in time. In longitudinal data, research subjects are followed and information is collected over multiple points in time.

3.5 Who are the three audiences for whom sociologists typically write, and how does sociological writing differ depending on the audience?

The three audiences for whom sociologists typically write include academic audiences, policy makers and stakeholders, and community partners. Writing for academic audiences tends to be very technical, including details and specialized terms. Writing for policy makers and stakeholders and community partners is less technical, and makes the research accessible to a wide audience.

KEY TERMS

applied research (p. 42)

cases (p. 47)

cohort data (p. 49)

community-based research/community action
    research (p. 42)

cross-sectional (p. 48)

cycle of research (p. 41)

descriptive research (p. 40)

evaluation research (p. 42)

explanatory research (p. 41)

exploratory research (p. 39)

hypotheses (p. 41)

longitudinal (p. 48)

panel data (p. 49)

peer review (p. 51)

qualitative (p. 43)

quantitative (p. 43)

trend data (p. 49)

unit of analysis (p. 47)

AP Photo/Charles Krupa

4

CONTEMPLATING THE ETHICAL DILEMMAS OF SOCIAL RESEARCH

Steven E. Gunkel

STUDENT LEARNING QUESTIONS

4.1 What is human subjects research, and what special considerations does it require?

4.2 What are some of the key examples of unethical research in the medical and social sciences? What are some of the ethical problems of these studies?

4.3 What are the major ethical policies and resources for social scientists pursuing research?

4.4 Why might sociologists want to deceive research subjects, either implicitly or explicitly? Under what circumstances is some degree of deception ethically permissible?

4.5 What ethical obligations guide sociological scholarship?

4.6 What are some of the special ethical considerations of community-based research and evaluation research?

HOW I GOT ACTIVE IN SOCIOLOGY

Steven E. Gunkel

I originally thought that I was going to college to become a high school math teacher. I had not heard of sociology until I took an Introductory Sociology class at the local community college. I found sociology to be fascinating and, in particular, the field of criminology. Criminology looks at the ways we define, measure, explain, and control criminal behavior, and I have focused on that in my teaching and research interests—ranging from juvenile delinquency to white-collar crime. I can't think of a better way to spend a career—teaching undergraduates about crime since 1986!

If your friend told you that she was planning a research project in which she would test the effects of consuming radioactive food by feeding radioactive oats to disadvantaged children, hopefully your sense of ethics would kick in. Probably, you would tell her it was a bad idea. If she persisted in planning this experiment, hopefully you'd tell Child Protective Services and they would put an end to it.

Imagine that another friend told you that, for a class project, he was going to try to find people who have impersonal sex in public bathrooms, and then secretly follow them home to learn more about their everyday lives. Hopefully your sense of ethics would kick in then too. Likely, alarm bells are going off as you consider these examples because you intuitively suspect that harming and deceiving people in the course of scientific research is wrong.

Yet, for the scientists pursuing these and countless other research projects, alarm bells did not go off—at least not immediately. In the 1940s and 1950s, researchers at MIT fed radioactive oats, milk, and calcium to cognitively challenged boys at the Fernald School while telling them that they were

57

receiving a "special diet" as part of a select "science club" (Boissonault, 2017). The researchers did this because they wanted to be able to determine how the nutrients in oats traveled throughout the body. The effect of the radiation was equivalent to 30 consecutive chest X-rays. In 1995, President Bill Clinton issued a public apology to the former students of Fernald School and, in 1998, a $1.8 million settlement was reached with 30 of the men whom the researchers had deceived.

And, in the 1960s, sociologist Laud Humphreys conducted a study of the "tea-room trade," where he served as a "Watch Queen" for men having sex with men in public bathrooms. He wrote down their license plate numbers as they left the facility, and later visited (unannounced and uninvited) the homes of the men he observed. Conducting the study at a time when gay men and other sexual minority groups were highly stigmatized and often living closeted lives, he reasoned that the deception was necessary to gain entry into this hidden community. Although the identities of the men were never revealed, Humphreys acknowledged later in life that he was not sure that he could have kept this information secret if authorities had compelled him to turn over his records (DuBois, 2020).

Most, if not all, of us have a moral compass, but history is filled with examples where researchers' moral compasses have failed tremendously. As discussed in greater detail later in this chapter, vulnerable people, disadvantaged groups, and communities have suffered the consequences. Learning about research ethics and following the guidelines for ethical research are crucial for ensuring that similar abuses do not occur again.

This chapter provides an overview of research ethics for sociologists. An important first step in appreciating the importance of research ethics is learning about historical ethics violations. So, we begin there. We then look at how researchers, educational institutions, and governmental organizations have responded to their troubled history, and the policies in place today to promote ethical research. Different forms of sociological research sometimes require different ethical considerations. The last section highlights some important ethical considerations for socially engaged research.

HUMAN SUBJECTS RESEARCH

Sociologists must attend to ethical issues in all types of projects, but ethical considerations are particularly important in research involving human subjects. As defined by the National Institutes of Health (2020), a human subject is a living individual about whom an investigator (whether professional or student) conducting research:

- Obtains information or biospecimens through intervention or interaction with the individual, and uses, studies, or analyzes the information or biospecimens; or

- Obtains, uses, studies, analyzes, or generates identifiable private information or identifiable biospecimens.

What is known as human subjects research includes a broad spectrum of research. Interview research, ethnography, and participant observation certainly involve human subjects, but so too do online surveys—even when they do not ask for personally identifying information.

Research with human subjects requires a number of special considerations. First, social researchers should *do no harm*. The research project should not harm research subjects either physically or psychologically. Second, the participation of research subjects must be *voluntary*. Participants must have freely chosen to participate in the research and must be able to withdraw at any time without penalty. Third, researchers must not use deception to secure initial participation or to promote ongoing participation. We are called to be honest in all of our dealings with research subjects. Fourth, people who participate in social research must first give their informed consent. Researchers must provide potential participants with sufficient information about the research study, so that those who agree to participate understand the potential risks, benefits of participation, and what their participation entails. Fifth, researchers must exercise special care when conducting research with vulnerable populations. Vulnerable populations include prisoners, children, undocumented immigrants, and other groups for whom the risks of study participation might be particularly high and those who—because of age, citizenship status, or other reasons—may not be in a position to give their informed consent.

CONSIDER THIS...

Why do you think children and prisoners are considered "vulnerable populations" in social science research? What other social groups do you think might be particularly vulnerable?

DOING SOCIOLOGY 4.1

Identifying Human Subjects Research

In this exercise, you will use your knowledge to determine whether or not particular projects fall within the category of human subjects research.

Sociologists conducting research with human subjects are required to have approval from their college, university, or institute prior to the beginning of their research. Determine whether the following projects fall within "human subjects research." Then, explain what ethical issues the researcher should consider before beginning their proposed project.

1. A sociologist is interested in how U.S. newspapers portray issues related to climate change. They plan to identify all of the *New York Times* articles from 2020 that use the terms *climate change* or *global warming*. They intend to read these articles carefully, focusing on the emotions authors use to discuss the issue.

2. A sociologist is interested in understanding why some students participate in volunteer activities and others don't. They plan to interview 12 students, asking questions about their family, religious, and political backgrounds, their history of volunteering, and their future career goals.

3. A sociologist is interested in how people present themselves and interact with others in social media. They plan to make a pretend profile and join an online dating site and analyze all of the interactions they have with others. As part of this, they will record the profile details of everyone with whom they interact.

4. A sociologist is interested in analyzing presidential tweets about the Middle East. They plan to collect and analyze all of the tweets from the president that mention countries and leaders in the Middle East. They intend to publish the results of the analysis in a book.

Check Your Understanding

1. What is human subjects research?
2. What are some of the main ethical principles researchers should consider when doing human subjects research?
3. What is informed consent?
4. What are vulnerable populations in social science research?

UNETHICAL RESEARCH: KEY HISTORICAL EXAMPLES

Although the 20th century saw unprecedented scientific advancements, it also saw some of the worst violations of human rights and dignity. In this section, we review some of the most notable ethical failures in social scientific and medical research. Learning about these cases is important for a number of reasons. First, knowledge of ethical violations of the past can help to prevent similar ethical violations in the future. Second, as discussed more in the sections that follow, many of these historical examples led to the development of legal policies and procedures designed to protect the rights and dignity of research participants. Third, knowledge of these historical ethical violations—along with those in the current day—underscores the importance of scientific humility. These examples remind us of the importance of following ethical protocols because even well-intentioned, brilliant researchers sometimes have blind spots and are unable to fully assess the ethical implications of their research. The ethical policies and procedures that we have today help to ensure that participants are protected, now and in the future.

The Eugenics Movement

In the late 1800s and early 1900s, many doctors, policy makers, and scientists endorsed eugenics—the idea that future societies would benefit if some people were allowed to have children, and if others were denied the opportunity. Proponents of eugenics believed that by selecting who was able to have children, and who was not, they could increase the proportion of children born with socially desirable traits such as intelligence and decrease the proportion of people with traits that were socially undesirable.

You may already be aware of some of the flaws of this perspective, but they are worth stating, nonetheless. First, what constitutes a "desirable" and "undesirable" trait is not at all objective. Instead, ideas about desirability stem from historic inequalities of class, race, ethnicity, nation, and disability. Second, people in positions of relative privilege were able (and remain able) to exercise more power and control over which characteristics were deemed undesirable. Third, many of the "undesirable" traits that eugenicists sought to eliminate were not individual traits at all! Eugenicists considered people who were poor or unable to read, for example, as holding "undesirable traits," when in reality poverty and illiteracy stem primarily from structures of inequality and opportunity. Fourth, forcing people to be sterilized and denying them their ability to have children not only violates the principle of "do no harm" but is also a violation of human rights.

As the ideology of eugenics took hold in the early 1900s, states across the U.S. passed laws to permit forced sterilization. Thousands of poor people, people of color, and people with disabilities were sterilized. Eugenics was in fact so accepted in the early 1900s that the U.S. Supreme Court supported the practice. In the case of *Buck v. Bell* (1927), the Court actually reaffirmed the legality of forced sterilization.

Carrie Buck, a white woman from an impoverished background, was doing quite well in her studies, but was forced to leave school in the fifth grade in order to help her foster family. Tragically, the nephew of her foster mother raped her, and Carrie became pregnant. Carrie's pregnancy, along with her mother's alleged prostitution, were used to argue that she had inherited a moral defect—and both were incarcerated at the Virginia State Colony for the Epileptic and Feeble Minded. She was subsequently sterilized by the state of Virginia to prevent her from passing along her "immorality."

Sterilization programs like that in Virginia became firmly institutionalized across the country. The number of forced sterilizations virtually doubled, hitting over 12,000 in the 6 years following the *Buck* case—and the programs continued well into the 1970s in several states (such as North Carolina; Public Broadcasting Service, 2018). Given structural inequalities of race, class, and gender, this practice frequently targeted poor, African American women.

On a massive scale, this represents an egregious abuse of power that violated key ethical principles regarding psychological and physical harm, voluntary participation, and vulnerable populations. Only in the last two decades have state officials offered public apologies to those forcibly sterilized and provided some financial compensation to these victims.

The Tuskegee Study

The Tuskegee study represents yet another important example of unethical conduct in the name of science and the public good. In the early 1930s, researchers at the Public Health Service (the forerunner of the Centers for Disease Control and Prevention, or CDC) were interested in analyzing the physical impact of untreated syphilis on African American males. The men were selected from a predominantly African American, largely illiterate, impoverished, and rural county in Alabama.

In what was called the Tuskegee study researchers identified 399 African American men who had syphilis and 201 who did not, and then denied treatment to those afflicted with the disease (at the time, some people believed that the effects of syphilis were different for African Americans than they were for whites). As the CDC notes on its website dedicated to this tragedy (2020), "Even when penicillin became the drug of choice for syphilis in 1947, researchers did not offer it to the subjects."

Researchers lied to patients, telling them they were being treated when, in fact, they were not—a horrendous violation of informed consent. The Tuskegee study lasted for 40 years. As late as 1969 the CDC, and local chapters of the American Medical Association (AMA), expressed written support for the study's continuation. It resulted in the deaths and permanent disability of many of the men, as well as a massive loss of trust for the medical community. As a result of litigation, the state of

Participants of the Tuskegee syphilis study.
ASSOCIATED PRESS

Alabama awarded each of the 70 survivors $37,500 (or approximately $2.50 per day for the 40 years in which their medical needs were ignored) in 1993. And President Bill Clinton also issued a formal apology (Brown et al., 2019, pp. 424–425). Similar to the forced sterilization programs, the Tuskegee study violated several ethical principles regarding physical harm, informed consent, and protection for vulnerable populations.

CONSIDER THIS. . .

In the 1900s, the forced sterilization of disadvantaged social groups, withholding medical treatment from them, and practicing medical experimentation upon them were rarely questioned by privileged groups. Why do you think privileged groups failed to speak against these practices?

The Milgram Experiment

Like the medical sciences, the social sciences are also filled with examples of studies that violate our core ethical principles. Researchers have often assumed that their scientific goals were sufficiently noble to outweigh any harm done by their studies. The Milgram experiment is a classic case. In the early 1960s at Yale University, Stanley Milgram conducted a controversial study on obedience to authority to attempt to understand the horrors of the Nazi Holocaust. Why would individuals simply follow orders from their superiors when asked to perpetrate acts that most people would find repugnant? Milgram wondered if ordinary individuals would inflict harm on others if they were ordered to do so by an authority figure.

In his study, participants were instructed, by a person wearing a lab coat, to administer increasingly painful electrical shocks to an unseen "learner" when they responded incorrectly to a series of questions. However, both the authority figure (in the lab coat) and the learner were actually actors working for Milgram. But the participants did not know this—and believed they were indeed shocking the learners. The learner would scream out in pain each time a shock was presumably delivered—and eventually fall silent, as if incapacitated. Two-thirds of the study participants believed they had administered

Psychologist Philip Zimbardo is best known for conducting the Stanford prison experiment.

Everett Collection Inc/Alamy Stock Photo

lethal electrocutions in response to the directions of the authority figure. Although Milgram's experiment demonstrated the power of authority for inducing obedience, it relied on the deception of research subjects, and, even with debriefing, it created psychological trauma as human subjects believed that they had seriously harmed others.

The Stanford Prison Experiment

Philip Zimbardo's now-infamous Stanford prison experiment is another ethically problematic and well-known study. Like Milgram, Zimbardo thought his research goals were noble. Zimbardo was interested in prison reform and, in 1971, recruited 24 male students enrolled at Stanford University to participate in a study examining the psychological effects of prison life. The students were paid $15 per day and (by the flip of a coin) were assigned the role of either prisoner or guard. Zimbardo also recruited some former convicts to consult on the project, in order to better understand the conditions of prisons at the time.

Wanting to understand how people would respond to prison life, Zimbardo constructed a jail in the basement of Stanford's psychology building and had students play the part of prisoners and guards. After only 2 days, "guards" became overzealous and sadistic in their duties. Some "prisoners" became overwhelmed by the conditions of their confinement. And while the study was supposed to run for 2 weeks, it had to be terminated after only 6 days (Zimbardo, 2020).

As in Milgram's experiment, researchers did not fully inform research participants of the psychological trauma that they might encounter, and subjects felt obligated to keep participating—even when they were uncomfortable doing so. Although Zimbardo was well intentioned, he and his research team deceived and harmed the study participants.

Forced sterilization, untreated syphilis, and medical experimentation all point to the consequences of a faulty moral compass that was deeply woven into the most powerful institutions of the day—medical, legal, and military. Sadly, we could add to this list many other cases including the unwarranted use of psychosurgery (such as brain lobotomies) to control mood and behavior (see Pfohl, 1994, pp. 148–149); the harvesting of cancer cells without a patient's knowledge or permission (Skloot, 2011); inducing stuttering in unsuspecting orphaned children (Reynolds, 2003); and using conscientious objectors (to military service) to study the effects of starvation (Tucker, 2006). Fortunately, the ethical tide was about to turn in response to the glaring absence of protections and safeguards for participants in medical and social research.

DOING SOCIOLOGY 4.2

Studying Prison Life in an Ethical Way

In this exercise, you will think through the process of designing an ethical research study.

Zimbardo designed the Stanford prison experiment to assess how people responded to life in prison, but his research resulted in mistreated and traumatized participants, and had to be cut short. But creating a prison in the basement of a university building isn't the only way to assess how people respond to life in prison.

Choose one of the following research methods: (1) interviews, (2) ethnography, or (3) surveys, With this method in mind, answer the following questions:

1. How might a researcher use one of these methods to assess how people respond to life in prison?

2. What are limitations of this approach, relative to Zimbardo's study?

3. What are the benefits of this approach, relative to Zimbardo's study?

> **Check Your Understanding**
>
> 1. What did eugenicists hope to achieve through forced sterilization? How did this policy conflict with modern-day ethical principles?
> 2. What did the Public Health Service hope to achieve through the Tuskegee study? How did this research violate research ethics?
> 3. What did Milgram hope to understand through his research? How did his experiment violate research ethics?
> 4. What did Zimbardo hope to understand through his research? How did his experiment violate research ethics?

POLICIES AND RESOURCES TO PROMOTE ETHICAL RESEARCH TODAY

It is difficult to pinpoint the exact "turning point" in the history of research ethics, but in the 1970s, public officials and academics began seriously questioning the unethical practices that had become all too common in the name of science—and officially recognized our ethical obligations to protect human dignity in all research.

In 1974, Congress held hearings on the Tuskegee study, in particular, and subsequently passed the National Research Act. This federal law called for the formation of a special commission to examine ethical issues concerning scientific research involving humans. The formation of the National Commission for the Protection of Human Subjects of Biomedical and Behavioral Research followed. This Commission's members included ethics experts, medical doctors, legal scholars, social scientists, and leaders of advocacy groups (for example, those charged with protecting racial and ethnic minority groups—e.g., the National Council of Negro Women, Inc.).

The specific charge for the Commission was to consider the similarities and differences between behavioral and biomedical research; assess risks and benefits of research involving humans; develop guidelines for selecting people to participate in research; and provide for informed consent for study participants. After extensive deliberations, in 1979, the Commission published what is referred to as the *Belmont Report*. This extensive report serves as the blueprint for the ways in which we conduct social and biomedical research today. Let's consider some of the key aspects of the *Belmont Report* and the ways its content has been translated into ethical guidelines for sociologists in particular.

Federal Oversight and Provisions for the Institutional Review Board

The publication of the *Belmont Report* in 1979 represents a significant turning point in the development of ethical standards governing biomedical and behavioral research. It outlines three basic ethical principles: "respect for persons," "beneficence," and "justice" (United States Department of Health, Education, and Welfare, 1979).

Respect for persons specifies that researchers must protect the freedom of individuals to choose to participate in a study, and details the steps that must be taken to protect vulnerable populations—those who are vulnerable or perhaps unable to freely choose to participate in a study (e.g., children or prisoners). Beneficence refers to the criterion that research does not harm the individual, *and* that it maximizes possible benefits and minimizes possible harms. The principle of justice incorporates the notion that benefits and burdens should be shared equally, and carefully scrutinized in instances when they are not (e.g., when benefits accrue to the wealthy but burdens are borne by the poor). In fact, the *Belmont Report* explicitly cites the aforementioned case of experimentation on unwilling African American men in the Tuskegee syphilis study, as well as experiments conducted on prisoners of Nazi concentration camps. These three principles find their way into respecting our research subjects by requiring that we gain participants' informed consent, inform them of the potential risks and rewards of participating in studies, and guaranteeing fairness in the selection of, and outcomes for, research subjects.

You might be asking yourself, But how do sociologists know how to put these standards into practice? Who determines when a research project is sufficiently respectful of subjects' rights? Who determines what constitutes an unreasonable level of risk for participants?

An extension of the *Belmont Report*, referred to as the "Common Rule,", was established in 1991 by the U.S. Department of Health and Human Services (HHS) to provide such guidance and to ensure compliance with these ethical standards. It was through the "Common Rule" that institutional review boards (IRBs) were created (United States Code, 2014).

IRBs are units within universities and other research organizations that review all research proposals and determine whether they provide sufficient informed consent, pose a risk to research subjects (and if the project minimizes such risks), and if they adhere to all existing ethical standards. As such, an IRB plays a pivotal role in reviewing research proposals. Such proposals may involve clinical trials evaluating the effectiveness of drugs or medical therapies. Alternately, they may outline behavioral research that examines human behavior in a variety of settings: laboratories, groups, organizations, institutions, or online (Internet-based).

IRBs are concerned with whether the researcher conducting research abides by the ethical principles of do no harm, voluntary participation, no deception, informed consent, and protection of vulnerable populations. In addition, IRBs require that researchers provide participants informed consent forms that provide details of the study (all aspects of the research design, risks and benefits of participation, and possible compensation). Researchers must: (1) disclose to potential research subjects information needed to make an informed decision; (2) facilitate an understanding of what has been disclosed; and (3) promote the voluntariness of the decision about whether or not to participate in the research (United States Department of Health and Human Services, 2019). Consent forms need to be written in a language that is familiar and "accessible" to the research subjects. If research involves children, "assent forms" may be provided to them to solicit their affirmative agreement to participate in a research study—after parents have signed a consent form in their capacity as guardian.

A key component of informed consent is understanding what personal information will be gathered during the research, and how personally identifying information will be handled. In some cases, researchers collect data anonymously—even the researchers themselves do not know the names, addresses, or other identifying information of the people providing the data. In other cases, researchers do know the identities of the people involved, but keep the participants confidential, meaning they promise not to disclose the names or any identifying information to anyone. Researchers who guarantee confidentiality must think carefully about the ways in which identifying information about research subjects could be accidentally shared. Especially in the era of online security breaches and identity theft, it is crucial for researchers to make a plan with their IRB to protect and store sensitive data.

CONSIDER THIS. . .

Data cannot be both anonymous and confidential. Why is that?

Along with securing participants' informed consent before the start of the study, researchers also frequently offer a "debriefing" for research subjects when their participation ends. Ideally, researchers should debrief participants fully and immediately upon completion of their participation in the research project. Researchers will sometimes provide their subjects with copies of their research results (in either final reports or publications).

Negotiating Ethics in Social Network Research

To see the IRB process "in action," we might consider the experiences of researchers negotiating some of the guidelines cited above. The process often proves more complicated than it might appear at first glance. A noteworthy example could be drawn from the work of Emily Dworkin and Nicole Allen (2017), who examined sorority social networks and support for victims of sexual violence. These researchers highlight the challenges that social scientists who examine sensitive topics often encounter when seeking IRB approval for their projects.

Dworkin and Allen had hoped to use social network analysis (SNA) to understand how sororities facilitated the recovery process for members who were sexual assault survivors. SNA allows sociologists to map the networks in which their subjects are situated and gather information about these networks. In these studies, an individual research subject may inadvertently disclose sensitive information about other people or groups who have not explicitly agreed to participate in the study. For instance, sorority members who chose to participate in the study might inadvertently name, without their consent, other sorority sisters who had been victims of sexual assault.

This study highlights the tensions that arise when ethical principles primarily focus on the well-being of

Institutional review boards require that participants complete informed consent forms.
iStockphoto.com/nito100

the individual research subject without weighing the potential risks for individuals, groups, or organizations that are not officially research participants. When reviewing Dworkin and Allen's proposed research, their university IRB raised concerns about precisely these sorts of risks for sorority members who had not explicitly agreed to participate in the study. The IRB also raised several other concerns that highlight the ethical dilemmas that might arise in the research. Dworkin and Allen had planned to depend on sorority leaders to recruit participants—but members *could* feel coerced to participate because they might feel that saying no to a person holding a position of power within the organization could create future conflict or a loss of status. They had also planned to conduct in-depth qualitative interviews with some of the individual research subjects—but any confidentiality breach could potentially divulge particularly sensitive information about these subjects.

In short, the research could have violated several ethical principles—the study could have caused psychological harm, encouraged involuntary participation, and undermined informed consent. In an interesting twist, the authors elected to withdraw their initial proposal and work with the IRB to redesign their study. Specifically, they chose not to depend on sorority leaders to recruit participants—and thereby lessened the potentially coercive aspect of participation; they used a "truly informed consent" form that included a detailed statement about the risks of participating in the study (e.g., explicitly identifying the ways in which confidentiality could be breached); and they dropped the in-depth qualitative interview altogether. The second proposal was approved by their IRB as a result of these changes.

The American Sociological Association's "Code to Live By"

In addition to adhering to the principles of the *Belmont Report* and following the guidelines set forth by their institutional review boards, sociologists are bound by the code of ethics of the American Sociological Association (ASA). These ethical standards "set forth enforceable rules of scientific and professional conduct for sociologists."

The first official ethical standards, the *Code of Ethics* of the American Sociological Association, were established in 1970 (American Sociological Association, 2018). In order to capture the many activities and roles sociologists play, and the changing nature of research and teaching, sociologists have updated the Code many times since.

The *Code of Ethics* governs all aspects of the discipline of sociology. It requires sociologists to: be competent and remain abreast of developments in the discipline; adhere to the highest principles in teaching; observe fair hiring of graduate and undergraduate students (if they become part of research teams); speak in a professional capacity and consult only on matters for which they have expertise; conduct research in an ethical fashion; and abide by principles of fair employment in hiring and promotion decisions. Ethical violations can lead to expulsion from the American Sociological Association, disciplinary actions by universities (such as suspension or termination), and civil and criminal sanctions.

Collective Risk

Increasingly, social scientists weigh not only the costs and benefits for those individuals who participate in our research projects but also the collective risk this research might create for groups, organizations, and society as a whole. You might recall, from earlier in this chapter, the difficulties that Dworkin and Allen encountered with the IRB approval process for their study on sororities and social support for victims of sexual violence. For their IRB, the key concern was the damaging consequences for individuals if confidentiality were breached.

Beyond these concerns, Dworkin and Allen deliberately considered the ways in which the information provided by their participants might damage friendship networks or the sororities in which they were involved. For example, participants might reveal that their sororities did not offer much support for members who were sexually assaulted, or collectively bought into rape myths that blame the victim. The reputational costs that sororities potentially faced as a result of this study could jeopardize the prospect of future research that might provide a deeper understanding of these problems. The high-stakes impacts of these kinds of findings are not merely hypothetical. Harvard recently banned fraternities, in part, because of research that revealed these organizations fostered "high levels of sexual entitlement" among their members.

Ethical provisions for doing no harm, informed consent, vulnerable populations, and voluntary participation all become more complicated when research potentially creates collective risks. In a particularly troubling case, Steven Picou recounts the legal difficulties he encountered when he studied the communities most affected by the 1989 Exxon Valdez oil spill in Prince William Sound, Alaska (Picou, 1996). Picou had faithfully followed the ASA *Code of Ethics* in ensuring confidentiality, but he found that the promises he had made to local residents were jeopardized when Exxon attempted to counter the damage claims it was facing for the spill—the largest and most ecologically destructive in U.S. history.

Exxon issued a legal subpoena for the survey results that Picou had collected from his respondents. This legal maneuver threatened to expose the identities of those who had participated in Picou's study as well as other personal information provided by subjects. Fortunately, Exxon was denied access to his data, but as Picou later explained, sociologists can sometimes find themselves as "unwilling informants" and should take extra precautions and care in honoring the promises they make to safeguard confidentiality (1996, p. 149). Sadly, when news of the legal struggles between Picou and Exxon became public, one study participant actually committed suicide as a result of the stress created. According to Picou, this strengthened his resolve to protect the identities of all the community residents he had surveyed (1996, p. 152).

DOING SOCIOLOGY 4.3

The General Principles of the ASA *Code of Ethics*

In this exercise, you'll reflect on how sociologists live up to professional ethics.

Sociologists in the United States are bound together and by the ASA *Code of Ethics*, which provides explicit statements regarding professional obligations for all sociologists.

1. The first three General Principles of the *Code of Ethics* emphasize professional competence (i.e., understanding the need for continuing training and education, consulting other professionals and appropriate sources, knowing one's personal limitations); integrity (i.e., acting with respect and fairness toward others in all types of work, honesty and truthfulness in reporting); and responsibility (i.e., adhering to all scientific and professional standards, working to maintain public trust in sociology). What obligations do these Principles create for sociologists?

2. The last three General Principles delineated in the Code of Ethics emphasize respect (i.e., recognizing the dignity and worth of all people, being sensitive to cultural and individual differences, not tolerating any form of discrimination); rights (working to advance human rights globally); and social responsibility (i.e., working to contribute to the public good, avoiding harming individuals or groups). What obligations do these Principles create for sociologists?

3. Can you think of situations in which sociologists might have conflicts or difficulty in abiding by these ethical standards?

> ### Check Your Understanding
>
> 1. What is the significance of the Belmont Report?
> 2. How should our research reflect the principles of "respect for persons," "beneficence," and "justice"?
> 3. What is an institutional research board (IRB), and what role does it play in social research?
> 4. How do ethical guidelines shape the work of sociologists?
> 5. What is collective risk?

AUTHENTICITY AND DECEPTION

Social scientists conducting research today have access to clear ethical principles and guidelines from their colleges and universities as well as from the federal government. Even so, there are cases in which researchers, in consultation with their IRB and others, must make difficult decisions about ethics, carefully weighing the risk of benefits of research decisions. Let's take a look at a few examples.

Authenticity in Social Research

Establishing trust with the research subjects is often necessary for gaining entry into communities and gathering information (see Allen, 1997). Researchers benefit when study participants feel comfortable sharing their beliefs, uncertainties, and experiences. And particularly with sensitive topics and experiences (for example, participating in deviant behavior), it is only after trust is established that participants truly open up about the details of their lives (Burton, 2010). As a result, researchers often have an incentive to be the person their participant would like them to be: a trusted friend and confidant; someone who is on their side.

But serious ethical problems emerge when researchers present a false representation of themselves in order to gain the trust of people, groups, or communities. One such example is Carolyn Ellis's ethnography of two fishing communities along the Chesapeake Bay. Ellis befriended her research subjects and gained their trust by helping them with housekeeping and babysitting (Allen, 1997). She examined kinship ties and religiosity in the two communities, as well as their isolation from broader society. She then wrote the book *Fisher Folk*, in which she depicted the villagers as illiterate and backward, garnering much anger among those she detailed in the book. Plus, even though Ellis relied on pseudonyms in the book, participants were able to identify themselves and others in Ellis's text, so confidentiality was destroyed.

A second case concerns Richard Leo's participant observation study of policing practices (Allen, 1997). As Leo tried to gain the trust of police officers, he pretended to share their biases and views. When he encountered police who supported the death penalty, for example, or expressed homophobic views, he did the same. Ironically, Leo was studying the police to understand their use of deception in interrogation tactics. After earning advanced degrees in sociology and law, he now serves as an expert witness in cases involving police deception and forced confessions. In fact, Professor Leo appears in the recent Netflix mini-series version of John Grisham's *The Innocent Man* (2006), in which he details the ease with which police deception can translate into wrongful convictions—some of which carry the death penalty!

These two examples illustrate the problems that emerge when researchers present inauthentic versions of themselves or misleading descriptions of their research to study participants. Ellis identified herself as a researcher at the very beginning of her study, but she failed to remind the villagers of her identity and aims (and secretly recorded her interactions with them). Leo identified himself as a researcher but misrepresented his beliefs and values in order to gain the trust of the police officers he studied.

CONSIDER THIS...

Do you think it is ever justifiable for researchers to present inauthentic versions of themselves to study participants?

Research Requiring Explicit Deception

Some research projects—particularly experimental research studies—require a degree of deception as part of the research design. Hiring audits, used to test for labor market discrimination, represent one such set of studies.

In one of the most important recent audits, sociologist Devah Pager (2003) used this approach to document discrimination against men with criminal records. In her study, she asked Black and white men to pose as job seekers (testers), sending them to apply for the same entry-level jobs in a large American city. They submitted, in person, job applications that indicated they had similar educational credentials (a high school diploma) and similar work histories (low-skill jobs). They were also trained to appear and act in the same way when they applied for jobs. Finally, one man in each pair was instructed to indicate he had a criminal record.

Pager was then able to assess how both a criminal history and racial inequality affected the likelihood of getting a callback from prospective employers. She found that men with a criminal record were significantly less likely to receive a callback, but racial disparities were equally significant. White job applicants without a criminal record were called back about 34% of the time; whites with a criminal record were called back only 17% of the time. But Black applicants without a criminal record were called back even less frequently—14% of the time. And finally, Black men with a criminal record were called back only 5% of the time.

Deception was central to Pager's study. The job applicants were not who they said they were, and they were not intending to accept the positions to which they had applied. The study increased the workload of employers who were trying to fill the positions, since they had to review additional applications. But Pager, and importantly her university IRB, determined that these burdens were limited in scope, and the rewards to society significant. And Pager, in consultation with the IRB, determined that there was no other equally valid way to gather this evidence of discrimination.

For some sociologists, the use of deception is never justified; it threatens the credibility of the research project itself and may undermine the legitimacy of the discipline of sociology as a whole (Allen, 1997). Interestingly, this absolutist stance actually stands in contrast to ASA ethical standards that allow for the use of deception in research, albeit under strict provisions for its use. Figure 4.1 shows an excerpt from the ASA *Code of Ethics*, which explains that deception in research is allowable when the data cannot be gathered using other methods, when it poses minimal risk to research subjects, and when it is overseen by an IRB.

Devah Pager's 2003 study required the use of deception in order to determine if discrimination exists in hiring.

iStockphoto.com/fizkes

> **FIGURE 4.1   ■   Excerpt From the ASA** *Code of Ethics (p. 14)*

11. Informed Consent

11.4 Use of Deception in Research

a. Deception can include misleading participants about the research procedures and/or not providing all relevant information about the research. Sociologists do not use deceptive techniques unless they have determined that the following conditions have been met

1. the research involves no more than minimal risk to research participants;

2. deception is justified by the study's prospective scientific, educational, or applied value;

3. equally effective alternative procedures that do not use deception are not feasible; and

4. they have obtained the approval of an authoritative body with expertise on the ethics of social science research such as an institutional review board.

b. Sociologists do not deceive research participants about significant aspects of the research that would affect their willingness to participate, such as physical risks, discomfort, or unpleasant emotional experiences.

c. When deception is an integral feature of the design and conduct of research, sociologists attempt to correct any misconception that research participants may have as soon as possible, and no later than at the conclusion of the research. This debriefing may be waived if correcting the deception can potentially cause problems for the participants or if debriefing is not possible.

d. Sociologists generally disclose their identities to research participants. On rare occasions, sociologists may need to conceal their identities in order to undertake research that could not practicably be carried out were they to be known as researchers. Under such circumstances, sociologists undertake the research if it involves no more than minimal additional risk for the research participants, and if they have obtained approval from an authoritative body with expertise on the ethics of social science research such as an institutional review board. Under such circumstances, confidentiality must be maintained.

Source: American Sociological Association (2018)

DOING SOCIOLOGY 4.4

"Protecting Our Research Participants"

In this exercise, you'll learn how sociologists address the trade-offs associated with deception and authenticity in sociology.

Read this scenario and then, drawing on what you know about research ethics, answer the questions that follow.

Alicia and Daniel are university students who are beginning a job conducting telephone surveys for a professor in their university. The professor for whom the pair are conducting interviews is evaluating the impact of a local prisoner reentry program. Alicia and Daniel will be calling program participants and asking them about their experiences in the program and in life more generally.

In their spare time, Alicia and Daniel also volunteer at a local nonprofit agency that provides services to low-income people in their community. Alicia and Daniel suspect that some of the people they know from their volunteer work are also participants in the prisoner reentry program. They are concerned that, if they introduce themselves to telephone survey participants and use their real names, the survey participants might recognize them and may be embarrassed for Alicia and Daniel to know their history of incarceration. Alicia and Daniel are considering using stage names to conduct the interviews, so that participants don't recognize them.

1. Do you think Alicia and Daniel's use of stage names would be a form of deception? Explain why or why not.

2. If Daniel and Alicia do use stage names, do you think they have a responsibility to tell the survey participants that they are using stage names? Explain why or why not.

3. Does the use of stage names compromise informed consent? Explain.

4. Do you think the use of stage names is consistent with the ASA *Code of Ethics*? Explain why or why not.

1. Why might sociologists be motivated to present inauthentic versions of themselves to their study participants?
2. How have sociologists used deception in their research?
3. Under what circumstances does the American Sociological Association sometimes permit the use of deception in sociological research?

ETHICS IN THE PUBLICATION OF RESEARCH

Attention to ethics is vital for designing social science research, but it is also vital for sharing the results. Sociologists are required to report their research results accurately and truthfully—whether that is in government reports, journal articles or books, or research presentations. Three of the most common breaches of publication ethics are plagiarism, counterfeit research, and failure to disclose conflicts of interest.

Plagiarism

Plagiarism involves presenting the words or ideas of another person without giving them credit. When researchers, students, or anyone present someone else's ideas, arguments, data, or analyses as their own, this constitutes plagiarism. Sadly, some sociologists along with other social scientists, academics, and governmental officials have recently been found guilty of plagiarism.

In some cases, academics plagiarize what they themselves have previously published. In cases of self-plagiarism, researchers reproduce what they published previously, but present it as new, original research—without citing their previous work. This presents a problem because when researchers submit a manuscript to a journal editor or publisher, they are required to certify that the manuscript is original research. One of the main goals of academic publishing is to advance scholarly understanding of an issue or problem. The publication review process is lengthy and requires the labor of editors, reviewers, and publishers. Misleading publishers about the originality of their research violates professional research ethics.

CONSIDER THIS...

If you were a coauthor on a published study and you discovered that one of your coauthors had plagiarized the section that they had contributed to the article, what would you do?

Counterfeit Research

In addition to plagiarizing, researchers sometimes misrepresent their work or their findings. These, too, are considered highly unethical research practices. In some particularly outrageous cases, researchers have simply fabricated their entire study!

In one recent example, Helen Pluckrose (an editor at an online magazine), Peter Boghossian (a philosopher), and James Lindsay (a mathematician) wanted to discredit the fields of Gender Studies, Critical Race Studies, and Queer Studies by showing that journals associated with these fields published low-quality scholarship. In what is now known as the "Sokal Squared" scandal, Pluckrose, Boghossian, and Lindsay fabricated several academic articles—based on non-existent studies—and submitted them for publication at multiple academic journals. The journal editors, who did not know the articles were baseless, subjected these articles to the peer-review process, and seven of the 20 made-up articles they had submitted were ultimately accepted for publication (Beauchamp, 2018). The authors not only lied to the journal editors, reviewers, and potential readers, but also wasted their limited time and resources.

In addition to violating publication ethics, by targeting journals and fields associated with marginalized groups, their prank undermines the valuable and important work being done in these fields. Unfortunately, bogus research has made its way through the peer-review publication process and into print in many fields, including Andrew Wakefield's now infamous—and entirely discredited—study linking vaccines to autism, which was published in one of the world's leading medical journals, *The Lancet.* Pluckrose and her colleagues

Having a financial relationship with the subject of a study is a conflict of interest.
iStockphoto.com/PeopleImages

argued that they were trying to promote scientific integrity, but by targeting Gender, Critical Race, and Queer Studies they instead put forth a narrative that undermined the scholarship of disadvantaged social groups and communities.

Conflicts of Interest

Another critical issue underlying the publication process is the ethical obligation for sociologists to report any possible conflicts of interest that may attach to their research. Sociologists are required to report any financial relationship (or sponsorship) they share with the individuals or organizations they are studying. Abiding by this ethical principle ensures the integrity of the research process and demonstrates that they have conducted their research in a fair and unbiased fashion. Sociologists are to abide by all provisions governing the disclosure of conflicts of interest specified by the university, government, and ASA.

A poignant example of this type of ethical violation was covered by Geis et al. (1999) in their case study of Professor Charles Thomas. Professor Thomas was a sociology professor at the University of Florida. Geis and colleagues revealed that Thomas held 30,000 shares in a private-prisons company, Corrections Corporation of America (CCA), which was valued at $660,000. Thomas was an ardent supporter of private prisons and had also been hired as a consultant with a CCA-affiliated entity, Prison Realty Board, for which he was paid $3 million (Geis et al., p. 380).

Thomas coauthored an article in *Crime and Delinquency* (1999) that claimed a lower recidivism rate for those inmates released from two private prisons versus those released from a state prison. However, Thomas failed to disclose these forms of financial compensation from CCA (and related entities) at the time of this publication—a major conflict of interest!

Retraction

We know that academic journals across fields occasionally publish research that is low quality, fabricated, or produced by scholars with a conflict of interest. When this is discovered, journal editors can retract these publications—issuing formal notifications for potential readers that the studies were deeply flawed and should be disregarded.

The process of investigating and discrediting plagiarism and other types of fraudulent work can be seen on the website *Retraction Watch*. This website highlights those studies that have been peer-reviewed and published, but which were subsequently discredited.

DOING SOCIOLOGY 4.5

Plagiarism and Deception in Student Work

In this exercise, you will consider the similarities and differences between ethics in the context of socio-logical publishing, and the ethics of conducting and submitting student work.

Colleges and universities across the United States have established codes of ethics for their students. Sometimes this is called an "Honor Code," and in other cases it might be called an "Honors Policy," "Student Code of Conduct," or something similar. Even though schools have such policies, students violate these policies with surprising regularity.

With this and your own school's code of ethics in mind, answer the following questions:

1. Think about the various demands put on students and the stresses they encounter throughout the semester. Under what structural circumstances do you think students are most likely to plagiarize or submit counterfeit work?

2. Do you think any of these structural circumstances are similar to those that might encourage professional researchers to commit academic dishonesty?

3. What college- or university-level changes might help to reduce instances of plagiarism or academic dishonesty more broadly?

Check Your Understanding

1. What is plagiarism?
2. What is counterfeit research? What are some key examples?
3. What is a conflict of interest when it comes to scholarly publication?
4. What does it mean when a scholarly article is retracted?

ETHICAL CONSIDERATIONS FOR ENGAGED RESEARCH

Sociologists have worked to promote the public good from our earliest days as a discipline. Some of the most effective ways we can do so are exemplified in "applied research"—community-based research and evaluation research. These two strategies carry with them certain ethical issues that are not fully anticipated in the ASA *Code of Ethics* and represent challenges for the researcher.

Community-Based Research

Sociologists seeking to promote the public good sometimes rely on "community-based research" (CBR), which is also referred to as "participatory action research" or "empowerment research." In CBR, community members and researchers share their collective knowledge, perspectives, expertise, and other resources to investigate and address an issue of mutual concern or interest.

Although CBR can yield tremendous benefits for communities, this type of research also brings the potential for unforeseen collective risks. In some cases, it may actually work to the detriment of the community or segments within that community if, for example, the results of the research depress property values, reinforce stereotypes of crime-prone neighborhoods, produce a "brain drain," or increase the frequency of police patrols.

Sociologists may find themselves facing numerous ethical challenges when it comes to community-based research (Banks et al., 2013). We must be attentive to who speaks for the community, and we must consider the possibility that some voices (or viewpoints) might be omitted or given greater weight than others. We must also recognize the possible loss of anonymity for those members of the community who elect not to participate but who reside in the community being studied. And we must be mindful of tensions underlying the power dynamic between researcher and research subject and how this influences the collaboration that is at the heart of CBR.

You might recall from the beginning of this chapter that the sociologist Laud Humphreys, who studied the "tea-room trade," was not so sure that he could continue to conceal the identities of the men he studied. Similarly, for collective risks, the protection of the identities of groups, organizations, or entire communities, like those in Prince William Sound, is a critical consideration. Some professions—like health care providers, clergy, and psychologists—are not subject to legal requests to turn over confidential information in courts, unless their client or parishioner is a threat to themselves or others. However, sociologists are *not* exempt from providing testimony, and can be compelled by subpoenas to release their notes and findings or face jail time. In fact, with an eye toward protecting the confidentiality of members of an animal rights group he studied, Rik Scarce served 159 days in jail for his unwillingness to provide notes (a stance supported by ASA in a "friend of the court" brief). Be sure to keep this in mind as you consider the potential pitfalls of any research study, but in particular community-based research.

SOCIOLOGISTS IN ACTION
DAN ROSE

Dan Rose

Photo courtesy of Dan Rose

I'm interested in the ways that evictions disrupt the lives of renters. People who get evicted struggle to find new housing. They face higher rates of homelessness, job loss, disease, domestic violence, suicide, and depression (Desmond, 2015; Desmond & Gershenson, 2016; Fowler et al., 2015; Gold, 2016). Their children, who often must change schools, are at risk of diminished academic performance.

Evictions are evidence of our system of racial and economic inequality doing harm to the most vulnerable among us. Eviction rates for Black and Latinx renters are higher than those of whites (Desmond & Gershenson, 2017). As a sociologist who sees the human impact of these structural problems up close, I'm interested in systemic change that would make housing a human right. And with most landlords seeing housing primarily as a source of profit, I understand this contradiction through the lens of conflict theory.

Many tenants feel that the legal system is confusing, intimidating, and biased against them. So, I combine my efforts to understand their experiences with efforts to provide knowledge they might be lacking. I give tenants "Know Your Rights" information from a local housing justice group and encourage them to contact Legal Aid. Tenants with legal representation fare better in eviction cases than those without (Desmond, 2016). This is not just an interesting piece of academic knowledge. I see it as my duty to help.

Am I objective in my research? No. I don't pretend to have a neutral stance on evictions. I'm against them. Many people think if you're not objective, you cannot do good research. But even the research questions we choose are value-laden; every researcher has interests that guide their inquiry. As sociologist Max Weber (1904) stated, "All knowledge of cultural reality, as may be seen, is always knowledge from particular points of view." I'm interested in the tenants' point of view. Is this unethical? I don't believe it is. If I were to distort, misrepresent, or lie about what tenants experience, that would raise moral issues. Researchers make deliberate choices about what they focus on, but they must also accurately report the data they collect. I report the data from my studies accurately, but I'm also concerned with helping tenants fight back. As historian Howard Zinn (2018) stated, "You can't be neutral on a moving train."

Dan Rose is assistant professor of sociology at Winston-Salem State University, whose research focuses on housing inequalities, rights, and evictions.

Discussion Question

What is the difference between objectivity and accuracy in research? Is objective research possible in sociology?

Evaluation Research

Evaluation research is another form of applied research in which researchers must consider the ethical implications of how their research might be used. Recall that evaluation research assesses whether various policies, programs, or other social interventions produce their intended outcome.

Many sociologists, and especially criminologists, conduct research that informs crime control policies. The emerging standards for evaluating crime control policies are "evidence-based practices" (EBP)—meaning the policies that we implement should be those that are backed by empirical evidence that they actually work. If, for example, research shows that people who commit a crime are less likely to reoffend when they are given probation, compared to those who are sent to prison, then we have evidence that probation is a more effective crime control tool.

Evaluation research can directly affect people's lives. If studies show that early childhood education promotes health, well-being, and employment later in life, then policy makers are more likely to support and fund these programs. If studies suggest that policies, programs, or services are ineffective or even simply less effective than funders would like, then the resources and services upon which people depend can be cut. Social scientists who practice evaluation research must be extremely careful in their research designs as well as in communicating their results so that they do not inadvertently undermine support for effective programs.

In addition, researchers conducting evaluations of particular organizations must be attuned to how any inequities within the organization might generate ethical concerns. Researchers must take great care to ensure that workers in lower-level positions are free to decide for themselves whether and how to participate in the research. Researchers must give extra attention to issues of confidentiality. Especially if the organization is small, or if there are only a few people in particular types of positions or social status (like gender, religion, race, or ethnicity), then it might be easy to trace survey responses or interview quotations back to individual people.

CONSIDER THIS. . .

How might sociologists use community-based research or evaluation research to understand the consequences of the COVID-19 pandemic? What are some of the ethical issues that might emerge in using these methods to understand the virus?

DOING SOCIOLOGY 4.6

Committing to Community-Based Research

In this activity, you will gain a better understanding of community-based research as well as the special ethical considerations for this type of research.

W.E.B. DuBois, arguably one of the most influential American sociologists, lived in the Seventh Ward of Philadelphia and went door to door to interview residents regarding their experiences with inequality. This culminated in the publication of *The Philadelphia Negro* (1899), which has had a profound influence on how sociologists understand racial inequality as well as the link between research and social justice.

In his book *The Philadelphia Negro* and elsewhere, DuBois argued that public policies and private initiatives working for social good need to be rooted in careful and rigorous sociological research in order to be successful (1899). He produced such research and participated in and indeed led a number of social justice organizations to advance racial equality.

Consider your own community as you answer the following questions:

1. Are there any challenges that your community is facing? Are there any challenges to which your community is contributing?

2. Choose one of the challenges you identified in Question 1. If you wanted to conduct interviews with community members to better understand this issue, about what would you question them?

3. What ethical considerations would you want to think about when asking these questions and presenting the results?

4. What are some collective risks that you would need to consider before conducting this research?

Check Your Understanding

1. What distinctive ethical issues does community-based research raise for sociologists?
2. What distinctive ethical issues does evaluation research raise for sociologists?

CONCLUSION

As we saw at the beginning of this chapter, the history of observing, experimenting, and controlling human behavior has been a troubled one. Horrific instances could be seen and often magnified the already marginal status of minority, disadvantaged, and impoverished populations, in addition to other vulnerable groups such as children or people with mental illness or disabilities. Prior to the 1970s, there was a virtual absence of ethical concerns when it came to the well-being and safety of humans as research subjects or as objects of social control. This was reflected in a wide variety of troubling abuses in the academy, the government, and the broader society.

However, in response to these abuses and specific missteps in the behavioral sciences such as Humphreys's "tea-room trade" or the Stanford prison experiment, starting in the 1970s, we saw the emergence of ethics in social research. These ethical standards provide for broad protections of human subjects and promote sound conduct on the part of sociologists in everything they do. In the contemporary context, we also observed those instances in which sociologists have not always met their ethical responsibilities related to deception, misrepresentation, and conflicts of interest. Lastly, we examined the ways in which professional ethics both compel and influence our efforts to promote social justice through community-based research and evaluation research. We must exercise caution, however, when these efforts might create a heightened risk for the communities involved.

As you will see in the next chapter, potential ethical issues may inform our selection of observations, especially if those observations are based on the use of unethical "push polls" and the ways these distort our understanding of attitudes, values, beliefs, and behavior.

REVIEW

4.1   What is human subjects research, and what special considerations does human subjects research require?

Research involving human subjects involves a broad spectrum of strategies used by sociologists to intervene, interact, interview, and obtain information from individuals, groups, and organizations. Because this research involves humans, special ethical considerations take into account the respect, dignity, and well-being of our subjects. To this end, researchers should promote informed and voluntary participation of research subjects, especially when research involves vulnerable persons.

4.2   What are some of the key examples of unethical research in the medical and social sciences? What are some of the ethical problems of these studies?

We can point to several examples of ethical lapses in research involving human subjects such as the eugenics campaign and forced sterilization, the Tuskegee syphilis study, Milgram's study examining obedience to authority, and the Stanford prison experiment. A common thread for these studies is their failure to inform subjects of risks posed by the study and, in the case of Tuskegee, irreparably harming subjects to the point of death.

4.3   What are the major ethical policies and resources for social scientists pursuing research?

Many ethical policies emerged in the 1970s that emphasize informed consent, voluntary participation, and minimizing risks for individuals and groups alike. Several resources promote ethical research such as federal policies, institutional review boards, and the *Code of Ethics* of the American Sociological Association.

4.4   Why might sociologists want to deceive research subjects, either implicitly or explicitly? Under what circumstances is some degree of deception ethically permissible?

Sociologists sometimes use deception in order to gain rapport with their research subjects, elicit responses to sometimes objectionable questions, or gain information related to discriminatory practices (such as employment). Deception may be permissible provided that no other strategy could gain the information, poses minimal risk to the research subjects, and is approved and supervised by an institutional review board.

4.5   What ethical obligations guide sociological scholarship?

Sociologists should represent their research accurately and truthfully; their scholarship should not involve plagiarism or falsification of results; and, whenever present, potential conflicts of interest should be disclosed by the researcher.

4.6   What are some of the special ethical considerations of community-based research and evaluation research?

Sociologists should be aware of distinct ethical challenges posed by community-based research as it may exclude some voices in the community, can jeopardize the anonymity of community residents, and can pose collective risk for the community and its well-being. Evaluation research can also jeopardize anonymity of research subjects, and it may create unforeseen risks if programs being studied are found to have limited impact, thereby eliminating these programs and services for potentially vulnerable communities or individuals.

KEY TERMS

anonymously (p. 64)

Belmont Report (p. 63)

beneficence (p. 63)

collective risk (p. 66)

confidential (p. 64)

conflicts of interest (p. 71)

eugenics (p. 60)

human subject (p. 58)

human subjects research (p. 58)

informed consent (p. 58)

informed consent forms (p. 64)

institutional review board (p. 64)

justice (p. 64)

plagiarism (p. 70)

respect for persons (p. 63)

retract (p. 71)

self-plagiarism (p. 70)

Stanford prison experiment (p. 62)

Stanley Milgram (p. 61)

Tuskegee study (p. 60)

vulnerable population (p. 58)

SELECTING OBSERVATIONS
Jennifer A. Strangfeld

SELECTING OBSERVATIONS

Imagine that you were interested in learning more about members of the LGBTQ+ community (people who identify as gay, lesbian, bisexual, transgender, or queer) who have experienced instances of homophobia (discrimination because of their sexual identity) in the United States. How would you find them? Would you try to talk to every single LGBTQ+ person who has ever experienced homophobia? If that seems impractical, then to how many people would you talk? And how would you decide to *which* people you would talk?

Each of these questions is one that, at its core, is about sampling. More often than not, the research questions sociologists have are about a group or set of social artifacts (material things that humans create like movies, books, social media posts, etc.) that are much larger than what we have the time and resources to study in their entirety. In all likelihood, we don't have time or resources to collect information from every LGBTQ+ person about their experience of homophobia. But, we do have the ability to ask *some* people about their experiences. The process of deciding who to include, and who by extension not to include, is what sampling is all about.

HOW I GOT ACTIVE IN SOCIOLOGY
Jennifer A. Strangfeld

I had never heard of sociology until I went to college. In my first year, I enrolled in a gender studies class to fulfill a general education requirement. My instructor was a sociologist and the class centered on gender, race, and sexuality in particular. It was the first time in my educational experience that I got to think and talk about these things in a critical way and I was both fascinated and nervous at the same time. I felt like the class gave voice to some of my own experiences as a white, working-class, queer student while also challenging some of my assumptions about racial oppression and privilege. I could not believe that I got to talk about these issues for an entire semester. Afterward,

I started looking through the course catalog and figured out that there were actually entire majors devoted to these topics! I took some classes in sociology and gender studies and completed my undergraduate degree in gender studies. However, when I went to graduate school, I chose sociology. I chose sociology because I like how it gives me a framework and language to discuss how institutions and culture reflect inequalities and oppression, and how we can try to end these problems.

Sampling is a much more complicated process than just picking a group of individuals or social artifacts to study. Who or what we include in our study will impact our findings. For example, let's go back to the first question above, which was how to find people who have experienced instances of homophobia. LGBTQ+ people live in all types of communities throughout the United States, but we know that some cities and neighborhoods—like the Castro District in San Francisco or Boystown in Chicago—have a higher proportion of LGBTQ+ people than do other cities. A researcher wanting to study experiences of homophobia might first consider locating LGBTQ+ people in those areas. However, these places tend to have a higher percentage of residents who are gay men compared to those who are lesbian women. In the case of the Castro District, residents are also more likely to be white and earn higher than average incomes (Compton & Baumle, 2012; Ghaziani, 2014).

Consider how focusing only on residents in these LGBTQ+ neighborhoods might affect our research project—do gender, race, and income influence life experiences? Absolutely. So, if we only select residents from these neighborhoods, we might *think* that our research is about the experiences of the LGTBQ+ community as a whole, but there would be a good chance that our research findings would more accurately represent a subset of this group: that is, the experience of white, upper-class gay men. Moreover, even if we were able to get a balanced and racially diverse group of men and women from these neighborhoods, the type of prejudice and discrimination that people encounter in liberal urban environments differ from the types of mistreatment LGBTQ+ people experience in rural and more conservative areas. Importantly, it is fine to research residents in these neighborhoods, and a lot of good research has been done this way. But the point is for us to understand how our choice of *whose* experiences to study shapes our research questions and findings. Many of the experiences of urban white gay men differ from those of lesbian women, LGBTQ+ individuals of color, and lower-income members of the LGBTQ+ community living elsewhere (Cohen, 1997; De Pedro et al., 2018). Thus, we need to be aware of how well our study participants represent the broader group or population we are trying to study.

Consider a very different example. A researcher wants to determine how issues of climate change have been covered in the U.S. news media in recent years. They compile all of the stories from the Fox News website that contain the terms *global warming* or *climate change* in the subject line or lead. They conclude based on this sample of news media that the U.S. news media are dismissive of climate change in more than half of their stories, and reject the idea of humans contributing to climate change in more than 30% of their stories. While the researcher's analysis of the stories they collect might be completely correct, a focus on sampling leads one to ask, "Do stories from Fox News accurately represent the U.S. news media more generally?" In fact, a recent study shows that Fox News differs significantly from both CNN and MSNBC in its coverage of climate change (Feldman et al., 2012). The research findings may accurately represent how Fox News represents climate change, but their findings do not apply to other cable news outlets, nor to the media more broadly.

What both of these stories reveal is that who or what we include in our study matters. In fact, one of the ways to critically evaluate any particular research study is to look at who or what the researchers collected data from, how they collected it, and whether that fits well with the scope of their claims. In short, for quality research, decisions about who or what to include in the study must be thoughtfully, carefully, and deliberately considered.

How might you study the different experiences of LGBTQ+ individuals?

Populations and Samples

Any sociological research study must define its population: all of the elements (e.g., individuals, groups, organizations, social artifacts, etc.) that *could* be included in a study depending on what the research is about. In the examples above, the population might be people who identify as lesbian, gay, bisexual, transgender, or queer in the United States. In the case of the news media example, it would be stories from all Internet, radio, and television sources, big and small, local and national, over a specified period of time. If a researcher is interested in studying U.S. women in professional workplaces, then the population would include all U.S. women who hold professional jobs. Notice that the population is determined by the research questions being asked and thus it varies across studies. Even two studies on women in professional jobs might have different populations if, for example, the studies define professional jobs differently or if one study included an additional criterion such as women of color in professional jobs or millennial women in professional jobs. In those studies, the population of professional women will be further defined by racial identity or age group.

Determining a population specifies who or what the study is about. However, as noted previously, in most cases a researcher cannot study everyone in the population because of time and/or resource limitations. Thus, researchers generally study a subset—or sample—of a given population. By analyzing a sample, researchers can learn something about a population while balancing work, time, and financial restrictions. There are a number of techniques that a researcher can use to collect a sample. The choice of which technique is best depends upon the researcher's questions and goals.

CONSIDER THIS...

Populations can be big or small, depending on the research question. What's a research question that would have a large population? What's a research question that would have a smaller population?

DOING SOCIOLOGY 5.1

Distinguishing Samples and Populations

In this exercise, you will consider the differences between samples and populations.

Consider each of the following examples and identify whether the research is using a sample or a population. Explain how you arrived at your decision.

1. The registrar at Pastoral University, who has access to the records of every student, is analyzing them to see what the typical course load is for undergraduate students at your university.

2. The Anti-Racism Coalition at Pastoral University is interested in assessing the amount of racial discrimination and harassment at their school. They are interested specifically in undergraduate students' perspectives and send a short survey to all undergraduate students. Half of the students respond to the survey.

3. The local Parks and Recreation Department wants to know who is using the local parks, and specifically if there are socioeconomic, racial/ethnic, and or disability-based patterns in the usage of public parks. For one week, surveyors stand at the entrance to the most popular park and give a survey to everyone who enters. They collect completed surveys as people exit. Remarkably, everyone who receives a survey completes it!

4. A researcher collects data from the U.S. Census on all of the towns and cities in North Carolina to investigate patterns of education and poverty in the state. They use a spreadsheet and enter data about the number of people living in each place, the average educational attainment of community members, the racial/ethnic composition of each community, and the percentage of the community living in poverty.

CHOOSING A SAMPLE SIZE

The overall number of respondents or artifacts to include in a sample is referred to as the sample size, often abbreviated with the letter *n*, for "number." Sample sizes vary greatly across sociological studies. Researchers' questions, methods, and goals drive their decisions about sample size. Quantitative studies focused on identifying trends in a large population will typically have larger sample sizes (often 1,000 cases or more). Qualitative studies typically have smaller samples (around 100 cases or less), but often draw a greater depth of knowledge from each case. In some cases—for example, in a content analysis project—researchers are able to determine the sample size early in a study design. In other cases, the sample size remains unknown until later in the data collection process.

Why Larger Samples?

Larger samples are most commonly associated with quantitative studies, though researchers conducting qualitative work sometimes use large samples as well. Quantitative researchers are often interested in identifying patterns, trends, and differences across large populations. To accomplish this, it is important that the characteristics of the sample they analyze be as similar as possible to the population in which they are interested. Of course, no sample is identical to the population from which it is drawn. Researchers use the term sampling error to describe the discrepancy (or error) that exists between the characteristics of a sample and a population. In simple terms, a larger sample generally has a greater chance of reducing sampling error because it can better capture population diversity.

Imagine that a researcher wants to know more about the experiences of first-generation college students—students who are the first in their families to attend college. They are particularly interested in the challenges that face first-generation college students in the United States. In this case, the researcher will likely want a sample that closely matches the population of these students. If the population varies in terms of gender, race/ethnicity, sexual identity, class, age, region, and other traits of interest, then the sample will need to be large enough to adequately capture that diversity. If all first-generation college students were essentially the same, then our sample could be smaller because there would not be much diversity in the population. In this case, we could more easily apply our results from a small group to the larger population. But this is not the case, and thus a larger sample is better able to capture the diverse population of first-generation college students. In a study like this, the researcher would determine a desirable sample size at the onset of a research project and then proceed with data collection.

CONSIDER THIS...

Why are researchers better able to capture the diversity within a population when they use larger samples?

Why Smaller Samples?

Sometimes the primary goals of a study are about understanding something in-depth, or understanding the deep meanings people attach to things, or understanding the complexity of a particular circumstance. This is often the case with qualitative studies.

For example, a sociologist studying the Black Lives Matter movement might want to describe and analyze what meaning participation in the movement has for the activists themselves. In such cases, researchers might spend time observing and interviewing activists for extended periods and maybe even at multiple times. Depending on the research question, the researcher's focus might be understanding the perspective of long-term members and leaders or the motivations of activists who joined the movement once it was established. In studies like this, "coverage" is more important than sample size (Jones et al., 2014). In other words, a researcher is more concerned with choosing participants who are best able to speak about the meanings of the movement rather than focusing primarily on obtaining a large sample. Sample size varies widely in these studies, sometimes reflecting fewer than 100 respondents and in some cases even fewer than 20. A common guideline is that researchers stop collecting data when they are no longer learning new information from their respondents. This reinforces the key point that a researcher has to have a clear understanding of *what* they want to know and what they want their research to achieve in order to accurately determine when they have reached that point.

The experiences of first-generation college students vary based on a number of factors. A study of such students would require a larger sample size to capture that diversity.

©Kentaroo Tryman/Getty Images

Smaller sample sizes can sometimes be determined at the onset of a study in the same way that larger sample sizes are. Yet, in some cases, it might be difficult to know exactly how many people to include in the sample until the researcher has spent time in the field. Since exploratory research investigates new and emerging issues, situations, identities, or other social phenomena, researchers enter the field with relatively little knowledge of their subject. They learn and analyze as they go, and their research may continue until they run out of resources or they reach the point of saturation—when information from new participants mimics that provided by earlier participants, and thus provides little additional information.

DOING SOCIOLOGY 5.2

Larger and Smaller Samples

In this exercise, you will consider how the research questions, methods, and/or goals influence the sample size you pursue.

Consider the research question, method, and/or goal in each of the following examples. Identify whether you would pursue a larger sample size (about 1,000 or more) or a smaller sample size (about 100 or less), and why.

1. The nonprofit Equality for Workers is interested in learning more about levels of satisfaction with union membership among U.S. workers. The goal is to survey workers from diverse gender and racial identities and age categories, as well as include both private and public sector union workers.

2. Student University wants to better understand how experiences with racism on campus impact students' sense of belonging. Researchers interview students at length because they want to gain in-depth understanding of students' experiences. The researchers are primarily interested in learning about the meanings students attach to their experiences and are less focused on generalizing their findings to the larger student population.

3. A researcher is interested in learning from self-identified "fat activists" about how they manage negative stereotypes associated with fat bodies. The researchers conduct a series of focus groups with activists to talk about their body experiences and attitudes. The primary goal of the research is to develop a more in-depth understanding of the complexities associated with participants' lived experiences and perceptions.

4. A team of researchers is investigating how a recent health pandemic impacted service workers financially across the country. The researchers want to survey people in all four of the U.S. Census–designated regions; people in rural, urban, and suburban areas; and people in different types of service work (namely, transportation, hospitality, health care, and financial services).

PROBABILITY SAMPLING

When researchers know they cannot gather the information they are seeking about an entire population, they have to think carefully about determining from which subset of the population they will gather data—that is, which cases to include in their sample. There are two broad types of samples: probability samples and nonprobability samples. A probability sample is one in which the elements of the sample (people, objects, schools, newspaper articles, etc.) are chosen based on mathematical chance. In nonprobability samples, the probability of inclusion for any particular case is unknown.

Imagine a researcher is conducting a study on student satisfaction. They focus on one school, with a student population of exactly 1,000 people, and intend to interview 100 students. They have a list of students in the school, and randomly selects the names of 100 students. This list of all possible individuals or artifacts in a defined population is called a sampling frame.

In this example, each student in the population has an equal probability of being selected for inclusion in the study. Notice that to guarantee each person has an equal chance of being included, the researcher must have access to a full list of a population. If a researcher does not know how many people are in the population, then they cannot be certain that everyone has the same mathematical chance of being included in the sample.

In short, probability samples require that researchers select sample cases by mathematical chance and that each case has the same chance of being selected. To accomplish this, researchers use sampling frames (e.g., lists of individuals, families, schools, organizations, etc.) to draw their samples. Researchers can use probability samples in any type of study, though they are used most often in quantitative studies, which typically rely upon survey data, experiments, and/or content analysis. In these types of studies, generalizability and random assignment tend to be closely tied to the goals of the research.

Generalizability refers to the ability to apply (or generalize) findings from the sample to the larger population from which they were selected. It is also the primary strength of probability sampling. A researcher whose sample is not a probability sample might claim that their results can be generalized to a larger population, but using probability samples gives the researcher greater confidence that the sample characteristics are reflective of the population. There is always a chance that the characteristics of the sample differ from the larger group. But a researcher who uses probability sampling can make a better estimate of the characteristics in the larger population. This is because the laws of probability allow researchers to estimate the level of sampling error that occurs in a given sample. There are four main types of probability samples, each of which we will now discuss.

Simple Random Sampling

Probability samples are based on random selection. In a simple random sample, each sample element is assigned a number and then a researcher generally uses a computer or random number generator to select the desired number of elements in the sample. Done correctly, a simple random sample should be reflective of the population from which it is drawn.

In the context of sampling, the meaning of the term *random* differs from its common usage. In our everyday life, the word *random* typically means "haphazard"—something that is done without a particular aim or rule. We might say that we approach a random person on the street to ask a question, for example. But, in the context of research, asking questions to people we happen to meet on the street doesn't count as "random." This is because the term *random* in sampling refers to the property of having equal mathematical chance. If we approach people on a certain street corner to answer a survey, then people who are not on that street corner at that particular time have no chance of being included in our sample. Consequently, we cannot say that everyone has an equal chance of being included in our sample, and thus our sample is not random.

Even if every member of a population under study were located in one place, approaching people unsystematically and haphazardly still does not result in a random sample, because our conscious or unconscious bias may affect the people we choose to approach. Perhaps we are more comfortable talking to people who share some commonality with us. Perhaps we have an unconscious apprehension about talking to certain people. It is possible that this type of bias is influencing who we approach and who we let pass by.

Simple random samples have two important limitations. First, groups who constitute a small proportion of the overall population are likely to constitute a small proportion of the sample. A small proportion of the sample may translate into only a handful of actual cases, making it difficult for researchers to draw meaningful conclusions about this group. A given population might have a low percentage of people who identify as people of color—say, less than 10%. In a large population, this might equate to thousands of people in the population but in a sample of 100 people, that might mean fewer than 10 people. Thus, a researcher runs the risk that the trends or experiences of the minority group may be overshadowed by the trends or experiences of the dominant group. Stratified random sampling, discussed next, is one way to address this concern.

A second potential limitation is that a simple random sample is only representative of the population from which it is drawn. An October 2016 *Cosmopolitan* magazine story reported that a survey of randomly selected online subscribers supported Hillary Clinton for president. The data were collected specifically from female Cosmpolitan.com subscribers between the ages of 18 and 34 years (Thomson-Deveau, 2016). Although the data were randomly selected, they were chosen from a very narrow population. The magazine story makes note of this, but also uses the data to make a broader statement about millennial women. This is problematic because although the Compolitan.com survey was a random sample, the information is only generalizable to the population from which it is drawn—namely online subscribers, not all millennial women.

Systematic Random Sampling

Sometimes the conditions under which sample elements are accessible make it impractical to generate a sample from a random number generator. A common example of this is in the case of voters casting ballots on election day. A researcher may have a list of all registered voters, but not all registered voters actually cast votes in any given election. To address this, a researcher could stand at precinct sites and collect a sample of people who cast ballots at that location on that day. But this information would not be collected neatly in some list from which the researcher could select a computer-generated sample. In such cases, researchers can instead choose every *nth* person (every 10th or every 20th, for example) who leaves the polling station and ask them about their voting choices. Everyone who votes at that precinct should have an equal chance of being included in the sample (random), and selecting every *nth* individual (systematic) helps diminish the impact a researcher's conscious or unconscious bias may have on the selection of sample participants. Researchers often use this technique to conduct exit polls on election days.

Another common use of this sampling technique involves researchers sampling a general population by sampling every *nth* household in a given neighborhood (Haj-Yahia et al., 2012; Zandee et al., 2013). This is particularly useful when population records are inaccurate or incomplete. The value of the *nth* interval—for example, every fourth house—depends on the size of the population and the desired sample size. If there are 1,000 homes in a neighborhood, and the desired sample size is 100 households, then the researcher might approach every 10th house (population size divided by desired sample size equals the *nth* interval). A word of caution: This method is not effective if the elements are arranged in some interval pattern (called periodicity). If every eighth house is uniquely different from the other houses—for example, in terms of size—a researcher could end up with either an over- or underrepresentation of those houses. This could bias the resulting data. Zandee et al. (2013) addressed this by flipping a coin to determine whether the investigator started with house number one or house number two on any given street. Data

When conducting a systematic random sample, researchers must be aware of period-icity within a population to ensure there is not an over- or underrepresentation of those elements in the sample population.

©iStockphoto.com/BrianAJackson

that are ordered alphabetically or numerically are not nec-essarily a problem as long as the ordering does not have a specific pattern to it.

In comparison to simple random samples, system-atic random samples are not as purely tied to the math-ematical principles of probability. However, the choice to use a simple random sample versus a systematic ran-dom sample generally depends on which method is most practical for any given research study and the limitations of available data.

Cluster Sampling

Cluster sampling is useful when a listing of individual elements is not available or selection of a random sample is impractical but sampling elements are grouped into clusters from which we can collect a random sample. For example, people of religious faith in the United States are often associated with specific religious institutions (like mosques, temples, or churches). Students are similarly associated with, or clustered in, schools.

Cluster sampling is a two-step process. In the first stage, a researcher selects a random sample of clusters from all possible clusters (e.g., a random sample of all mosques). In the second stage, a researcher collects data from each element within the selected cluster (e.g., each individual who worships at the mosque). A variation of this is for researchers to select a random sample of individuals in the second stage instead of collecting data from all individuals in the cluster. In this approach, sampling occurs at more than one stage (a random sample of clusters and then a random sample of individuals). This is known as multistage cluster sampling.

The World Health Organization manual recommends this approach for collecting data on popula-tion immunization rates (particularly in nonindustrialized countries where population records may be unavailable or incomplete) based upon the premise that individuals are typically clustered in cities, towns, or villages. For example, researchers interested in immunization rates among 2-year-old indig-enous children in Queensland, Australia, began with a random sample of 30 areas selected from the state's 153 designated indigenous areas (Vlack et al., 2007). They then randomly selected seven eligible children from each of the designated 30 areas for inclusion in the sample.

One of the primary reasons to use cluster sampling has to do with practicality. By focusing on clus-ters of elements, researchers can more realistically reach a broad range of elements given the time and resource constraints that typically impact research. For example, in the immunization research cited above, if the researchers had used a simple random sample of indigenous children in Queensland, they likely would have had to travel to many more than 30 geographic areas to obtain the same sample size. Cost and time associated with this amount of travel are generally too much for researchers to manage. Or consider research on college students in the United States. A simple random sample could require researchers to travel to hundreds of schools around the country. Although it might be theoretically desirable to do that, it is often not practical. Instead, researchers might select a random sample of states, then select a random sample of universities within each state, and finally select a random sample of stu-dents within each university. This would be an example of multistage cluster sampling.

A second reason to select a cluster sample has to do with availability of information. In instances where a listing of all possible sampling elements—the sampling frame—is unobtainable, researchers can often use cluster sampling as an alternative to a simple random sample. In the example of individu-als who worship at mosques, researchers cannot access a list of people who actually meet this criterion. However, they can still collect a sample based on probability by selecting a random sample of mosques.

Cluster sampling is considered a probability sample because all elements have at least *some* prob-ability of being included in the study. Again, in the Queensland study, all eligible indigenous children had some chance of being included in the study because all indigenous areas were included in stage one of sampling. However, in stage two, children whose geographic areas were not selected for the sample no longer had a chance of being included in the study. Thus, the probability of inclusion was not the same for all children. For this reason, cluster sampling is not as purely tied to the principles of probability as simple random sampling. Remember, though, that sampling techniques are chosen based on their ability to meet the goals and questions of a research study. While adherence to the mathematical principles of probability is not absolute, cluster sampling may offer the most cost-effective or most realistic opportunity to meet the research goals or answer the research questions.

Stratified Sampling

In applying the principles of probability to sampling, researchers intend to collect a sample that represents the larger population. One consequence of this is that traits that are less common in a population will be less common in a representative sample. For example, a researcher may be interested in investigating people in corporate leadership positions. Women and people of color tend to be underrepresented in these positions and therefore a representative sample will produce the same results. But what if researchers are primarily interested in how the experiences or attitudes of corporate leaders vary by racial and gender identities? In such instances, researchers might design a stratified sample.

In a stratified sample, researchers select particular strata, or categories, of a population and choose random samples from each of those strata. In the preceding example, rather than select a simple random sample of corporate leaders, researchers might split the sample into particular racial groups and then select a random sample for each group. Researchers decide how much of the sample each stratum will represent, and this decision is based on the goals of the research question. For instance, research by Malcolm and Dowd (2012) examined the impact of student debt on graduate school enrollment for students who completed a STEM degree in college. In order to include meaningful comparisons across racial–ethnic groups, sample data were collected from four specified racial groups (African American/Black, Latinx, Asian, and white). African American/Black and Latinx students, in particular, tend to be underrepresented in STEM fields and are more likely to come from lower-income backgrounds. A simple random sample runs the risk of minimizing the representation (and thus experiences) of these racial groups who may have very distinct roadblocks that impact their graduate school attendance. Including a greater share of these groups in the sample than would otherwise appear in the population is known as a disproportionate stratified sample.

CONSIDER THIS. . .

In addition to racial/ethnic minority groups, what other social groups could benefit from a national survey that used disproportionate stratified sampling?

In some cases, researchers will select strata that reflect the relative proportions of each in the general population. Imagine that a researcher wants a random sample of college students to complete a survey and wants to ensure that the sample is representative of the adult student population in terms of age groups. A large percentage of university students tend to be younger-aged adults (18–24 years), though there are a number of older students enrolled in these schools as well. With a simple random sample, it is possible that the sample will not adequately capture the age diversity on a given campus. To address this concern, the researcher can collect data from a random sample of each designated age group separately with a target sample size for each that represents their population proportion.

For example, suppose at University A, 45% of students are 18–21 years, 30% are 22–24 years, 15% are 25–29 years, and 10% are 30 years of age or older. Suppose also that the researcher wants a sample of 1,000 students that reflects these percentages. Among those 1,000 students, the researcher can randomly select 450 from those who are 18–21, then randomly select 300 from those who are 22–24, 150 from those who are 25–29, and 100 from those who are 30+. In this example, the same proportion or percentage of each identified age group in the population is reflected in the sample. This is known as a proportionate stratified sample.

DOING SOCIOLOGY 5.3

Assessing Probability Samples

In this exercise, you will weigh the benefits and limitations of different types of probability samples.

Imagine that the superintendent of your local school system contacts you for help. They would like to know whether students, faculty, and staff find the classrooms in their district to be inclusive, safe, and welcoming environments for working and learning.

Answer the following questions:

1. What is the population in which the superintendent is interested?

2. What would a simple random sample of this population look like in this situation? What would be the benefits and limitations of using this sampling design?

3. What might a cluster sample look like in this situation? What would be the benefits and limitations of using this sampling design?

4. What might a stratified sample look like in this situation? What would be the benefits and limitations of using this sampling design?

Check Your Understanding

1. What is the difference between a random sample and choosing a sample haphazardly?

2. What is a systematic sample and why might a researcher choose this method over a simple random sample?

3. What is a stratified random sample and why might a researcher choose this method?

4. What is the difference between a proportionate and a disproportionate stratified sample?

NON-PROBABILITY SAMPLING

Nonprobability samples do not adhere to the principles of mathematical chance evident in probability sampling. But this does not mean that researchers give no consideration to the population from which they are sampling. In fact, in most cases, researchers make significant efforts to reflect at least some key aspect of their population within the sample and thereby improve their ability to speak about the experiences of a larger group. Nonprobability samples offer important opportunities to study hidden populations or populations in which not all members are clearly known. It is also common to see nonprobability sampling in qualitative studies (such as interviews, participant-observation, and some content analysis), where the goals are focused more on depth of knowledge rather than broad generalizations. There are four main types of nonprobability samples, discussed next.

Convenience Sampling

Convenience sampling is sometimes referred to as availability or volunteer sampling because it involves sampling members or artifacts of a population that are available at a given moment (such as stopping people on the street) or who volunteer for a study. As the name implies, this technique is indeed convenient, and a desirable trait of this approach is that generally, people who volunteer for a study are very motivated to provide information. Sometimes academic researchers will recruit study participants by offering extra credit to students in large lower-division classes (like Introduction to Sociology, for instance). This is certainly a convenient way to motivate participants to join a research study.

Convenience sampling has some significant drawbacks, though. For one, relying on people to volunteer for a study gives the researcher very little control over who is included in the study. Perhaps those who volunteer feel very strongly about a topic, and the researcher who relies on the data from these enthusiastic volunteers will miss the attitudes or experiences of more ambivalent members of the population. Or perhaps the researcher is only getting students who need extra credit in a class rather than a representative sample of typical students.

A second consideration is that volunteer samples make it more difficult to do comparisons of different subpopulations (for example, comparing commuting students versus students who live on campus, or nearby but off campus) because the researcher cannot guarantee participation from all desired groups. Before opting for a convenience sample, a researcher should critically reflect on whether such a sample is the best way to meet those goals. When researchers do use convenience samples, it is important that we recognize the weaknesses of this sampling technique and their potential impact on the findings of a study.

Although convenience samples have significant limitations, there are instances in which using a convenience sample is a good option. For example, a convenience sample might be a useful way to pre-test survey or interview questions without having to expend too much time and financial resources. Or perhaps a researcher is still trying to learn more about a topic or population to better design a more rigorous research project. In practice, when using convenience samples, it is generally better to consider them as a first-stage practice rather than a primary sampling approach.

Convenience samples are often the basis for reader or listener polls. Magazines, newspapers, or radio shows, for example, might ask subscribers or audience members to answer survey questions on a particular topic, such as dating/sexual behavior or voting choices. In these cases, respondents volunteer to participate in the poll and offer their perspectives. In reporting the results of these polls, media outlets are generally not intentionally trying to deceive readers or listeners with false information. Nonetheless, readers who consume that information uncritically can misunderstand the findings.

Magazines often use convenience samples—their readers—which can lead to skewed survey results.

©Retro AdArchives/Alamy Stock Photo

For example, a reader poll might declare that 52% of respondents have cheated on their sexual partner, which might give the reader the impression that cheating is common (e.g., something that more than half of us have done). But this poll captures only those people who are interested in this topic, are readers of the magazine, and took the time to answer—which is a very particular group of people in society and certainly not representative of the larger population. So, in actuality, all we know is that 52% of people who responded to the poll indicated that they have cheated on a sexual partner. This is a very different conclusion than suggesting that more than half the population has cheated on a sexual partner. In sum, results presented from convenience samples generally require an even higher level of scrutiny than other types of sampling techniques.

CONSIDER THIS...

So many of us use online reviews to make decisions about purchasing things. How could understanding the difference between probability and nonprobability sampling help people to better understand online reviews?

Purposive Sampling

In a purposive sample, participants or artifacts are purposefully chosen because they meet some sort of important or specific criteria. A purposive sample requires the researcher to know something about the population, group, or artifacts that they are interested in studying to ensure that the sample is indeed purposeful. Additionally, a researcher should be able to justify why a purposeful sample is appropriate for a given study. This, again, illustrates how sampling is tied to the study goals and questions.

There are many examples of studies in which the goals of a research project are well-matched with a purposive sample. For example, if the goal of a research project is to understand the motivations of leaders in a particular social movement, then a purposive sample would likely be beneficial. Movement leaders often have unique traits, deeper levels of commitment, or different perspectives than the broader movement participants, so it makes sense why a researcher might wish to focus on this group. The sample of movement leaders will not provide data that are generalizable to the larger movement population, but that is not the goal of this kind of research.

A researcher interested in how a topic is portrayed in the print news media might also choose a purposive sample. For example, they might purposefully choose to sample newspaper articles only from particular news sources like the *New York Times* and *Washington Post* based on the kinds of news coverage these papers provide (e.g., national and international news coverage) and their prominence in the industry. Sometimes researchers are interested in studying people who have experienced a specific condition or event, such as people who have experienced a school shooting. In such cases, a purposive sample would be both useful and efficient. Whatever the context for using purposive samples, the researcher should be able to articulate a clear explanation for why such an approach is appropriate.

Snowball Sampling and Respondent-Driven Sampling

Snowball sampling involves a researcher locating some members of a particular population and then asking those members to recommend other members of the population who might be interested in participating in the study. The metaphor of a "snowball" describes the process by which a researcher starts with a few participants and then builds the size of the sample through participant recommendations, much like you might start with a small snowball and keep rolling it until it picks up much more snow. This sample technique is useful when members of a population are hidden or otherwise difficult to locate. For example, this could include individuals who are unauthorized immigrants, participants of organized sex or play parties, punk subculture members, and many other groups. In such cases, it is generally impossible to select a probability sample because there is no list (or sampling frame) of population members. Likewise, it is difficult to conduct a purposive sample on a relatively hidden or unknown population.

For snowball samples, the researcher must generally take the time to develop an initial inroad into the target community in order to establish the initial contacts. Additionally, researchers generally need to establish trust and rapport with their target population before members will willingly volunteer information about themselves or others in their community. For example, Joanna Dreby (2015) was interested in the experiences of families with mixed immigration and citizenship status. She participated in a youth program with her own children for an entire year in Ohio before approaching other families in the program who met her research criteria.

In some instances, researchers also solicit the help of gatekeepers—key participants who are known and respected in a community and can provide information about the community, identify potential participants, and build trust between participants and researchers. In Dreby's study mentioned above, though she was active in the youth program, she also hired a research assistant who had a long history with mixed-status families in the community. The research assistant contacted families to explain the study's goal as well as vouch for Dreby's trustworthiness. This was particularly important given that families in the study had at least one member who was unauthorized to be in the United States. The vulnerability associated with their status required Dreby to make an exceptional effort to establish trust and rapport.

One weakness of a snowball sample is that the sample will reflect only those population members who are directly or indirectly connected to the initial contact, called a network. There may be characteristics of this network that are unique to that group, rather than reflective of the larger population. For example, immigrants, both authorized or unauthorized, tend to settle in communities where they have a preexisting connection or contact, such as a family member or friend. Consequently, it is common for immigrants in a particular city or region to have ties to the same community of origin. Thus, a researcher using a snowball sample to study unauthorized immigrants may end up with a sample of individuals that originate from a similar place and similar set of circumstances rather than a broader range of immigrant experiences.

To address this problem, one strategy is the use of respondent-driven sampling, whereby a researcher selects at least 5–10 sample participants—called *seeds*—and then asks each seed to recruit additional participants through a coupon system that financially rewards their efforts. In short, seeds give potential recruits coupons with basic information about the study and the researcher's contact information and receive compensation for each successful recruit they bring to the study. New recruits are provided with similar coupons to facilitate a new recruitment cycle. The logic underlying this approach is that each seed represents a potentially different network of individuals in the population. By pursuing respondents from different networks, the researcher has a greater chance of getting a more diverse representation of the target population. Not all seeds will produce a fruitful network, but the greater number of seeds, the greater chance that more networks can be accessed.

The process of respondent-driven sampling can continue as long as the researcher wishes to collect data and new participants can be recruited. Consequently, this method has significant potential to achieve larger sample sizes. But often with this approach, the researcher likely will not know beforehand exactly how many respondents will be included in the sample. If research goals favor smaller sample sizes, a researcher can start with a larger number of seeds and have fewer recruitment cycles. For example, Ghaziani (2018) started with 20 seeds in his study of gay and lesbian residents and business owners in Chicago's Boystown and Andersonville "gayborhoods." The study questions necessitated in-depth interviews of residents and business owners and aimed to have around 100 participants. Starting with 20 seeds allowed Ghaziani to maximize the number of different networks despite limiting the sample size.

SOCIOLOGIST IN ACTION
STEPH LANDEROS

As an undergraduate, I started attending local drag shows when I had some free time. Eventually, I got to know some of the performers through interactions at the shows and on social media. I noticed that their lives appeared quite different from the lives of drag performers seen on popular television shows like *RuPaul's Drag Race* (RPDR). For instance, local performers were not earning the financial success displayed in the television shows. Additionally, they embraced and showcased gender diversity differently than what appeared on RPDR. Given that, I was curious about why they do the performance work. For my senior capstone project, I had the opportunity to conduct an original research project, so I decided to interview local drag performers about their experiences. I was unsure whether the performers would be willing to participate in my study, but having attended shows regularly proved to be advantageous in this regard. First, I approached a participant I knew well from both the shows and social media and who was also a prominent local performer. She acted as a gatekeeper in recommending other drag performers for the study. Second, when I introduced myself to recommended performers, they recognized me from the shows, which helped to quickly establish trust and rapport.

When I began my master's degree program, I decided to build upon this research project by comparing the experiences of drag performers in different communities. I did not have the same personal connection with or access to performers at the shows, which made it difficult to find individuals willing to participate in my study. But I knew the community would have a strong social media presence and so I started developing relationships there first. Eventually, I developed a rapport with a performer who then introduced me to other performers in the community. In both my undergraduate and graduate research, having a gatekeeper proved extremely advantageous and helpful in gaining access to this community.

Steph Landeros holds bachelor's and master's degrees in sociology. They are currently pursuing a PhD in sociology at the University of Nevada, Las Vegas.

Discussion Question

What role did gatekeepers play in helping this sociologist interview drag performers?

Quota Sampling

Quota sampling is a type of nonprobability sampling where researchers specify a particular number of participants (a quota) that meet a specific characteristic or set of characteristics important to the study. The principles of quota sampling are similar to those of stratified probability samples. For example, imagine a researcher who wants to assess how people of different religious traditions link their faith to issues of climate change. They might want to ensure that a sample includes equal proportions of people who identify as Protestant, Catholic, Jewish, or Muslim. In such a case, they would determine the overall target sample size and attempt to include an equal proportion of respondents from each religious tradition. Researchers choose this sampling technique most often when the goal is to provide some sort of comparison among groups. The process by which a researcher selects respondents for each quota (e.g., snowball sampling or convenience sampling) should be consistent for each one.

Quota sampling can be used to create a sample that is fairly representative of the population on some measure. For example, if a researcher knows the approximate proportion of each religious group in a given population, they might select those proportions for the sample even though a list is not available to generate an exact proportion. However, it is important to note that the researcher is only specifying respondents by one or two variables (in this case, religion) rather than the diversity of human characteristics present in a population. Therefore, a sample may be reflective of a population in terms of religion but not necessarily by other characteristics such as age or race.

DOING SOCIOLOGY 5.4

Identifying Research Goals and Sampling Strategies

In this exercise, you will identify how research goals and questions impact decisions about sampling.

Read the following research summary and then answer the questions that follow.

A study of Filipino methamphetamine drug users by Laus (2013) explored in-depth the extent to which connections that Filipinos have with others in their community affect their methamphetamine use. Knowledge about drug use in this community is limited because of how shaming tends to lead users to hide their drug use. Additionally, previous research tends to make broad generalizations about the Asian American community even though important differences exist within this population (such as more recent waves of immigration). In this study, Laus interviewed 14 Filipino Americans in Northern California with a history of methamphetamine use. Participants were selected through a network of personal contacts and an organization specializing in rehabilitation and counseling for people with a history of drug use.

1. What are the goals of the research?

2. How did the researcher find study participants?

3. Did the researcher use a probability or nonprobability sample?

4. How does the sampling technique reflect the goals of the research? What are some of the strengths and limitations of the sampling approach Laus used?

Check Your Understanding

1. What is a convenience sample and when might it be a useful sampling strategy?
2. What are purposive samples and what kinds of research questions are they useful for addressing?
3. What is the difference between a traditional snowball sample and a respondent-driven sample?
4. What benefit does respondent-driven sampling have compared to traditional snowball sampling?
5. What is a gatekeeper and why might they be important in a researcher project?
6. When might a researcher use a quota sample instead of a stratified probability sample?

SAMPLING VULNERABLE POPULATIONS

At all stages of any study, researchers must continually evaluate potential and emerging ethical concerns. This responsibility takes on heightened importance when we are researching vulnerable populations. As you learned in Chapter 4, a vulnerable population is one in which the individuals are at greater risk of harm or who have limited power to give consent or otherwise require greater consideration than the average person. In social science research, this would include children, recent immigrants (particularly if they are unauthorized), people who are poor or with low incomes, historically oppressed racial groups, and other groups with physical, mental, economic, legal, or political vulnerabilities. Ethical concerns are at the heart of issues related to informed consent, but researchers should have heightened concern for ethical research when sampling vulnerable populations as well.

Connell (2018) recounts an experience she had interviewing gay and lesbian K–12 school teachers for her dissertation research. She collected participants through snowball sampling whereby respondents provided names to her of other potential gay or lesbian respondents who might willingly participate in the study. This approach of providing names to researchers is a common technique in snowball sampling. Nonetheless, it inadvertently raised an ethical concern when one recruit (identified as Peter) became notably upset that another teacher had essentially "outed" him without his consent. Peter was denied the opportunity to decide whether he wanted a stranger (Connell) to know about his sexual identity. Additionally, gay and lesbian teachers have historically been vulnerable to homophobic attacks from school personnel and other teachers, which in some cases has led to their termination. Consequently, "outing" a member of the gay and lesbian community, even inadvertently, can have both personal and institutional consequences. In this situation, Connell had to immediately rethink her sampling approach. Going forward, she instead asked participants to pass on her information to other teachers who then could decide whether to initiate contact. Connell notes that this method was less efficient in building a research sample (because she had to wait for respondents to reach out to her), but the ethical responsibility to protect participant privacy outweighed concern for efficiency.

Recruitment of vulnerable populations is no simple task. As another example, consider research by Strangfeld (2019), which centered on the reasons why some first-generation college students plagiarized their academic assignments. Given the stigma colleges and universities attach to plagiarism, as well as the penalties schools can impose against students who plagiarize, Strangfeld's approach to participant recruitment required exceptional ethical consideration. In her study, she sent recruitment emails to a sample taken from all first-generation students enrolled at a particular university. In the email, students were explicitly informed that receipt of the email in no way suggested that they had ever committed acts of plagiarism. Consequently, it was up to the student to consider whether they met the criteria of the study population and to contact the researcher if they wished to participate. As in Connell's case, this was arguably a less efficient method in terms of time, but it nonetheless reflects the ethical sampling considerations necessary for protecting vulnerable participants.

Past research studies indicate that involving members of vulnerable communities in the research process can also help address issues of ethical concern in sampling. For example, in their study of sexual behavior and HIV risk among Hispanic migrants in Durham, North Carolina, Parrado et al. (2005) included members of the Latinx community in various stages of their research project, including recruitment of participants. Researchers had to contend with the fact that not only was the population itself vulnerable by virtue of their migration status, but the topic itself involved disclosure of deeply personal and sensitive information on sexual behavior. Consequently, community members guided the researchers on aspects of cultural and gender dynamics within the community that affected participant recruitment.

There is no single method for how a researcher should go about sampling vulnerable populations. Instead, it is important to understand that a commitment to ethical research extends to all aspects of research, including sampling, and that consideration of ethical strategies is an ongoing process. In the case of Connell, she did not initially anticipate the ethical dilemma that arose during her sampling and data collection process. Indeed, this sometimes happens in the course of a research project. But notice that once the issue arose, she redesigned her sampling approach. This happens only when researchers recognize that consideration of ethical standards is an ongoing process.

CONSIDER THIS...

What are some examples of other hidden or vulnerable populations that might require enhanced ethical scrutiny when recruiting participants?

DOING SOCIOLOGY 5.5

Ethical Considerations in Recruitment

In this exercise, you will consider potential ethical concerns that can arise in recruitment of participants and how you might approach recruitment differently.

Read the following scenarios, then answer the questions.

Scenario 1: Imagine that you wanted to recruit participants for a study that focused on opioid addiction among students at your school. You post a flier with pullouts containing your contact information in public spaces around school.

Scenario 2: A researcher is interested in learning more about the experiences of people who have struggled with anxiety disorders. After meeting a few people who meet this criterion, the researcher asks them for names of people they know who have had similar experiences. The researcher then contacts those people.

Scenario 3: You are interested in interviewing students who have experienced incarceration. You make an announcement in each of your classes informing students about your project and asking them to approach you after class if they are interested in participating.

1. What ethical concerns might be raised by the recruitment approach in each scenario?

2. What is another recruitment approach you could use for each scenario?

> ### Check Your Understanding
>
> 1. What is a vulnerable population?
> 2. What is an example of an ethical problem arising during the sampling stage of research?
> 3. What is at least one strategy a researcher can use to protect vulnerable populations during the sampling or participant recruitment stage of research?

CONCLUSION

In conducting quality and ethical studies, researchers make important and thoughtful decisions when collecting data from a sample of a given population. Often circumstances do not allow a researcher to collect data from an entire population, but researchers nonetheless want to be able to convey knowledge and information about a group that is larger than just the sample participants. This is easier to do in some cases than others, but in all circumstances the decisions we make affect the outcomes of our study. This is why the sampling method we choose must correspond with the primary goals and questions of our research. Studies that intend to make broad generalizations about a population will use different sampling techniques and have different sample sizes than studies that are focused on in-depth understanding of particular circumstances. Paying attention to sampling strategies not only helps produce better-quality and ethical research, but also helps us to critically evaluate the results of other research studies. In this way, we improve both our research skills and our information literacy. In the next chapter, you will explore another important dimension of research that is common to all sociological studies: the measurement of concepts.

5.1   What are samples, and why do researchers use them?

A sample is a subset of a population; scientists conduct research using samples when time and resources do not allow for the study of a population or the members of a population are not entirely known.

5.2   How and when does a researcher determine the appropriate size of a sample?

Sample size depends on the research questions and goals. Studies focusing on generalizability to the larger population will be larger while studies focused on in-depth understanding will typically have smaller samples. Additionally, sometimes it is appropriate for researchers to determine a desired sample size at the onset of a study while other times the sample size is not determined until much later in the data collection process.

5.3   What are the primary types of probability samples, and what are the strengths and limitations of each?

The primary types of probability samples include a simple random sample, a systematic sample, cluster sampling, and stratified sampling. A simple random sample can be used when researchers want a sample that does not require guaranteed representation from subgroups with the population. A systematic sample is similar but would be used when the sampling frame cannot be inputted into randomized sample-generating software, such as voters who show up on voting day (as opposed to all registered voters). A cluster sample is appropriate when the individual elements in a population are clustered together in some way. For example, students are clustered in schools and people of religious faith may be clustered in places of worship. Finally, researchers use stratified samples when the goal is to have guaranteed representation of specific groups in the sample.

5.4   What are the primary types of nonprobability samples, and what are the strengths and limitations of each?

The primary types of nonprobability samples include convenience samples, purposive samples, snowball and respondent-driven samples, and quota samples. Convenience samples are useful in exploratory stages of research or to pre-test survey and interview questions. Purposive samples target particular individuals or artifacts based on their unique positions or knowledge of the study focus, such as leaders in an organization. Snowball and respondent-driven samples rely upon participants to refer others to the study and thus are particularly useful when studying hidden populations. Finally, quota samples are used when the goal is to guarantee representation of certain target groups.

5.5   What are some possible sampling approaches or considerations to use when researching vulnerable populations?

Researchers might use respondent-driven sampling, which allows potential participants to reach out to the researcher rather than being approached by a stranger. Another approach would be to involve community members in the research process itself to provide guidance on how best to recruit study participants. Researchers should continually evaluate their sampling methodology and make adjustments as needed when problems or concerns arise.

disproportionate stratified sample (p. 87)

gatekeepers (p. 90)

generalizability (p. 84)

multistage cluster sampling (p. 86)

nonprobability sample (p. 84)

periodicity (p. 85)

population (p. 81)

probability sample (p. 84)

proportionate stratified sample (p. 87)

respondent-driven sampling (p. 91)

sample (p. 81)

sample size (p. 82)

sampling error (p. 82)

sampling frame (p. 84)

saturation (p. 83)

6 AUTHENTICATING CONCEPTS AND MEASURES

Kimberly Tauches

STUDENT LEARNING QUESTIONS

6.1 How do sociologists conceptualize variables, and what are the main challenges in measuring sociological concepts?

6.2 How do sociologists operationalize variables?

6.3 How do sociologists conceptualize and measure variables when conducting inductive and deductive research?

6.4 What are the two types of composite measures, and how do they differ?

6.5 What are the main characteristics of good measures?

HOW I GOT ACTIVE IN SOCIOLOGY

Kimberly Tauches

I grew up in suburban Long Island in an environment that kindled in me a curiosity about how inequality plays out in society and culture. From an early age, I witnessed all around me the push to assimilate and conform in a white, wealthy, suburban area. My understanding of inequity was based on multiple juxtapositions of both privilege and oppression, and as a youth I had a sense of this, if not the vocabulary to express myself. When I left for college, I quickly found a new home in the Sociology Department at Drew University—where I began honing this nascent critical lens. Sociology gave me the language and tools that I needed to understand my own positions of power and privilege, as well as the ways in which systems of oppression operated in and through me.

In my senior year of college I took an Introduction to Women's Studies course that sparked a strong desire to pursue a PhD in order to learn more and teach students about these aspects of privilege and oppression—particularly how they were related to gender, sexuality, race, and class. Since then I have worked at multiple colleges and universities, where my primary goal is to work with students in order to gain a clear understanding about how we can understand social inequality through a sociological lens in order to help create a more just society.

Sociologists measure things. A lot! Some things are relatively easy to measure. For example, the number of people in a classroom, the square footage of a house, or the number of public parks in a community. Most aspects of the social world—and some concepts most central to sociology—are more difficult to measure, however. Macro-level social characteristics like the degree of inequality, democracy, and social cohesion, and micro-level characteristics like individual people's health, socioeconomic status, and social connectedness could each be measured in a variety of different ways. Some measures are better than others, of course, and an important part of the sociological research process is ensuring that the measures sociologists use are as effective as possible.

This chapter describes how sociologists develop, refine, and measure the complex elements that make up the social world. We begin with the process of conceptualization—defining the concept as clearly as possible—and then turn to operationalization—linking the definition to measurement. We consider how these processes differ in the context of inductive or deductive research. We end with the concepts of validity and reliability—properties of vital importance if we are to have good measures.

CONCEPTS AND CONCEPTUALIZATION

Sociologists begin their research by formulating a research question and developing hypotheses in consultation with existing theory and research. Once done, the next step is to think carefully about the meaning of each of the concepts in the research question and hypotheses, and to specify precisely what each one means. This process is called conceptualization.

Researchers define their concepts as clearly as possible, clarifying their boundaries by specifying what falls inside of each definition and what falls outside of it. For example, researchers trying to conceptualize activism may decide that participation in a public protest falls within their definition of activism, but that maintaining a blog about politics does not. Other researchers might decide that working at a nonprofit social justice organization falls within their conceptualization of activism, but that working for a labor union does not. Researchers need to make these decisions carefully, and keeping a written record of why they make the decisions they do can often be helpful. When the research project is finished, and the researchers communicate their results with others, critical audiences may ask the researcher to describe their decision-making process and justify their conceptual definitions.

One of the best strategies for developing a conceptual definition is to review the existing research to see how others have defined the concepts. Knowing how others have defined concepts can help researchers to clarify their own ideas. When reviewing literature as part of building a conceptual definition, a researcher might ask themselves: How have others defined this concept? What are the relative strengths and weaknesses of these definitions? Which definition makes most sense for my question and hypothesis? It is also important to remember that the meaning of concepts can change over time and may vary across different situations. It is important for researchers to ask: Does this conceptual definition make sense in this context and for the group or groups I'm studying?

In some cases, the process of conceptualization is relatively simple. For example, a researcher might examine the relationship between parental status and self-reported happiness. They might ask the question, as indeed sociologist Robin W. Simon (2008) has asked: Do parents report better mental health than adults who are not parents? A conceptual definition of parents might be someone who is or has been the legal parent or guardian of a person under the age of 18. Note, however, that this is not the only conceptual definition of parenthood possible, and that this definition does not include the experiences of those who may be highly involved in the lives of young people but who were not legally recognized as parents or guardians. Further questions arise when one considers how foster parents and stepparents fit into this definition—not to mention sperm and egg donors! Even though the term *parent* is one we use in our everyday lives, formulating a conceptual definition requires careful consideration.

Challenges of Conceptualization

Developing a formal definition of the most central concepts in one's research project can be challenging for a number of reasons. For one, many of the most important things that sociologists measure are immaterial and do not exist in physical space. Their boundaries are not easily identified and may be actively disputed. Consider again the issue of political activism. Self-described activists and nonactivists often disagree on what counts as activism. And activists themselves—even within the same social movement and same organization—might vehemently disagree with one another! Conceptualizing characteristics of groups, institutions, and societies can be similarly contentious. Imagine trying to come up with a conceptual definition for social justice, a cohesive neighborhood, a democratic country.

A further challenge of conceptualization stems from the fact that many of the concepts most central to sociology vary over time and place. Imagine a researcher who was planning a study of deviance.

Her central question might be, "Are young adults in the United States today more likely to engage in deviant activities than were young adults in the 1950s?" To answer this question, the researcher would first have to identify "young adult"—the meaning of which has changed drastically in the past 70 years (Furstenberg, 2000). And then they would have the further difficulty of trying to define and measure "deviance"—the meaning of which has also changed a great deal! To successfully compare historical levels of deviance among young adults in the United States—or anywhere else—a researcher must first establish a clear definition of their key concepts that is attentive to the specifics of history, geography, and culture.

Conceptions of deviance change over time. To compare deviance among teens today to teens in the 1950s, researchers must define key concepts.

iStockphoto.com/CREATISTA

Specifying the Dimensions of a Concept

Most of the concepts that sociologists study—things like health, social class, social cohesion, or inequality—have many dimensions or components. Scholars actively disagree with one another about how many dimensions each of these concepts have and further disagree about which dimensions are the most important. For example, is the most important component of social class an individual person's wealth? Or is the wealth of their immediate or extended family most important? Is education an important component of social class? What about social capital—the network of people who can provide someone with information, resources, and if need be, a way out of trouble? Sociologists have been defining, redefining, and debating how best to measure social class for more than a century, and the debate continues today.

Consider a researcher interested in analyzing the relationship between democracy and social well-being. Political theorists have argued there are two main dimensions of democracy (Dahl, 1971). First is contestation: the ability of citizens to have meaningful preferences to speak their mind, and to receive equal consideration by governmental officials. And second is inclusiveness: the proportion of people who are able to participate in a meaningful and equal way. Social well-being also has multiple dimensions, and could include individual people's longevity and quality of life; their individual rights and freedoms; the extent to which diverse cultural groups thrive and are able to maintain their values, traditions, histories, and where relevant, their land. With concepts that are very broad and have multiple dimensions, researchers may not be able to account for all of these dimensions in any one particular research project. But even when analyzing each dimension is impossible, researchers nonetheless need to be aware of the dimensions for each of their key concepts, and state explicitly which dimensions they include in their analysis and which they do not. Often, they also include a discussion about why those specific dimensions are included. By specifying the dimensions of the overall concept, the researcher can clarify which dimensions they are most interested in examining and then develop a strategy for assessing each.

CONSIDER THIS...

What other sociological concepts can you think of that have multiple dimensions? What are the dimensions of these concepts?

Conceptualization is a crucial step in the measurement process because it is impossible to measure something in the social world without first establishing what it is that we are trying to measure. Identifying and specifying the dimensions of a concept is an important aspect of conceptualization, as it can help researchers to pose more precise research questions and hypotheses.

DOING SOCIOLOGY 6.1

Conceptualizing Community Engagement and Activism

In this exercise, you conceptualize the ideas of community engagement and activism.

Community engagement and activism are both central ideas in sociology. Sociologist Émile Durkheim was very concerned with what societal-level characteristics promoted a high level of engagement (and disengagement) among community members. Many modern sociologists inspired by Karl Marx, W.E.B. DuBois, and movements for social justice research the factors associated with political activism. With this in mind, answer the following questions:

1. How would you describe what it means for a person to be engaged in their community versus being a community activist?

2. Are there multiple dimensions of being engaged in one's community, and being a community activist? If so, what are they?

3. What is your conceptual definition of community engagement?

4. What is your conceptual definition of political activism?

Check Your Understanding

1. What does it mean to develop a conceptual definition?
2. Why is developing a conceptual definition important for social science research?
3. What does it mean to say that some concepts have multiple dimensions?

OPERATIONALIZATION

Once researchers establish conceptual definitions of the key concepts in the research question and hypotheses, the next step is to develop a more concrete, working definition in a process known as operationalization. Operational definitions specify precisely how each abstract concept is measured. By developing an operational definition, researchers specify exactly how each concept in their study is represented in their data.

If the researcher's main concept is relatively simple, then developing an operational definition is relatively straightforward too. Imagine a researcher who is interested in the relationship between age and life satisfaction, who conceptualizes age as a person's age in years, based on their date of birth. When developing an operational definition of age, the researcher would provide a detailed account of how they acquired information about the participants' age, and how this information is represented in their data and analysis.

Interviewers might ask participants, "What is the month, day, and year of your birth?" Once the researcher has this information, they can easily and precisely calculate respondents' age in years and use this age in their analyses. Alternatively, researchers could also ask participants about their age in years directly: "How old are you?" or "What is your age?"

CONSIDER THIS...

Are there situations in which one approach to asking someone's age on a survey is more beneficial than others?

Operationalizing more complex social phenomena is more challenging. Let's think about the example of financial well-being in the United States. This can be a very difficult concept to operationalize for a number of reasons. First, there are different dimensions of financial well-being. Personal income—the amount of money a person earns from wages, salary, and other sources of income—is one dimension. But there are others too. Family income—the income of all people living in a person's family—is another important dimension, as is wealth—the amount of money and assets, including the value of property, that a person or family has accumulated. Researchers might also be interested in people's *perceptions* of their financial situation, instead of, or in addition to, other more objective indicators.

Figures 6.1, 6.2, and 6.3 show excerpts from the Questionnaire for the 2018 General Social Survey (GSS)—a survey that sociologists often use to analyze the social world. In this survey, interviewers ask respondents numerous questions about their financial resources, including their personal income, their family income, and the perceptions of their own financial well-being. Researchers using this survey might use any or all of these indicators of financial well-being to operationalize socioeconomic status.

FIGURE 6.1 ■ Personal Income	
In which of these groups did your earnings from all sources for 2017 fall? That is, before taxes or other deductions.	
A. UNDER $1,000	N. $22,500 to 24,999
B. $1,000 to 2,999	O. $25,000 to 29,999
C. $3,000 to 3,999	P. $30,000 to 34,999
D. $4,000 to 4,999	Q. $35,000 to 39,999
E. $5,000 to 5,999	R. $40,000 to 49,999
F. $6,000 to 6,999	S. $50,000 to 59,999
G. $7,000 to 7,999	T. $60,000 to 74,999
H. $8,000 to 9,999	U. $75,000 to $89,999
I. $10,000 to 12,499	V. $90,000 to $109,999
J. $12,500 to 14,999	W. $110,000 to $129,999
K. $15,000 to 17,499	X. $130,000 to $149,999
L. $17,500 to 19,999	Y. $150,000 to $169,999
M. $20,000 to 22,499	Z. $170,000 or over

Source: GSS Data Explorer, https://gssdataexplorer.norc.org/

FIGURE 6.2 ■ Family Income	
In which of these groups did your total family income, from all sources, fall last year—2017—before taxes, that is.	
A. UNDER $1,000	N. $22,500 to 24,999
B. $1,000 to 2,999	O. $25,000 to 29,999
C. $3,000 to 3,999	P. $30,000 to 34,999
D. $4,000 to 4,999	Q. $35,000 to 39,999
E. $5,000 to 5,999	R. $40,000 to 49,999
F. $6,000 to 6,999	S. $50,000 to 59,999
G. $7,000 to 7,999	T. $60,000 to 74,999
H. $8,000 to 9,999	U. $75,000 to $89,999
I. $10,000 to 12,499	V. $90,000 to $109,999
J. $12,500 to 14,999	W. $110,000 to $129,999
K. $15,000 to 17,499	X. $130,000 to $149,999
L. $17,500 to 19,999	Y. $150,000 to $169,999
M. $20,000 to 22,499	Z. $170,000 or over

Source: GSS Data Explorer, https://gssdataexplorer.norc.org/

FIGURE 6.3 ■ Perceived Financial Well-Being

Thinking of your household's total income, including all the sources of income of all the members who contribute to it, how difficult or easy is it currently for your household to make ends meet?

1. Very difficult
2. Fairly difficult
3. Neither easy nor difficult
4. Fairly easy
5. Very easy

Source: GSS Data Explorer, https://gssdataexplorer.norc.org/

In their operational definition of financial well-being, a researcher analyzing data from this survey or any other source of data would need to specify how the information about participants' financial well-being was obtained. Using the GSS or a similar survey, the researcher would need to specify both the question wording, as well as the response categories available to participants. If the researcher combined information from different response categories together in their analysis—for example, lumping those with personal incomes under $10,000 per year together—then this information would also be included in their operational definition.

Let's consider an even more complex concept—gender ideology. Sociologists and social psychologists use this term to describe the system of gender-related beliefs that a person or group holds. There are many dimensions of gender ideology, including beliefs about gender inequality; gender roles in the context of heterosexual relationships; beliefs about women in politics; beliefs about whether gender differences are innate or socially produced; and support for transgender issues (Harnois, 2015; Risman, 2018). Researchers investigating gender ideology need not simultaneously analyze all of these dimensions but should be up-front about which aspects of gender ideology are their focus, and which are not.

Researchers can and have drawn from many methods to advance our understanding of gender ideology, including both qualitative and quantitative techniques, but one of the most common is statistical analyses of survey data. When this is the case, researchers can either design their own survey and administer it to a group of their choosing, or they can turn to an existing survey like the General Social Survey (GSS), the American National Election Study (ANES), or the World Values Survey. The GSS includes several questions about respondents' gender beliefs. Figure 6.4 shows several of them.

Again, sociological concepts are often complex and multidimensional. Trying to come up with a way to capture all dimensions of a concept can be a daunting task and is often impractical or impossible, given resources limitations. But this doesn't mean a research project is doomed. Rather, researchers should simply indicate the limitations of their measures, noting that some dimensions are captured and others are not, and explaining why this is the case.

DOING SOCIOLOGY 6.2

Operationalizing Community Involvement and Activism

In this exercise, you will create measures for different dimensions of a concept.

Imagine that a nonprofit organization in your community was interested in identifying potential leaders for the community. They ask you to design a short survey that will assess people's level of community involvement as well as their level of community activism because, they reason, those who are already involved and those who are community activists will likely be good future leaders.

1. What are the different dimensions of community involvement?
2. As a researcher, how would you measure each dimension of community involvement that you identified?
3. What are the different dimensions of community activism?
4. As a researcher, how would you measure each dimension of community activism that you identified?

FIGURE 6.4 ■ Sample Questions From the General Social Survey Related to Gender

Beliefs about gender roles in heterosexual relationships:

1. Now I'm going to read several more statements. As I read each one, please tell me whether you strongly agree, agree, disagree, or strongly disagree with it: It is much better for everyone involved if the man is the achiever outside the home and the woman takes care of the home and family.
   Response options: (1) Strongly agree, (2) Agree, (3) Disagree, or (4) Strongly Disagree

2. Now I'm going to read several more statements. As I read each one, please tell me whether you strongly agree, agree, disagree, or strongly disagree with it: A working mother can establish just as warm and secure a relationship with her children as a mother who does not work.
   Response options: (1) Strongly agree, (2) Agree, (3) Disagree, or (4) Strongly Disagree

Beliefs about same-sex parenting:

3. To what extent do you agree or disagree with the following statement? A same sex female couple can bring up a child as well as a male-female couple.
   Response options: (1) Strongly agree, (2) Agree, (3) Disagree, or (4) Strongly Disagree

4. To what extent do you agree or disagree with the following statement? A same sex male couple can bring up a child as well as a male-female couple.
   Response options: (1) Strongly agree, (2) Agree, (3) Disagree, or (4) Strongly Disagree

Beliefs about women in politics:

1. Tell me if you agree or disagree with this statement: Most men are better suited emotionally for politics than are most women.
   Response options: (1) Agree, (2) Disagree

2. Do you agree or disagree with this statement? Women should take care of running their homes and leave running the country up to men.
   Response options: (1) Agree, (2) Disagree

Source: General Social Surveys, 1972–2018: Cumulative Codebook, 2019, National Data Program for the Social Sciences Series, no. 25.

Check Your Understanding

1. What does it mean to develop an operational definition?
2. Why is developing an operational definition important for social science research?

DEDUCTIVE AND INDUCTIVE APPROACHES TO MEASUREMENT

As we have discussed earlier in this text, inductive research questions are those that result from specific observations of facts that a researcher thinks might point to a general tendency, whereas deductive questions start with a theoretical premise that a researcher hopes to verify by examining specific observations in the social world. While conceptualization and operationalization are key aspects of both types of research, they take different forms in deductive and inductive research.

Within deductive research, a researcher begins with the process of conceptualization, and once they have their conceptual definition, they then operationalize it, specifying precisely how each abstract concept is measured. The concept, its operational definition, and its measurement remain consistent throughout the research process as the researcher attempts to test their hypothesis. Someone using the General Social Survey to assess whether there is a relationship between financial well-being and emotional well-being, for example, could be said to be doing deductive research. A researcher examining the frequency with which single-parent families have been represented in children's books over the past 30 years would be another example of this approach. In both cases, researchers would clearly state their hypotheses, conceptualize and operationalize their key ideas, and then conduct their analyses to test their hypotheses.

Within inductive research, the process is much more cyclical. Researchers revisit and refine their concepts throughout the research process, and often introduce new concepts in the process. When researchers conduct in-depth interviews or ethnographic research for an extended period of time,

How does gender play out in schools?

Klaus Vedfelt/DigitalVision/Getty Images

they listen and learn from study participants and in so doing, gain a better understanding of how respondents make sense of themselves and the world around them. Researchers need to keep an open mind about which concepts are most central to their research, because in many cases they uncover new concepts—and concepts that are crucial for understanding their research question—in the process of doing the research. This can happen while researchers are collecting data or when analyzing the data, depending on the information that is collected.

One example of inductive research in which concepts have been revised and refined in the research is in Barrie Thorne's book *Gender Play: Girls and Boys in School* (1993). As a researcher, Thorne was interested in studying gender in schools—and this concept was understood in greater complexity as a result of her measurement. For example, Thorne noted different ways to understand gender in schools, including how schools helped to structure gender in very specific ways, such as creating divisions between girls and boys in the classroom by pitting girls and boys against each other. But she also noted the ways in which gender became an aspect of play for girls and boys. This became an important focal point for her book, and she gained a deeper understanding of how children create meaning through her research, as well as a shift in how we might define gender. Thorne's conceptualization of gender changed from something that was "top down," where schools produce gender differences by lining up girls and boys in separate lines, for example, to a "bottom up" approach, where children play with and inform the meanings of gender.

Open- and Closed-Ended Questions

When sociologists conduct interviews or administer surveys, they ask research participants questions with the goal of generating data that will ultimately help the researcher to answer their research question. There are two broad types of questions upon which sociologists rely: open-ended questions and closed-ended questions. Open-ended questions do not have any answer choices specified—the person answering the questions come up with their own answers, rather than picking from a list of answers. Open-ended questions are typically used for inductive research—such as when someone conducts in-depth interviews to explore a new social phenomenon. They may not yet know what types of responses to expect, and therefore allow participants to answer in their own words. Closed-ended questions-specify answer choices—the researcher provides a set of answers from which the respondent chooses. Closed-ended questions are often found on surveys, which are a useful tool when the researcher already has a sense of what a list of potential responses might include. Such research tends to be more deductive in nature, because the researcher is often attempting to test a theory.

In the context of social research, resource limitations are always important to consider. While open-ended questions often provide more nuance and meaning, closed-ended questions are often easier for respondents to answer—particularly if they are designed well—and are less time-consuming to analyze once the data are collected. Consider, for example, the questions in Table 6.1, which are questions that are included in the American National Election Study, a survey administered each 4 years around the time of the U.S. presidential election. The survey is administered to several thousand people and includes hundreds of closed-ended questions. The information gleaned from the survey is less nuanced than the information that might be gathered in the course of open-ended questions, as you can see by comparing the right and left sides of Table 6.1. But open-ended questions take longer for respondents to answer and provide more complex answers that are more difficult and time-consuming to analyze, and so open-ended questions require more financial resources. Thus, there is always a trade-off between being able to ask more closed-ended questions to a larger number of people, and asking more open-ended questions where each answer may generate a more nuanced and complex answer.

CONSIDER THIS. . .

Why do open-ended questions require more time for respondents to answer and more resources for researchers to analyze?

TABLE 6.1 ■ Comparing Closed- and Open-Ended Questions

Closed-Answer Questions and Hypothetical Answers	Open-Answered Questions and Hypothetical Answers
Question 1: How many organizations are you currently a member of?	1) Are you currently a member of any organizations, and if what are they?
Response options: 0, 1, 2, 3, 4, 5, 6, 7, 8, 9, 10, 11, 12 or more	Response Options: Infinite
Anne's Answer: 2	Anne's Answer: Well, I guess it depends on what you mean by an organization. If you count my church group and my book club then that would be two. But truthfully, I don't go to either that frequently, only when I have extra time on my hands, and face it who has time for that these days? I do belong though and am technically a member. I should say that I also do hang out with my friends every day, which is important, but I guess that's not so much an organization. Is it?
Mark's Answer: 0	Mark's Answer: I'm not part of any organized group, per se. But my friends and I meet up twice a week for pick-up basketball. It's not like an official organization, just a group of us who have been getting together for the past maybe 5 years.
Question 2: During the past 12 months, have you worked with other people to deal with some issue facing your community?	Question 2: During the past 12 months, have you worked with other people to deal with some issue facing your community? If so, can you tell me more about that?
Response options: Yes, have done this in the past 12 months; No, have not done this.	Response options: Infinite
Anne's Answer: no	Anne's Answer: No. I don't think the people in my community are really facing that many issues right now that I could help with. Maybe they are but I just don't know about them? They seem OK. Not sure.
Mark's Answer: yes	Mark's answer: Yeah, my family and I work with other folks from our church go to the food pantry once a month to help the folks who are struggling in our town. That's something that I like to do because it's a way of helping out other people, looking out for each other, in case that might happen to me one day where I'm in a position where I need help, well then maybe someone will be there to help me.

The research question, whether inductive or deductive reasoning is being used, the specific question being asked, and the type of methodology chosen are all considerations when selecting whether open-ended or closed-ended questions should be used.

DOING SOCIOLOGY 6.3

Comparing Open-Ended and Closed-Ended Questions

In this exercise, you will think through the different types of information that can be generated with open- and closed-ended questions.

When researchers ask open-ended questions, the answers respondents provide—and the information contained within them—are sometimes surprising! Take another look at Table 6.1 and compare the answers Anne and Mark provide to the closed- and open-ended questions. Then answer the following questions:

1. What do we learn about Anne and Mark's individual levels of community involvement from the open-ended questions that we missed in the closed-ended questions?

2. What information do we learn about Anne and Mark more generally from the open-ended questions?

3. How might Anne and Mark's responses to the open-ended questions help researchers to more clearly conceptualize and operationalize community involvement?

Check Your Understanding

1. How are the processes of conceptualization and operationalization different in deductive and inductive research?
2. What is an open-ended question, and why is this type of question well-suited to inductive research?
3. What is a closed-ended question, and why is this type of question well-suited to deductive research?
4. What are the limitations and benefits to using open-ended questions as opposed to closed-ended questions?

COMPOSITE MEASURES

In the case of deductive research, especially that which is quantitative, researchers sometimes combine several indicators into a single measure, called a composite measure. There are two broad types of composite measures. The first is an **index**, in which several different measures are *added* together to create a combined score. If a researcher is working with a unidimensional concept, they might create an index using multiple measures of that dimension. But a researcher could also create an index to assess a multidimensional concept by asking a series of questions that address each of the various dimensions. In an index, each of the indicators is treated as having the same weight; in other words, each indicator contributes equally to the measurement of the concept.

Imagine a researcher who was interested in gender ideology as it relates to parenting. They might create an index using the first four questions presented in Figure 6.4. The GSS assigns each of the response categories a number: strongly agree (1), agree (2), disagree (3), and strongly disagree (4). To create an index, a researcher should first make sure that the responses are all in alignment with what higher and lower values represent.

In the case of gender ideology in parenting, it is important that higher values for each variable indicate either more progressive or more restrictive ideas about parenting. Either way is okay, but they all have to be in the same direction. Then the researcher can easily add up the numeric values across the variables of interest. That number will indicate the extent to which respondents have more restrictive or more progressive ideas about parenting. Indexes are a good way for researchers to get an overall picture of where a respondent stands with respect to a particular concept, even when that concept has many different dimensions.

Scales are another type of composite measure. Scales are like indexes in that they combine a number of indicators that speak to dimensions of a concept. However, indexes simply sum up the series of responses, whereas scales allow the weight of the various items to vary prior to being summed. Let's break that down.

Imagine your school has asked you to assess the level of academic engagement of students across the school year. A crucial first step would be to conceptualize academic engagement, which we might define as the overall level to which someone participates in and feels connected to academic life at their school. This is a multidimensional concept as there are many ways students can participate in and feel connected to academic life. When assessing a student's level of academic engagement, we might consider how often they attend class; how often they complete the reading assignments for their classes; how often they ask questions in class; how many times they have visited their teachers during office hours; how many hours per week they study. We might also ask them about their self-assessed engagement: how connected they feel to their school, their peers, and their teachers; how excited they are to come to school; the extent to which they feel valued and respected in school.

CONSIDER THIS...

What are the benefits of using an index relative to using a single indicator of a concept?

As you develop your measure of academic engagement, you might decide that some aspects are more important than others. So perhaps attending class is a more important indicator of academic engagement. You could make that indicator count for more than the other indicators in your measure by weighting it more in the overall measure's calculation.

In the case of gender ideology in parenting, we might decide that the first two questions – beliefs about the bread-winner home-maker family model and beliefs about working mothers' relationships with their children—each describe a unique element of gender ideology in parenting, but that the two questions concerning beliefs about same-sex parents as compared to female-male couples really tap the same underlying ideology (and in fact there is a very high degree of correlation (0.94) between the two based on the GSS data). Rather than counting each of the four variables with equal weight, it might make more sense to give the two questions about same sex parenting a little less weight in the overall composite measure.

DOING SOCIOLOGY 6.4

Creating an Index

In this exercise, you will create indicators that can be combined to make an index.

Social science researchers often work with concepts that are multidimensional in nature. Therefore, it is important to be able to conceptualize and then operationalize the dimensions of a concept. Consider the following example regarding hypermasculinity, which can be defined as the exaggeration of male stereotypical behavior, such as an emphasis on physical strength, aggression, and sexuality.

Survey:

Please indicate your response to the following statements, using the following response categories: Strongly Disagree, Disagree, Neutral, Agree, Strongly Agree. The following questions are designed for use with male-identified individuals.

● *Any man who is a man needs to have sex regularly.*

● *So-called effeminate men deserve to be ridiculed.*

● *I'd rather gamble than play it safe.*

- *In conflicts with others, I fight to win.*
- *When I have a few drinks, I look for trouble.*

    The example survey shows how a series of statements can be used to "tap into" a concept. Think about the dimensions of one of the following concepts, and use it answer the questions.

- Happiness
- Political engagement
- Body image
- Academic success
- Depression
- Job satisfaction
- Religiosity
- Health

1. What concept have you chosen and what are the main dimensions of that concept?

2. What are five statements or questions you could use to measure the dimensions of your chosen concept? Be sure to identify which statements or questions correspond to each dimension.

Check Your Understanding

1. What is a composite measure?
2. What is an index measure, and how is it created?
3. What is a scale measure, and what are its benefits relative to an index variable?

CHARACTERISTICS OF GOOD MEASURES

Defining concepts and planning how to measure them are issues at the heart of sociological research. However, researchers think carefully about conceptualization and measurement because they want their research to be accurate. That is, researchers are seeking the answer to a research question that is as "truthful" as possible and can be verified. This means that researchers have to carefully plan and think about what information they get from their measurements. They are concerned with measurement quality—how accurate their measures are. Validity and reliability are aspects of measurement quality that researchers have to think about when planning ahead for a study, and sometimes in the midst of their research.

Mutually Exclusive and Exhaustive Categories

If the researcher decides that closed-ended questions are needed, then they have to consider what answer choices to provide. When using closed-ended questions, researchers must consider two factors: mutual exclusion, and exhaustion. The response categories for a question have to be *both* mutually exclusive *and* exhaustive. Mutually exclusive means that the respondent should only be able to classify themselves into *one* category. Exhaustive means that *every* respondent should be able to find a category that describes their answer to the question. Consider this example regarding the variable income.

Please select the category that best describes your annual income:

$10,000–$20,000

$20,000–$30,000

$30,000–$40,000

$40,000–$50,000

These response categories are problematic because they are neither mutually exclusive nor are they exhaustive. If a person earned $20,000 per year, then their response could fall into either the first or the second category. This means that the answer choices are not mutually exclusive. Also, if a person makes less than $10,000 or more than $50,000 they would not be able to choose any options— meaning the answers aren't exhaustive. In order to fix the issue with the answer choices not being mutually exclusive, the researchers should fix the answer choices so that none overlap.

Please select the category that best describes your annual income:

$10,000–$19,999

$20,000–$29,999

$30,000–$39,999

$40,000–$49,999

In order to ensure that the variables are exhaustive, the researcher should be sure to include more categories so that everyone would be able to answer the question.

Please select the category that best describes your annual income:

<$10,000

$10,000–$19,999

$20,000–$29,999

$30,000–$39,999

$40,000–$49,999

$50,000–$59,999

$60,000–$69,999

$70,000–$79,999

$80,000–$89,999

>$89,000

In this last example, the answer choices are both mutually exclusive and exhaustive—all respondent answers would fit into one category, and all respondents would be able to answer the question.

DOING SOCIOLOGY 6.5

Is This Measure Mutually Exclusive and Exhaustive?

In this activity, you will determine whether a series of questions and statements have mutually exclusive and exhaustive categories.

Carefully examine the following examples of closed-ended questions. Make a determination as to whether they are both mutually exclusive and exhaustive.

1. Is this question mutually exclusive and exhaustive?
   What year in college are you?
   A.   First year
   B.   Sophomore
   C.   Junior
   D.   Senior

2. Is this question mutually exclusive and exhaustive?
   With which of the following religions do you identify?
   A.   Christianity
   B.   Catholicism
   C.   Protestantism
   D.   Judaism
   E.   Hinduism
   F.   Islam

3. Is this question mutually exclusive and exhaustive?
   What is your educational attainment?
   A.   High school
   B.   Associate degree
   C.   Bachelor's degree
   D.   Master's degree
   E.   Professional degree

4. Is this question mutually exclusive and exhaustive? If not, how would you fix it so that it is both mutually exclusive and exhaustive?
   How old are you?
   A.   18–25
   B.   25–35
   C.   35–45
   D.   45–55
   E.   55–65

Validity

Measurement validity is a type of measurement quality that focuses on accuracy. There are different ways to measure the accuracy of a specific measure. Consider the most basic type of validity—face validity. The basic premise of face validity is to look at a measure "on its face"—that is, do you think the measurement is accurate just by looking at it? If a researcher asks a survey question about age— "How old are you?"—this measure appears to have face validity. When assessing measurement validity you might ask, "Does this look like it measures the concept I hope to measure?" For the same concept, asking college students about what year they are in school is not a good measurement for age. Although year in school might correspond well to age in some colleges and universities, this would not be the case for institutions that serve many returning students, who may not fit the "typical" age range for undergraduates. Basically, age is best answered through a question about age specifically. Although we can sometimes rely on face validity to evaluate our conceptualization of variables, many other types of validity exist. In fact, some academic papers are all about how to validate a measure! Let's look at a few of these other types of validity now.

Criterion validity looks at a measure to determine its quality based on how it has been measured in the past. As discussed earlier, the first place to look when conceptualizing is prior literature. But other researchers don't only define concepts—they also measure them. Criterion validity looks at how accurate one measure is for a research project when compared to other research projects that have already been published. Researchers studying anxiety know that asking a single question about anxiety on a survey isn't likely to produce accurate results—however, there are a series of questions, called the GAD-7, that have been proven to be valid measures of anxiety. What if a researcher wanted to study anxiety but didn't want to use the full GAD-7 test? If they used a different series of questions that were then compared to results for the GAD-7 for the same people taking both surveys, then they would have criterion-related validity because the results of the two different surveys would be the same, and the new questions would be deemed comparable to the GAD-7. When researchers use measures that produce accurate results in comparison to already proven measures, they have criterion-related validity.

Content validity looks to determine whether the full range of meaning of a variable is being measured. More complex concepts may use several different measures to determine the full range of the meaning. Indexes and scales are good choices for measuring multidimensional concepts. For example, when measuring happiness, researchers note that there are different life arenas in which respondents might consider their happiness, such as in their significant relationships, in their friendships, and at work. Content validity determines how well these measures fit with each to help determine how happy an individual is.

Construct validity looks at the extent to which our measurement accurately reflects our original concept. In their article "Who Is Multiracial?" Harris and Sim (2002) note that there are differences in how adolescents identify based on the context in which they are asked the question. That is, if a multiracial student were asked their race at home, some students answered one way, but if asked that same question at school, those students would give a different race. This leads researchers to note that conceptual definitions of race need to allow for differences in how people identify based on location.

Multiracial Americans, such as Vice President Kamala Harris, choose how they racially identify. For some multiracial individuals, how they identify may change based on the context.

DOD Photo/Alamy Stock Photo

Cross-cultural validity is a fifth type of validity that looks at the ways in which measures can be compared across different cultures. An illustrative example comes from the 1980s and 1990s, when researchers were trying to understand the HIV/AIDS epidemic and the notion of cross-cultural validity became a pressing issue. Most of the research centered around the very specific populations at highest risk for the disease, for example, gay men. When researchers studied HIV/AIDS in the "gay" population of non-Western cultures they ran into a serious roadblock: Not every man who had sex with men identified as gay. While this was a concern in the United States, in other cultures where the definitions of sexuality aren't always based on same-sex/opposite-sex attraction, the question of how to reach groups for advocacy and health care became a serious concern. This represents a moment in which we have to take into consideration the similarities and differences between cultures. Having faced this measurement issue, Parker (2001) noted the importance of using terminology based on the culture that is being studied, rather than that which is used in the researcher's own culture.

CONSIDER THIS...

Imagine a dartboard where the bulls-eye represents maximum accuracy. If a measure is both valid and reliable, what would the pattern of darts on the dartboard look like? If a measure is invalid, what would the pattern of darts look like? If a measure is unreliable, what would the pattern of darts look like?

Reliability

Reliability is another factor to consider in measurement quality. Reliability is about repeatability—if a researcher were to conduct the same research project again, in the same way, would they find the same answers? There are different types of reliability—test–retest reliability, inter-item reliability, and inter-rater reliability. The research that is being conducted influences the type of reliability that might be used.

Test–retest reliability seeks to determine how well different measures of the same variable are in accordance with each other. If a professor gave a quiz in a class and then gave the same exact quiz again to the same students a few days later, each student should get very similar grades on both quizzes, if they had truly learned the material and the test were reliably measuring that information. The same grade would indicate high test–retest reliability—the test would be seen as reliable. But, if many students got an A on the first test and then failed the second test, then the test would have low test–retest reliability.

Inter-item reliability focuses on the ways in which different measures fit together to measure a more complicated concept. Have you ever taken a long survey, and you get to a question that seems very familiar? It seems like it's asking the same thing as a question that was asked earlier in the survey, but it's worded just a *little* differently? If this has happened to you, then you've probably encountered inter-item reliability. For example, if there is a survey question that asks someone to enter in their age, and then there's another survey question asking for that person's date of birth, then researchers are likely making sure that there is reliability between the items. Researchers can look at the two measures to determine how reliable the measures were—that is, the two answers to these questions should lead the researchers to the same age for the respondent. If it doesn't, then there is an issue with one or both of the measures. Both test–retest reliability and inter-item reliability are used when researchers are measuring variables by asking questions.

Inter-rater reliability is used when researchers are using some form of observation. Let's suppose that you and another student are tasked with determining how many people who are using the library are studying. First, you and the other student would have to determine what "studying" looks like. Once you agree on what it looks like you would likely want to both walk through the library together, to see if you agree on whether each person or group of people look to both of you like they are studying. Once you've done an initial walk-through together you could both go through the library separately on a different day to count the number of people studying. If you both separately, while studying the same thing, had the same number at the end, then you would likely have a high inter-rater reliability. Inter-rater reliability is used for observations of individuals or organizations, and it can also be used when looking at recorded information. That is, if two researchers were watching the same television show to determine how often characters express "surprise" and they came up with the same number and instances, there would be high inter-rater reliability. If they both had very different moments in the show when they thought the characters were surprised, they would have low inter-rater reliability. This is most important when there are multiple researchers collecting data through observation.

<hr>

Check Your Understanding

1 What does it mean for a measure to be mutually exclusive?
2 What does it mean for a measure to be exhaustive?
3 What does it mean for a measure to be valid?
4 What does it mean for a measure to be reliable?

CONCLUSION

This chapter described how sociologists develop, refine, and measure the complex elements that make up the social world. We began with the process of conceptualization, which is the process of defining a concept as clearly as possible. Conceptualization allows researchers and their audiences to be on the same page when it comes to what is included in a concept and what is not. It is vital to have a shared definition of concepts, especially those that are potentially ambiguous. Next, we reviewed operationalization—linking the conceptual definition to measurement. In creating an operational definition, we specify precisely how we will actually measure the concept, such as writing a survey question, interview question, or defining what counts as an observation. We then considered how conceptualization and operationalization differ in the context of inductive or deductive research. Within deductive research, the concept, its operational definition, and its measurement remain consistent throughout the research process as the researcher attempts to test their hypothesis. Within inductive research, the process is much more cyclical. Researchers revisit and refine their concepts throughout the research process, and often introduce new concepts in the process. Researchers need to keep an open mind about which concepts are most central to their research, because in many cases they uncover new concepts when collecting data or when analyzing data. Composite measures were then introduced. Indexes, in which several different measures are *added* together to create a combined score, are useful for measuring multidimensional concepts, as are scales. Scales differ from indexes in that they allow for some dimensions of a concept to carry more weight than others. Finally, we ended with the concepts of validity and reliability. Measurement validity is a type of measurement quality that focuses on accuracy. We want to make sure that we are measuring what we think we are measuring. Reliability refers to making measurements that are consistent and replicable. Both are necessary when doing quality research. You should now be well-equipped to understand measurement as a part of the social science research process.

SOCIOLOGISTS IN ACTION
TANGELA TOWNS

Tangela Towns

Courtesy of Tangela Towns

As a scholar, teacher, and administrator, I use sociological research methods every day. I ask my students to do the same!

I research issues of food insecurity, health disparities, race, and poverty. These complex sociological concepts can be measured in a variety of different ways. One approach to assessing food insecurity is to make use of existing data. The U.S. Department of Agriculture, for example, provides a survey that measures household-level food security and insecurity. The survey includes questions such as, "In the last 12 months, did you or other adults in the household ever cut the size of your meals or skip meals because there wasn't enough money for food?" and "In the last 12 months, did you lose weight because there wasn't enough money for food?" (2021).

In one of my projects, I combined data from two different sources, Census Bureau data and city-level data, to analyze the food environment. These data were then integrated by the Geographic Information Systems (GIS) to determine the average distance of grocery stores, food pantries, and other food sources varying by income and race. The analyses showed that high- poverty areas are more likely to lack grocery stores, general stores, and food pantries. Moreover, concentrations of grocery stores occur most frequently in non-Black neighborhoods, leaving Black neighborhood residents having to travel further to grocery stores.

In my teaching, I guide my students in their own investigation of food insecurity, health inequities, and racial inequalities. In my African American Health and Society course, students conduct a Service Learning Project that incorporates quantitative data analysis with other research methods. Students learn about health in African American communities and the structural inequalities that contribute to food insecurity and health inequalities. They analyze data from the United States Census Bureau and create visualizations that illustrate patterns of health-related racial inequality. They investigate the extent to which the average distance to grocery stores in our community varies by race and poverty level. In addition, they review existing scholarly literature research to understand diverse food environments and the determinants of food insecurity among African Americans.

Volunteering at the local food bank gives the students further information for understanding and contextualizing the data. Students participate in food sorting, egg grading, and compiling orders to be shipped to local food pantries. They journal about their experiences and use reflective learning methods by comparing their own experiences with the theories and research findings of other sociologists. In the process of gaining this hands-on experience, they learn more about what food insecurity entails, and how better to conceptualize this phenomenon. At the end of the semester, students complete a research paper integrating everything they have learned about food insecurity and associated health outcomes in the African American community.

Dr. Tangela Towns is associate professor of sociology in the Department of Behavioral Science at Winston Salem State University, and the interim director for the Office of Student Research.

Discussion Question

How does Dr. Towns use sociological research methods to address social inequalities?

REVIEW

6.1 How do sociologists conceptualize variables, and what are the main challenges in measuring sociological concepts?

Conceptualization is when researchers think carefully about the meaning of each of the concepts in the research question and hypotheses, and specify precisely what each one means. Researchers define their concepts as clearly as possible, clarifying their boundaries by specifying what falls inside of each definition and what falls outside of it. One challenge in measuring sociological concepts is that many of the most important things that sociologists measure are immaterial and do not exist in physical space. Their boundaries are not easily identified and may be actively disputed. Furthermore, many of the concepts most central to sociology vary over time and place. Finally, most of the concepts that sociologists study—things like health, social class, social cohesion, or inequality—have many dimensions or components. Scholars actively disagree with one another about how many dimensions each of these concepts have and further disagree about which dimensions are the most important.

6.2   How do sociologists operationalize variables?

Once researchers establish conceptual definitions of the key concepts in the research question and hypotheses, the next step is to develop a more concrete, working definition in a process known as operationalization. Operational definitions specify precisely how each abstract concept is measured. By developing an operational definition, researchers specify exactly how each concept in their study is represented in their data.

6.3   How do sociologists conceptualize and measure variables when conducting inductive and deductive research?

Within deductive research, a researcher begins with the process of conceptualization, and once they have their conceptual definition, they then operationalize it, specifying precisely how each abstract concept is measured. The concept, its operational definition, and its measurement remain consistent throughout the research process as the researcher attempts to test their hypothesis. Within inductive research, the process is much more cyclical. Researchers revisit and refine their concepts throughout the research process, and often introduce new concepts in the process. Researchers need to keep an open mind about which concepts are most central to their research, because in many cases they uncover new concepts—and concepts that are crucial for understanding their research question—in the process of doing the research. This can happen while researchers are collecting data or when analyzing the data, depending on the information that is collected.

6.4   What are the two types of composite measures, and how do they differ?

There are two broad types of composite measures. The first is an index, in which several different measures are *added* together to create a combined score. If a researcher is working with a unidimensional concept, they might create an index using multiple measures of that dimension. But a researcher could also create an index to assess a multidimensional concept by asking a series of questions that address each of the various dimensions. In an index, each of the indicators is treated as having the same weight; in other words, each indicator contributes equally to the measurement of the concept. Scales are another type of composite measure. Scales are like indexes in that they combine a number of indicators that speak to dimensions of a concept. However, indexes simply sum up the series of responses, whereas scales allow the weight of the various items to vary prior to being summed.

6.5   What are the main characteristics of good measures?

When using closed-ended questions, researchers must consider two factors: mutual exclusion and exhaustion. The answer choices for a question have to be *both* mutually exclusive *and* exhaustive. Mutually exclusive means that the respondent should only be able to classify themselves into *one* category. Exhaustive means that *every* respondent should be able to find a category that describes their answer to the question. Measurement validity is a type of measurement quality that focuses on accuracy. Face, criterion, content, construct, and cross-cultural validity all allow researchers to establish accurate measures. Reliability is about repeatability—if a researcher were to conduct the same research project again, in the same way, would they find the same answers? There are different types of reliability—test–retest reliability, inter-item reliability, and inter-rater reliability. The research that is being conducted influences the type of reliability that might be used.

KEY TERMS

closed-ended questions (p. 104)

conceptualization (p. 98)

exhaustive (p. 108)

face validity (p. 110)

index (p. 106)

measurement validity (p. 110)

mutually exclusive (p. 108)

open-ended questions (p. 104)

operational definitions (p. 100)

operationalization (p. 100)

scales (p. 107)

CAUSALITY AND THE ROLE OF EXPERIMENTAL DESIGNS

R. Saylor Breckenridge

HOW I GOT ACTIVE IN SOCIOLOGY
R. SAYLOR BRECKENRIDGE

I started college as a pre-med major. I had been a good student in mathematics and the physical and biological sciences when I was in high school and my teachers and counselors put me on the medical track. However, once I was in college, while I still enjoyed mathematics, I found chemistry and biology to be uninspiring. My Introduction to Sociology course was fascinating to me, both in terms of the basic ideas of the discipline— power and social structure, status and role, work and organizations—and relative to methodology. As I learned more about how questions were asked and answered in social science, and their analogs in other sciences, I became increasingly fascinated. A sociology professor learned of my continuing pursuit of mathematics, convinced me to apply it to the world of sociological inquiry, and I was sold: I became a double major in mathematics and sociology. I went on to graduate school, where I embraced the use of mathematical models to understand the success and failure of organizations. After earning my PhD, I worked for the United States' National Science Foundation (NSF) as both the Director of Methodology, Measurement, and Statistics and the Director of Sociology. Now, as a professor teaching sociology methodology and statistics courses for over 20 years, I work to reveal the techniques and strategies that we can use to most effectively answer the questions that help us to understand the social world and solve some of its pressing problems.

UNDERSTANDING PROBABILISTIC CAUSALITY

The word *cause* is deceptively complicated. It is a part of everyday language and used by English-speakers with such ease that there is rarely a need to question the precise implications of its use. But that ease is hiding a great deal of ambiguity. Consider the relatively common, accepted, and generally understood statement: "Smoking cigarettes causes lung disease." Does this statement mean that anyone who ever smokes a cigarette will develop lung disease? Does it imply that if someone smokes enough cigarettes, some large number, then they will definitely develop lung disease? For either light smokers or heavy smokers, would they immediately develop disease, or would it be something that would develop over the years after or while smoking? Does the statement mean that anyone who develops lung disease must have smoked a cigarette (or many cigarettes) in their past? All of these questions are reasonable ones stemming from that original statement. However, the answer to all those questions is "no." And figuring out why that is, and the real meaning of that statement about the relationship between smoking and lung disease, is crucial to understanding what the words *cause* and *causality* mean when researchers use them in sociology and other scientific contexts.

The punchline to untangling this complexity, one that will be a guiding light through this chapter, is that the statement "smoking cigarettes causes lung disease" actually means "smoking cigarettes *increases the likelihood* of acquiring lung disease." You may well have already known that, or maybe you aren't too surprised by this interpretation, but it is one of the essential ways that researchers need to interpret and untangle what "cause" can mean. When scientists use the word *cause*, they are very often referring to what is known as probabilistic causality, the condition where there is a general trend that one thing has an effect on another, but the size of the effect may differ case by case, and, in some occasions, there may be no observed effect at all. When analyzing the relationship between lung disease and cigarettes, medical science has shown that the more cigarettes a person smokes, per day and over time, the more likely they are to develop lung disease. While some people develop lung disease without ever smoking, and others smoke extensively but never develop it, the generally observed pattern is that the more people smoke, the higher the likelihood of disease.

Imagine a social science example with a statement that links gender socialization to jobs: "Gender socialization causes men and women to pursue training for different sorts of jobs." That's a pretty straightforward sociological idea that fits with popular knowledge, so it can be used to help illustrate this core idea of probabilistic causality. What that sentence intends to reveal is that while men and women can and do choose all sorts of different careers, for all sorts of different reasons, it's still the case that socialization encourages people to pursue different types of educations, and different types of careers, depending upon their gender. But relying on the word *cause* doesn't make that specifically clear. Instead, the phrasing "in general, gender socialization increases the likelihood that men and women will pursue different sorts of job training" clarifies the social process described by being more precise about the probabilistic nature and direction.

Recall from Chapter 2 the terminology of independent and dependent variables. When scientists are talking about these in their simplest form, they use X and Y as shorthand terms for independent and dependent variables. And they might say things like "X causes Y" (i.e., "the independent variable I'm studying causes the dependent variable I'm studying") or "X increases the likelihood of Y" or "X has a positive effect on Y" or maybe the finding is "X has a negative effect on Y." And sometimes in these conversations, if someone chooses the "X causes Y" phrasing, another scientist will chime in and ask, "What do you really mean by cause?" and then the first scientist will reply, "Oh! It's a probabilistic relationship. I really mean that in general, X has a positive effect on Y," or "I really mean that in general X has a negative effect on Y." These clarifying statements illuminate some detail of scientific finding and are a reflection of the potential for ambiguity when simply using the word *cause*. Focusing on probabilistic causality and the direction of the relationship between independent and dependent variables is often essential for making a clear statement that reveals a scientific finding. So "smoking cigarettes causes lung disease" is a shorthand phrase that really means "smoking cigarettes increases the likelihood of lung disease" where smoking is the independent variable, lung disease is the dependent variable, and there is a positive relationship between the two.

Probabilistic causality can help us understand how gender socialization impacts the jobs men and women pursue.

Returning to the relationship between exposure to gender socialization and the jobs men and women pursue, "gender socialization" is the independent variable and "the jobs men and women pursue" is the dependent variable. In doing research to attempt to find a causal relationship, a scientist might pose the question, "Does X cause Y?" But an even better question, one that captures probabilistic causality, might be, "In general, does X have an effect on Y?" In this case, "Does exposure to gender socialization about jobs increase the likelihood that the actual jobs men and women pursue will conform to gender norms?" This phrasing helps to make it clear that a probabilistic relationship is expected.

Components of Causality

When scientists want to claim that there is a causal relationship between the two variables, they must reveal a set of key characteristics about the variables: temporal priority, correlation, mechanism, and nonspuriousness.

One essential condition of causality is temporal priority. This means that the independent variable, X, must occur prior in time to the dependent variable, Y. The independent variable must occur before the dependent variable in order for there to be a causal relationship between the two. Essentially, this is referring to the idea that the future cannot affect the past. Time is linear and the independent variable must occur before the dependent one. Y depends on X, so X must happen first.

Correlation is the idea that the two variables are related to each other in some way. There is a statistic called the correlation coefficient that you may be aware of and it captures just this idea. Both X and Y must vary together in some measurable manner. Maybe, in general, one goes up and the other goes down in matching ways, or maybe they both go up or both go down, but there is some way that two variables change in matching ways. There is a common critique of scientific findings where someone might claim "you've only shown correlation, but not causation." It's worth reflecting on this as a weak critique because correlation is actually a requirement to show causation. If X and Y aren't correlated, then they can't possibly be causally related! It's a big step toward causation to be able to show correlation.

A mechanism is a process that explains why X and Y are causally related. Recall that a theory is an understood way in which phenomena are related to each other, based on evidence. This is distinct from a hypothesis, which is a claim or question about what we might expect to find in a new situation or case, based on the theories we already know. Theories are accepted explanations and hypotheses are the questions that stem from them. A mechanism is, then, the theoretical (meaning scientific, evidence-based, and accepted) explanation for why X might be causing, or having an effect on, Y. The mechanism is the process that makes us understand the relationship between X and Y as something other than just coincidental; it's the reason for the relationship.

Finally, nonspuriousness is an idea that is related to correlation and mechanism. If two variables are correlated, that relationship could be coincidental—meaning that either there is no proposed mechanism between them or that the proposed mechanism is incorrect. If this were the case, it would be a spurious relationship, and it undermines claims of causality between X and Y. Similarly, if X and Y are correlated, there could be a third variable, Z, that is actually affecting both X and Y simultaneously.

DOING SOCIOLOGY 7.1

Considering the Components of Causality

In this exercise, you will practice applying and assessing the components of causality to causal relationships.

Consider some of the following probabilistic relationships.

1. Students who receive positive feedback from a teacher at the beginning of a course tend to do better throughout the course of the academic year.

2. People who own pets are more likely than people who don't own pets to report higher levels of happiness.

3. Compared to nonparents and parents of older children, people who are parents of young children report having less time for relaxation.

4. People who regularly spend time in nature report lower levels of anxiety and higher levels of calm.
   For each of the situations, answer the following questions.

1. What is the independent variable? What is the dependent variable?

2. Does the relationship meet the criterion of temporal priority? Why or why not?

3. What do you think is the mechanism linking the two variables? Explain.

4. Do you think the relationship between the two variables is spurious? Why or why not?

A classic example of this is the relationship between the rate of ice cream consumption and the rate at which people go swimming. In almost any city, it turns out that these two rates are positively correlated: As ice cream consumption increases, people also swim more frequently. But establishing a mechanism between the two is quite difficult, so perhaps it is a coincidental, or spurious, relationship. And, really, there is a third variable, air temperature, that affects them both: Air temperature is positively correlated with rates of ice cream consumption, and it is also positively correlated with rates of swimming—and there is a very reasonable mechanism to explain both those relationships. With this in mind, we describe an independent and dependent variable as having a nonspurious relationship when they are correlated and there is a mechanism that can accurately explain that relationship. The relationship between air temperature and rates of ice cream consumption is nonspurious. The relationship between air temperature and rates of swimming is nonspurious. But the relationship between rates of ice cream consumption and rates of swimming is spurious.

CONSIDER THIS. . .

How does knowing the mechanism between air temperature and ice cream consumption or swimming help us to identify spuriousness between ice cream consumption and swimming?

Necessary Conditions and Sufficient Causes

There are a few more technical aspects of causality that can be useful toward understanding the relationship between an independent and a dependent variable. Two basic forms of causes that are frequently discussed in science are necessary conditions and sufficient causes. If there are two variables, X and Y, the independent and dependent variables, there might—on very rare occasions in sociology—be some absolute, nonprobabilistic relationships between them. For example, if X absolutely must always occur first before Y can occur, then X is necessary for Y. Here, if X happens, then Y may or may not occur, but Y can't possibly occur unless X does: Y requires X in order to occur. X is a necessary condition for Y. An example of this is the relationship between being married and getting divorced. Being married is a necessary condition to getting divorced, but not everyone who is married will become divorced.

Alternately, if it is the case that every single time X occurs it is followed by Y also occurring, then X is a sufficient cause of Y. Here, Y can occur for many reasons, but if X occurs first, then Y will surely follow. X is a sufficient cause of Y. Going to prison can happen for many reasons, but being convicted of first-degree murder will always lead to prison. That conviction is a sufficient cause of being sent to prison, but not a necessary condition. People can be sent to prison for many other reasons too.

It is possible for X to be both a necessary condition and sufficient cause of Y. In this case, Y occurs if, and only if, X occurs. If X happens, then so does Y. And if Y happens, then X must have occurred beforehand.

It isn't very common in sociology that X is either a necessary condition or sufficient cause of Y. Typically, the independent and dependent variables occur in correlation with each other, but their relationship isn't an absolute one. These are the cases where there is a probabilistic cause. Here, if X occurs, then Y might occur some proportion of the time, but not at other times. And, similarly, if Y occurs, then X occurred first in some measured number of cases, but not others. While this might seem messy, this sort of causality is at the core of the science of sociology and is the most common sort of causal relationship.

Let's reflect on our two examples in terms of these types and components of causality. Recall that the link between smoking cigarettes and lung disease is neither necessary nor sufficient—lung disease can occur for many different reasons in addition to smoking cigarettes, and smoking cigarettes doesn't always lead to lung disease; the link is probabilistic. Similarly, the relationship between gender socialization and the jobs people of different genders pursue is also probabilistic. It's not that a high level of gender socialization is either sufficient or necessary for anyone holding any particular job. In reality, it's a general trend where social norms about gender are one of many forces that play a role in how people become interested in and pursue training to hold certain jobs. Recall the phrasing "in general, gender socialization increases the likelihood that the actual jobs men and women hold will conform to gendered norms." That statement implies, and clarifies, a probabilistic cause between the independent variable, X, or in this case, "exposure to gender norms" and the dependent variable, Y, which in this case is "the jobs people hold."

The question embedded in all this is, "How do we actually do the science to test whether or not any sort of causal relationship exists between X and Y?" The answer to that starts with an understanding of experimental design, a core feature of how science is actually done and a great starting point for thinking about the work of doing sociological science.

Check Your Understanding

1. What is probabilistic causality?
2. What are the four components of causality?
3. What is a necessary condition?
4. What is a sufficient cause?

EXPERIMENTAL DESIGN

The term experiment is one of the first that people learn as a component of doing science. When we think of experiments, we might imagine scientists in white coats trying novel combinations of chemicals in laboratories with test tubes, or with patients and new drug treatments. Sometimes nothing happens and other times there are explosions or improvements to patients' health. In reality, we all often conduct casual experiments in our day-to-day lives: "Will it taste different if I dip my french fry in mayonnaise instead of ketchup?" "Will people treat me differently if I shave my head?"

At their core, experiments serve as a way of designing research that allows us to answer a question by detecting causal relationships. They are designed to focus attention on whether an independent variable, X, has an effect on a dependent variable, Y. In the language of experimental design, this "X" variable, the new element being tested, is referred to as the treatment. In the examples provided earlier, mayonnaise and a shaved head are treatments being tested to see if they produce new, different outcomes for you.

Reflecting on a casual understanding of science laboratories is a valuable starting point to conceptualizing the importance of more rigorous experimental design. Laboratories are often clean and sterile; they are very controlled places where scientists are precise and pay close attention to examining how the treatment, and only the treatment, has an effect on what is being studied. There is an attempt to avoid contamination by dirt or germs or other chemicals in order to assuredly focus on the effect of the treatment alone. While this brings to mind images of chemistry or medical experiments, the basic

We often associate experiments with chemistry, but there are many different types of experiments—including those conducted by sociologists.

©SDI Productions/Getty Images

idea is the same in social science: Experiments are designs for research that create a controlled and uncontaminated environment in which scientists can introduce a treatment to examine how it might cause an effect.

The ability to isolate the effect of the treatment, to control all other possible factors that could affect the outcome, is the central strength of experimental design as a means of detecting causality, and this requires some standard rules about how scientists recruit, organize, treat, and interact with participants.

Research Questions and Treatments

Let's reconsider the sociological question, "Does gender socialization cause men and women to pursue training for different sorts of jobs?" Using an experimental design to study this relationship, sociologists would identify a way to create a treatment related to gender socialization that, akin to a new drug in a medical experiment, could be tested to see if it affects people's interest in particular jobs.

Sociologist Shelley Correll did just this in her 2004 article "Constraints Into Preferences: Gender, Status, and Emerging Career Aspirations." While it is difficult to create a simple treatment that captures the grand scope of gender socialization, she crafted a single item of information, a simple statement promoting inequality by indicating that, typically, men performed a certain task better than women. She used this as a treatment. The information was given to some participants, but not others. Then they were all given the task and asked how well they thought they performed. Do you think those who did and didn't receive the statement thought of their performances differently? Could it have affected men differently from women? These questions will be answered later in the chapter, but for now, imagine that this process is precisely analogous to medical researchers giving patients a new drug and then asking how it affects their health.

For sociologists, experiments typically have individuals as the unit of observation. They might assess social–psychological forces like how an interactional experience affects their behaviors or, as in Correll's study, the impact of a new piece of information on participants' attitudes. But whatever the treatment might be, it needs to be easily manipulated in a controlled setting by the researchers so that its effect can be isolated. The sociological laboratory setting is typically a separated space within a university building where participants enter one at a time or in small groups and take part in the experiment. They may meet with the researchers, they might complete a questionnaire, they might play a game on a computer, or researchers might carefully observe them in order to measure aspects of their opinions or behaviors. Researchers then apply the treatment and examine the participants a second time to see if any changes have occurred. Isolating the effect of this treatment is at the core of experimental design and is achieved by following a few key guidelines.

Treatment and Control Groups

In their simplest form, experiments involving human participants focus on a comparison of two groups of participants, those who receive a treatment—the treatment group—and a comparison group who do not receive the treatment—the control group. In medical experiments that test the effectiveness of new drugs, scientists analyze whether those participants who receive a new drug treatment improve, or are unaffected or possibly become more ill, in different ways from those who do not receive the drug. In these types of studies, participants who do not receive the new drug are given a placebo instead. A placebo is an alternate to the treatment that the researchers expect to have no effect, but that makes recipients think they may be receiving a treatment. If the two groups consist of identical types of participants, having identical experiences in the laboratory, except for receiving the new drug or a placebo, then the difference in outcomes between them reveals the effect of the drug treatment. The same process applies to sociological experimentation: One group of participants receives some sort of new treatment, while another group does not, and then the two groups are compared. The process of organizing participants into these groups follows some standardized rules that serve to isolate the treatment and allow its measurement.

CONSIDER THIS...

Why are control groups important for experimental design? Why might it be a problem if a treatment group consists only of young adults and the control group consists only of elderly people?

DOING SOCIOLOGY 7.2

Considering Experimental Design

In this exercise, you will apply some of the basic ideas of experimental design to understanding a real sociological experiment.

For her 2004 article, "Constraints Into Preferences: Gender, Status, and Emerging Career Aspirations," Shelley Correll performed an experiment using volunteers who were undergraduate students at her school. As part of the experiment, she told all the participants that they were going to take a test and, beforehand, told some of them that men typically performed better on the test than women and told others that gender did not affect test performance.
Answer the following questions based on this example.

1. What is the treatment being applied?

2. What is the "placebo" in the control group?

3. Consider the order of events as described. Do you think this meets the conditions of temporal priority? Why or why not?

Check Your Understanding

1. What are the features of treatment groups in experiments?
2. What are the features of control groups?

STAGES OF SOCIOLOGICAL EXPERIMENTS

Experimental research using human participants always requires the approval of an ethical review board, such as a university or college's nstitutional review board (IRB). Once this is obtained the research proceeds in four steps: recruitment, informed consent, assignment to treatment or control group, and designing experiments for validity.

Recruitment

Recruitment refers to the process through which participants learn of and agree to participate in a research study. In sociological experiments, the participants are volunteers who agree to take part in the research. Scientists use a variety of techniques to solicit people to volunteer including posted fliers, hand-delivered mail, email, and publicly promoted Internet sites. When research is conducted on university campuses, professors may ask students to participate. These recruitment strategies produce a sample of participants, some of whom will become members of the treatment group and others of the control group.

The number of participants necessary for an experimental project can vary, but the larger the sizes of the groups—and the more times the experiment can be rerun with new groups—the more confidence researchers can have in their results. In some medical experiments, the groups may have as few as 10 participants in each, while in sociology there are sometimes hundreds of people in the groups, with the experiment being replicated many times before researchers are confident in the results. Size varies, in part due to the practical details of the experimental work (e.g., the actual size of the laboratory and the amount of time the researchers have to complete the project), the research questions asked (e.g., the research might require diverse respondents or, alternately, only those who are women or people under the age of 30 or those with hourly-wage incomes or some other key characteristic), and it is ultimately limited by the number of participants who actually volunteer to take part in the experiment. This last issue is of great importance because recruiting participants can sometimes be challenging.

Recruitment of volunteers requires making potential participants aware of the project and providing them with an opportunity to volunteer to take part in it. In medical research, researchers will often inform participants of what health condition they are studying, encouraging people who might benefit from the research due to their own state of health to participate. However, sociological research more often uses financial compensation, and in some cases extra credit for students, as a means of soliciting participants. And actual monetary payment is often presented in particularly enticing ways, using language such as, "Participants are guaranteed at least $10 for 30 minutes of participation, but may earn more, up to $50, depending on project outcomes." This extra enticement helps to increase willingness to participate and to follow the rules of the experiment.

CONSIDER THIS. . .

Have you ever been asked to participate in a social science or medical experiment? If so, what factors influenced your decision to participate or not? If you haven't been asked, what do you think might influence your participation?

Informed Consent

It is also the case that participants who agree to take part in the experiment must be allowed to drop out at any time, even after they have started the process. This ability to volunteer and drop out is a condition of the ethics of research on human subjects known as informed consent. Participants must be informed, in at least general terms, of what will take place in the experiment, what physical and emotional risks they might face, and what compensation they might receive. They must voluntarily agree to participate, and they must be allowed to remove their consent and leave the experiment at any time during the process. All this information is included in a document that each must sign prior to participation.

Assignment to Treatment or Control Group

Once researchers recruit their participants, they must then assign them to either the treatment group or the control group. The goal of this step is to make sure that the characteristics of the participants in each group are matching. Any characteristics of the participants that might impact the study should be distributed identically among the members of each group. In sociology, this often means that the composition of the two groups should be the same in terms of gender, race/ethnicity, age, education, occupation, and other background characteristics. As an example, the two groups should have equal distributions of gender, because if the treatment group consisted solely of men and the control group solely of women, then it wouldn't be possible to isolate the effect of the treatment—differences in the outcomes for the two groups could be the result of either their gender differences or the treatment and it wouldn't be possible to separate the two.

There are three typical strategies to achieve this equal distribution. If the set of participants is very large, they may be randomly assigned by the researchers into each group such that the process of randomization would produce equal distributions of all characteristics in the two groups. If simple randomization isn't possible, then a matching process might be pursued that would place people with matching characteristics into the two groups. For example, 10 women, randomly selected from all the women participants, would be placed into each of the control and treatment groups, then 10 men. But this might become a difficult task if the sample is small. Finding an equal number of people in each key demographic category combination would be impossible. Needing to make sure to recruit an equal number of men and women of different ages and educational levels and any other general characteristics can be difficult. The third strategy is quite common in sociological (and medical) research: requesting or selecting a constrained sample of participants, one that has a specific lack of variation so that the treatment and control group are assuredly matched relative to that parameter (e.g., only selecting women into both groups so that they are assuredly matched by gender). Because sociological experimentation is typically performed by professors at universities, recruiting college students constrains variation in age and educational attainment, which then makes the use of randomization and matching easier as a means to produce an equal distribution of other demographic characteristics in the treatment and control groups. This would mean selecting/constraining on age and education, then randomly selecting a number of men and an equal number of women, then randomly assigning half of each of those sets of respondents into either the control or treatment group.

Designing Experiments for Validity

In order for experimental research to produce valid conclusions, it is important for researchers to consider and control the process of experimentation as much as possible. The actual series of events, the history, that participants experience should be the same. In addition, any components of the experimental environment that could affect participants' attitudes and responses should remain consistent between the groups. For example, the tone of voice of the experimenter who is giving instructions, the temperature and comforts of the rooms, and all the minutiae of the experience that could affect attitudes should be kept as identical as possible for all participants. The duration of the experiment should also be kept the same so that participants mature over time in similar ways. Many experiments take place only over the course of a few minutes or hours, but some may take days or weeks, or longer. It is especially true in those latter cases that equal timing and opportunity for change to occur should be maintained.

DOING SOCIOLOGY 7.3

Social Media and Social Connectedness

In this exercise, you will think through the complexity and importance of designing experiments for validity.

Imagine that a researcher was conducting an experiment to determine whether time spent on social media affects people's sense of connection to others. They wonder, does spending more time on social media make people feel more connected to others, or more isolated? They plan to recruit a sample of 40 adults from their community, none of whom use social media regularly. The researchers will hold six in-person hour-long sessions over the course of 3 weeks for 20 participants. Prior to the start of the first session, researchers will ask participants about how socially connected they feel, and they will ask them again at the end of the 3 weeks. During each session, participants will be given an iPad and instructors will teach them how to create a profile on Instagram, Facebook, and Twitter. Instructors will also teach participants how to interact with other people, including other study participants, online.

The researcher is considering a variety of possible scenarios for the 20 people in the control group:

1. Asking them to report how socially connected they feel at two time-points 3 weeks apart, but without any instruction, activity, or contact in between.

2. Asking them to report how socially connected they feel at two time-points 3 weeks apart and in between having them attend six in-person hour-long sessions where they are given an iPad and taught business skills such as how to make an effective PowerPoint presentation.

3. Asking them to report how socially connected they feel at two time-points 3 weeks apart and in between having them attend six in-person hour-long cooking classes.
   Answer the following questions:

1. Which of these control group options do you think will maximize the validity of the experiment? Explain.

2. The researcher knows that it is important for the control group and the treatment group to be as similar as possible. What personal characteristics do you think are important for the researcher to consider when designing the two groups? Why are these important characteristics?

3. Consider the timing of the experiment for the two groups. Should the 3 weeks of social media classes be held during the same 3-week interval as the activities for the control group, or should the researchers focus on one group and then the next? Explain.

These broad concerns of creating equal experiences can apply to a myriad of conditions that are impossible to list completely. Good attention to this is part of the general practical procedure of administering an experiment: Make sure the experiences of the participants are as equal as possible.

There is, nonetheless, a set of specific issues and terminology that focus on key aspects of these concerns for maintaining the validity of experiments.

When it comes time to administer the treatment, it should be done in a manner whereby no participant knows whether they are being placed in the treatment or control group. Researchers should not ask participants to volunteer for one group over the other, nor should they tell participants into which group they have been assigned. Those in the control group should receive a placebo. In medical science, we can imagine the use of an empty pill capsule given to those in the control group, while the treatment group receives the new drug. The same is the case in sociological science, where some nontreatment is given to the control group to deceive them into thinking they are receiving a treatment.

Much like the problem of comparing a sample of men in the treatment group with a sample of women in the control, where the effect of the treatment cannot be isolated from the effect of gender, if participants assuredly know to which group they have been assigned, then the effect of the treatment cannot be isolated from the effect of knowing that treatment is occurring relative to knowing that no treatment has occurred. In sum, when participants believe that they are part of the treatment group, it may have an effect on how they respond in the experiment, so care must be taken to make sure they are unaware of their assignment. This enables isolation of the treatment effect from the **placebo effect**—which is not a false finding, as it is sometimes erroneously considered, but a real psychological and physiological effect that stems from cognition and emotion that a treatment is being received. If people want to experience the effect of the treatment and think they are receiving the treatment, then they may experience the effect due to that psychological state, regardless of whether the treatment is actually having an effect itself.

Making sure that this placebo effect is equally distributed among the members of both the control and treatment groups is very important. This is typically achieved by **blinding** participants from the knowledge of whether they are in the treatment or control group, so they don't know if they've received the treatment or the placebo. This means that the placebo effect, the effect of knowing that they might be receiving a treatment, will be equally distributed among all participants so that the true effect of the treatment can be isolated. The second step toward ensuring that the experience of the treatment and control

Double-blind experiments help to prevent biased outcomes.

group are identical is to blind the lead researchers as to which participants are in the treatment and control groups. Double-blind experimentation, where neither participants nor researchers are aware of assignments, prevents the lead researchers from incorrectly inferring some outcome in the treatment group because of their own desire for that outcome to occur. Researchers might be unconsciously biased toward hoping for an outcome and the double-blind process prevents that from occurring. One way of achieving this is by having different members of the research team make the group assignments, administer the treatment and placebo, and examine the outcomes of the experiment.

Debriefing

As we've seen, experimental design has many rules to follow in order to capture its goal: the isolated effect of the treatment. However, you may have noticed that two of the rules we discussed are in conflict with each other. Informed consent requires that participants know about and agree to take part in the experiment, but the need to blind the experiment prevents them from truly knowing what will happen to them. This deception is accounted for within the informed consent document by providing the participants with a general assurance that the events of the experiment will not be harmful—with support from the researchers' IRB—and that there will be a debriefing at the end of the experiment in which its details will be revealed.

> #### Check Your Understanding
>
> 1. What are the stages of experimental research?
> 2. How do researchers assign participants to treatment and control groups?
> 3. Why is it important for participants not to know whether they are in the treatment or control group?

MEASURING THE EFFECT OF THE TREATMENT

The effect of the treatment is measured by comparing changes in the participants in the experimental group against those in the control groups. Recall that the groups should be matched in some way, perhaps through random assignment, so that their members are similar to each other. The process should be double-blinded so that neither the participants nor the researchers know whether a respondent is in the experimental or control group. Then after administration of the treatment or placebo to the respective groups, it is the difference in outcomes between the groups that reveals the isolated effect of the treatment. It is this idea of isolation—separating the effect of the treatment from any other possible causal force—that is the strength of experimental design.

Two-Group Pre-Test and Post-Test Design

The classic experiment follows a two-group pre-test and post-test design. There are two groups, treatment and control; all participants take a pre-test (e.g., a questionnaire measuring their attitudes about whether their gender affects their success at task); they receive a treatment or placebo (e.g., new information that gender typically does affect success at the task or that gender does not affect success); and then they retake the questionnaire. The difference between the pre-treatment test (pre-test) and post-treatment test (post-test) determines how much the treatment or placebo affected each group, and the difference between the groups isolates the effect of the treatment from all the conditions of the experiment that could affect the survey. As long as all conditions are maintained identically for the treatment and control groups, then this process of comparison will isolate the treatment effect.

Table 7.1 illustrates this example and helps reveal a mathematical process by which to measure the isolated effect. A and C are the average scores on the pre-test for the control and treatment groups, respectively. B and D are their average scores on the post-test. The effect of the treatment is:

Effect of the treatment = (D-C) – (B-A)

TABLE 7.1 ■ Diagram of the Two-Group Pre-Test and Post-Test Experimental Design			
Group	Pre-Test Score		Post-Test Score
Control	A	Placebo	B
Treatment	C	Treatment	D

If all the guidelines of good experimental design are followed, this is net of (i.e., separated from) the placebo effect, the effect of the variables that match the samples, and the effect of history and maturation in the laboratory setting. In other words, the effect of the treatment on the test score is being measured separately from all other forces that could be affecting the score.

Eliminating the Pre-Test

When assignment is handled well, so that the samples of participants found in the treatment and control groups are representative of each other, then it is not necessary for the researchers to conduct the pre-test. Because the two groups have the same characteristics, their scores on the pre-test, prior to administration of the treatment or a placebo, should be approximately equal. So, as presented in Table 7.1, A = C, and as a result:

Effect of the treatment = D – B

So, a well-designed experiment can follow what is outlined in Table 7.2.

TABLE 7.2 ■ Diagram of the Two-Group Post-Test Experimental Design			
Group	Pre-Test Score		Post-Test Score
Control	– not administered	Placebo	B
Treatment	– not administered	Treatment	D

Multiple Treatment Groups

Experiments can also be constructed with more than just two groups. All the guidelines of good experimental design still apply, and treatment groups can receive variations of the treatment. For example, if the treatment is providing information to respondents to study how it affects attitudinal change, different treatment groups could receive different information.

TABLE 7.3 ■ Diagram of the Multigroup Post-Test Experimental Design			
Group	Pre-Test Score		Post-Test Score
Control	– not administered	Placebo	B
Treatment 1	– not administered	Treatment 1	D
Treatment 2	– not administered	Treatment 2	F

The effect of treatment 1 = D – B
The effect of treatment 2 = F – B
The difference between the effects of treatment 1 and treatment 2 = F – D

If time, resources, and participants are sufficiently large, this design could be used for a large number of different treatments. As many as is practical.

CONSIDER THIS...

Imagine a sociologist conducting experiments about how practicing meditation affects interpersonal relationships. The treatment group will be asked to meditate twice a week, while the control group could be asked either to (a) take no specific action, or (b) take a brisk walk twice a week. What are the advantages and disadvantages of each option?

Causality and Generalizability in Experiments

When all the guidelines of good design are met, experiments allow researchers to make claims about how the treatment (i.e., the independent variable) has a causal effect on that which is being measured in the post-test (i.e., the dependent variable). This cannot be understated as one of the most important components of practical science: Within a perfectly designed experiment, the treatment is causing the outcome.

However, experimental findings may not be generalizable to broader populations and environments outside of the laboratory. The experiment itself might only be generalizable to the population represented by the samples in the treatment and control groups. Even in a perfectly designed experiment, these might be selected to be representative of each other with constrained populations such as only college students or only men; then the results of the experiment are not necessarily generalizable beyond those populations. In other words, the conclusions that the researcher draws based on their experiment may not apply to different social groups or in other social contexts. While the process of using a constrained, selected sample can simultaneously enhance the ability to make a claim about a causal relationship, it also undermines the ability to make that claim generalizable. Similarly, the entire laboratory experience is not like "real life," so the findings of an experiment may hold certainly true within that environment, but be less assured in the complex, uncontrolled world of a lived social system.

Every bit of imprecision in design (e.g., shortcomings in history, maturation, blinding, or sampling) affects the validity of the causality claim. While the controlled experiment itself and the size and characteristics of the sample of participants limit generalizability, these limitations are not fatal flaws! This is the reality of practical science. A single research project, regardless of design, is rarely the final word in determining a scientific finding. Experiments are an excellent strategy for isolating an independent variable toward establishing the existence of a causal relationship in at least some cases, but then that finding may need to be retested via other methods (e.g., ethnography) in order to assess how much it applies in the everyday world of our social lives.

DOING SOCIOLOGY 7.4

How Does Volunteer Work Influence Happiness?

In this exercise, you will identify and weigh the advantages and disadvantages of different research designs.

Dr. Palley is a sociologist interested in studying how participation in volunteer work affects personal happiness. They work at a large state university in the United States and have access to many sections of first-year introductory sociology courses. They decide to use students from those classes as the participants in the experiment.

Another sociologist, Dr. Chen, is replicating this experiment but uses a set of volunteers drawn from public library patrons.

Answer the following questions:

1. Why might Dr. Palley's strategy for selecting participants be problematic for generalizability?

2. Why might Dr. Palley's strategy for selecting participants be advantageous for identifying causality?

3. How might Dr. Chen's strategy for selecting participants be an improvement over Dr. Palley's sample?

4. How might Dr. Chen's strategy for selecting participants be disadvantageous relative to Dr. Palley's?

1. How is the effect of the treatment measured in a classic experiment?
2. When is it allowable to remove the pre-test from the classic experimental design?
3. Why might experimental designs enhance validity but limit generalizability?

EXPERIMENTS OUTSIDE OF THE LABORATORY

The foundations of experimental design revolve around the notion of control. The procedures associated with sampling, maintaining consistent history, using treatment and control groups, and double-blinding experiments are all associated with scientists' ability to control the process of the research. But this has the shortcoming of being distant from, and perhaps not representative of, the messy realities of social life. There are, however, opportunities to apply the logic of experiment design in looser frameworks that, while a bit less controlled and able to assuredly identify causality, are more representative of lived social life and, as a result, more generalizable to an understanding of the social world.

Field Experiments

Field experiments are those where, instead of a laboratory setting, experimental designs are applied to analyze a real-world social process. This research plan is often engaged to capture an understanding of society that is difficult to isolate in the laboratory, but at the cost of sacrificing control of history or other strategies of experimental design. One of the most common techniques of field experimentation is known as an audit study. In this design, members of the research team engage in social activities outside of the laboratory in real-world settings, each performing a slight variation on otherwise identical roles, in order to detect different responses. An oft-cited modern example is Devah Pager's 2003 article titled "The Mark of a Criminal Record." For her research, Dr. Pager had four men assisting with her research who pretended to be job applicants. They were two Black men and two white men, and all presented with nearly identical (and completely fabricated for the sake of the experiment) résumés, save that one from each racial group was identified as having a criminal record while the other did not. Her goal was to determine how differences in race and criminal records affected receiving a callback for an interview after applying for a job. Here, the participants are the businesses seeking new employees, and "race" and "criminal record" aspects of the applicants and their résumés are treatments in a four-group design with no pre-tests. Pager was able to compare the number of callbacks for each "treatment," meaning each applicant, received. In doing so, she found that by using the group who received a résumé from a white applicant with no criminal record as the "control" case for comparison, Black applicants had a lower rate of callback than white applicants, and those applicants identified as having a criminal record had lower rates of callbacks than those without a record. And, perhaps most interestingly, the effect of race was stronger than the effect of a criminal record.

This design does not follow all the guidelines for optimal experiments. It isn't precisely controlled and the selection of participants, the businesses, is not easily randomized or evenly matched—and they aren't able to engage in informed consent or debriefing, either. These are real limitations on the ability to assuredly claim necessary or sufficient causality between race, criminal record, and job access, but the project is embedded in the real world, is more generalizable, and provides excellent evidence to support a probabilistic relationship that supports existing theory and establishes a trajectory for continued research.

DOING SOCIOLOGY 7.5

Reexamining the Mark of a Criminal Record

In this activity, you will consider ways of adjusting the design of an experiment and how it might be useful to inform social policy.

Reflect on Devah Pager's field experiment, "The Mark of a Criminal Record" described in the preceding section. Pager's analysis focused on how having a drug-related offense on their record affected the Black and white men's chances of getting a callback for a job. An important finding within sociology, however, is that social groups often experience the world, and even particular events in the world, in different ways. In this case, we might wonder whether the "mark of a criminal record" has the same effect for people of diverse genders, age groups, and religious groups, for example.

Answer the following questions:

1. If you were to redesign Pager's study for today, what changes could you make to the research design to make the results more generalizable?

2. Would you change the gender, racial/ethnic, or other characteristics of the pretend job applicants? Why or why not?

3. Would you change the crime that they are shown to have committed? Why or why not?

4. Do you think that the results of this experiment could help to inform social policy and promote social equality? Why or why not?

Surveys as Quasi-Experimentation

The multigroup design of experiments presented in Table 7.3, combined with field experimentation, is a useful framework to think about other sorts of research design. Imagine a multigroup design with 10 groups or 50 groups or 500 groups, each receiving some slightly different treatment. Instead of simply the pairing of race and criminal record as described in Devah Pager's research, imagine if she had added binary gender so that there were eight applicant categories—the four for men as described in the project and another four for women. Imagine a project that extended beyond binary gender to include a multitude of gender categories, and beyond Black and white racial categories to include another multitude and, because we might expect it to affect job interview callbacks, a variety of levels of educational attainment as well. We might quickly be able to recognize the need for hundreds, or more, possible types of résumés and applicant-actors who would need to be part of such an experiment. The multiple group figure would include those hundreds of rows; there would be hundreds of treatment groups.

As interesting as this may sound as a method of understanding how the nuances of how gender, race, education, and a criminal record might combine to impact callbacks for job interviews, it is not practical to pursue as an audit study—nor would any research of this scale and scope be easily engaged via classical experimental methods. However, this is something survey methodology can attempt to approximate. Survey questionnaires can be administered to large populations with vast amounts of variation across large sample sizes. Each respondent can fit into one of the treatment groups—each would answer questions about gender, race, and the other factors in which we are interested along with a question about applying and being interviewed for jobs. A statistical analysis, such as a regression analysis, would enable scientists to assess these relationships and make claims about the probabilistic effects of the independent variables on the dependent one. For example, a researcher could study the effect of years of education on annual earnings, controlling for gender, by conducting a questionnaire survey that measured each of those three variables—independent, dependent, and control—for a large, representative sample of the population.

Large-scale surveys do not meet many of the guidelines of good experimentation—group assignments, history, maturation, double-blinding, and other strategies are not followed. But they can nonetheless be understood as quasi-experiments because they are comparing respondents who have different levels of the relevant independent and dependent variables that can be isolated via the use of control variables. And, in large-scale surveys, the entire set of respondents could be representative of the broader population. As such, this wouldn't be particularly effective at capturing necessary or sufficient causes, but would be excellent at making generalizable, probabilistic claims.

CONSIDER THIS. . .

There are methodological similarities among laboratory experiments, field experiments, and survey research. How do field experiments and surveys use the logic of treatment and control groups?

Check Your Understanding

1. What is a field experiment?
2. What are the advantages of a field experiment relative to a laboratory experiment?
3. What are the advantages of a laboratory experiment relative to a field experiment?
4. What are the advantages of a large-scale survey relative to a laboratory experiment?
5. What are the advantages of a laboratory experiment relative to a large-scale survey?

SOCIOLOGISTS IN ACTION

MARCUS HILL

Equitable Clinical Trial Recruitment

I serve as the grassroots recruitment specialist for a national clinical trial, studying ways older adults might be able to protect themselves from memory loss, Alzheimer's disease, and other dementias through adopting healthier lifestyles. This trial is recruiting 2,000 participants across five regions within the United States for a 2-year study. The healthy lifestyle intervention involves a prescription of healthy eating, exercise, socializing, health monitoring, and cognitive stimulation for individuals particularly at risk for cognitive decline. Study participants are older individuals (60–79 years in age), not regular exercisers, and not currently experiencing cognitive problems but have risk factors for future decline (family history of memory loss, or slightly high blood pressure, cholesterol, or blood sugar). This combination of high-risk, poor physical health, and functional cognitive health allows the trial to track the efficacy of the intervention (are people actually getting healthier via this prescription?) and the incidence of decline (are fewer people experiencing cognitive decline over this time period than would be expected without the intervention?).

Accessibility is essential to the success of this study, so it must ensure that participants have access to healthy food, places in their communities to work out, neighborhood spaces to meet with their teams for socializing, and so on. As such, it relies on a broad network of community partners to host workouts, team meetings, and lead the intervention. It is structured in this way—with attention to accessibility—because if the study proves successful and supports the hypothesis that healthy lifestyles can protect against cognitive decline later in life for those among us most at risk, the healthy lifestyle intervention needs to be a programmatic service than can exist in the community long after the study itself ends. As such, this trial is not merely a scientific excursion but intends to see real social change toward ending Alzheimer's and other dementias.

The other aspect of accessibility is the trial's intentional inclusion of nontraditional clinical trial participants. African Americans, for instance, are recruited at far lower percentages in dementia-related clinical trials than white participants even though they are two to three times more likely to develop Alzheimer's disease according to the Alzheimer's Association. In order for this study's findings to be relevant to the American population as a whole— particularly our community members with elevated risk—it is essential this trial be demographically representative of the U.S. population. This means a cohort composition of roughly 23% of participants from communities of color with an emphasis on communities with particularly elevated risk (Native American, Black/African American, and Hispanic/Latinx).

Much of my role has been developing our outreach strategy for these communities of interest consisting of the following: community presentations for potential participants and for community leaders and potential community-based advocates; shared, paid, and earned media outreach (including social medial and local news campaigns); assembling community advisory boards across our five regions consisting of community members that can inform outreach and provide feed-back; and participating in larger, collaborative community events with community partners (health fairs, etc.). This strategy includes metrics, progress tracking from grassroots outreach activity, regular coaching, training on cultural competency, humility, and trust-building, and infrastructure development for participant retention so we can better respond to daily realities for many of us like transportation needs and food access issues. This is all accomplished through working closely with our main study sponsor, our study Coordinating Center, each of our five regional sites, study team leadership, and the grassroots outreach team assembled at each site.

Marcus Hill has a bachelor's degree in sociology from Wake Forest University, a master's degree in public health from Yale University, and is broadly interested in studying and enabling participatory social systems.

Discussion Question

How might the described recruitment strategies improve general understanding of lifestyle inter-ventions as protections against memory loss and dementias?

CONCLUSION

Identifying causal relationships between independent and dependent variables is often a goal of socio-logical research. The nature of causality requires that researchers reflect on it as something that is far more often probabilistic, with various possible effect sizes, rather than being one of absolute determin-ism. Experimental designs for research become one possible strategy for identifying these relationships. The creation of a controlled environment wherein a specific treatment can be tested enables research-ers to isolate and measure its effect. This isolation is an aid in identifying causal relationships, but it can come at the cost of generalizability because it is so distinct from the complex realities of everyday life. The process of science, though, is rarely complete with a single research project and, so, the theo-ries that are developed from experiments often are further studied, and often refined and sometimes refuted, by research that is more generalizable, such as survey designs, or more embedded in the details of social systems, such as ethnographic methods.

REVIEW

1. **What is probabilistic causality? What are the components of causal relationships?**

     Probabilistic causality refers to the condition where an independent variable affects the likelihood or level of a dependent outcome. The components of causal relationships are temporal priority, correlation, mechanism, and nonspuriousness.

2. **What are the main features of treatment and control groups in experimental design?**

     Experimental design includes a set of participants assigned to either treatment or control groups using a double-blind procedure. Those in the treatment group receive the treatment being tested while those in the control group receive a placebo.

3. **What strategies do sociologists use to measure the effect of a treatment on an outcome?**

     The effect of the treatment is measured by comparing the difference in outcomes for the treatment and control groups.

4. **In what ways is experimental design good for determining causal relationships but potentially problematic for generalizability?**

     Classic experimental design isolates the effect of the treatment, the independent variable, from all other forces and enables a valid claim about its effect on the outcome. This same isolation and the typically small and nondiverse sample being studied can also limit the ability to generalize this observed effect to the broader population.

5. **How do sociologists use the ideas of treatment groups and control groups outside of laboratory settings?**

    Comparing outcomes among groups who receive different levels of an independent variable is a strategy incorporated into field experiments done outside of the laboratory. This is also a helpful way of understanding how survey research operates by comparing respondents' scores on variables in a quasi-experimental manner.

KEY TERMS

audit study (p. 130)

blinding (p. 126)

control group (p. 122)

correlation (p. 119)

double-blind (p. 127)

experiment (p. 121)

field experiment (p. 130)

history (p. 125)

mechanism (p. 119)

necessary conditions (p. 120)

nonspuriousness (p. 119)

placebo (p. 122)

placebo effect (p. 126)

probabilistic causality (p. 118)

recruitment (p. 123)

sufficient cause (p. 120)

temporal priority (p. 119)

treatment (p. 121)

treatment group (p. 122)

oor

DK/NA/RF

On a scale of 1 to 5 where
would you rate your leve

1   2   3   4
☐   ☐   ☐   ☐

On a scale of 1 to
would you rate y

SURVEYING THE SOCIAL LANDSCAPE

William J. Scarborough and Allyson L. Holbrook

8.1 What are the benefits of surveys? When and why should we use them? What types of errors can surveys produce?

8.2 How do you design survey questions that measure social phenomena in ways that minimize measurement error?

8.3 What are the advantages and disadvantages to each potential survey mode or combination of modes? How do you determine the best mode for a particular research question?

8.4 How do you identify a sampling frame and sampling approach that is best suited for the research question and population of interest?

8.5 What are some key considerations in survey implementation?

HOW I GOT ACTIVE IN SOCIOLOGY

WILLIAM J. SCARBOROUGH

My road to sociology began with a deep curiosity about the causes of social inequality. Why are women paid, on average, less than men? Why is racial residential segregation so common in American cities? Why is it harder for mothers to be hired for jobs than equally qualified fathers? Viewing these questions from a sociological perspective allowed me to adopt a lens by which to understand the dynamic factors reproducing systems of inequality and has given me the tools to further investigate them. Using survey data on gender attitudes, I've explored how changing views toward women's and men's family responsibilities has affected their respective opportunities in the labor force. Analyzing large-scale census data, I've examined how local economic conditions relate to gender wage gaps through influencing the types of opportunities women and men experience. Generating new knowledge through data analysis has allowed me to inform public discourse on these topics, providing key information that may be used to reduce social inequality. I publish my research in academic journals that advance scientific study, as well as public outlets (newspapers and magazines) so that my research may benefit individuals working outside of academia. Analyzing inequality from a sociological perspective enables me to provide a unique contribution to society that focuses on how structural aspects of society, meso-conditions of organizations, and individual-level preferences collectively influence social patterns in ways that may reproduce, or challenge, systems of inequality.

HOW I GOT ACTIVE IN SOCIOLOGY

ALLYSON L. HOLBROOK

My research and interests are interdisciplinary and include sociology, social psychology, political science, and survey methodology. As an undergraduate and graduate student, I studied political science and social psychology; my research examined how people form attitudes about political candidates and issues, and how those attitudes motivate (or don't motivate) action like voting or engaging in activism. During graduate school, I also developed an interest in survey methodology. As a professor, I teach people how to do better surveys. I also use surveys in my own work, and I study the social and cognitive processes involved in considering a survey request and in answering survey questions. One current interest of mine is connecting other sources of data (e.g., census data, crime statistics, etc.) with survey data. This has led to a number of collaborations with sociologists that focus on the interaction between individual-level factors (e.g., a person's demographic characteristics, beliefs, or attitudes) and contextual factors (e.g., the racial composition or crime level of the neighborhood in which they live).

Each day, social statistics can be found in news headlines across the world. From regular updates on unemployment rates to constant appraisals of the president's approval ratings, news media rely heavily on statistics to keep the public informed. But where do these numbers come from? And how do we know whether they can be trusted?

Every time you read a social statistic in the news or hear a numerical indicator about attitudes or behaviors on the radio, chances are these numbers were generated from a survey. The unemployment rate, which makes headlines every month when the Bureau of Labor Statistics releases regular jobs reports, is made possible by the Current Population Survey. The president's approval rating is generated through regular surveys performed by Gallup, and much of what we know about people's political orientations or attitudes about race and gender are compiled by ongoing social science surveys such as the American National Election Survey and the General Social Survey.

In this chapter, we explore the world of survey research as an invaluable social science tool that researchers use to make inferences on population trends, general attitudes, and associations between social phenomena. In many ways, survey research provides the information used in countless critical decisions. Political leaders' policy positions are shaped by the results of public opinion polls, business leaders make decisions according to the results of product surveys, and economic decisions are informed by data derived through ongoing population surveys. Surveys, however, are much more than generating questions and getting people to answer them. Methodologists help to ensure that surveys ask questions that can be understood and answered by the general public, represent key constructs of interest, and can be used to make inferences about a population based on a sample of that population. There is an extensive science behind these practices, represented by the field of survey methodology. In this chapter, we provide a broad overview of the key concepts and ideas from this field to illustrate how surveys work and why they are such a valuable tool in the social sciences. Importantly, we also differentiate good surveys from bad surveys. Those failing to follow the key principles of survey research produce misleading statistics that may cause damage when used to inform policies or decisions.

In each section, we provide multiple examples of questions used in established surveys. The activities located throughout the chapter will guide you through the development of our own survey. Although large, national-representative surveys can be quite cost-prohibitive, valuable information can still be obtained from surveys done on a smaller scale, and on a budget. As will be discussed throughout the chapter, even the largest surveys with the most resources have to balance survey costs with survey design. To introduce the basic principles of survey research, we'll walk through each step of the research process: from developing a research question that is suitable for surveys, constructing survey questions, specifying the population you wish to describe, establishing a sampling frame, selecting and recruiting from that frame, and fielding the survey.

WHY SHOULD WE USE SURVEYS?

Are surveys the right research tool for the questions you're asking? As you will learn in other chapters, qualitative research methods like ethnography and interviews are excellent tools to understand social processes, mechanisms, and personal motivation. But they do not inform us about how generalizable trends are across the population. This is where survey research comes in. The central purpose of surveys is to make *inferences to a broader population*. The term inference means to describe characteristics of a population using pieces of information from a carefully selected group of people. Survey research uses two primary tools to make inferences.

First, surveys reduce the complexity of social life into a shorter number of closed-ended, answerable questions. For example, researchers may ask respondents to rate their health as "excellent," "very good," "good," "fair," or "poor." It may take a respondent 30 seconds to answer this single item on a survey. This expedient design allows survey researchers to ask a much larger number of respondents than would be possible in ethnography or interviews. This benefit, however, does come at some expense. Survey methodologists make great efforts to ensure survey items measure exactly the phenomena in which they are interested (discussed later). Nonetheless, the need to reduce phenomena, such as attitudes or beliefs, into survey questions comes at the cost of complexity.

The second way that surveys are used to make generalizable inferences to a population pertains to the statistical process of sampling respondents who are representative of the general population. This topic is of central importance to the process of inference, and Chapter 5 is devoted to sampling. Nonetheless, we touch on this important aspect here because it is a critical component of survey research. We can create perfect survey items that provide excellent measures of social phenomena, but if we ask these questions to an unrepresentative group of respondents, the information we obtain is of little value in describing larger trends. As a result, survey methodologists undertake significant efforts to ensure the people they sample are representative.

In summary, there are two main components of survey research (Groves et al., 2009). Measurement refers to the process of capturing social phenomena through survey items and collecting this information from respondents. Here, the focus is on the construction of valid survey items and the modes of fielding the survey. Representation focuses on the process of selecting survey respondents who are representative of the broader population. This involves the definition of a population that is of interest for your research question, identifying a frame from which to sample that population, recruiting respondents in a systematic way, and using statistical techniques to improve the generalizability of estimates.

Developing Survey Research Questions

The first step to using surveys for social science is specifying research questions. Survey researchers need to have an idea of for what they are looking before they start collecting information. Research questions inform the design of survey questions and the sampling of respondents. Once a survey is fielded, it's often too late or too expensive to change questions and re-administer the survey to obtain further information. Thus, a strong research question is a critical first step for any study using surveys.

Research questions should contain two aspects corresponding to the strengths of surveys. First, research questions explore a particular social phenomenon. In survey research, the social phenomena motivating the study are known as constructs. Constructs are *what* the survey is designed to measure and can have varying levels of abstraction. Some, such as the unemployment rate, are relatively straightforward. Others, such as individuals' opinions about racial equity, can be more abstract and ambiguous. Constructs represent the social characteristic we are interested in measuring.

The second component of a research question specifies the target population we are describing. The target population is *who* will be answering the survey questions. If we're interested in the gender attitudes of college students, our research question should specify a focus on individuals enrolled in college. The Monitoring the Future Survey,

Students are sometimes the target population of surveys, such as the Monitoring the Future Survey, which focuses on high school students.

©iStockphoto.com/mediaphotos

for example, is an ongoing survey of high school students. Research using data from this survey ensures that inferences are limited to high school students, rather than the population at large. Specifying the population of study is a function of research motivation and is influenced by research constraints. Those without a large budget to pay for nationwide data collection may need to field their survey on a single university campus. In these instances, the population may be restricted to a single university.

Below are a number of example research questions that are well-suited for survey research:

- *What is the unemployment rate of the U.S. population?*

- *How do Chicago residents feel about racial equity in their city?*

- *Do students at the University of North Texas feel welcome on campus?*

Each research question specifies a population and a construct. At the most generalizable level, the first question seeks to make inferences about the U.S. population as a whole. Research questions around unemployment motivate the Current Population Survey administered by the Census Bureau and the Bureau of Labor Statistics. These entities have a large budget allowing for regular surveying of a representative sample of the U.S. population. The second research question pertains to racial attitudes among Chicago residents. The construct, racial attitudes, is much more abstract than rates of unemployment. Nonetheless, surveys are frequently used to measure these types of social phenomena. Even researchers with no research budget can develop questions that shed important insight on more local phenomena. Many colleges and universities regularly conduct climate surveys to investigate whether students, staff, and faculty feel welcome and supported on campus. These surveys provide critical insight for how schools can improve the services provided to students in aiding their educational advancement, while also ensuring all staff/faculty have positive work environments. Students and researchers interested in these issues can develop research questions focused on a local context.

DOING SOCIOLOGY 8.1

Writing a Survey Research Question and Clarifying Constructs

In this activity, you will develop a measure of a social construct.

1. Write a research question appropriate for surveys that generates information on a topic, social issue, or phenomenon in which you're interested.

2. Evaluate your construct of interest. Write a short description defining your construct of interest and address the following questions:

   - Could you make it more specific?
   - Could you add clarification?
   - Might there be multiple dimensions to the construct?

CONSIDER THIS. . .

When was the last time you completed a survey? What was its purpose? What would you say were the strengths and limitations of the survey?

SOCIOLOGISTS IN ACTION
THOMAS FILE

As a senior special assistant at the U.S. Census Bureau, my professional goal is to help inform the American people about themselves. I do this in multiple ways, all using surveys. In the beginning of my career at the U.S. Census Bureau, I helped manage the 2010 Census in New York City. This included collecting detailed social and demographic data from individuals residing in the largest metropolitan area in the U.S. After gaining first-hand experience collecting survey data on a large scale, I moved into my current role, where I now focus on analyzing survey results and reporting them to the public. I do this in two ways. First, I work on teams that help repackage survey data so that researchers, policy makers, and students can analyze census data and learn about their communities or topics of interest. This work involves making sure the data are accurate, but also involves creating tables, reports, and interactive data tools that provide key statistics from the U.S. Census for different enti-ties, such as cities, states, occupations, or certain demographic categories. Repackaging the data from individual survey responses to aggregated levels helps data users find the specific information they need, without having to go through individual survey-responses themselves.

The second part of my job entails communicating key survey results to the public. I create data visualizations illustrating interesting trends that emerge from the data we collect. Sometimes these products show the geographic dispersion of certain characteristics (such as language trends or technology use) across the U.S. In other instances, they illustrate how a characteristic we mea-sured in a survey (such as registering to vote) differs by demographic characteristics such as race, gender, or level of education. Coupled with these visualizations, I also write reports based on the results of surveys. Currently, I am working on a project examining the characteristics of voters in the U.S. based on data from the Current Population Survey (administered through the U.S. Census Bureau). I've written reports based on my analysis of these data to inform the public about who voted in previous elections, and have also worked to improve the way that we measure voter turn-out. Over my career, I've had my work cited by the Supreme Court, and have been quoted and cov-ered in national media outlets, including the Associated Press, the *New York Times*, CNN, CSPAN, and National Public Radio.

My favorite part of my job is communicating statistical survey results to nonstatistical audi-ences, showing the public why statistics matter, and helping them digest survey results. My degree in sociology gave me the methodological training I needed to collect, analyze, and interpret the results of survey data, affording me the opportunity to be a part of the important work at the U.S. Census Bureau.

Thomas File is a senior special assistant at the U.S. Census Bureau.

Discussion Questions

1. What sorts of research questions might you ask if you were using census data?
2. Envision yourself doing this type of work. What part of Thomas File's job would you like most?

The Total Survey Error (TSE) Approach

Once we've developed an appropriate research question (i.e., decided *who* and *what* we want to ask), the next step is designing and fielding the survey. The science of survey methodology focuses on ensur-ing that surveys measure what they intend to measure and that responses are representative of the population of study. Deviations from these ideals are referred to as error. In survey research, error is the difference between the true information we intend to collect (e.g., median household income in the population) and the actual information gathered (e.g., median income in the survey sample). Error can enter surveys at any stage, from the creation of survey items that are misinterpreted by respondents to the use of a sampling technique that unintentionally leaves out certain segments of the population.

In survey methodology, the total survey error (TSE) framework is an approach used by researchers to reduce error across all aspects of research (see Biemer et al., 2017; Groves & Lyberg, 2010). This framework outlines possible sources of error in surveys that will be covered in this chapter. We list key terms used to describe aspects of the TSE framework in Table 8.1 and discuss them in more detail. Adopting this framework, survey researchers consider how the decisions they make regarding measurement and representation influence error. By using TSE to identify sources of error, survey researchers can edit their approach to achieve greater accuracy in their findings.

Sometimes, however, the cost of reducing survey error is too large. Although collecting data from a nationwide random sample is the gold standard for obtaining a nationally representative sample, many researchers do not have the budget to employ the statisticians needed for sample selection, or the interviewers required to recruit respondents and field the survey. In these cases, researchers must think creatively about how they can reduce survey error while staying within their budget. Because all researchers operate with budgetary, time-related, and other constraints, there is always a balance between creating the ideal survey and reducing costs (Groves, 1989).

Check Your Understanding

1. What is the main goal of survey research? How is this goal achieved?
2. What sorts of questions are appropriate to survey research?
3. What are representation and measurement? How do they relate to survey questions?
4. What is the Total Survey Error (TSE) approach to surveys?

TABLE 8.1 ■ Total Survey Error (TSE) Framework	
Total Survey Error	A framework used by researchers to evaluate all aspects of surveys, from their design to data analysis and reporting of findings, to ensure that data are as accurate as possible. Error refers to the difference between the information obtained through surveys and the actual phenomenon under study. Surveys with low error closely capture their intended subject, while surveys with high error may intend to study a particular topic, but factors related to question wording, data collection, or limitations in data analysis reduce the accuracy of results.
Construct Validity	A concept describing how well survey questions measure the social phenomenon they are intended to measure.
Measurement Error	Error in survey responses caused by question wording or response options.
Processing Error	Error caused through mistakes made by respondents or interviewers in the collection of surveys, such as through checking the wrong response to a survey question or when multiple researchers inconsistently code survey responses.
Interviewer Effects	When responses to surveys are influenced by characteristics of interviewers. This may occur when respondents try to appeal to an interviewer who they assume will feel a certain way.
Coverage Error	When researchers use a list of individuals to draw a sample (a sampling frame), but that list does not include all relevant or eligible individuals; the survey is no longer representative.
Sampling Error	Error is always involved when a sample is used instead of the entire population of interest. Uncertainty stemming from the sample is usually described through a margin of error, providing an estimated range within which the true population estimates will fall.
Nonresponse Error	Error that occurs when not all selected respondents participate in the survey or answer all questions in a survey.

QUESTION DESIGN TO REDUCE MEASUREMENT ERROR

Measurement begins with defining the constructs of the research question. The process of defining constructs through survey items is known as operationalization. For some constructs, there is an established method of operationalization. The unemployment rate, for example, is defined as the percentage of the civilian labor force that is seeking work but has not obtained it. Measuring this construct, therefore, requires survey items that measure current employment status, civilian status, and, if not currently employed, whether the respondent is currently seeking work.

Other constructs are more abstract and require significant thought. Take, for example, a study on gender attitudes. Are we interested in a particular aspect of gender attitudes? Do they pertain to gender roles in heterosexual dating? Gendered expectations in the workplace? The division of labor in the family? If we are interested in broad gender attitudes, it may be important to include several questions measuring different components. But this would come at the expense of lengthening our survey, increasing its cost, and decreasing the likelihood that respondents will complete all the questions.

Considering these issues, it's best to be as specific as possible in defining constructs. Although we may start with a general interest in gender attitudes, thinking more deeply about it, we may discover that our true motivation is in understanding individuals' attitudes about the gendered division of family labor. Here, the construct "attitudes about the gendered division of family labor" is much more specific and, therefore, easier to measure in the next step. Construct validity is the extent to which a measure assesses what it is intended to measure. Poor construct validity is one source of error in survey estimates (see Chapter 6 for a more in-depth discussion of measurement).

As a general rule of thumb, a good starting point is to see how previous researchers have operationalized the construct in which you are interested. Gender attitudes, for example, have been studied extensively, and four items in the General Social Survey (GSS) are widely established measures of gender attitudes. If it is well-suited, using the four GSS items may be enough to achieve your research purposes. In addition to being fully established measures, the benefit of using survey questions from previous research is that it allows you to compare your results to those of previous work. Often, however, survey researchers wish to build from existing operationalizations to explore new facets of constructs. Other times, there are no existing ways to measure constructs of interest. In these frequent instances, researchers make significant efforts to generate survey questions that measure the construct in which they are interested. The design of questions and question wording is a major area where survey error can be introduced. Error that is introduced as part of the process of asking and answering survey questions is known as measurement error. The process of identifying and remedying sources of measurement error is critically important for survey researchers. Measurement error reduces the effectiveness of survey questions to gather information on the topics that interest you.

To identify sources of measurement error, survey methodologists consider the steps respondents take when answering a survey question. Much research has studied how people read questions, interpret their meanings, and offer responses. This body of literature has identified four basic steps people take when completing a survey item (see Tourangeau et al., 2000, for a review):

1. *Comprehension of the Question:* The first thing respondents do when completing a survey question is read the instructions (if applicable) and define the task required by the question.

2. *Retrieval of Information:* After comprehending the purpose of the question, respondents retrieve information from their memory in order to make a judgment on how to respond.

3. *Estimation and Judgment:* Respondents apply their memories to the survey question, assessing relevance and formulating a response.

4. *Reporting:* Respondents select a response option that best corresponds to their personal viewpoint or memory.

Considering these four steps of survey response in the construction of questions can help researchers identify measurement error that can be introduced when respondents interpret different meanings

Many adults have or have had credit card debt. Constructing a clear survey question can help ensure accurate responses about current or past debt.

©iStockphoto.com/kitzcorner

of survey questions (comprehension), have imperfect memory of previous events asked in a survey (recall), are influenced by a desire to give socially acceptable answers (estimation and judgment), or are given response options that do not correspond to their answers (reporting).

Refining a Survey Question: Measuring the Experience of Credit Card Debt

As an example of how we can use respondents' process of answering a survey question to improve the measurement of these questions, we'll go through the steps of designing a question intended to measure whether respondents have experienced credit card debt. Our research question could be something like, "How many people have ever experienced credit card debt?" To examine this research question, we could start with a relatively simple survey item:

In your adult life, have you ever had credit card debt?

- *Yes*

- *No*

While this question is short and directly related to the construct of interest (experience of credit card debt), there are at least two sources of error related to varying types of comprehension of the question. First, respondents may have different interpretations of "adult life." Some may consider this to be the age of 18 or older, others may think age 21 qualifies one as an adult, while some may believe adult life starts after the completion of education. Therefore, respondents' interpretation of the question may be in reference to varying points of their life. Another source of measurement error may refer to the definition of the construct "credit card debt." Some respondents may define credit card debt as the monthly balance they owe prior to their regular payments. Others may feel that credit card debt only occurs when they have missed a payment or when they are unable to pay the full balance. Thus, varying interpretations of the definition of "credit card debt" may influence responses to the question in ways that are unrelated to our research interests. Adjusting for these aspects, an alternative wording could be:

Since the age of 18, have you ever been unable to pay off your credit card balance at the time it was due?

- *Yes*

- *No*

In the course of answering this question, respondents will have to retrieve information from their memory. Error may be introduced to the survey if respondents have a difficult time remembering if they ever missed a credit card payment. One strategy used by survey researchers to aid respondents in the retrieval of memories is adding cues to survey questions. Cues are words that may trigger memories relevant to the question. In the case of credit card debt, it is possible that respondents were unable to pay their balance during a period of financial hardship. Therefore, inserting this type of cue may help increase response accuracy. Along with recalling memories, respondents engage in judgment of their responses. Here, they may be less likely to report that they have experienced credit card debt because this is seen as socially undesirable. The tendency for respondents to answer survey questions in ways that portray them in a positive light is known as social desirability bias and can have a negative impact on response accuracy. A strategy used to reduce social desirability bias is to frame questions in ways that make negative responses seem more common. Considering how respondents recall memories in order to answer survey questions and make judgments on how to respond, we can edit the original question to include a statement that may both cue relevant memories and reduce social desirability bias by making it seem more common to have credit card debt:

Many people experience financial hardship that makes it difficult to pay bills from time to time. Since the age of 18, have you ever been unable to pay off your credit card balance at the time it was due?

- *Yes*

- *No*

During recall and judgment, respondents have identified their position with respect to the survey question. Now they must report that decision onto one of the question's response options. This is the step where defining response options is of critical importance. Prior to fielding the survey, researchers must identify a limited number of ways respondents may answer the question. Most survey researchers prefer response options to be exhaustive—meaning that they cover all possible responses. Evaluating the response options to the survey question on credit card debt, we find that limiting responses to the dichotomous "yes," "no" options is not exhaustive because it does not account for respondents who have never owned a credit card. For these individuals, they may skip the question, leaving researchers unaware as to why they didn't answer, or they may choose the "no" option, but their reason for choosing "no" would be very different than those who make regular payments. Therefore, variation between question answers is due to both people's financial responsibility in paying off credit cards (the construct of interest) and their owning of a credit card (not pertaining to the construct and a source of error). To reduce this form of measurement error, we can include an additional question to avoid asking respondents a question that does not apply to them:

Since the age of 18, have you ever had a credit card in your name?

- *Yes*

- *No*

[IF YES] Many people experience financial hardship that makes it difficult to pay bills from time to time. Since the age of 18, have you ever been unable to pay off your credit card balance at the time it was due?

- *Yes*

- *No*

Although the questions above seem straightforward, measurement error can also be introduced if respondents are unable or unmotivated to carefully think about their answers. When this occurs, respondents may look for strategies to answer questions with little effort. Acquiescing, or agreeing with assertions, is one such strategy that can result in acquiescence response bias—or a bias toward agreeing with or saying yes to questions that are framed in this way. The questions above only ask about one possibility—having a credit card and not being able to pay off one's balance. To avoid acquiescence response bias, more balanced response options could be used:

Since the age of 18, have you ever had a credit card in your name or have you not had a credit card in your name?

- *I have had a credit card*

- *I have NOT had a credit card*

[IF YES] Many people experience financial hardship that makes it difficult to pay bills from time to time. Since the age of 18, have you ever been UNABLE to pay off your credit card balance at the time it was due, or have you NEVER been UNABLE to pay off your credit card balance at the time it was due?

- *Have been UNABLE to pay off credit card balance*
- *Have NEVER been UNABLE to pay off credit card balance*

There are, however, several instances where researchers may not want to use exhaustive categories. In the study of public opinion, survey researchers often use a forced response to make respondents express an opinion on a topic and removing an option for them to report "don't know" or "no opinion." This approach has the advantage of gaining information on "fence-sitters"—people who don't really feel one way or another—by identifying in which direction they lean. The disadvantage of forced response, however, is that it equates everyone's opinion as equal, even if they are unlikely to voice those opinions in public or, in the case of electoral politics, vote on them. Including a "don't know" or "no opinion" response option also gives respondents another strategy for answering a question with little effort. This is why it is generally a good idea, when possible, to omit explicit "don't know" or "no opinion" options from such questions and to follow a forced response question with a question measuring opinion intensity. Often, opinion intensity is measured with a question worded as "How strong is your opinion on this topic?" with response options "Extremely strong," "Very strong," "Somewhat strong," "Not very strong," and "Not at all strong."

DOING SOCIOLOGY 8.2

Writing and Evaluating Survey Questions

In this activity, you will write and evaluate a survey question.

In the course of developing survey questions, methodologists often conduct interviews where they ask respondents to complete a survey question and then follow-up with a number of questions about how the respondent interpreted the meaning of the question, the response options, and the process by which they went about answering the question.

1. Write a *survey question* that collects information on a topic you are interested in.

2. Evaluate your research question by following the four steps respondents usually take when answering a survey question.

3. After evaluating your survey question, write a short paragraph assessing the design of the survey question. What worked well? In what ways might measurement error be introduced based on question wording?

4. Use the information obtained in question evaluation to edit your survey item in ways that reduce measurement error by ensuring it is interpreted the same way across respondents and collects the intended information. What changes did you make, and why were these changes potentially important?

Additional Sources of Measurement Error

There are two additional sources of measurement error with which survey researchers are generally concerned. The first has to do with respondent satisficing—the tendency for some respondents to go through the process of answering questions quickly and with minimal effort in order to finish a survey as fast as possible (Krosnick, 1991). Respondents who satisfice may not read the full question or all of the response options, and their answers may not be very thoughtful or accurate. Acquiescence response bias is one strategy survey respondents use to satisfice when asked yes–no or agree–disagree questions. Selecting an explicitly offered "no opinion" or "don't know" response option is another such strategy.

In contrast to satisficers, optimizers are respondents who read each question thoroughly, deeply consider their answers, and do their best to provide the most accurate responses possible.

In general, a sample will have both optimizers and satisficers, and their different answering style can artificially amplify differences between groups in the construct you're trying to measure. In other words, statistical differences observed in their answers to survey items may be due to the varying levels of effort they put into answering the question, rather than actual differences in the construct of interest.

Satisficers pose a challenge for survey researchers, and many strategies have been suggested to account for these respondents. One approach is to design a survey so as to remove the opportunity for common strategies used by satisficers (e.g., avoiding yes–no and agree–disagree questions; omitting explicit no opinion or don't know response options). Another way to do so is to avoid the use of long batteries of items that use the same response options. Using the same response options in the same order for multiple questions can help respondents move through the survey efficiently. A related strategy is to use question matrices, such as those illustrated in Figure 8.1. Question matrices can be helpful when measuring respondents' opinions on social/political topics, as topics can be listed alongside indicators for levels of agreement. However, it is best to limit the number of items in a matrix or the number of items in a row that use the same response options, because nondifferentiation—defined as using a single response option or a small range of response options—is another strategy used by satisficers and may introduce measurement error.

CONSIDER THIS. . .

Some surveys do not follow the scientific standards described in this chapter but, nonetheless, pretend to produce important information. How can we differentiate good surveys from bad ones?

A second strategy for dealing with satisficers is identifying and removing them from the survey or analysis. New technology used in Web surveys allows researchers to time how long respondents take on each question or how long it took for respondents to complete the entire survey. If a respondent finishes a 10-minute survey in less than 2 minutes, chances are they were satisficing. This may warrant their removal from survey analysis. Another way to identify extreme satisficers is to include "check" questions in the survey. These are questions designed to identify respondents who are not reading question directions. For example, a check question may read, "In this question, please select the fourth response option below." There is a clear answer to this question, and respondents who answer incorrectly are highly likely to be those who are not reading questions and giving invalid responses across the survey.

Another source of measurement error pertains to the construction of survey items that unintentionally include more than one construct. These types of items are known as double-barreled questions. The following survey question is an example of a double-barreled question:

FIGURE 8.1 ■ Example of Question Matrix

Please indicate your satisfaction with the following aspects of your experience in our restaurant.					
	Very satisfied	Somewhat satisfied	Neither satisfied nor dissatisfied	Somewhat dissatisfied	Very dissatisfied
Your interaction with the servers	○	○	○	○	○
Your wait time in receiving your meal	○	○	○	○	○
The quality of the food you ordered	○	○	○	○	○

Do you support the increased funding of public schools through raising property taxes?

- Yes

- No

This question poses a problem for respondents who believe school funding should be increased, but not through property taxes. There are, essentially, two questions being asked here: (1) Do respondents support increased school funding? and (2) Should school funding come from property taxes? By including them in the same survey item, we are unable to know whether answers are based on respondents' feelings about school funding (the first part) or property taxes (the second part). Hence, the term *double-barreled*. When evaluating survey items, it is crucial that each question pertain to a single construct. Editing the question above, we can turn it into two survey items:

1. *Do you support or oppose increased school funding?*

2. *[IF SUPPORT] Should increased school funding come from property taxes or from some other source?*

A final source of error that is introduced in the survey data collection process is processing error. This occurs when an error is made when the survey answer is recorded by the respondent or interviewer. Processing error can also occur when data are entered from paper-and-pencil questionnaires into an electronic format.

> ### Check Your Understanding
>
> 1. What are the four cognitive steps respondents usually take when answering survey questions?
> 2. Identify at least four sources of measurement error.
> 3. What strategies are available for reducing these forms of error?

MODES OF DATA COLLECTION

In conjunction with the design of survey questions, researchers also consider the best way to administer the survey to respondents. There are several modes of data collection, the major ones being: face-to-face interviews/computer-assisted personal interviews (CAPI), computer-assisted telephone interviews (CATI), mailed surveys, and Internet surveys. Each mode has different strengths and limitations. The limitations of each mode pertain to the introduction of error—the difference between what we intend to measure and what we actually measure. Survey errors arising from the mode of data collection are called mode effects. There is no "best" survey mode. Instead, the mode of data collection should fit the needs of the research question and the topics of the survey.t

Face-to-Face Structured Interviews

Face-to-face structured interviews occur when trained interviewers approach potential respondents for participation in a survey. Respondents who agree to participate receive the survey via the interviewer who reads each question and response options and records the answer. Today, many face-to-face interviews are administered with a computer, where the interviewer will use computer software that aids in reading questions and recording responses. This specific form of data collection is called computer-assisted personal interviewing (CAPI).

Face-to-face structured interviews have the highest rates of participation across all survey modes. People are much less likely to decline survey participation when asked by a person than when asked through mail, over the phone, or online. High rates of survey participation reduce unit nonresponse error—survey error that occurs when survey respondents are different from the general population (assuming that some form of random sampling has been used). Thus, face-to-face interviews excel at reducing this form of error. Therefore, they are ideal for collecting information on topics that people may be less excited about, such as population demographics or health care. Other topics, such as local politics or schools, garner much interest among the general public and have a less difficult time in recruitment.

Another strength of face-to-face structured interviews is that they have very low rates of item nonresponse error—survey error that occurs when respondents skip questions in the survey. By virtue of having each question administered by an interviewer, respondents cannot skip items in the survey. Interviewers are also trained to encourage respondents to give legitimate responses to each survey question. In other words, respondents might initially report that they don't feel one way or the other about a political issue—to which an interviewer may ask, "If you had to choose, would you say you agree or disagree with this stance?"

Face-to-face structured interviews are more susceptible to social desirability bias, since respondents may be less likely to disclose sensitive information or unpopular viewpoints to interviewers than they would in an online or mail-in format. This may bias survey results toward more acceptable answers. One way to avoid this issue is for interviewers to give respondents their computers to fill out sections of the survey that are more vulnerable to social desirability bias.

Surveys using face-to-face structured interviews often employ multiple interviewers to conduct surveys. Differences between interviewers in personal characteristics or style of conducting the interview can create variation between survey responses that is due to the interviewer, rather than the constructs of interest pertaining to the respondents. This form of survey error is known as interviewer effects. Providing extensive training to interviewers can decrease these sources of error by ensuring that all survey questions are asked in the same way and that interviewers respond in the same manner to respondent questions. Through no fault of interviewers, however, certain characteristics of interviewers can affect how respondents answer survey questions. For instance, white respondents may be more likely to report that they support policies like affirmative action if they are interviewed by a Black survey-taker who they assume would be in favor of such policies. Research has also found that the gender of survey-takers can influence survey responses, with both women and men expressing more support for equal gender roles when interviewed by women (Kane & Macaulay, 1993). To account for this form of error, researchers can record interviewer characteristics for each survey and statistically control for these effects in post-survey analysis.

Computer-Assisted Telephone Interviews (CATI)

In another common survey mode, respondents are contacted via telephone and asked to participate in a survey. Those agreeing to participate are interviewed over the phone. The interviewer is often assisted by a computer program providing them with the survey question and response options and allowing them to input responses (known as computer-assisted telephone interviewing [CATI]).

This survey mode shares many of the strengths of face-to-face interviews while avoiding the cost of site transportation. Interviewers may ensure low item nonresponse error by encouraging respondents to complete all survey questions. Interviewers are also trained to answer any clarifying questions that may come up during survey questions to ensure they are measuring the intended construct. As a strength when compared to face-to-face interviews, CATI are less susceptible to social desirability and interviewer effects as respondents cannot physically

CATI allows interviewers to more easily conduct surveys from a distance, bearing many of the same results as face-to-face interviews.

©vm/Getty Images

see the interviewers and may, therefore, be less inclined to portray themselves in an overly positive light. Yet some research has shown that interviewer effects can still play a role as the gender, and sometimes the race, of the interviewer are assumed by respondents.

Historically, the drawback of telephone surveys was that they did not include segments of the population that did not own phone lines. This concern has decreased in recent years, now that nearly the entire population owns either a landline or a cell phone. Furthermore, enhanced sampling techniques allow researchers to create sampling frames that include both landlines and cell phone lines—accounting for the fact that these different forms of telephones may correspond to important variation between respondents. Instead of population coverage, the major concern with CATI surveys is low response rates. The proliferation of spam and sales calls means that many surveys contacting respondents over the phone will be inadvertently blocked by filters on phones or avoided by respondents who assume an unknown caller is spam. This increases the likelihood that respondents participating in the survey are different from the general population—unit nonresponse error.

Mailed Survey

Traditionally, one of the most common modes of survey administration is the mailed survey. Researchers would randomly select a sample of postal addresses from a sampling frame and send a paper-based survey to the address with prepaid postage that respondents could use to return the completed survey. This form of survey mode provides the most extensive coverage of respondents since nearly all of the population has an address. Another strength of this mode is that it avoids any survey error associated with interviewer effects, since all respondents will receive the same paper-copy of the survey.

Like telephone surveys, however, mail surveys suffer from high levels of nonresponse. Mailed surveys are very easy to ignore, since there is no person (face-to-face or on the phone) to decline—the respondent need only throw the survey away. Incentives may help mitigate low response rates, as respondents mailing in a completed survey could be entered to win a prize in a raffle, or could be sent a gift card for a major retailer.

Mail surveys benefit from increased standardization across respondents due to the absence of interviewers, but may also have the consequence of decreasing response accuracy as respondents are not able to ask clarifying questions. Mail surveys are also more susceptible to satisficing and item nonresponse error where respondents complete the survey as quickly as possible or skip items in the survey, respectively.

Web Surveys

Web surveys are the fastest-growing field of survey methodology (Tourangeau et al., 2013). The proliferation of the Internet and the ease of research software in designing, administering, and cataloging survey data have made this mode of data collection the most popular. In some respects, Web surveys have revolutionized survey methodology by offering a new suite of capabilities and reach. Yet the proliferation of Web surveys by those who are not engaged in the science of survey methodology or who wish to generate data to serve personal interests, rather than to create valid information, pose serious problems not just to the legitimacy of this survey mode, but to the field of survey research more broadly. We discuss these problematic uses of surveys later in this chapter.

Web surveys have many advantages. They are inexpensive and easy to design and conduct. They allow survey respondents to answer questions at their own pace and to complete the survey in more than one sitting, if necessary. They also allow for visual presentation of complex stimuli (e.g., pictures of faces or videos), which can be

Web-based surveys are popular for several reasons, such as their ease of dissemination and low cost of creation. Have you ever completed a Web survey?

useful for studying many social topics (e.g., examining the effect of skin tone on perceptions and evaluations of people from different racial or ethnic groups).

On the other hand, it can be difficult to conduct Web surveys with some populations. They require literacy (unlike interviewer-administered surveys) and Internet access. Thus, they may exclude members of already marginalized groups (e.g., low-income or low-education) from participating. It is also difficult to conduct a Web survey with a representative sample of many populations (e.g., American adults) because there is no national registry of email addresses, nor is there a one-to-one association between individuals and email addresses. Web surveys are therefore ideal for closed populations where email addresses can be obtained (e.g., employees at a specific organization or students at a specific university).

In order to conduct Web surveys with larger, more general populations, a number of organizations have constructed standing panels of individuals to participate in surveys. These fit into three broad categories. The best and most expensive of these recruit panel members using probability sampling (see section below on sampling) methods to ensure a representative sample of the adult population (e.g., GfK's KnowledgePanel and NORC's Amerispeak Panel). New panel members are constantly being recruited and participants are typically sent a small number of surveys. In these cases, respondents are usually recruited via initial telephone or face-to-face contact, and households without access are sometimes provided with Internet access to ensure representativeness. The rigorousness of this approach is most important when a goal of the survey is to *describe* the population (e.g., 45% of American adults disapprove of the job the president is doing).

Other organizations recruit panel members through more opportunistic means such as ads on webpages or volunteers (e.g., SSI, Harris Interactive). These organizations send a survey to a sample of panel members who look like the population of interest on key demographic characteristics (measured when they join the panel). This approach is less rigorous than the first approach described above, but also less expensive.

Finally, there are organizations that recruit individuals to participate in surveys as a form of employment (e.g., Amazon's Mechanical Turk). These organizations post opportunities to participate in a survey and respondents (or "workers") self-select into participating. These surveys are the least rigorous in terms of being representative of a population of interest, but the least expensive to complete. Web surveys that are completed using these kinds of panels are not good for describing a target population, but they are well-suited to conduct experiments (see Chapter 7) and for collecting preliminary or exploratory data.

Multimodal Surveys

In some cases, a survey might be conducted in more than one mode. This might happen in a number of different configurations and is typically done to minimize cost and potential sources of error. Different contact information might be available for different potential respondents (e.g., telephone numbers versus email addresses). Respondents may be given the opportunity to participate in different modes either as an initial choice (e.g., telephone or face to face) or in follow-ups with those who do not initially participate (e.g., respondents who do not participate in response to an initial invitation for a mail survey might be contacted via telephone). Respondents may initially be contacted in one mode but asked to complete the survey in another (e.g., a letter inviting respondents to participate in a Web survey). Alternatively, respondents in a longitudinal survey that is done multiple times over a period of time may be asked to initially participate in a survey in one mode (e.g., face to face) and then asked to complete subsequent surveys via a different, less expensive mode (e.g., Web or telephone).

Advancements in technology and changes in how humans communicate with one another are constantly changing the mode options for conducting surveys. For example, options to conduct surveys via SMS or a video conferencing platform like Skype or Zoom or using bots or artificial intelligence applications are all being explored. Similarly, the way Web surveys are presented and constructed has changed as more individuals are completing them via mobile devices rather than laptop or desktop computers. The potential of existing modes has also changed over time as people's use of technology has changed (e.g., telephone surveys conducted via landlines are increasingly less useful as many people now rely exclusively on cell phones).

CONSIDER THIS. . .

Given the myriad forms of digital communication available today, do you think it's easier to conduct surveys now than in the past? What are some new challenges that survey researchers face in administering surveys with contemporary forms of communication?

Weighing the Costs and Benefits of Survey Modes

There is no "best" mode for conducting surveys—only the one that ideally fits the purposes of your study. In determining this fit, it's important to do your best to minimize survey error while also staying within your budget. Is your research question focused on rural populations that have less access to the Internet? If so, choosing a Web survey mode may introduce a problematic degree of unit nonresponse error. Do you have the budget to hire and train interviewers? If so, what's your timeline for the study? Do you need data to be collected immediately? If this is the case, face-to-face interviews may not be ideal since they take longer, while CATI surveys can be completed faster. What if you have a low budget, or no money at all? If you have time and require a small sample, you could conduct face-to-face interviews on your own. If your population of interest is well-represented online, and if you have chosen a creative sampling technique (such as emailing a listserv), Web surveys can be a cheap and effective way to administer surveys. There are several websites that allow you to build surveys and administer them via a sharable link (e.g., surveys.google.com or Survey Monkey) for no cost whatsoever. Using these free resources, it is possible for creative researchers to conduct surveys with no budget at all. Yet it is important to be forthcoming about the limitations inherent in whatever mode you decide to use.

DOING SOCIOLOGY 8.3

Selecting the Right Mode

In this activity, you will weigh the different strengths of various modes for collecting survey data.

1. Write a research question that you could answer with surveys. This could be a topic related to individuals' attitudes, perceptions, behaviors, or well-being.

2. Considering your research question and the population it involves, what mode of survey administration would be best suited for collecting information?

3. Imagine you have a large budget and can afford any mode of data collection; which would you choose?

4. Which mode would you choose if you had no budget? In the case of having no budget, what are some creative strategies you might use to administer your survey?

Check Your Understanding

1. What are the basic modes of survey administration and their strengths and weaknesses?
2. How can you determine the best type of survey for your research question and research goals?

SAMPLING AND RECRUITMENT

Once you have decided who the target population for your research is, you need to determine how you're going to identify and contact members of that population. This is called sampling. There are two broad categories of sampling approaches: probability sampling and nonprobability sampling.

In probability sampling approaches, every member in the target population has a *known and non-zero probability of being selected* for the survey. Probability sampling techniques start by obtaining or constructing a sampling frame, or a list of all members of the population and any information available about them. For example, one might obtain a list of the names and email addresses of students at a university where a climate survey is going to be conducted. One might obtain a list of organizations with nonprofit tax status in order to conduct a survey of nonprofits.

If a frame is not available, you may have to construct one. For example, if you are interested in conducting a survey with women faculty members employed in STEM disciplines in the United States, you could construct a sample frame by compiling a list of such individuals from university websites. Coverage error affects survey estimates when the sample frame excludes some of the target population. For example, a sample frame of U.S. residential addresses excludes the homeless, people who are incarcerated, and those in other institutional living situations (e.g., college students living in dorms).

Once a sampling frame has been obtained or constructed, a sample is then selected from the sampling frame. The size of this sample is determined by the goal for the final survey sample size and best estimates of the response rate (or the percentage of eligible cases who are contacted who participate). For example, if conducting a climate survey with university students, you might invite 1,000 randomly selected students (from a sample frame of approximately 20,000) to participate if your goal is 500 completed surveys and you believe 50% of those who are contacted will participate.

Although samples from a target population can be used to efficiently draw inferences about the population (e.g., political surveys of 1,000–1,500 individuals are often used to make statements about "American adults"), there is error introduced into survey estimates whenever a sample (and not the entire population) is surveyed. This is called sampling error. Unlike some other sources of error, sampling error for probability samples can be estimated. When surveys, particularly political or preelection surveys, are reported in the media, sampling error is captured as the margin of error (see https://www.pewresearch.org/fact-tank/2016/09/08/understanding-the-margin-of-error-in-election-polls/).

Probability sampling techniques include simple random sampling, cluster or stratified sampling, and systematic sampling (see Chapter 5 for a more in-depth discussion of these approaches). Probability sampling techniques help to ensure that the sample is representative of (i.e., looks like) the target population. This is particularly important when you want to describe the target population.

Nonprobability sampling techniques are those where the probability that a particular individual or case (e.g., in surveys of organizations) is not known. Nonprobability sampling techniques include convenience sampling and snowball sampling (see Chapter 5). Sampling error cannot be estimated for nonprobability samples (although see Baker et al., 2016, for recent developments on this topic). Nonprobability sampling techniques are often used when probability sampling is impossible, impractical, or too expensive, or when the goal of the research is exploratory. For example, nonprobability sampling techniques are often used to find relatively rare or hard-to-identify populations (e.g., political extremists, members of the LGBTQ+ community).

One of the biggest challenges facing survey researchers today is lack of participation in surveys. Rates of survey participation have been declining for decades. This is important because it increases the costs associated with surveys and makes them more challenging to conduct. It also threatens the ability of surveys to describe a target population. It is common for different types of population members to participate at different rates, and that can introduce nonresponse bias. For example, consider conducting a survey about gender attitudes. You identify and contact 500 potential respondents from a population that is 50% women and 50% men—so 250 of those you sample are women and 250 are men. Forty percent (a total of 200) of these 500 participate. If 100 of these are women and 100 are men, your sample looks like the population. Although you have nonresponse (i.e., not everyone participated), you don't appear to have nonresponse *bias* on the dimension of gender. However, if of the 200 who

Nonprobability sampling techniques help researchers to find individuals who are members of hard-to-identify populations.

©iStockphoto.com/VioletaStoimenova

participated, 150 are women and 50 are men, your estimates of gender attitudes are more likely to be affected by nonresponse bias.

CONSIDER THIS...

What do you think are the reasons why people do not participate in surveys as much anymore? What sociological theories or findings (e.g., about civic engagement or social capital) might be helpful in explaining this reduction?

Designing a survey also involves decisions about strategies or techniques for increasing successful contact of potential respondents and gaining their cooperation. In interviewer-administered surveys, interviewers are trained in how to present themselves professionally and to address concerns respondents might have about participating. In mailed or Web surveys, materials are developed to communicate the importance and legitimacy of the survey. In all modes, multiple contact attempts can also be used to increase participation, and incentives (either prepaid incentives sent with the survey request or promised incentives given to respondents once they've completed the survey) can also be used to increase participation. All of these strategies can increase participation, but typically also increase the cost of the survey—either the length of time needed to complete the survey or the monetary cost.

DOING SOCIOLOGY 8.4

Recruiting for Your Survey

In this activity, you will consider the different strengths and limitations of recruitment strategies.

Consider that you are conducting a survey study on college students' sense-of-belonging at your university.

1. What would be a suitable sampling technique for your survey? Identify both the sampling frame from which to draw as well as a method for selecting/recruiting participants from that sampling frame.
2. What are the strengths and weaknesses of your approach?
3. After selecting a sampling frame and recruitment strategy, what steps would you take in survey implementation to reduce sources of error such as interviewer effects or processing errors?

Check Your Understanding

1. What role does a sampling frame play in survey implementation?
2. How can coverage error in the sampling frame bias the results from surveys?
3. What are some ways to increase participation in a survey?
4. Under what conditions would nonprobability sampling be appropriate?

SURVEY IMPLEMENTATION

You've carefully identified a sampling frame, recruited respondents from a selected subset of the sampling frame, and successfully recruited a number of them to participate in your survey. The next step is collecting data from respondents through fielding the survey. In face-to-face or CATI interviews, interviewers will be in charge of reading questions and recording the answers of respondents. In mail or Web surveys, tools (websites or mailing-packages) will be used to record information. In either case, it is crucial that data be collected in a standardized way across respondents so that variation in survey responses is due to differences in the phenomena of interest and not to the way the question was asked.

As noted earlier, both face-to-face and CATI mode surveys are susceptible to interviewer effects where responses may be affected by the presence of an interviewer. Identifying the potential sources of interviewer effects and mitigating their impact can help reduce the role of these biases. Perhaps the most consequential source of interviewer effects occurs through differences in how interviewers read survey questions or answer queries from survey respondents. Differences between interviewers in voice inflections during the reading of survey questions, for example, may influence which responses respondents feel are most desirable. Oftentimes during a survey, respondents will ask interviewers questions to clarify survey items. Differences in how interviewers respond to these questions can introduce bias to the survey, since they deviate from respondents' own perceptions and are shaped, instead, by differences in how the question is interpreted.

Interviewer training is the best way to reduce these sources of bias. At a minimum, a training will go through each survey question to instruct interviewers on how the question is to be read. During trainings, interviewers are also instructed on how to respond to potential questions from respondents so that they are able to reply in the same way. The most obvious respondent questions are often intentionally prepared for. For less expected questions, interviewers are often instructed to respond with a standardized answer, such as, "You may answer the question in whatever way you interpret its meaning."

Other sources of interviewer effects are due to characteristics beyond the control of researchers, such as interviewers' race or gender. For example, research has unsurprisingly found that respondents are less likely to report anti-Black racial attitudes to a Black interviewer than a white interviewer (Schaeffer, 1980). No amount of interviewer training may reduce this effect. Instead, some researchers plan to match the characteristics (such as race or gender) of interviewers and respondents, with the idea that answers will be more truthful, particularly when surveys include potentially sensitive topics around race or gender attitudes. Another common approach is to record interviewers' characteristics for each survey respondent. This allows for the estimation of interviewer effects during data analysis, ensuring that results are adjusted to account for the potentially confounding effects of interviewer characteristics.

Although Web and mail surveys do not require the training of interviewers, they come with another host of considerations. For Web surveys, the use of different types of online devices can introduce error when survey questions look differently when answered on a phone versus a tablet versus a computer. Web surveys designed on a computer, for example, may unintentionally omit response options when completed on a mobile device. Such occurrence introduces error to surveys, since responses may be due to the format of the survey item rather than the phenomenon in question. To account for this aspect, researchers ensure that Web surveys are properly formatted for multiple devices. Additionally, researchers may record the device on which the survey is completed in order to estimate and account for biases results from variation in devices.

Another issue specific to Web surveys is ballot-stuffing, where a single respondent will complete multiple surveys. This is more likely when the survey offers incentives. Some online survey builders (such as Qualtrics) record device IP addresses to prevent ballot-stuffing, yet this doesn't prevent respondents from completing the survey multiple times from different devices. The best method for avoiding this potential source of error is to assign unique usernames and/or passwords to respondents or, if invitations are emailed, a unique link to the survey that can only be used once.

DOING SOCIOLOGY 8.5

Managing Interviewer and Design Effects

In this activity, you will consider the different interviewer and design decisions made in the course of designing a survey study.

Consider three different types of survey studies:

- Research on illicit drug use
- Family research on children's recreational activities
- Political research on attitude toward controversial topics

Answer the following questions with each of the three studies in mind:

1. How might each study be more or less susceptible to interviewer or design effects?

2. What strategies could you adopt to reduce these types of error?

Across modes, fielding a survey also requires sample management. This involves tracking the status of each selected case for two primary purposes. First, it allows efficient and sensible use of recontact attempts to focus only on cases where a completed survey has not yet been obtained (e.g., you wouldn't want to have telephone interviewers call numbers where someone had already been interviewed or send reminder emails to those who've already completed a Web survey). A second reason for tracking the status of cases is that it allows you to assign a final disposition code to all cases and to estimate the response rate for the study (AAPOR, 2016). The response rate is the proportion of eligible cases that resulted in completed surveys. It is estimated in slightly different ways for surveys in different modes, but is considered an important indicator of the quality and rigor of a survey as well as an indicator of the potential for nonresponse bias (i.e., error introduced by differences between the survey sample and the population).

After receiving answers to survey questions, researchers then process these responses so that they can be analyzed. For many questions, this is as simple as assigning a predefined numeric code to each response option and putting together a codebook matching codes to definitions. Some questions, however, require more data management. Open-ended questions where interviewers record respondents' statements on an issue or respondents type a response (usually one or two sentences) into an open-ended online survey item, are often coded by research staff into categories or assigned values. Processing error occurs when research staff assign similar responses different codes. For example, a survey may ask respondents their occupation with an open-ended question. One respondent may reply that they are a student while also working as a research assistant at the university. Processing error in coding this response may arise if one research staff member were to record this respondent's occupation as "student," while another would code it as "research assistant." Extensive training on how to deal with responses can reduce this source of bias. Additionally, having multiple research staff code these types of questions can help identify disagreements in classification that need to be addressed.

From collecting data in the survey to processing it into usable code, the most important thing to remember when implementing a survey is that survey items should be standardized in both how they are asked and how they are recorded. Whether through the way it was worded by an interviewer, presented on a website, or input on a spreadsheet, consistency between respondents and their answers is crucial to ensuring the survey is collecting information purely on the phenomenon of interest and not aspects of how the data were collected. Once all the important steps have been taken to obtain information with the least amount of error, researchers then turn to data analysis to uncover themes and investigate their original research questions.

Identifying Bad Surveys and Nonsurveys

One challenge to conducting surveys (and to getting people to participate in them) is that there are many instances when something that is called a survey is actually not a survey. Although these practices are condemned by professional survey organizations and researchers, in many cases they persist. One example is SUGGING, or Selling Under the Guise of conducting a survey. This is when survey respondents are contacted not with the goal of collecting data, but with the goal of selling a product or service. Similarly, FRUGGING is Fund-raising Under the Guise of conducting a survey. Here, organizations connect fund-raising efforts with a "survey."

One last example would be "push polls" that are often conducted by political campaigns and candidates. Push polls are surveys that are designed to change public opinion rather than to measure it. For example, a push poll conducted by one political candidate might call to conduct a "survey" that actually is designed to provide respondents with harmful information about their opponent. Push polls are designed to contact a large number of people, and meaningful data are not collected from respondents.

"Push polls" are distinct from message testing often done by campaigns to test their messages with small numbers of people. The former is considered an unethical practice because it involves using surveys to influence the outcome of an election, whereas the latter is an acceptable practice.

Other surveys are designed to collect data, but do so with little rigor or focus on data quality. Examples of these include entertainment surveys and other opt-in surveys. Entertainment surveys are often conducted by news organizations. Viewers or readers of a particular news outlet are invited to participate in a survey or sometimes just answer a single question. Opt-in surveys are similar in that people are invited to participate through flyers, advertisements, word-of-mouth, or some other platform like Twitter. In both entertainment and other opt-in surveys, little effort is put into getting responses from a representative sample of a target population, and access is not restricted to sampled participants. As such, the same person could participate more than once, and it is difficult to draw meaningful conclusions from the findings.

Political campaigns, such as those in support of candidates running for president (like Donald Trump, seen here), often utilize push polls to influence voters. Have you ever come across such a "survey"?

© Visions of America, LLC/Alamy Stock Photo

For example, if I want to conduct a survey about city residents' satisfaction with the local government of City X, I might conduct an opt-in survey by posting flyers inviting participation in my Web survey by providing a website for interested respondents to visit to participate in the survey with a $5 incentive for doing so. I stop the survey after 100 completed surveys. In this scenario, I cannot ensure that the 100 surveys are from people who live in City X or that they're even from 100 separate people. The sample may also be biased toward unhappy residents who see this as an opportunity to express why they're unhappy with the government of City X. As such, this survey doesn't allow me to say very much about how satisfied residents are.

CONSIDER THIS...

Have you ever experienced a push poll, SUGGING, or FRUGGING? If so, what do you believe were the pollsters' actual intentions?

Check Your Understanding

1. What are interviewer effects? Provide at least two examples.
2. Why is it important to track the status of each selected case that has been recruited and interviewed for the survey?
3. What are some examples of push polls, SUGGING, and FRUGGING?
4. What effect do push polls, SUGGING, and FRUGGING have on survey research?

CONCLUSION

Surveys play a central role in our understanding of the world around us. Information from surveys is featured daily in the media, used to make consequential decisions at all levels of government, and inform our perceptions of the political climate. In this chapter, we've reviewed key aspects of survey methodology to highlight how surveys function to inform nearly all aspects of society. With this knowledge, you can evaluate the presentation of data in the media to decipher whether it is produced from a well-implemented survey and can be trusted, or if it suffers from numerous forms of error that undermine its usefulness. You may also become a producer of knowledge yourself through designing and implementing surveys to collect information on topics that have not yet been studied, but about which you feel passionate. To begin, it may be advantageous to start locally—asking questions about your school and community. Using surveys to collect information on these nearby and easy-to-reach populations could be an effective way to produce data that inform public policy and improve social life.

REVIEW QUESTIONS

1. **What are the benefits of surveys? When and why should we use them? What types of errors do surveys produce?**

   Surveys are intended to make inferences about a broader population. By collecting information from a large, representative number of people, surveys describe generalizable social trends and relationships. In this chapter, we've covered the following sources of error:

   Measurement error occurs when answers to survey questions are affected by factors other than the construct of interest. *Processing error* occurs when responses are inconsistently coded by research staff. *Coverage error* comes into play when the people who complete a survey are different from the population we intend to describe. *Sampling error* pertains to the uncertainty of survey findings that are based on a sample, rather than the entire population. *Nonresponse error* occurs when not all selected respondents participate in the survey or answer all questions in a survey.

2. **How do you design survey questions on social phenomena in ways that minimize measurement error?**

   Scholars have identified four steps respondents take when answering survey questions: (1) Comprehension of the question, (2) Retrieval of information, (3) Estimation and judgment, and (4) Reporting the answer. Considering how each of these steps will occur when respondents view a survey question can help to identify possible sources of error. In addition to behavior by respondents, error can be introduced by interviewer effects and in the course of data processing. Training to standardize survey implementation and coding can help reduce these sources of bias.

3. **What are the advantages and disadvantages to each potential survey mode or combination of modes? How do you determine the best mode for a particular research question?**

   Face-to-face interviews have higher response rates, but take longer and are more expensive. CATI, meanwhile, can be conducted faster, but have far lower response rates and potential sampling error when only landlines are used. Web surveys are cheap and effective for online users. Yet compiling a sampling frame for Web surveys is difficult unless there exists an available listserv. Also, Web surveys systematically leave out those without Internet access. Finally, mail surveys have broad coverage, but have high nonresponse. It is common for researchers to use multiple modes in the same study to compensate for their different strengths and weaknesses.

4. **How do you identify a sampling frame and sampling approach that is best suited for the research question and population of interest?**

   In general, researchers try to minimize survey error while staying within budget. If a researcher does not have the funds to hire a large staff of interviewers, selecting a more specific population to study that is more accessible (such as students in a classroom or employees at a particular workplace) is a viable alternative that can produce valuable insight, if only with a more limited scope.

   The sampling frame should correspond directly to the research question to ensure the people recruited for participation in the study are the relevant population. As with survey mode, however, selecting a sampling frame is a function of both research questions and budget. If there is not a large enough budget to generate a nationally representative sample, restricting the sampling frame to a more local or accessible population is a common approach.

5. **What are some key considerations in survey implementation?**

   After defining the research question, constructing valid survey items, and identifying suitable sampling frames and sampling approaches, the final steps in survey research include collecting and analyzing data. When collecting data, researchers are cognizant of the different sources of error pertaining to modes of data collection. Face-to-face and CATI modes are susceptible to interviewer effects where responses are potentially influenced by the presence of an interviewer. Training interviewers and statistically adjusting for interviewer characteristics can mitigate these effects. Web and mail survey modes can be influenced by design bias stemming from respondents' use of different Internet devices that format surveys in varying ways, or the different context in which respondents complete mail surveys. Once surveys are completed, some error may also be introduced during data processing as research staff may code open-ended responses in different ways.

Three forms of illegitimate surveys pose as social science but have other motivations. SUGGING (selling under the guise of conducting a survey), FRUGGING (fund-raising under the guise of conducting a survey), and push polls (framing survey questions in ways intended to sway public opinion) do not follow scientific methods of survey methodology and do not produce reliable information.

KEY TERMS

ballot-stuffing (p. 155)

climate surveys (p. 140)

construct (p. 139)

construct validity (p. 143)

coverage error (p. 153)

cues (p. 144)

double-barreled questions (p. 147)

error (p. 141)

exhaustive (p. 145)

final disposition code (p. 156)

forced response (p. 146)

FRUGGING (p. 156)

inference (p. 139)

interviewer effects (p. 149)

item nonresponse error (p. 149)

margin of error (p. 153)

measurement (p. 139)

measurement error (p. 143)

mode effects (p. 148)

nonresponse bias (p. 153)

operationalization (p. 143)

optimizers (p. 147)

probability sampling (p. 152)

processing error (p. 156)

push polls (p. 156)

representation (p. 139)

response rate (p. 156)

sampling (p. 152)

sampling error (p. 153)

sampling frame (p. 153)

satisficing (p. 146)

social desirability bias (p. 144)

standardized (p. 156)

SUGGING (p. 156)

total survey error (TSE) framework (p. 142)

unit nonresponse error (p. 149)

9 WATCHING, TALKING, AND LISTENING

Kathleen (Casey) Oberlin

LEARNING QUESTIONS

9.1 What is qualitative research, and how does it differ from our day-to-day experiences of watching, talking, and listening to one another?

9.2 What is fieldwork observation? How and why do sociologists use this method to collect data?

9.3 What are social science interviews? How and why do sociologists use this method to collect data?

9.4 What are group interviews, or focus groups? How and why do sociologists use this method to collect data?

QUALITATIVE RESEARCH APPROACHES

We all watch, talk, and listen to other people daily. But qualitative research differs from our everyday conversations and our observations of others. In day-to-day interactions, the goal might be to get hired for a job, find a romantic partner, or make new friends. The goal of qualitative research, however, is to better understand social processes among individuals, groups, organizations, and even countries. To meet this goal, qualitative researchers observe and ask questions carefully and systematically.

Qualitative research is the analysis of nonnumerical data. Researchers focus on what people do, say, or express in other ways. It is an approach that often links data collection, analysis, and theory throughout the research process. Typically, quantitative approaches are more focused on examining the *"what"* in terms of pattern frequencies. Qualitative research focuses mostly on the *how* and the *why*. Researchers seek to learn about people in-depth and on their own terms.

Qualitative research is designed to identify patterns through careful observation. Diane Vaughan's book *The Challenger Launch Decision* (1996) provides a good example. As you may know, in 1986, the National Aeronautics and Space Administration (NASA) launched the space shuttle *Challenger,* which exploded shortly after takeoff and killed all the crew members on board. After the disaster occurred, it was revealed that NASA knew the shuttle design was flawed before it launched. Vaughan's research asked, "Why did NASA continue with the launch if they knew the design to be flawed? Why did NASA launch the *Challenger* against the eve-of-launch objections of engineers?" In order to answer these questions, Vaughan extensively reviewed documents and interviews available from NASA. She found that NASA's organizational culture explained away errors by normalizing them over time, rather than altering technical production or launch timelines. The process unfolded incrementally, rather than as a result of last-minute organizational misconduct.

A very different example is Barbara Risman's qualitative study of U.S. millennials in the 21st century. In her book, *Where the Millennials Will Take Us* (2018), she poses the question, "Just how does the millennial generation understand gender today?" Through in-depth interviews with more than

100 young adults, she finds that millennials approach gender in a variety of different ways. Some are pushing the boundaries of gender, embracing flexibility and fluidity, while others are holding on to more traditional gender ideals. These examples underscore the wide variety of pressing societal issues that qualitative research approaches can address.

Table 9.1 lists elements of social life that sociologists often study using qualitative research. As you can see, they use qualitative research to study all sorts of things. To do so, they collect and analyze different types of data. Like all approaches to social science research, it is important to collect and analyze qualitative data systematically.

Case Selection

After identifying a research topic, constructing key research questions, and selecting a method, the next step in the qualitative research process is case selection. What kinds of observations (such as individual, community, or organizational) would help the researchers address the research question? Qualitative researchers typically rely on samples of less than 100 people or fewer than 10 groups. In the case of ethnographic field research (discussed later in this chapter), researchers might study just one or two institutions or organizations. Determining which cases to include in the analysis is a crucial decision that needs to be thought through carefully.

HOW I GOT ACTIVE IN SOCIOLOGY
KATHLEEN (CASEY) OBERLIN

I always loved people-watching. I enjoyed sociology courses in high school and college because they helped me contextualize the types of people I thought were so fascinating to watch. But it was only after I took a research methods course that I became hooked. The ability to collect data (rather than just make assumptions) in order to better understand why people do what they do, and how the broader context in which they are making decisions matters, was really powerful for me. I became a college professor because I enjoyed sharing with students the wide range of tools they could use to seek out answers to their own sociological questions. Recently I transitioned into the user experience research field, where I now use my sociological perspective and skillset to research the role technology plays in all our lives.

Some researchers build their samples through a process of convenience sampling. They recruit research participants through flyers, message boards, social media, and word of mouth. This approach tends to be inexpensive and requires few resources. An important limitation to this approach is that

TABLE 9.1 ■ Elements of Social Life Qualitative Researchers Study, With Examples
● **Practices**: exercise habits, reading a book to a child
● **Life Episodes**: divorce, crime, illness
● **Encounters**: people meeting and interacting in a business
● **Roles**: occupations, family roles
● **Relationships**: friendships, romantic partners
● **Groups**: school cliques, sports teams, work groups
● **Organizations**: hospitals, schools
● **Settlements**: neighborhoods, communes
● **Social worlds**: "Wall Street," "the sports world"
● **Lifestyles (or subcultures)**: vegan, drag culture
● **Symbols and artifacts**: protest signs, clothing

convenience samples often result in biased samples lacking in diversity. Flyers posted on college campuses are likely to recruit college students, for example. Studies recruiting only through social media apps are more likely to reach middle-income respondents and unlikely to reach lower-income respondents who may not have easy access to the Internet. In response to this limitation, researchers often collect and analyze data with an analytical sampling approach.

Researchers using an analytical sampling approach focus on collecting and assessing data from critical cases, typical cases, and deviant cases. Critical cases are unusually rich in information pertaining to the research question. Typical cases are regarded as standard, and deviant cases are in stark contrast to others. Imagine a researcher wants to examine how small, local business economies are responding to shifts in the global economy. That researcher could approach coffee shops as a population; they could then sample across a range of local, independent shops as well as branches of corporate franchises. A critical case in their study might be a shop that was developed locally, perhaps with a nonprofit mission or explicit goal in mind (e.g., a local food pantry or religious organization). A typical case would be a nearby independent coffee shop, but one could reasonably exchange it with many coffee places in other locations. A deviant case for this research project would be a corporate franchise like Starbucks, since it is not unique to a particular location and is not locally owned. It's not the focus of the research, but rather, the case is used as a critical comparison.

CONSIDER THIS. . .

How would you find out more information about the different types of coffee shops in your community, if any? What kind of data would you need to collect in order to evaluate how these different types of coffee shops operate day to day?

Another strategy for case selection is to construct an "inconvenient sample" (Duneier, 2011). An inconvenient sample is one that is designed specifically to challenge prevailing theories or dominant beliefs about the topic. Consider the debates surrounding neighborhood gentrification. A common argument is that gentrification is associated with increased development and expanded neighborhood amenities. Often developers portray this as a benefit for residents, since it increases the economic activity in a neighborhood. An *inconvenient* sample of community members might seek out people who recently moved out of the neighborhood, whose lives were *not* enhanced by the new development. What do these residents have in common? What are the contextual circumstances that led residents to move out? How do they perceive the changes in the neighborhood compared to new residents? By focusing on specific cases that run *counter to* the expected narrative, researchers may create new theories, fine-tune existing explanations, improve empirical insights into ongoing phenomena, and develop new research questions.

Whatever sampling approach, you might be asking yourself, When do I stop collecting data? How many cases do I need? Researchers are always constrained to some extent by time, funding, and other resources, but qualitative researchers aim to collect data until they reach the point of saturation. Saturation occurs when collecting more data yields little new information. If spending more time in the field, interviewing more people, or conducting more focus groups is no longer generating additional information, then researchers have reached the point of saturation and it's time to move on to analysis.

DOING SOCIOLOGY 9.1

Qualitative Research Design

In this exercise, you will gain practice developing a research question and considering different types of qualitative data that could be collected and analyzed to answer the question.

Recall that qualitative research can be used to study many different aspects of society and human behavior. Consider one of the following elements of social life:

- **Practices**: for example, exercise habits, reading a book to a child
- **Life Episodes**: for example, divorce, crime, illness
- **Encounters**: for example, people meeting and interacting in a business

Answer the following questions with your chosen element in mind:

1. What is a research question that could help researchers better understand this element of social life?
2. What type of qualitative data could a researcher collect to help answer this question?
3. What type of sample could a researcher use for this study?
4. What do you think the results would reveal?

Check Your Understanding

1. What is qualitative research, and how does it differ from the day-to-day experiences of watching, talking, and listening to one other?
2. What is analytic sampling, and why is it useful for case selection in qualitative research?
3. What is an inconvenient sample?
4. What is the point of saturation in qualitative research?

FIELDWORK OBSERVATION

Researchers sometimes immerse themselves in a specific group, organization, or community for an extended period of time to collect detailed, accurate, holistic data on all that they observe. The process of collecting and analyzing this data is called ethnographic research, or ethnography. Ethnographic research is time-consuming; it rests on the idea that in order to really understand what is happening and why, one needs to understand the situation from the perspective of an "insider."

In order to understand why busy adults participate in volunteer activities, for example, a researcher might simply ask adult volunteers, "Why do you volunteer?" But the answers that the researcher might receive—"To help people," "For religious reasons," or "To build my network"—likely only tell part of the story. By attending volunteer events and the numerous organizing activities that go on behind the scenes, and by talking with volunteers throughout this process, researchers can get a much fuller picture of why the volunteers do what they do.

Participant observation requires the researcher both to interact with and observe the individuals being studied.

© FS Productions/Getty Images

Although they seek an "insider" status, ethnographers need to maintain the ability to be a detached observer, an "outsider." Maintaining an outsider status is important because researchers should routinely step back and assess what they observe from a variety of perspectives, considering a range of different ideas. For example, the researcher described above might find it helpful to step back from their analysis of adult volunteers and think critically about the diversity of volunteers represented in their study. Are they all retired? Or do they all only volunteer with one organization? When researchers immerse themselves in a group, community, or organization, it sometimes becomes difficult to fairly assess the values, behavior, or language of group members. Ethnographic researchers must carefully balance their need to be close, and to build rapport with those they study while maintaining the ability to step away.

Participant observation is a type of ethnographic research designed to gain a close and intimate familiarity with a given group of individuals and their practices. As the name suggests, in participant observation, researchers both participate and observe. For example, a researcher practicing participant observation in the study of adult volunteerism would join in their volunteer activity.

Researchers use participant observation to collect data regarding a range of social issues and phenomena. Typically, units of observations include:

- *Practices*, such as those of workers at a nano-technology manufacturing plant;

- *Attitudes and beliefs*, like the extent to which an individual supports the legalization of marijuana or their beliefs about fairness within the criminal justice system;

- *Symbols*, like the Confederate flag.

Participant observation is particularly effective for assessing practices and tacit knowledge—that which is unspoken and sometimes so taken for granted by those who are doing it that they do not recognize it. Examples of this include the ways in which people teach their children to cook simply by being in the kitchen; how a clinical lab manager teaches their research intern how to work a centrifuge; or how a teacher encourages some students, and maybe discourages others, in the course of day-to-day classroom interactions.

An important idea in all ethnographic fieldwork is that group members have different experiences and perspectives. By teasing out such differences, the researcher can understand both the varying aspects of what participants say and believe *should* happen (the formal system) and the discrepancies between the formal system and what *actually* does happen (the informal, everyday system). In the end, one person can never accurately represent or speak for the whole group. All groups are diverse in one way or another, and most, if not all, contain people with varying levels of power and prestige. It is important to attend to these differences in the course of ethnographic research by developing a strategy for which types of people you will want to observe and engage with during fieldwork, and importantly how you will frame the data you collect (and keep in mind who you do not observe, talk with, or otherwise engage).

Entering the Field

Gaining access to a social setting is one of the most integral, yet difficult, steps in ethnographic fieldwork. How to gain access differs by setting, but a key consideration is whether the site(s) is open to the public or situated in a closed setting not open to the public such as companies, schools, or private clubs. When the field site that a researcher would like to study requires permission to enter, a gatekeeper is needed. A gatekeeper is someone who can help the researcher gain access. For example, if you would like to observe an office setting, you would almost certainly need to go through a department manager. To observe a classroom, you would need to get permission from the school's principal, the teacher, and potentially students and their parents as well. Researchers doing fieldwork need to be able to explain to other people (depending on the kind of project, this could be a gatekeeper, participants, etc.) why they are there, what they are doing while there, and what they plan to do afterward. This information should be thought through before entering the field and is referred to as an account.

The level and type of involvement a researcher creates during their fieldwork shapes the participant observation. In covert participant situations, researchers may choose not to disclose their identities *as researchers*. Those with whom they interact may not know that they are being observed for the purposes of research, which presents ethical implications related to deception. As discussed in Chapter 4, researchers should never conduct ethnographic research, or any other form of research involving human subjects, without first obtaining the approval of their institutional review board (IRB) or similar ethical oversight. When acting as a covert participant, or as a complete observer (like a fly on the wall with intentional distance from participating in the field site), the researcher will need to be as unobtrusive and unassuming as possible. In either of these cases, asking a lot of questions could be very difficult. When acting as a covert participant, the other people in the field site will assume that you already know what is happening, since you are actively involved in the activity or setting; therefore, your questions could be viewed as odd and could possibly reveal your identity as an outsider. As a complete observer, you want to have as little effect on what is happening as possible, since you are just hanging out as an audience member. So, in this case, asking direct questions is not advisable because it would violate what is expected from your stated role.

In contrast, when acting in the role of an overt participant, the researcher is known as such to the participants and has more ability to ask questions. In these instances, it is a good idea also to conduct interviews with informants in order to check whether you have correctly interpreted what is being said, expressed, or done in a setting. A key informant is a person in the field who can provide "behind the scenes" insight into the interactions and other elements of social life that you are observing. Sometimes a gatekeeper will also act as a key informant. It is important to keep in mind that the goal of fieldwork is to learn from the perspectives and experiences of participants, and from their interactions with one another.

DOING SOCIOLOGY 9.2

Participant Observation in the Workplace

In this exercise, you will gain a better understanding of participant observation.

Read through the following situation and then answer the following questions.

Trey is interested in studying how race and gender influence the work experiences of call center employees. They connect with the president of a customer service center that gives help to people who experience poor Internet connection. Trey thinks that even though race and gender are not directly seen in customer service interactions, they will nonetheless structure the organization of the workforce, interactions between customer service representatives and their employers, as well as interactions between customer service representatives and those calling in. The president introduces Trey to all of the employees, describing them as a researcher interested in workplace operations. The president gives Trey permission to listen in on phone calls, to move freely around the call center for a month, and to talk with anyone they encounter. Trey speaks with many employees and finds that Linda, a mid-level manager whom other workers confide in and trust, is a particularly valuable source of information.

1. Would you describe the research as overt or covert participant observation?

2. Who is the gatekeeper?

3. Who is the key informant?

4. What kinds of things (if any) do you think Trey might count in order to orient their focus on racial and gendered experiences? What kinds of things might they ignore?

Field Notes

Once you enter the field, you may wonder how to decide on what details to pay attention. What should you write down? How are you going to gather data systematically without drawing attention to yourself and disrupting the situation you are trying to observe? Field notes are written or recorded descriptions capturing what the researcher hears, observes, and otherwise experiences while on site. They are records of both important events and day-to-day happenings. It is important to include commonplace things that initially seem unimportant. Observations like the general flow of students through a school's hallways, or where the boss sits during a meeting, and who sits to their right and left may seem like minor details, but even these small details could gain more significance later on.

Researchers make a series of important decisions while taking notes—jotting down what is happening while it occurs and noting questions to follow up on later. Researchers also include personal reflections in their field notes. Recording how they are feeling and their in-the-moment thoughts about the situations they encounter can be important points of data for analyses later on. But what's most important is to capture what you observe during fieldwork as soon as possible, either while it is happening or shortly afterward (within 24 hours), since recall becomes harder and harder with time.

Since there is a lot going on in any given field site, and no researcher can document everything, two common strategies help orient a researcher's focus. *Counting* offers a sense of magnitude and internal reliability for claims (how often does this action occur, or how many people attended). *Mapping the scene* is the process of outlining a geographic layout to orient what else is happening socially. This process not only records the spatial aspects of the observed situation but may also draw the researcher's attention to details that might otherwise not be observed, such as what types of people gather together where (how many and what groups of students sit where in the cafeteria), or what else is near the site of observation (the principal's office is closer to one side of the cafeteria; Dewalt & Dewalt, 2011, p. 83). Counting and mapping the scene allow researchers to take note of key details that may at first seem insignificant but later prove to be important.

Theory, Data, and Approaches to Fieldwork

Researchers take different approaches to connecting ethnographic fieldwork data with theory. Although the approaches below are presented as different ends on a spectrum, in reality, most ethnographic researchers fall somewhere in between. They move back and forth between data collection and data analysis to refining theory and hypotheses throughout an iterative, or cyclical, process.

On one end of the spectrum, grounded theory is an example of inductive research (Glaser & Strauss, 1967). Researchers try to bracket their theoretical guide and enter into their fieldwork with the goal of understanding participants on their own terms. The analytic categories they develop emerge from observational data. In what range of activities do children engage during recess? How do they decide who's going to do which tasks for a classroom project? Researchers using a grounded theoretical approach let the theory emerge from their data, "from the ground up," but frequently engage with existing theories after the data are collected and analyzed.

Ethnographic researchers describe the site and its participants with close attention to detail—a process called thick description (Geertz, 1973). The goal is to understand the individuals or groups within the field rather than to generalize across a variety of field sites. Grounded theory tends to focus less on case selection and data collection since it tends to be largely constructed in practice via convenience sampling (Jerolmack & Khan, 2018, p. xv). It is an approach that informs not just sociological fieldwork, but also many other disciplines from nursing to computer science (Tavory & Timmermans, 2014, p. 10).

On the other end of the spectrum is the extended case method (Burawoy, 1998). Rather than bracket theoretical questions at the beginning, this approach puts them front and center. Researchers using this approach typically use ethnographic data to test hypotheses formulated in other research. Existing theory drives not only the research question, but also the case selection, data collection, and analysis. Their research asks, "Do fieldwork observations line up with a given explanation in existing social science research?"

Research using the extended case method approach often spans multiple sites (groups, organizations, or communities) in order to see how external, and more macro-level factors shape social activity on the ground locally. Researchers using this approach might ask, "What are the conditions on the factory floor, and how do they vary across economic contexts in Zambia, Sri Lanka, or Hungary?" Or, "How do industrialized countries socialize children for their future career aspirations within classrooms in the United States, Sweden, and Japan?" Ultimately, the aim is to generalize across cases and contexts by challenging existing theoretical explanations and developing new analytical insights.

Reflexivity

Researchers reflect upon their own position in the field through a process known as reflexivity. This process helps others determine how a researcher's perspective may influence their observations and maybe some conclusions by reporting how and why they did what they did in the field. Researchers situate themselves in their field notes—noting their location during the rally, festival, or meeting; how they think others perceive them, often noting how their social location (such as gender, race, or age) aligns with their participants or stands apart (Connell, 2018). Researchers also consider external cues they have to support their observations about how they are perceived. What did participants say or indicate about the researchers' presence? Reflexivity is important because it helps provide context for how researchers conducted their fieldwork and allows others to evaluate the validity of the resulting data and analysis.

CONSIDER THIS...

What social identities do you hold? To which groups do you belong? How could your position influence your ability to gain access to groups you want to study?

Check Your Understanding

1. What is the difference between open and closed fieldwork sites?
2. What kinds of observations should be documented in field notes?
3. What are three approaches to ethnographic fieldwork?
4. What is the role of reflexivity in fieldwork?

SOCIAL SCIENCE INTERVIEWS

Interviews are everywhere in our day-to-day lives. Journalists and informal reporters conduct interviews for magazines, television, newspapers, and social media. We read or watch excerpts of interviews on the news, online, or in print. Typically, these interviews are designed with the goal of having the interviewee share their expertise or perspective with the readers or viewers. Interviewers might ask biographical questions so that the audience can have a better understanding of their life story. In other cases, interviewers ask experts to share their perspectives on current events or to speculate about the future.

Social science interviews are quite different. Sociologists conducting interview research may also ask interviewees about their background and experiences. But sociologists conducting interviews typically ask dozens of people a series of questions, in a similar order. When sociologists analyze their interview data they seldom take the words of their interviewee at face value. And when communicating the results of their interviews, they hardly ever share entire interview transcripts. This is because the experiences and perspectives of a single person seldom provide sufficient evidence for answering a sociological research question. Sociologists seek to identify patterns or trends in interviewees' attitudes, beliefs, experiences, and perceptions. This requires conducting and analyzing data from multiple people.

Interview Formats

Social science interviews range in structure from formal to unstructured. Formally structured interviews often include closed-ended or restricted choice questions. These standardized questions are presented in a fixed order, along with a range of possible response options in a questionnaire format. You can imagine sitting down with someone who is reading a survey aloud to you and recording your selection from a list of predetermined answers to the questions. The goal is to capture variation consistently.

In contrast to structured interviews, the goal of unstructured interviews is to allow respondents more room to open up and develop the conversation in their own words and at their own pace. This format is frequently used in conjunction with ethnographic fieldwork to discuss sensitive topics or to delve into people's lived experiences. As a result, unstructured interviews are often only loosely planned. In fact, they may only consist of a single guiding question or statement! An example might be, "Tell me about a time when you experienced conflict." From this initial prompt, a skilled interviewer can use follow-up questions to continue to engage the respondent in a conversation that elicits more details about this particular experience. Having these potential follow-up questions thought out prior to the interview is important, however.

Situated in between these two types of interviews, semi-structured interviews are the most common format for social science interviews. Semi-structured interviews consist of a series of planned questions that are open-ended and allow the respondent to answer in their own words. Overall, semi-structured interviews are more flexible than structured interviews; they emphasize the interviewee's point of view and seek rich, detailed answers. Interviewers seek to create a comprehensive sense of the interviewee's background, attitudes, and actions. "Rambling" is often encouraged, since it can yield insight into related issues or topics that the researcher may not have anticipated when the interview schedule was created. The semi-structured format requires similar interviewer skills to those

ITV Hub, courtesy of Harpo Productions/CBS

Talk show host Oprah Winfrey, seen here interviewing Prince Harry and Meghan Markle, is a master of leading semi-structured interviews.

© ASSOCIATED PRESS

used in unstructured interviews, where the interviewer should actively listen to explanations, follow up with tailor-made questions, and unpack any complex issues mentioned. Depending on the project, some interviews might last just 20 minutes, while in other projects interviews might last for 3 hours or more. This approach is well-suited to when a researcher will not have the opportunity to interview someone more than once or twice, and when an efficient use of time is important (e.g., administrators, public officials, or community leaders).

Semi-Structured Interview Guides and Questions

When researchers schedule a semi-structured interview with a participant they use an interview guide, which is a written list of questions in a particular order. It is a guide to "work through" rather than rigidly adhere to the exact questions in the same precise order each time. For instance, a degree of flexibility is needed when an interviewee addresses multiple questions in one response or offers an unexpected, new insight that was not anticipated. The greater number of interviewers on a team, the more structured the guides become. The goal is to produce reliable, comparable data across interviews.

Interview guides include a variety of question types and probes (Bernard, 2018). Introductory questions are easy to answer for the respondent and often focus on gathering some descriptive information about the interviewee such as where they live, what they do in a particular organization, or what they enjoy doing in the community. Grand tour questions try to elicit lengthy narratives, and should be asked early in the interview. The goal is to engage the respondent in the topic of interest. Although most folks like talking about themselves (even if they think they do not!), grand tour questions can help the interviewer establish rapport (Spradley, 2016). Rapport is a feeling of good-will and trust that is created when the person being interviewed feels comfortable both with the process and the interviewer. An example of a grand tour question is, "What are all the things you need to do to prepare for a typical workday?" Note that answering this question might involve a lot of consideration on the part of the respondent and may solicit a lengthy answer. Finally, interpretative questions encourage the interviewee to assess a scenario or informational statement related to the interview topic: "What would you do if you received a $60,000 community loan—how would you spend it to improve your neighborhood?" or "How would you respond to a news report that announced scientists cloned a human being?"

CONSIDER THIS. . .

Why is establishing rapport with interviewees important for soliciting meaningful information from respondents?

Probes are additional questions to explore an interviewee's answers. Direct probes involve clarifying what an interviewee said, such as, "I'm not sure I understand X…would you explain that a little more to me?" These kinds of probes may also ask why an interviewee provided a particular response, how they think a situation unfolded, or a request for them to provide an example, such as, "Could you provide an example of Y that you remember?" or "What happened then?" Indirect probes often include neutral utterances such as "uh-huh," "mm-hmm," or "interesting" to indicate the interviewer is listening without steering the conversation in one direction or another. Otherwise, it may be useful to express empathy: "I can see why you say that was a challenging situation"; or repeating back what the respondent said: "So if I got that right, you were age 50 when you were laid off."

Regardless of the question type or probe format, biased questions that lead participants toward a certain response should be avoided. Table 9.2 shows some examples of how to tweak the same kind of question to be more or less biased.

Other considerations during an interview include deciding on how to document the interview itself. If you are going to audio record, then think about where you want to hold the interview, how you will record it—through a device, a smartphone, or an online platform for digital interviews. You will also need to think through what to do with your body and voice. Demonstrate your interest in terms of tone, body language, and a sense of being "on" throughout the interview. How you show this will be culturally specific, but in many contexts, an upbeat tone, upright posture, and semi-frequent amount of eye contact are signs of engagement.

What to Ask—and What to Avoid Asking

People new to interview studies often struggle with determining what questions to ask and what questions not to ask. It is tempting to want to ask interviewees every question imaginable—*tell me everything!*—but this is not possible. Interviewers and interviewees both have a limited amount of time and energy, and when inviting people for an interview, researchers should provide potential interviewees with an expected timeframe for interview completion. So researchers must plan ahead and be judicious with their choice of questions. It is important to complete at least one practice interview before jumping into the research project. In many cases, a practice interview will reveal aspects of the interview that can be improved.

One of the classic blunders for first-time interviewers is asking their research question directly to the interviewee, in hopes that they will provide a straightforward answer. For example, a researcher wanting to know about how social class influences students' high school experiences might ask students, "How, if at all, did social class influence your high school experience?" While this question could be used in conjunction with other questions in an interview, it is crucial to remember that interviewees' *perceptions* of how their social class influenced their high school experiences are just that: perceptions. Collecting and analyzing information about people's perceptions are definitely important. But perceptions may or may not be accurate.

Consider, for example, the wealthy student, whose parents and grandparents are lawyers and doctors, who responds that social class had no influence on his attending and graduating from an elite private high school. Now consider, for example, a student whose parents work under the table as farm-laborers, who responds that social class had no influence on her attending and graduating from a public

TABLE 9.2 ■ More and Less Bias in Interview Questions	
Biased Questions	**Less-Biased Questions**
Most smart people in this community always recycle, don't they?	I've heard some people in this community say that most smart people recycle all the time, and others say that they know smart people who don't think recycling is as helpful as other environmental strategies. What do you think?
Was one reason that you wanted to transfer schools because you were trying to avoid failing out?	Why did you want to transfer schools? Potential follow-up question: 'What were you hoping to change by transferring?'

high school with comparatively fewer resources. Both respondents' accounts are likely inaccurate. What we could learn from asking this question and listening to interviewees' responses is how these students understand their own successes, their experiences, social class, and structural inequality more generally. When researchers ask many students from a variety of life backgrounds to reflect on the same question, they can uncover patterns about ideology, identity, and the processes through which people make meaning in their lives.

DOING SOCIOLOGY 9.3

Developing and Refining Interview Questions

In this exercise, you will develop your skills in critiquing and fine-tuning interview questions.

Tom is interested in how parents of different socioeconomic statuses think about children's social activities and playtime. He thinks that middle- and upper-class parents are more likely to enroll their children in formal activities such as organized sports, academic enrichment programs, and music lessons, while lower- and working-class parents are more likely to encourage their children toward unstructured social activities like hanging out and playing at one another's houses, in parks, and organizing their own games of sports. He wants to understand how parents interpret their children's play activities, and how their beliefs about their children's activities feed back into their own assessment of themselves as parents. He develops an interview guide and plans to ask parents of varied socioeconomic statuses the following questions:

- How would you describe your socioeconomic status?
- Can you tell me about the activities in which your children participate?
- Do you think your social class influences your approach to parenting?
- Do your children's activities influence your perception of yourself as a parent?

Rob reviews Tom's interview questions and offers the following revised questions:

- Can you describe the work that you do and your educational background?
- How would you describe yourself as a parent? How is your approach to parenting similar or different from other parents you know, or from your own parents?
- How do your children spend their days outside of the school day? What do they do for fun, relaxation, or for social activities? With whom do they spend time?
- How do you feel about the way your children spend their time? Do you wish they were doing more or less of anything, or do you think they've got it right? Why?

Think critically about the two sets of interview questions and the types of information they may solicit. Then answer the following questions:

1. Do you think that Tom and Rob's sets of questions would solicit different types of answers? Why?
2. Which set of questions do you think parents would feel more comfortable answering? Why?
3. Which set of questions do you think gives the interviewee more opportunity to share their experiences and perceptions? Why?
4. Which set of questions do you think would be more valuable in answering the research question? Why?

SOCIOLOGISTS IN ACTION
SARA GOLDRICK-RAB

Using Research to Inform Social Change

Sara Goldrick-Rab discusses how she puts her research into action and working with policy makers.
How do you use interviews in your work?

Sara Goldrick-Rab

Photo courtesy of Sara Goldrick-Rab

I get all my joy from doing the qualitative work. My main purpose in doing interviews is to figure out what I don't know.

How do you approach interviews?

If I were to kick off an interview about how a student's doing in college, I would start with, "How did you get here?" "What brought you here?" Anything. I won't tell them to talk to me about their college admissions process because for many of them that wasn't even a thing to them. It might be, "I've known I was going to go to college since the day I was born" to "I have no idea how I got here. I just ended up here," which is a vastly different perspective. And then I ask them things like, "What has college been like for you?" And I usually don't have to ask a question after that, incredibly. It just goes. The only thing is if I'm going to get a lot of irrelevant material and they start talking about a boyfriend or a girlfriend, I'll redirect. But I really follow where they get excited. Where they get unhappy. Where they are hesitant. Again, I follow their emotions. That has opened up so many avenues and answers for why college isn't working for so many people.

In the policy sphere, what kind of research do you draw upon?

I'm usually talking to policy makers about one of three things. First, prevalence estimates, where I'm just saying, "I counted." This is how many food-insecure students we found when we sent out this survey. ... The second most common thing I'm talking to them about is students' perspectives. And these come from interviews. I would argue a bit of my credibility is that I can actually speak to the experiences of humans. Policy makers talk to a lot of economists, who we all know that they take seriously, but there's a difference between just being taken seriously because of your degree and becoming the kind of person that policy makers turn to when they really need your help. ... I'm the kind of person now where people will call me and say, "I'm really nervous about something," or "I have a problem and I need an ear." I have to hold their confidence and give them good advice. I think the reason is they do view me as being a good listener since I listen to students. I'm so known for it now. I'm glad since that's who they should be listening to ... that's one reason why I still do a ton of my own interviewing.

Sara Goldrick-Rab is a professor of higher education and sociology at Temple University and the founding director of the Hope Center for College, Community, and Justice.

Discussion Question

How do interviews help Dr. Goldrick-Rab in her advocacy work?

1. How do the types of interviews in popular media (online, televised, magazines) differ from social science interviews?
2. What are three different formats for social science interviews?
3. Why does the type of questions asked in interviews matter?
4. What else beyond interview questions should you keep in mind while conducting an interview?

GROUP INTERVIEWS/FOCUS GROUPS

Focus groups are group interviews with a facilitator leading multiple participants—typically six to eight—in a discussion of a particular issue, object, or phenomenon. Researchers develop a series of questions prior to the interview. The facilitator, also called a moderator, asks the questions and participants share their answers with the facilitator and one another. In focus groups, participants often engage with one another—sometimes agreeing, sometimes disagreeing, and sometimes asking for clarification.

The researcher pays close attention not only to the views of individual participants, but to the interactions among them, to gain a nuanced understanding of participants' perspectives, feelings, and beliefs. Researchers often conduct three to six focus groups (Guest et al., 2016). They then identify and analyze the themes within and across the interviews.

A good example of focus group research comes from sociologist McDonnell (2010), who used focus groups as part of a larger study on public information campaigns related to HIV in Ghana. McDonnell knew that governmental and health care organizations were interested in reducing the spread of HIV in Ghana and had committed significant resources to educating the public and providing contraception such as condoms. McDonnell wanted to understand *how* people interpreted and used the information and resources they were given, how the social and geographic context shaped all of this. In addition to ethnographic work and individual interviews, he also conducted a series of focus groups: three with school teachers, two with people living with HIV/AIDS, and three with everyday Ghanaians. During the interviews, people discussed images that had appeared on HIV/AIDS educational materials.

A very different example of focus group research comes from political scientist Betina Cutaia Wilkinson. Wilkinson (2015) was interested in race relations in the United States, and in particular how people understand racial groups other than their own. In addition to analyzing large-scale survey data about racial attitudes, she conducted focus groups with white, Latinx, and Black people, to get a better sense of how each racial group perceived the others—as "partners or rivals."

Focus groups are an important tool in the social science toolbox, but market researchers use them frequently as well. Market researchers use focus groups to try out new products and advertising campaigns. They ask participants about their feelings and associations with particular words, slogans, and products. Participants' responses to the facilitator's questions, their comments about the remarks of other participants, and even their body language can provide important insight into how potential consumers may respond to products and advertisements.

Two-way mirrors are sometimes used so researchers can watch focus groups being conducted.
© iStockphoto.com/EvgeniyShkolenko

CONSIDER THIS. . .

Imagine that a company has designed a new advertisement campaign for a restaurant and presents it to a focus group to see what they think. What body language would convey a successful campaign? What body language would convey an ineffective campaign?

Who's in the Group?

Focus groups involve multiple people in the same location, sharing their thoughts and feelings, asking questions, and responding to the comments of other participants. To be effective, participants have to feel comfortable expressing uncertainty, disagreeing with other participants, and sharing opinions that may be unpopular (Herrman, 2017). It is impossible to create an environment that guarantees complete comfort for all participants, but two rules of thumb can help.

First and foremost, the participants in any focus group should hold similar backgrounds. This is because people tend to be more comfortable discussing topics—especially sensitive topics—with people who are similar to themselves. Imagine, for example, if Betina Wilkinson had asked people to share their perceptions of other racial groups while sitting in a racially diverse setting. It is likely that people would feel uncomfortable talking openly and would self-censor their beliefs and attitudes. When researchers using focus groups want to compare the perspectives of diverse groups—be they gender groups, racial/ethnic groups, religious groups, or other groups—they create focus groups of people with similar group characteristics.

Second, participants in focus groups should also be strangers. This may seem odd, given that people might be more comfortable with people they already know. But when participants know each other several potential problems emerge. First, when participants have shared experiences, shared friends, or shared colleagues, they might rely too heavily on their shared knowledge when commenting. Imagine a participant saying, "Oh, it reminds me of the time Chris did that thing, remember?" and another responding, "Oh, I know, or when Tanya had her big ta-do?" The researcher would likely have no way to interpret this dialogue. Who is Chris? Who is Tanya? What did they do? The facilitator would have to spend precious time asking for the back-story.

Participants knowing each other can lead to a second challenge with focus groups —namely, concerns about privacy and policing. Participants might be less likely to disclose potentially controversial thoughts if they know other group members, fearing that others might think badly of them or share their thoughts with others. On the flipside, participants who know one another might also police what other participants say in the context of a focus group. Whether the topic is family life, experiences in fraternities and sororities, discrimination in the workplace, or an altogether different topic, some people might discourage others from discussing or even acknowledging certain topics. When participants are strangers to one another, this is less of an issue.

The Structure of the Interview

Just like with an individual interview, the group interview or focus group can be unstructured, semi-structured, or fully structured. The researcher chooses the level of structure depending upon their research question. If the research question is exploratory in nature, then an unstructured interview may be a good choice. If the research question centralizes a comparison, such as Wilkinson's analysis of racial attitudes, then it is usually best for the interview to be structured. Structured interviews make comparisons easier because participants respond to the same series of prompts in the same order.

All focus groups have a facilitator. The facilitator has three roles (Herrman, 2017). First, the facilitator promotes the involvement of all participants, making sure that no one is talked over, and that every person has a chance to express their perspective. Second, they also act as a prober—asking follow-up questions when something is unclear or if more information is needed. Finally, the facilitator functions as an encourager—encouraging people to express their ideas and perspectives, especially those that might differ from those previously expressed. In the case of projects that rely on multiple facilitators, facilitators need to coordinate beforehand to ensure that they have similar approaches to guiding the interview. If one facilitator probes and encourages a lot, and the other does not, then the interviewers are less comparable.

Facilitators have a lot to do and should not be expected to make notes of all of the relevant data from the interviews. Focus groups require either one or more people in the room (or behind a one-way mirror) to take detailed notes or require audio or video recording of the interview. Focus groups generate a lot of information in a short amount of time, and researchers are best able to analyze this when they have audio or video, and ideally, also have interview transcriptions.

Multiple Levels of Analysis

Often combined with other methodological tools, such as surveys, a particular advantage of group interviews, compared to individual interviews, is that they produce three distinct units of analysis from which to gather insights (Cyr, 2015). At the individual level, researchers assess viewpoints across the participants within a conversation. In other words, how do individuals articulate their own reasoning when they are in a group setting? The group level affords researchers an opportunity to unearth points of consensus or tension among the participants. How much does the group agree on a particular topic or policy? How much do they disagree? Group-level feedback can also be used to pretest survey instruments for validation. A researcher might use a focus group to determine how people in the group understand a particular set of questions about how much they trust public institutions, for example. Finally, the interactive level narrows in on participant dynamics that emerge throughout the conversation: What unexpected interactions occur among the participants when a question about student loans and debt is posed?

Focus groups have two additional potential advantages relative to individual interviews. First, since each group interview has between six and eight people, researchers can gather data from participants in a shorter amount of time. Researchers might conduct five or six focus groups, and in so doing, hear the perspectives of 30 or 40 people! A second advantage comes from the fact that researchers can observe disagreement, dialogue, and exploration among participants. Researchers can also gain a better sense of how to justify their positions, explain things to others, and observe shifts in the overall mood as different topics come up.

A downside to focus groups is that people sometimes suppress what they perceive as an unpopular attitude, or shameful experience, and instead go along with the group. Some participants may dominate the conversation and others say little at all. Group interviews can be a powerful tool, but they are most effective when participants feel comfortable discussing their positions without judgment. As such, it is important for researchers to put together groups of people with similar backgrounds, to design the interviews in a way that promotes confidentiality despite the group setting, to have effective moderation, and an interview structure and approach that are consistent across group interviews.

DOING SOCIOLOGY 9.4

Focus Groups Gone Wild!

In this exercise, you will identify problems in research design and propose solutions.

Read each scenario, then answer the questions that follow.

A. A researcher studying how people interact with their pets conducts focus groups and asks participants to discuss the things they most love about their pets. Four participants are dog owners and three are cat owners; there is no overlap. The dog owners insist that dogs are the best companions, promoting exercise, sociability, and overall improved health. The cat owners do not say much, but look grumpy. Analysis of the interviews shows that dog owners not only talked more, but also frequently interrupted and talked over the cat owners.

B. A researcher is interested in pledging practices of fraternities and sororities on campus. At each interview, participants include members of multiple fraternities and sororities as well as people who pledged but were unsuccessful in their bids, along with people who were once members but quit. All of the fraternity and sorority members wear shirts identifying the name of the organization to which they belong. At one point, a participant describes a hazing process she experienced, and another member shouts, "I can't believe you're talking about that! You can't talk about that!"

C. A research team has been hired to assess the experiences of people in a school. They are especially focused on issues of discrimination and inequality. Their focus group includes people at varying levels of the school: administrators, faculty, and students. When the facilitators ask, "What types of problems have you experienced here?" the students say virtually nothing, the faculty members say things that are mostly good, and the administrator reports that everything is terrific. The facilitator reports back to the research team that, based on her notes, everything seems pretty good.

Questions

1. For Scenario A, what problem(s) did the researcher encounter? What might the researcher have done differently to lessen the chances of this problem emerging?

2. For Scenario B, what problem(s) did the researcher encounter? What might the researcher have done differently to lessen the chances of this problem emerging?

3. For Scenario C, what problem(s) did the research team encounter? What might the research team have done differently to lessen the chances of this problem emerging?

Check Your Understanding

1. How do group interviews differ from individual interviews?
2. Why should focus group participants share backgrounds, but also be strangers?
3. What are the responsibilities of a focus group facilitator?
4. What are the different levels of analysis that could be studied using group interviews?

CONCLUSION

Qualitative researchers seek to unpack what processes are unique to a set of individuals within a given context, group, or organization and then return the focus outward to analyze how these cases may help explain a more general social problem. Sociologists use qualitative research in a variety of settings from the private sector, like user experience research, to the broader public sector to influence evidence-based policy reform. In Chapter 10, you will add to your sociological toolkit by learning how to analyze all the qualitative data about which you've learned throughout this chapter.

REVIEW

9.1 What is qualitative research, and how does it differ from our everyday conversations with, and observations of, people?

Qualitative research approaches like ethnography, interviews, and focus groups are tools for sociologists to observe and listen to how people behave in their day-to-day lives, and why groups make the choices they do. The systematic inquiry, ethical considerations, and examination of patterns across individuals, groups, and countries are what distinguish qualitative research from our everyday conversations and observations.

9.2 What is fieldwork observation, and how do sociologists use this method to collect data?

When researchers want to holistically understand a specific group, organization, or community in its own setting, they do ethnographic research. Various types of data are collected during fieldwork from the site where the group, organization, or community is located; data from fieldwork observations capture what is happening in day-to-day life, or during the process being studied.

9.3 What are social science interviews, and how do sociologists use this method to collect data?

Social science interviews emphasize the interviewee's point of view and seek rich, detailed answers. Interviewers focus on building rapport with the interviewee in order to unearth patterns, trends, and nuances across interviewees' attitudes, beliefs, perceptions, or understanding of an issue. Interview data often include transcripts and field notes capturing nonverbal information from the interviewee—eye contact, facial expressions, or other contextual details like where the interview took place.

9.4 What are group interviews, or focus groups, and how do sociologists use this method to collect data?

Group interviews include at least two or three interviewees in conversation with an interviewer. These kinds of interviews provide a research setting to explore a range of viewpoints expressed within a community and to spark a discussion among the interviewees. Focus groups are often videotaped in order to capture not only what is said verbally, but also to analyze how the interviewees relate to one another, as well as to the interviewer, when different topics transpire.

KEY TERMS

account (p. 165)

analytical sampling (p. 163)

complete observer (p. 165)

convenience sampling (p. 162)

covert participant (p. 165)

critical cases (p. 163)

deviant cases (p. 163)

direct probes (p. 170)

ethnographic research, or ethnography (p. 164)

extended case method (p. 167)

field notes (p. 166)

focus groups (p. 173)

gatekeeper (p. 165)

grand tour questions (p. 169)

grounded theory (p. 167)

group level (p. 175)

inconvenient sample (p. 163)

indirect probes (p. 170)

individual level (p. 175)

interactive level (p. 175)

interpretative questions (p. 169)

interview guide (p. 169)

introductory questions (p. 169)

Iterative (p. 167)

key informant (p. 166)

overt participant (p. 166)

participant observation (p. 165)

probes (p. 170)

rapport (p. 169)

reflexivity (p. 167)

saturation (p. 163)

semi-structured interviews (p. 169)

structured interviews (p. 168)

tacit knowledge (p. 165)

thick description (p. 167)

typical cases (p. 163)

unstructured interviews (p. 168)

COLLECTING WHAT'S ALREADY THERE: CONTENT ANALYSIS AND SOME RELATED METHODS

Edward L. Kain

LEARNING QUESTIONS

10.1 What are unobtrusive methods, and what is their benefit for sociological research?

10.2 What is content analysis, and what are some strengths and weaknesses of this method?

10.3 What are the steps for doing a content analysis?

10.4 How do you code data in content analysis, and how do you calculate intercoder reliability?

10.5 How do sociologists analyze historical records/documents and policy documents?

UNOBTRUSIVE METHODS IN SOCIOLOGICAL RESEARCH

While social scientists often observe people directly or gather data from them using interviews and questionnaires, sometimes their approach does not require direct involvement with people. Unobtrusive methods refers to modes of data collection that do not involve direct contact or interaction with human subjects. The term *unobtrusive measures* was first used by Webb and colleagues over a half century ago (Webb et al., 1966).

One of the biggest benefits of unobtrusive methods is that they allow the researcher to collect data without influencing the behavior that they are trying to analyze. When people are aware that they are being studied this can change their behavior. One example of this found in research using experimental design is called the Hawthorne effect. Researchers studying worker productivity in the Hawthorne electric plant improved the lighting and other working conditions and then carefully observed to see if worker productivity increased. Although productivity did increase for a short time, it was ultimately interpreted that workers' behavior changed because they knew they were being observed by the researchers.

In addition to avoiding the problem that people may change their behavior when they are being studied, unobtrusive methods have several other benefits. On average, they typically are more economical, both in terms of time and money. Surveys using nationally representative samples, for example, can be prohibitively expensive. The time involved in interviewing respondents, then transcribing and analyzing those interviews, or doing qualitative fieldwork can easily take multiple years. In addition, because unobtrusive research does not involve direct contact with human subjects, it typically does not require approval by an institutional review board (IRB). This can save a considerable amount of time in the early stages of a research project.

HOW I GOT ACTIVE IN SOCIOLOGY

EDWARD L. KAIN

My first college course in sociology had me hooked. Using a sociological lens, and combining the-ory and research to examine social relations, transformed my understanding of the world. Having grown up on a farm in rural Michigan, I had accepted the standard cultural messages. Sociology kept providing "aha" moments that challenged my world view. I clearly remember one of the first times this happened. During the first week of the semester, the professor used the example of "anyone can grow up to be president of the U.S.," then pointed out that all had been men, most had come from privileged backgrounds, most were married, all but one had been Protestant, and (at that point, in the pre-Obama years) all had been white. My research on families and social change focused on the importance of using data to counter mis-impressions we have about families, both in the past and the present. Research particularly came alive for me when I started to collect and analyze data with my students, often in the context of teaching Research Methods. Indeed, Research Methods has always been my favorite course to teach, since it gives students the skills they need to become active investigators of the world in which they live. It is the most practical of the courses in the sociology curriculum, and many of my former students talk excitedly about how well it prepared them for their jobs and for graduate and professional school.

One common approach to unobtrusive research is the analysis of existing statistics, which refers to the use of quantitative data that have already been collected and applying them to study some-thing from a sociological perspective. Sociological researchers often analyze numerical information collected by governmental organizations and international organizations, such as the U.S. Census, the Department of Labor, or the World Bank. Demographic researchers often analyze birth and death rates, unemployment rates, rates of marriage and divorce, rates of educational attainment, and often rely on governmental records to do so.

Electronic media also provide possibilities for unobtrusive methods. The use of Internet search frequencies, numbers of followers on Twitter and Facebook, analyses of tweets, and examination of blog posts all can provide data without direct interaction with the people who are being studied. Other types of unobtrusive methods include the analysis of historical documents as well as policy analysis.

Looking at tweets, blogs, and Facebook posts brings us to one of the most common types of unob-trusive methods used within sociology—content analysis. Because it is used so much, content analysis is the topic of the next section of this chapter.

CONSIDER THIS. . .

What do you think is the most important advantage of unobtrusive research methods? Can you think of some other advantages? What might be some other methods of unobtrusively collecting data?

DOING SOCIOLOGY 10.1

Identifying Unobtrusive Research Methods

In this exercise, you will gain practice identifying examples of unobtrusive research methods.

Read the following list of descriptions of methods used in research studies. Then answer the questions.

Description of Method Used in a Study

A. Children in a preschool are playing indoors. Without interacting with the children, researchers watch their play behavior and code whether or not there are gender differences in running, hitting, and cooperative behavior.

B. After a film festival, attendees are asked to fill out an anonymous online survey asking them to rank the quality of the films they saw at the festival.

C. A researcher compares the number, length, and topics of Facebook posts made by the top five candidates running for a local School Board election.

D. The text found on tombstones in an historic cemetery is used to estimate average life expectation and how that varies between women and men, as well as how it changes over time.

   1. Which of the studies use unobtrusive methods? Why did you classify these particular studies as such?

Check Your Understanding

   1. What are unobtrusive methods, and why might they be important to use in research?
   2. What types of unobtrusive measures are often used in sociological research?

CONTENT ANALYSIS

Content analysis is the systematic analysis of cultural products—print, visual, and electronic. This can include things such as books, newspapers, advertising, films, television, websites, blogs, diaries, political speeches, and social media such as Instagram and Twitter. It could also, however, include things like pieces of art, legal documents, and required school curricula.

Content analysis can be qualitative, quantitative, or a combination of the two. When researchers conduct a qualitative content analysis, they systematically identify themes and describe patterns in the material they are analyzing. Researchers taking a quantitative approach identify and count the number of times particular images, words, sentiments, or other things occur in the material, as well as the circumstances in which they occur, and then analyze these patterns numerically.

When Is Content Analysis an Appropriate Method of Data Collection?

Historical and Comparative Research

There are at least four situations in which content analysis is a particularly appropriate method for collecting and analyzing data. First, content analysis is particularly useful for making historical and/or cross-national comparisons. A study by Bernice Pescosolido and her colleagues (1997) provides a good example. They examined historical change in the images of Black people in children's books spanning seven decades in the 20th century. They counted the number of Black characters in children's books and also recorded how Black characters were represented. By connecting the images with the historical context in which they were produced, they found that the number of images of Blacks in children's books declined in historical periods of racial unrest.

In another example, sociologist Janice McCabe and collaborators (2011) used content analysis to examine the titles and main characters in over 6,600 children's books in three series over a period of 101 years. On all of their measures, the number of male characters (whether human or animal, adult or child) was higher than the number of female characters in all years and in all of the book series. Males were mentioned in titles around twice as much, and were lead characters approximately 1.6 times as often. By looking over a full century, the data illustrated that there was more equity by gender from 1900 through 1930, and in the period after the 1960s than from the 1930s through the 1960s. The authors suggest that this result is likely because of the impact of feminist activity, which was much more common in the earlier and later periods (McCabe et al., 2011, pp. 197, 217–218).

Sociologists have studied how media coverage of women's sports teams differs from coverage of male sports teams.

Jamie Schwaberow/Contributor/NCAA Photos/Getty Images

Differential Portrayal of Groups

A second time when content analysis is a very useful method is when you want to explore if, when, and how different groups are portrayed in different ways. Some examples of research questions like this would include: Are women and men portrayed differently in advertising? Has this changed over time? Does the portrayal of women and men in advertising vary by type of magazine/newspaper/television show/Web page/social media site? Do media portray Asian, Black, Latinx, Native peoples, and white male professional athletes differently? How about female athletes of different racial or ethnic groups? Differential portrayal often indicates inequality. Analyzing media representations of athletes and coupling this analysis with statistics on the payscale for professional athletes could be especially illuminating.

An example of this type of analysis comes from Shor et al. (2015), who used content analysis to examine the representation of women in U.S. print media. Examining approximately 200 newspapers, they argued that most media coverage focuses upon the upper echelons of the stratification system. Although women's social position has increased dramatically since the middle of the 20th century, women are still significantly underrepresented at the highest levels of the occupational and social structure. In addition, Shor and colleagues found that parts of the newspapers that have female editors as well as "newspapers whose editorial board have higher female representation" have significantly higher coverage of women. Correlation is not necessarily causation, however. They further examined newspapers where a male editor is replaced by a female editor and, interestingly, found that "women's coverage rates do not noticeably improve" (Shor et al., 2015, p. 960).

Since the early 1980s, scores of researchers have used content analysis to document the gendered nature of sports coverage. Researchers have examined live sports coverage and newspaper and magazine articles for a wide variety of sports. A very influential researcher in the field of sociology of sport is Michael Messner. An early article he and several colleagues wrote on sportscasting related to female and male athletes is very descriptive of their findings: "Separating the Men From the Girls: The Gendered Language of Televised Sports." They analyzed the commentary of 1989 U.S. Open tennis matches, and the 1989 women and men's NCAA basketball tournaments. Their content analysis found that the commentary was not as "overtly sexist" as described in earlier research. Nonetheless, in both sports, the verbal coverage was highly gendered. For example, during the televised basketball games, both in the verbal commentary and in the graphics used on screen, women's games were regularly labeled as just that—the "women's" basketball game. This *never* happened during the men's games. A second finding

TABLE 10.1 ■ Use of First and Last Names During Tennis Commentary			
	First Only	Last Only	First and Last
Women	304 (52.7)	166 (28.8)	107 (18.5)
Men	44 (7.8)	395 (69.8)	127 (22.4)

Note: Numbers in each column represent the total number of references during the verbal commentary. Numbers in parentheses represent percentages.

Source: Messner et al., 1993.

from their research had to do with naming. Female athletes were often referred to as "girls," while male athletes were *never* referred to as "boys." Instead, they were called "'men,' 'young men,' or 'young fellas'" (Messner et al., 1993, p. 127). They also found that female athletes were much more likely to be referred to using their first names only, and male athletes were much more likely to be referenced using only their last names. Table 10.1 provides some data on this pattern from their article.

CONSIDER THIS...

The research by Messner et al. was published several decades ago. Do you think the results of the research would be different if you collected similar data today? Do you think the results would vary by type of sport?

The title of Messner's early research was prophetic of the findings of dozens and dozens of articles published over the coming decades. Much more recent data by Schmidt use content analysis to examine a random sample of sports articles in five top circulation newspapers in Australia, England, and the United States, yielding 3,382 articles (Schmidt, 2018, p. 62). He found that men were the topic of 84% of the articles, while only 3% were about women athletes or women's sports. The remainder of the articles talked about both men and women (2.4%) or did not relate to men or women (10.5%) (Schmidt, 2018, p. 63).

Political Topics

A third situation when content analysis is a useful tool is when there are political situations where what is said by one group may differ from what other types of evidence suggest is the case. Vasi et al. (2015) were interested in the impact of an award-winning documentary film about fracking upon social movement mobilization against fracking, as well as local government bans on fracking. As part of a mixed methods approach, their work examined variables like Google searches on fracking, Twitter activity related to fracking issues, and newspaper coverage of the topic. They found that screenings of the film increased all three of these activities, and these in turn led to many local fracking bans.

Exploratory and Descriptive Research

Content analysis is particularly appropriate/useful for exploratory research in areas where very little previous research has been done. It is also particularly appropriate/useful for descriptive research, where the research question seeks careful descriptions of some social phenomenon.

DOING SOCIOLOGY 10.2

Analyzing an Academic Article That Uses Content Analysis

In this exercise, you will read and analyze an academic abstract in which the researcher uses content analysis.

Read the following abstract from a research article, then answer the questions that follow.

This content analysis of gender role portrayals in 49 episodes of 40 distinct United States tween television programs aired in 2011 examined two genres: teen scene (geared towards girls) and action-adventure (geared towards boys). This programming is of interest because tweens are a lucrative market, they watch more television than any other age group, and television programs are created specifically for them. Furthermore, members of this special group are in an important developmental stage in which social and intellectual schema are established and identity and gender are explored. The analysis focused on the numbers of male and female characters in both genres, and the gender role portrayals of characters in terms of appearance, behaviors, and personality characteristics in the two genres. Results show that females, compared to the U.S. population, were underrepresented in the action adventure genre, but that the gender distribution in the teen scene genre mirrored the male–female distribution in the U.S. population. Overall, compared to males, females were more attractive, more concerned about their appearance, received comments about their "looks." Females were presented similarly in both genres. Overall, males were shown in varying levels of attractiveness, and were portrayed more stereotypically in the action adventure genre. Exploring these results through the lenses of cultivation theory and social cognitive theory shows that tween viewers could potentially develop narrow conceptions about their range of possibilities in the world.

Source: Gerding & Signorielli, 2014.

Discussion Questions

1. What was the research question being addressed in the article?
2. What type of content analysis did the author(s) use—qualitative, quantitative, or both?
3. What are some of the key findings from this study?

Advantages of Content Analysis

For researchers trying to understand and analyze the social world, content analyses offer several advantages. First, content analysis can give you access to information about other times and places even when you cannot interview the people involved. The earlier examples of research on images of Black Americans in children's books (Pescosolido et al., 1997) and underrepresentation of women in printed news coverage (Shor et al., 2015) provide two illustrations of historical analyses using content analysis.

A second advantage of content analysis is that it is relatively inexpensive, both in terms of time and money. Unlike other methods, such as surveys, in which the development, pre-testing, and revisions of a questionnaire often take weeks or months, content analysis coding can be started with a relatively small amount of pre-planning. Data collection and transcription of interviews can take even longer—sometimes years! Administering a nationally representative sample of either a survey or a series of interviews can be especially costly and is not possible for most individual researchers. In contrast, a content analysis study can be performed by one researcher in a short amount of time, with little or no funds required, especially if the materials being coded are freely available.

A third advantage of content analysis is that researchers can analyze data that are publicly available. Since no human subjects are involved, researchers do not typically need approval of an IRB to conduct this type of work. IRB approval can often take a significant amount of time.

A fourth benefit of content analysis is that it is relatively easy to learn how to code data. This leads directly to a fifth advantage of content analysis—it is an excellent method for collaborative research. Students—both undergraduate and graduate—can learn how to code data, and work together with faculty to conduct collaborative work.

Disadvantages of Content Analysis

Many of the disadvantages of this method mirror some of its advantages. When using historical data, it may be the case that our contemporary eyes "read" the meanings of text or images in a different way than they were interpreted in other times. Words take on different meanings over time, identities change, and what may be offensive in one sociohistorical context may be normal and even empowering in another.

Similarly, when comparing text or images (whether it is print or electronic) from different cultures or countries, it may be easy to misinterpret their meanings. Coders, readers, and observers from different cultures have a different set of lenses for "reading" cultural products. Using the same example, what is defined as respectful behavior in Saudi Arabia may be very different than the cultural definition found in Japan, Kenya, or Canada. Thus, when doing comparative work using content analysis, great care must be taken in assigning meanings to the cultural products that are being coded.

A further limitation of content analysis is that, although it is relatively easy to describe the content, it is much more difficult to determine *why* the content is the way it is. Content analysis is good for answering "What?," "Where?," "How?," "When," and sometimes "Who?" Content analysis is much less able to definitively answer research questions that ask "Why?" or "What impact does this have on people?" Remember the example of Pescosolido et al.'s research on images of Blacks in children's books? It was relatively easy for the researchers to document what the images were, how they varied between types of books, and how they changed over time. Their study was not, however, able to determine how these images affected readers. Indeed, the researchers did not attempt to answer that important question at all. To do so would require different research methods. This again points to the importance of the use of multiple methods to study many research questions.

Thus, if you want to move beyond exploratory or descriptive research to explanatory research, which seeks to find empirical relationships between variables and explain why the patterns exist, you often need to pair content analysis with other methods of data collection and analysis.

> **Check Your Understanding**
>
> 1. What is content analysis?
> 2. When is content analysis an appropriate method for collecting and analyzing data?
> 3. What are some strengths of content analysis as a research method?
> 4. What are some of the weaknesses of content analysis as a research method?

WHAT ARE THE STEPS FOR DOING A CONTENT ANALYSIS?

When using content analysis, the research process is generally the same as that in any other type of data collection. Some aspects of the research, however, such as the choice of a sample and the process of conceptualization, have particular characteristics when doing content analysis. A good way to illustrate this is to follow a specific example throughout the process. In this case we'll explore using content analysis to study patterns and trends in the college curriculum in undergraduate sociology.[1]

Clarifying Your Research Questions

As discussed in Chapter 2, the first step in any study is to develop a clear research question or set of questions. By the early 2000s, nearly half of all undergraduate hours in sociology were taught in 2-year institutions, yet virtually no research had been done on sociology in that setting (Zingraff, 2002). As noted earlier, content analysis is often a useful research method for doing exploratory research when very few studies have been done on a topic. The absence of research on sociology curricula in 2-year institutions prompted a research team, including three undergraduate students, to conduct their own research on this topic.

The research questions were very straightforward: What sociology courses are taught in 2-year institutions in the United States? Do the courses have any prerequisites? And what is the total number of sociology courses offered by each institution? This research project is discussed further in the Sociologists in Action feature.

---

[1] To read more about this research, see Kain, 2017

SOCIOLOGISTS IN ACTION: DOING RESEARCH AS AN UNDERGRADUATE

LAUREN R. CONTRERAS

Lauren R. Contreras

Courtesy of Lauren R. Contreras

During my time as an undergraduate sociology major at Southwestern University, I had the opportunity to work with a team of undergraduate sociology majors and our professor, Dr. Ed Kain, to conduct research on sociology programs at 2-year higher education institutions. Dr. Kain introduced our team to content analysis, which allowed us to review institutional course catalogs for the number and types of sociology courses available at 2-year institutions.

As part of the research team, I learned how to code data, assisted with developing a codebook, and analyzed the course catalogs. Through this project, I also learned more about the structure of sociology departments at 2-year colleges. This project provided an important assessment of sociology at 2-year institutions, which could lead to more research on this topic.

Through this project, I also became aware of the limitations of content analysis. I learned content analysis is a good method to gather descriptive data, but there is also a need to dig deeper to better understand what the findings from content analysis reveal. In our study of sociology at 2-year institutions, looking at syllabi and enrollment numbers would give more context to our findings.

As a result of the work our research team did, we were able to submit a paper to the journal *Teaching Sociology*, which was accepted for publication (Kain et al., 2007). Before graduating from college, I was already a published author! With a publication on my CV, I had the confidence to apply to master's programs in higher education. Shortly thereafter, I received a master's degree in education in higher education from the Harvard Graduate School of Education.

The knowledge I gained through this content analysis project as an undergraduate helped me learn how to conduct research and gave me the confidence that I, too, could be a researcher.

Lauren R. Contreras is a 3rd-year doctoral student in higher education at the University of Denver, where she conducts qualitative research with her adviser and a research team.

Discussion Question

What are some of the benefits of doing research as an undergraduate that Lauren discusses?

Choosing a Sample

As with other research methods, the type of sampling design that you choose for a content analysis project depends upon the research question and the type of research. In all cases, you strive for your sample to be representative of the population of documents about which you want to draw conclusions. The type of sample chosen is particularly linked to whether your research question is exploratory, descriptive, or explanatory.

A key consideration when choosing your sample is to think about the population about which you want to draw conclusions. You are *not* trying to "prove" your point. Rather, you are trying to systematically examine the data and describe what you find in the content you analyze.

To collect a sample, it is helpful (though not always possible) to have a complete list of the entire population about which you want to draw conclusions. This is called a sampling frame. Content analyses typically rely on either quota samples or systematic samples. A quota sample—where researchers select a specified number of observations from specified subgroups—may have been problematic for the study of 2-year institutions. Although the researchers could have used this method to select a sample that was representative of the total population in terms of type of 2-year institution (public, not-for-profit; private, for-profit; and private, not-for-profit), this sampling strategy might have missed patterns based upon geographic variation or size of institution. Instead, the research team chose to use a systematic sample. The researchers used the Carnegie Foundation list of 2-year institutions as their sampling frame. This list sorts the institutions into the three groups listed above, then lists them alphabetically by state, with institutions in alphabetical order within each state. The researchers chose every 10th institution, resulting in a sample of 166 2-year institutions (Kain et al., 2007).

Because this 2007 research was the first done on the topic, it was exploratory in nature. The sample needed to aim at being representative so that it could provide a sense of the general structure of the sociology curriculum at 2-year institutions. Researchers Rowell and This (2013) later returned to this research question and moved to a more descriptive approach. They wanted more detailed analyses of sociology courses in 2-year institutions. As a result, they chose a different sampling scheme; indeed, they coded as many college catalogs as were available, limiting themselves to public institutions. This allowed them to move beyond the original exploratory analysis and examine state-by-state variation. Many of their findings replicated the earlier research, but they also found geographic variation that was influenced by articulation agreements between 2-year and 4-year institutions.

Conceptualization in Content Analysis—the Importance of Manifest and Latent Content

One of the first decisions to be made when conceptualizing variables in content analysis is whether your research will be quantitative, qualitative, or both. Researchers also need to decide if their focus is manifest or latent content. Manifest content is content that is on the surface—obvious and clear, and that does not require much interpretation to code. In contrast, latent content refers to underlying meanings and content that requires interpretation. In many cases, researchers are interested in both manifest and latent content.

In the case of research on sociology that is taught in 2-year institutions, it was relatively easy to conceptualize the key ideas. The research questions were focusing only upon manifest content, and no interpretation was needed to decide whether or not a course was offered at an institution. The research was quantitative, as the goal was to calculate what percentage of institutions in the sample taught each type of course—courses like

Manifest content is surface-level, such as the lily pads seen here, which are positioned on the surface of the water, but have underneath another world to be uncovered—like latent content for sociologists.

iStock.com/Jorge Villalba

Introductory Sociology, Social Problems, Family Sociology, and Statistics; identifying the percentage that had pre-requisites; and count how many courses were taught at each institution.

Work by Hilliard (1984) in the sociology of sport provides a good illustration of the contrast between manifest and latent content, and how an analysis of both can be especially informative. Like Messner, Hilliard was interested in gendered images of athletes. He focused particularly upon tennis, and identified 115 articles on top tennis players in mass circulation magazines over a 5-year period. Analyzing the manifest content was relatively straightforward. Article titles tended to mention the men rather than the women. More text was devoted to discussion of the male athletes, and they tended to be talked about first in the articles. The latent content was subtler. His qualitative analysis found that the themes of the stories tended to vary by gender. For example, while a common theme focused upon the strengths and struggles of athletes as they worked to attain being the top in their chosen sport, the flaws varied in stereotypical ways. When women have challenges, the discussion often turns to dependence upon others, or emotional difficulties. In contrast, men's flaws were more likely to include descriptions of bad behavior that was explained by their single-minded determination to succeed at the sport.

Operationalization in Content Analysis—Developing a Codebook

Once researchers decide what they are going to analyze, and how they are going to code the material, they must develop a codebook—a document that indicates numeric codes for each attribute or category of a variable in an analysis, as well as detailed directions about how to code each variable in the study. Returning to the example of studying the sociology curriculum at 2-year institutions, it was relatively easy to operationalize the variables. The team started by examining a set of college catalogs from 2-year institutions and listed all of the courses that were available. We developed a codebook for our variables and added to it if new courses were found during the coding process.

Figure 10.1 shows the first part of the codebook for this project. The codebook begins with an ID number, indicating the institution about which the data were collected. After that, each possible course that might be listed in a catalog became a variable. While looking at a college catalog, each course would be coded 1 if it was listed and had no pre-requisite, 2 if it was listed but had a pre-requisite, 3 if it was not listed, 8 if no courses in sociology were listed in the catalog, and 9 if the catalog was unavailable.

You will also note that each variable has been assigned a variable name, or acronym that refers to the variable. No two variables in the dataset have the same name. When developing a dataset for analysis using a statistical software program like Excel, SPSS, Stata, or R, these variable names will be at the top of the column in which those data are found. Each case also has a column number, indicating which column in the dataset will hold this information.

When operationalizing your variables and creating a codebook, it is important to keep two things in mind. First, the categories for the variable need to be exhaustive. Exhaustive coding categories cover all of the possible cases that apply to that variable. Second, the categories need to be mutually exclusive. Mutually exclusive coding categories do not overlap. If there is overlap, then coding is unclear.

Applying codes to images, behaviors, or people can sometimes be difficult, because coders do not always have sufficient information about the meanings associated with the objects they code, and the identities of the people to whom they apply codes. For example, researchers analyzing military recruitment advertisements may not know the racial, ethnic, and gender identities of the people who appear in the advertisements. They would also likely not know the people's ages or socioeconomic status. To develop exhaustive coding categories, and to acknowledge the researchers' limited information, they could develop coding categories that explicitly reflect uncertainty or ambiguity. For example, rather than coding people as simply "man" or "woman," researchers might code categories as "people who present as men," "people who present as women," and "people who present as nonbinary."

It can also be a challenge to make certain that your categories are mutually exclusive. For example, if you were coding the age of a person in a photograph on Facebook, if you had the following categories, they would *not* be mutually exclusive: 0–10 years old, 10–20 years old, 20–30 years old, and 30+ years old. If the image was someone who was 10 years old, you could place them in both of the first two categories. Because the categories overlap, they are not mutually exclusive.

FIGURE 10.1 ■ A Sample Codebook in Content Analysis—Examining the Sociology Curriculum at 2-Year Institutions

Column 1 Variable 1: ID Number: Refer to the list of institutions that are in the sample. Each college has been assigned an ID Number. Code this number on the coding sheet.

Column 2 Variable 2: INTRO Does the College Catalog List a Course in Introductory Sociology? Code the answer to this question using the following codes:

1 = Yes, there is an Introductory Sociology course listed in the catalog, and it has no pre-requisite.

2 = Yes, there is an Introductory Sociology course listed in the catalog, but it has a pre-requisite before a student can take the course.

3 = No, there is no Introductory Sociology course listed in the catalog.

8 = There is a college catalog, but there are no sociology courses listed in the catalog at all.

9 = Missing data. A college catalog could not be located, or this institution no longer exists.

PLEASE NOTE: The Introductory Sociology course may have another name, such as "Social Patterns and Processes", or "An Introduction to the Social World". Read the course description to determine if it is truly an introduction to the discipline of sociology.

Column 3 Variable 3: SOCPROB Does the College Catalog List a Course in Social Problems? Code the answer to this question using the following codes:

1 = Yes, there is a Social Problems course listed in the catalog, and it has no pre-requisite.

2 = Yes, there is a Social Problems course listed in the catalog, but it has a pre-requisite before a student can take the course.

3 = No, there is no Social Problems course listed in the catalog.

8 = There is a college catalog, but there are no sociology courses listed in the catalog at all.

9 = Missing data. A college catalog could not be located, or this institution no longer exists.

Column 4 Variable 4: FAMSOC Does the College Catalog List a Course in Family Sociology? Code the answer to this question using the following codes:

1 = Yes, there is a Family Sociology course listed in the catalog, and it has no pre-requisite.

2 = Yes, there is a Family Sociology course listed in the catalog, but it has a pre-requisite before a student can take the course.

3 = No, there is no Family Sociology course listed in the catalog.

8 = There is a college catalog, but there are no sociology courses listed in the catalog at all.

9 = Missing data. A college catalog could not be located, or this institution no longer exists.

CONSIDER THIS...

When operationalizing some variables, it can be challenging to have exhaustive and mutually exclusive categories. If you were coding images in advertising for race/ethnicity, how would you operationalize the concept of race/ethnicity? Are the categories that you have chosen exhaustive—do they cover all possibilities? Are the categories mutually exclusive?

DOING SOCIOLOGY 10.3

Recognizing Problems With Content Analysis Categories That Are Not Mutually Exclusive or Exhaustive

In this exercise, you will identify problematic codes and clarify the meaning of mutually exclusive and exhaustive response categories.

Imagine that John and Susan are using content analysis to examine the images on the cover of *Time* magazine's "Person of the Year" issues. This issue is published once per year. From 1927 through 1999 this annual issue was called "Man of the Year." Some of the covers have honored non-humans, and some have included groups of people rather than one person.

In the list of variables below, evaluate whether the categories that Susan and John developed are mutually exclusive and exhaustive. In cases where they are not, write a sentence indicating what needs to be changed to make the categories for the variables both mutually exclusive and exhaustive.

1. Consider Variable 1: Year of the Magazine. Are the categories exhaustive? Are they mutually exclusive? If they are not, what would you change to make them both exhaustive and mutually exclusive?

2. Consider Variable 2: Sex of the Person on the Cover. Are the categories exhaustive? Are they mutually exclusive? If they are not, what would you change to make them both exhaustive and mutually exclusive?

3. Consider Variable 3: Is the Person on the Cover an American? Are the categories exhaustive? Are they mutually exclusive? If they are not, what would you change to make them both exhaustive and mutually exclusive?

4. Consider Variable 4: What is the Approximate Life Stage of the Person on the Cover? Are the categories exhaustive? Are they mutually exclusive? If they are not, what would you change to make them both exhaustive and mutually exclusive?

Check Your Understanding

1. What are some appropriate samples for content analysis?
2. What is the difference between manifest and latent content? Give examples to illustrate your understanding.
3. What is a codebook?
4. What is meant by exhaustive categories for a variable?
5. What is meant by mutually exclusive categories for a variable?

CODING DATA FOR CONTENT ANALYSIS AND CALCULATING INTERCODER RELIABILITY

Once you have finished all of the earlier steps in the research process, you are ready to begin collecting data in content analysis. Once the codes are developed and compiled into an initial codebook, the next step is to create a coding sheet, which is a sheet of paper or electronic document such as a spreadsheet that records the results of your analysis. Each row of data on the coding sheet is all of the information for one case. Figure 10.1 in the previous section of this chapter gave an example of the beginning of the codebook for an analysis of what types of sociology courses are offered at 2-year institutions in the United States. Figure 10.2 shows a sample coding sheet based upon this codebook.

As you collect the data, the coding sheet is used in combination with the codebook to record the data. By themselves, the numbers on the coding sheet have no meaning. They only make sense in combination with the codebook.

During the early part of data collection, coders will often encounter unexpected things. New variables may need to be added to the codebook and coding sheet, or variables may need to be reconceptualized because the categories were not exhaustive or mutually exclusive. Thus, you will note that at the bottom of the sample coding sheet in Figure 10.2, there are directions indicating that the coders should write down any problems or issues they have while coding the data. In the sample coding sheet in Figure 10.2, the coder wrote that she found that many of the institutions offered a course or courses in criminology. As a result, she suggested this be added as a new variable in the codebook and on the coding sheet.

The Importance of Validity and Reliability in Content Analysis

As with other research methods, two important qualities of variables in content analysis are validity and reliability. Validity refers to whether or not a variable is actually measuring what it purports to be measuring. The most common test of validity in content analysis is face validity, which simply asks the question: "On the face of it, does this seem like it is measuring what I want to measure?"

FIGURE 10.2 ■ Sample Coding Sheet for a Quantitative Content Analysis on Sociology Curriculum at 2-Year Institutions in the United States			
ID	INTRO	SOCPROB	FAMSOC
1	1	3	2
2	1	3	2
3	1	1	3
4	1	2	2
5	1	1	2
6	3	1	1
7	1	1	3
8	9	9	9
9	1	1	2

The second important measurement quality in a variable is reliability. If a measure is reliable, that means it is repeatable. If another researcher used the same methods, they would come up with the same conclusions. Coding of manifest content typically has higher rates of reliability than coding of latent content. Similarly, quantitative coding schemes often have higher reliability rates than qualitative coding of content.

There is a tension between reliability and validity in content analysis. When you are creating codes for your categories, if you increase the number of categories, you increase validity—but you decrease reliability. A perfect example illustrating this tension would be if you were coding the age of the people found in advertising. To have the highest degree of validity (are you actually measuring what you want—the age of the people in the images), you might want to code the exact age, or perhaps 5-year age categories. It is highly unlikely, however, that two coders would choose the same age of the person in the image, or even the same 5-year age category. To increase reliability you would collapse categories, and perhaps code only decades—0–10 years old, 11–20 years old, 21–30 years old, etc. Although this would increase your reliability (repeatability), it would decrease the validity of your data.

Intercoder Reliability in Content Analysis

Intercoder reliability refers to the extent to which different coders assign the same scores or codes to an item. Assessing the level of intercoder reliability is the major way to measure reliability in a content analysis. Without some measure of intercoder reliability, it is difficult to know the quality of the data reported in content analysis. Using the same coding scheme, multiple coders score a subset of the sample. They then calculate intercoder reliability—the percentage of times they agreed in their coding. If rates of reliability are low, then they will modify the categories in their coding for each variable. As noted earlier, the development of a coding scheme is a process that takes place in several stages during the operationalization of your variables. A major part of that process is when you calculate intercoder reliability and it is low, thus leading you to reconceptualize your variables.

Using the example of age will again illustrate how this works. Imagine that two coders each coded full-page advertisements that had one human figure in them. The coders were using 10-year age categories. They found that they only agreed on the age of the models in the image five out of 10 times, for an intercoder reliability rate of 50%. Clearly that is a low rate of agreement. After talking about the issue, they reconceptualized the codebook so that instead of age, they would code broad developmental stages: infant/toddler, childhood, adolescent/young adult, adult, and older adult (agreeing that visible signs of aging such as wrinkles and gray hair needed to be present). They recoded the same 10 advertisements using the new coding scheme and found that they had the same scores for nine out of the 10 cases. Thus, their new intercoder reliability rate is 90%—a much more acceptable level of reliability.

CONSIDER THIS...

Why do you think reliability and validity are important in sociological research? Which do you think is more important? If you had to choose one or the other in a variable, which would you choose? Why?

DOING SOCIOLOGY 10.4

Calculating Intercoder Reliability in Content Analysis

In this exercise, you will practice calculating the rate of intercoder reliability.

Imagine that Adrian and Dylan are working together on a research project. They double-coded 10 cases for six variables. Their coding sheets are reproduced in Tables 10.2 and 10.3. The first two rates of intercoder reliability have already been calculated. Calculate the intercoder reliability for each of the remaining four variables. (Simply divide the number of times they agreed by 10, then multiply it by 100, and that will yield a percentage. If they agreed 10 out of 10 times, their intercoder reliability [IR] on that variable is 100%.) Reminder: Intercoder reliability = the number of agreements/10 x 100 to equal a percentage.

TABLE 10.2 ■ Scores on Adrian's Coding Sheet					
2019	1	4	3	7	1
2019	1	4	3	8	2
2018	1	4	2	6	2
2020	3	5	2	6	1
2017	8	5	1	7	1
2012	2	2	3	6	1
2021	4	1	2	7	2
2022	2	6	2	6	2
2019	2	3	2	8	2
2018	2	1	2	9	2

TABLE 10.3 ■ Scores on Dylan's Coding Sheet					
2019	1	4	3	7	1
2019	1	4	3	8	2
2018	2	4	2	7	2
2020	3	5	1	7	1
2017	7	6	1	7	1
2012	2	2	3	6	1
2021	5	1	1	7	2
2022	2	6	1	6	2
2019	1	3	1	8	2
2018	2	1	2	9	2

Column 1 Intercoder Reliability = 10 agreements/10 x 100 = 100%
Column 2 Intercoder Reliability = 6 agreements/10 x 100 = 60%

1. What is the Intercoder Reliability for Column 3?
2. What is the Intercoder Reliability for Column 4?
3. What is the Intercoder Reliability for Column 5?
4. What is the Intercoder Reliability for Column 6?

Check Your Understanding

1. What is a coding sheet, and how is it related to a content analysis codebook?
2. How are reliability and validity important in content analysis?
3. What is intercoder reliability, and how is it calculated?

ANALYZING HISTORICAL RECORDS, DOCUMENTS, AND POLICY

Content analysis is one of the most common forms of unobtrusive methods, but sociologists also routinely analyze policies, documents, and historical material. In these cases, the methods may vary from what has been described as content analysis. Some of the most common differences are described next.

Sampling

In many historical analyses and examinations of archival materials the researcher does not use a sample. Instead, they examine the full universe of available materials—that is, the population. Indeed, when looking at archival materials and historical documents, you often search diligently to find relevant information, and then use everything that you can find. Similarly, researchers analyzing policies typically analyze the full universe of documents and information related to a particular policy, rather than a sample of documents.

A Tendency to Focus Upon a Single Policy

The majority of policy analyses focus upon one policy, often tracing its change over time (Frank et al., 2010). Some examples would include policies on women's property rights, age at marriage, or gay marriage. Again, rather than sampling, the researcher's goal is to gather policy documents on the full population—all of the states in the United States, all of the provinces in Canada, or all of the countries in the world.

When researchers are doing an in-depth study of a single policy—a case study—researchers approach the policy with six key questions in mind: (1) Will the policy be effective? (2) Will it have unintended consequences? (3) Will it have different impacts on different stakeholders? (4) How much will it cost? (5) Is it feasible? And (6) Will different groups of stakeholders view it as acceptable? (Morestin, 2012, p. 3). Indeed, many policy analyses focus a great deal upon stakeholders—groups of people who support and oppose the policy, and who potentially gain or lose something from the enactment or change in a policy.

Content analysis can involve reviewing archival materials and other historical documents.

iStock.com/Ivan Pantic

DOING SOCIOLOGY 10.5

Examining a Policy on Your Campus

In this exercise, you will identify a policy and conduct the first steps of a policy analysis.

A full policy analysis involves a huge amount of research. Answering questions like, "Will the policy be effective?," "How much will it cost?," and "Is it feasible?" take a significant amount of expertise in a number of areas, including budgeting, economics, and politics.

For this exercise, you will reflect on two aspects related to stakeholders—how it might have different impacts on different stakeholders, and how those different groups might view the acceptability of the policy change.

For each of the items below, write a paragraph clearly addressing the question(s). Be prepared to discuss your answers with another person in class or online, as indicated by your instructor.

1. Consider the policy change involved in the legalization of recreational marijuana at the state level (for states where this has not already occurred).

2. Identify at least three different groups of stakeholders who might be affected by this change. Write a paragraph about each set of stakeholders. Make sure that you answer the question, "Will it have different impacts on different stakeholders?"

3. Related to your answers for Item 2, write a paragraph about each set of stakeholders you have identified, and predict whether or not different groups of stakeholders will view it as acceptable. Give support for why you make the arguments that you suggest.

Although the focus may be upon a single policy topic, the analysis can nonetheless be extremely complex. A good example comes from Taylor et al. (2018), who studied public policies affecting transgender people. Their book explored these policies in a wide set of domains. One chapter, for example, focuses upon education policy. The authors note that "Transgender students face a challenging environment throughout their education career" (p. 260). Even narrowing the focus to educational policy, they note that because U.S. education policy is decentralized, they must examine many different levels of policy—ranging from Title IX (requiring schools to provide "equal opportunities and resources for sex-segregated athletic programs") at the national level, through state policies, all the way down to local school districts. With some 130,000 schools nationwide, the challenge of analyzing this policy is daunting (pp. 261–271). One common approach for summarizing data in this type of policy analysis is to use mapping techniques, illustrating variation by county/state/province or country.

CONSIDER THIS. . .

Can you think of some social policies that have changed significantly during your lifetime?

If you were to study one topic area in policy, what would it be? If you could compare several countries on this policy, which few would you select for an interesting comparison?

Sociological analyses of polices can also be international. Although most policy analyses focus on one policy in one country, or make comparisons between only a few (usually Western) countries, Frank and colleagues (2010) took on a much more ambitious task: to examine "worldwide trends in the criminal regulation of sex, 1945 to 2005." As noted earlier, they do not use a sample. Their goal is to include information an all of the countries in the world, examining the full population, not just a sample.

Rather than focus upon a single policy, Frank and colleagues used policy analysis to explore a broad question. They argue that the "world-society" perspective suggests that "especially after World War II," societies around the world "have grown increasingly universalistic, rationalized, and global rather than particularistic, fragmented, and local." They further argue that "Sex shifted from an activity meant to propagate the collective...to an activity meant to enhance individual pleasure through self-expression" (p. 870). They examine the expansion and contraction of four different types of laws regulating sexual behavior. In two cases (adultery laws and sodomy laws) they predict contraction of the laws, and their predictions are borne out by the data. In the other two cases (laws related to rape and to child sexual abuse) they predict expansion of protections for the people who are being injured, and the data support their predictions. They suggest that "Clearly, states did not 'get out of the bedroom' during this period but moved from its collectivized to its individualized corner" (pp. 877–878).

A final example illustrates how multimethods research can combine a number of the research methods discussed in this chapter and elsewhere in this book. As a window to understanding some central issues about culture and social movements, Ghaziani and Baldassarri (2011) studied a set of LGBT+ marches on Washington, D.C. They note that "Washington marches leave behind paper trails, facilitating the collection of primary source materials.... Our data consist of 424 randomly sampled newspaper articles ... and more than 200 archival documents, all of which ... were] gathered from seven institutional archives and the personal papers of 14 activists" (p. 184). Again, for the historical research using archival documents and personal papers, they do not conduct a sample but use the full universe of materials. In contrast, for the content analysis of media coverage, they use a random sample of newspaper articles.

Ghaziani and Baldassarri tackle a set of complex questions in the study of culture and political dissent. They argue that the literature tends to see dichotomies—culture is either described as "coherent or incoherent," and political dissent is conceptualized as "unifying or divisive" (p. 179). Their multimethod analyses indicate a much more complex picture. By examining four different LGBT+ marches on Washington (in 1979, 1987, 1993, and 2000), they show that some themes, such as the importance of equality and community building, are very stable over all four marches. In contrast, some themes (including AIDS, and the importance of education) are much more variable over time.

Check Your Understanding

1. How does the analysis of historical and archival documents differ from content analysis in terms of sampling?
2. When examining policies, what are some of the most common types of analyses?

CONCLUSION

Content analysis and policy analysis are both great examples of unobtrusive methods, and both are valuable tools in the toolbox of social research methods. Both techniques can generate important information and insights on their own, but sociologists often combine these forms of analysis with other approaches. As is shown in the next chapter, "Mixed Methods Research," sociologists often use multiple methodological approaches in the course of a single study. Doing so allows them to see a question from multiple angles provide especially nuanced and comprehensive answers.

REVIEW

10.1 What are unobtrusive methods, and what is their benefit for sociological research?

Unobtrusive methods are any methods by which you collect data without directly interacting with the subjects of your study or letting them know that they are being studied. They have several benefits for sociological research, including avoiding problems with people changing their behavior because they know they are being studied. Another benefit is that they tend to be relatively inexpensive when compared to many other methods.

Some common types of unobtrusive methods are content analysis, analysis of existing statistics, examination of electronic media using measures such as search frequencies, analysis of historical documents, and policy analysis.

10.2 What is content analysis, and what are some strengths and weaknesses of this method?

Content analysis is the systematic analysis of cultural products, including text and images. It is a particularly appropriate method when doing historical or comparative research. Because you cannot travel to a different time and interview people, systematic analysis of cultural products from other historical periods can help you understand social behavior and patterns in other times. It is also the ideal method for describing when different groups are portrayed differently than each other. It is useful for exploring political topics, when different groups may make contrasting claims. It is also particularly appropriate for exploratory and descriptive research.

There are at least five advantages of content analysis: (1) t is ideally suited for many historical and comparative research questions; (2) it is relatively inexpensive both in terms of time and money; (3) it typically does not need approval by an IRB; (4) it is relatively easy to learn how to code data; and thus, (5) it is a method that is often suited for collaborative research between faculty and students.

One disadvantage of content analysis is that how a coder "reads" or interprets texts or cultural products may be highly variable over time and space. Great care needs to be taken when interpreting materials from other historical periods or cultures. A second disadvantage is that it is difficult for content analysis to answer research questions that ask "why?" or "with what effect?" Typically, it needs to be combined with other methods to address these questions. Great care needs to be taken when examining content in electronic resources such as Web pages or forms of social media.

10.3 What are the steps for doing a content analysis?

In content analysis the basic process of research is like any other method within sociology. You begin by developing your research question, selecting a sample, and specifying what you mean by your concepts and how you plan to measure them. Some aspects of the process, however, are unique to content analysis. Decisions about sampling differ from some other methods, and purposive samples, quota samples, and systematic samples are often used. Another example of this uniqueness is considerations of manifest and latent content during conceptualization and operationalization of variables. As with other research methods, it is important that the categories of variables are exhaustive and mutually exclusive.

10.4 How do you code data in content analysis, and how do you calculate intercoder reliability?

A coding sheet is a paper or electronic matrix, like a spreadsheet, on which coders score each variable for each case in their content analysis. Rows are cases and columns are variables. The scores or codes they use are taken from the codebook that has been developed during the conceptualization of the research.

Both reliability and validity are important in content analysis. Face validity (does the variable, on the face of it, appear to be measuring what it plans to measure?) is the most common type of validity in content analysis. Reliability, or repeatability, is typically measured by calculating intercoder reliability. Two or more researchers code the same set of data, then compare their answers. They take the number of agreements and divide them by the number of cases they double-coded, then multiply that by 100, yielding a percentage.

10.5 How do sociologists analyze historical records/documents and policy documents?

A major difference between the analysis of historical and archival records as well as policy documents and content analysis has to do with sampling. Most archival research as well as policy analysis does not use a sample. Either it examines the entire population of documents available, or sometimes focuses upon a single case study.

Policy analyses often focus upon the role of actors and stakeholders. Although often only one policy domain is being studied, the analysis can nonetheless be extremely complex. Mapping is one analytic technique that is often used in policy analysis.

analysis of existing statistics (p. 180)

codebook (p. 188)

coding sheet (p. 190)

content analysis (p. 181)

descriptive research (p. 183)

exhaustive coding categories (p. 188)

explanatory research (p. 185)

exploratory research (p. 183)

face validity (p. 196)

Hawthorne effect (p. 179)

intercoder reliability (p. 191)

latent content (p. 187)

manifest content (p. 187)

mutually exclusive coding categories (p. 188)

qualitative content analysis (p. 181)

sampling frame (p. 187)

unobtrusive methods (p. 179)

11 COMBINING QUANTITATIVE AND QUALITATIVE APPROACHES: MIXED METHODS RESEARCH

Maura Kelly

STUDENT LEARNING QUESTIONS

11.1 What is mixed methods research, and what are the different approaches to it?

11.2 What are the benefits of mixed methods research?

11.3 What are the challenges of mixed methods research?

11.4 What are the best practices for mixed methods research, and the steps necessary to conduct mixed methods research?

HOW I GOT ACTIVE IN SOCIOLOGY

Maura Kelly

I was introduced to sociology in a Sociology of Gender course at Bates College in the late 1990s. Emily Kane, the faculty member teaching the course, was a truly dynamic teacher who sparked my interest in studying sociology generally and gender specifically. Sociology appealed to me because of the focus on understanding the causes of inequality *and* identifying solutions to these problems. While I also encountered these ideas in courses in other departments, for me, sociological theories, methods, and research were the most compelling way to understand our social world (they still are).

This love of sociology saw me through my undergraduate sociology major, a master's degree in sociology, and eventually a PhD in sociology. Now, as a faculty member, I teach undergraduate and graduate courses and do research. Currently, I am collaborating on a variety of projects in Oregon and Washington related to gender, race/ethnicity, and the construction trades. This line of research primarily focuses on evaluating programs designed to improve the recruitment and retention of apprentices and promote a diverse construction workforce. For example, we are evaluating the effectiveness of several trainings designed to reduce job site harassment and discrimination. For these evaluation projects, we use interviews, focus groups, surveys, secondary data analysis, and we often employ mixed methods research designs. We like to use mixed methods in evaluation research because they allow us to present both the quantitative data needed to evaluate whether the programs are successful as well as the qualitative data needed to tell the stories of the construction workers impacted by these programs. While the statistical analyses provide critical information, we often find that it is hearing the stories that really moves people to make change.

MIXED METHODS RESEARCH

This chapter provides an overview of mixed methods research, which integrates quantitative methods (e.g., surveys) and qualitative methods (e.g., interviews) in the same research project. Throughout this chapter, you will find discussions of mixed methods case studies conducted by the author of this chapter (see Figures 11.2, 11.3, and 11.4). These case studies will be used to help you to understand the types of mixed methods design and how researchers implement them in real-world research. First up is a discussion of different approaches to mixed methods research.

Quantitative and Qualitative Methods

As described in previous chapters, research methods are often categorized as qualitative or quantitative. Qualitative methods (e.g., interviews; focus groups; content analysis or discourse analysis; and ethnography, observation, or field work) focus on thematic analysis and present data in the form of text, observations, and/or quotes. Quantitative methods (e.g., surveys, experiments, and quantitative content analysis) include statistical analysis of numeric data (generally performed using statistical software) with results typically presented in the form of tables and figures.

Each of these approaches has strengths and weaknesses. One strength of qualitative research is the use of data to understanding the complexities of populations, contexts, and experiences or processes, particularly those that are not already well known. Qualitative research is also well suited for providing rich descriptive and detailed data, often using the language and experiences of participants. Qualitative research generally has limited ability to generalize findings from a sample to a larger population. Quantitative methods, in contrast, are best suited to understanding broad trends and generalizing about relationships observed in the study sample to the larger population (in research designs with random samples). Research with quantitative methods has a limited ability to provide detailed information on individual participants.

Approaches to Mixed Methods: Convergent, Additional, Sequential

While mixed methods research indicates the use of both quantitative and qualitative methods, researchers can integrate different methods in a variety of ways. Broadly speaking, there are three approaches to combining methods: convergent, additional, and sequential (Morgan, 2014).

The Convergent Approach

In convergent mixed methods research, researchers use the same research question for both quantitative and qualitative research. We might symbolize this as: qualitative=quantitative. The findings from the multiple methods can be compared, and serve as a form of triangulation. Triangulation refers to the process of confirming findings by using different methods.

Consider, for example, a researcher who is interested in how socioeconomic status shapes people's access to nutritious and affordable food in western North Carolina. The researcher might begin by combining collecting information from the U.S. Census Bureau about the communities in western North Carolina, including the number of households in each, the average income in each, and the rate of households living in poverty. They might then collect data on the location of grocery stores in each community. Using a spreadsheet or database, they could determine whether more impoverished communities also had fewer grocery stores. They could combine this quantitative analysis with an interview study, asking people from the region to describe how often they go to the grocery store, how convenient it is to get there, what they ultimately purchase, and why. The interviews might find that people of lower socioeconomic status went to the grocery store less frequently, found the process of getting there to be less convenient, and buy food that is less nutritious because it less expensive.

As shown in Figure 11.1, though the findings from each portion of the study differ slightly, they both point to the same general conclusion. Taken together, they provide strong evidence that the access to nutritious food in western North Carolina was structured by socioeconomic status.

FIGURE 11.1 ■ The Convergent Approach in Mixed Methods Research

Data from Census and location of large grocery stores: High-income communities have a higher number of large grocery stores on average, and a higher number of grocery stores per capita. = **Data from interviews:** People in high-income communities report shopping at large grocery stores more frequently than people in low-income communities, and perceive this shopping to be more convenient.

The Additional Approach

In the additional approach to mixed methods research, researchers answer different (but related) research questions paired with each method. We might symbolize this as: qualitative + quantitative. For example, you might conduct a survey of a work organization that asks about a wide variety of topics and also conduct interviews to get more detailed information on one specific topic of interest. In the additional approach, the researcher must take extra care to justify how the two methods fit together in a single mixed methods research design.

Consider a recent study of television news coverage of welfare reform (see Figure 11.2). This research used an additional approach, asking different subquestions with the quantitative and qualitative data. The overall research question is: "How were the welfare reforms of the 1990s covered in television news media?" Subquestions answered by the quantitative content analysis included: How often was welfare covered in the news? Which specific policies were reported in the news? Which sources were quoted in favor and in opposition to these policies? Subquestions answered by the qualitative content analysis included: How were current and former public assistance recipients portrayed? How was the controlling image of the "welfare mother" leveraged in the news stories? Answers to both sets of questions are needed to fully show how welfare reforms of the 1990s were covered in the television news media.

The Sequential Approach

In sequential mixed methods research, the results of the first method inform the use of the second method. These types of projects can start with either a qualitative method or a quantitative method. We might symbolize this approach as: qualitative → quantitative or quantitative → qualitative.

In "qualitative first" sequential approaches, the qualitative method is implemented first and the quantitative method is implemented second; for example, a researcher might conduct an interview study with a small number of middle school teachers and then conduct a survey of all middle school teachers in the district. Qualitative first allows the researcher to ask open-ended questions at the start of the data collection, which allows them to better understand the population, context, or experiences being studied. In open-ended questions, participants can frame the issues in ways that make sense to them and inform the researcher about what is most important. Rather than the researcher assuming they already know how people think about an issue and what they think is important, the researcher can learn from the participants and design the next stage of their project with a more informed vantage point. These approaches also allow the researcher to identify which words and phrases will be most effective in the quantitative research. The exploratory nature of qualitative methods is particularly useful when studying a topic where little is known as well as studying experiences or processes in a new population or context. Finally, in these approaches, findings that are identified in the qualitative data can be assessed with quantitative data to determine if they are true for the larger population.

In "quantitative first" sequential approaches, the order is reversed. For example, a researcher might start with a survey of middle school teachers in a district and then follow up with a smaller number of interviews with a subset of those teachers. These approaches may also be used when a researcher uses secondary survey data (data collected by other researchers) and follow this by collecting new qualitative

---

FIGURE 11.2 ■ Mixed Methods Case Study, "Control Over the Reproduction and Mothering of Poor Women: An Analysis of Television News Coverage of Welfare Reform"

Research question: How were the welfare reforms of the 1990s covered in television news media?

Quantitative data and method: Quantitative content analysis of television news segments representing a random sample of television evening news segments over two minutes long, stratified by network (ABC, NBC, and CBS), between 1992 and 2007. Video segments were obtained from the vanderbilt Television Archive. (N = 40)

Qualitative data and method: Qualitative content analysis of television news segments (same data used in the quantitative analysis). (N = 40)

Source: Kelly, 2010.

data. There are several reasons for choosing quantitative first approaches. One purpose of the quantitative first approach is to use quantitative data to identify a research site for participant observation or identify participants to contact for interviews. Follow-up qualitative research can also illustrate quantitative findings, giving them more depth. This approach allows researchers to more fully understand the "why" behind quantitative findings. Finally, a quantitative first approach also allows researchers to identify findings from the quantitative data that are surprising or interesting and interrogate them further with the qualitative data. This can be useful in evaluation research with null findings, for example, when research does not demonstrate that the program being evaluated has the expected outcomes.

The study on African American women's attitudes toward science (see Figure 11.3) is an example of a quantitative first sequential approach. The project started with a quantitative analysis of survey data. The dependent variable (or outcome variable) was respondents' answer to the question: "Overall modern science does more harm than good, do you agree or disagree?" Researchers looked at a variety of independent variables (or predictor variables) that might predict attitudes toward science: gender, race, age, income, education, political views, and religion. In the quantitative analysis, the researchers found that African American women had more negative attitudes toward science than did African American men, white women, and white men. Based on this key finding, the researchers designed a qualitative interview study of African American women to further understand their experiences and beliefs about science.

Multistage Sequential Some sequential mixed methods projects have more than two methods; in these projects, each method informs the following methods. An example of a multistage sequential project is shown in Figure 11.4.

In this project, there were three distinct phases of data collection and analysis. In the article "When Working Hard Is Not Enough for Female and Racial/Ethnic Minority Apprentices in the Highway Trades," Kelly et al. (2015) describe research that had a quantitative→qualitative→quantitative approach. First, the researchers examined administrative records of registered apprentices in Oregon; these data were provided by the Bureau of Labor and Industries, the public agency partner funding this research. In this analysis, researchers assessed differences in recruitment and retention by race and gender. Building on the findings of the initial quantitative analysis, the researchers wanted to know why women and people of color have lower recruitment and retention rates. In other words, what are the challenges these apprentices face? To answer this question, researchers started with interviewing staff of trade organizations, including unions and employers. Next, they interviewed apprentices who

---

FIGURE 11.3 ■ Mixed Methods Case Study, "More Harm Than Good? A Mixed Methods Approach to Understanding African American Women's Attitudes Towards Science"

Research question: How do African American women's attitude towards science compare with other race/gender groups? What explains African American Women's attitudes towards science?

Quantitative data and method: General Social Survey (GSS), survey of a random sample of the U.S. population (N = 2,006)

Qualitative data and method: Qualitative interviews with African American women in Portland Oregon, recruited using flyers posted in public places in two historically African American neighborhoods (N = 10)

Source: Kelly et al., forthcoming.

FIGURE 11.4 ■ Mixed Methods Case Study, "When Working Hard Is Not Enough for Female and Racial/Ethnic Minority Apprentices in the Highway Trades"

Research Questions: What are the trends in recruitment and retention of women and people of color in apprenticeships in the highway trades in Oregon? What challenges do women and people of color face in completing their apprenticeships? What narratives do staff and apprentices use to explain the success (and failure) of apprentices?

Quantitative data and method: Quantitative analysis of administrative data on registered apprentices in Oregon (N = 2,000)

Qualitative data and method: Interviews with staff (N = 20) and apprentices (N = 24)

Quantitative data and method: Quantitative analysis of a mail survey of apprentices (N = 177)

Source: Kelly et al., 2015.

had either completed or been terminated from their apprentice-ships. The 24 interviews were divided so there were equal numbers of completed/terminated and also equal numbers of women of color, white women, and men of color. After completing the interviews, researchers used the findings to develop a mail survey. The purpose of the survey was to assess the trends observed in the interviews in the larger population.

As indicated previously, the research question is a critical component of mixed methods research design. For mixed methods research, there may be a single research question that is answered with both quantitative and qualitative data; one main research question with additional research questions for the quantitative and qualitative methods; or one research question for the quantitative portion of the study and a different research question for the qualitative portion. These decisions depend on the unique characteristics of the study and the methods being used.

A good research question must meet several criteria: (1) it can be answered with the *methods* being utilized; (2) it can be answered with the source(s) of *data* being utilized; (3) it includes research design details necessary to make the research question answerable with the method and data (e.g., population, location, time frame); (4) it is appropriate in scope for the proposed research design (i.e., not too broad, not too narrow); and (5) it does not make assumptions about what the findings will be (adapted from Kelly & Gurr, 2019).

Dr. Maura Kelly (left) and graduate research assistant Sasha Bassett (right) arrive at a construction job site at 6:45 a.m. on a Monday morning to administer surveys about job site harassment to 200 workers. Closed-ended questions on the survey included: "How many times in the last month have you seen others be called names, be yelled at, or be cursed at?" Open-ended questions included: "Please briefly describe harassment you've seen on this job site in the last month." In this mixed methods research, both closed-ended and open-ended questions provide important information to the researchers about job site harassment.

Courtesy of Maura Kelly

CONSIDER THIS. . .

Imagine that you have been asked to design a mixed methods study to assess student satisfaction on your college campus. What types of data would you collect? Would you use a convergent, additional, or sequential approach?

DOING SOCIOLOGY 11.1

Reading Mixed Methods Abstracts

In this exercise, you will examine how quantitative and qualitative data are used in sociological research.

Read the abstracts from the following three articles, then answer the questions that follow.
Article 1: Desmond, M. (2012). Eviction and the reproduction of urban poverty. *American Journal of Sociology, 118*(1), 88–133.

Combining statistical and ethnographic analyses, this article explores the prevalence and ramifications of eviction in the lives of the urban poor. A quantitative analysis of administrative and survey data finds that eviction is commonplace in inner-city black neighborhoods and that women from those neighborhoods are evicted at significantly higher rates than men. A qualitative analysis of ethnographic data based on fieldwork among evicted tenants and their landlords reveals multiple mechanisms propelling this discrepancy. In poor black neighborhoods, eviction is to women what incarceration is to men: a typical but severely consequential occurrence contributing to the reproduction of urban poverty.

Article 2: Armstrong, E. A., England, P., & Fogarty, A. C. K. (2012). Accounting for women's orgasm and sexual enjoyment in college hookups and relationships. *American Sociological Review, 77*(3), 435–462.

This article investigates the determinants of orgasm and sexual enjoyment in hookup and relationship sex among heterosexual college women and seeks to explain why relationship sex is better for women in terms of orgasm and sexual enjoyment. We use data from women respondents to a large online survey of undergraduates at 21 U.S. colleges and universities and from 85 in-depth interviews at two universities. We identify four general views of the sources of orgasm and sexual enjoyment—technically competent genital stimulation, partner-specific learning, commitment, and gender equality. We find that women have orgasms more often in relationships than in hookups. Regression analyses reveal that specific sexual practices, experience with a particular partner, and commitment all predict women's orgasm and sexual enjoyment. The presence of more sexual practices conducive to women's orgasm in relationship sex explains some of why orgasm is more common in relationships. Qualitative analysis suggests a double standard also contributes to why relationship sex is better for women: both men and women question women's (but not men's) entitlement to pleasure in hookups but believe strongly in women's (as well as men's) entitlement to pleasure in relationships. More attention is thus given to producing female orgasm in relationships.

Article 3: Waller, M. R., & Emory, A. D. (2018). Visitation orders, family courts, and fragile families. *Journal of Marriage and Family, 80*(3), 653–670.

Despite proposals to make parenting time a part of all new child support orders, limited research has examined why some unmarried are more likely than others to establish legal visitation agreements. This mixed-methods study draws on qualitative data collected from unmarried mothers and fathers living in New York (*N*=70) to develop hypotheses about the contexts in which parents set up visitation orders, which are then tested in a large sample of unmarried parents living apart (*N*=1,392). Both qualitative and quantitative findings show that disengagement, cooperation, and conflict in the coparenting relationship postseparation influence unmarried parents' decisions about whether to establish a legal visitation agreement. The qualitative data further illustrate how parents' distrust of the court system, preference for informal agreements, and uncertainty about the custody of nonmarital children inform their decisions. The article concludes by considering approaches for helping low-conflict coparents set up visitation agreements outside of family court.

1. What is the main research question that each article addresses?

2. What quantitative data did the authors of each article use to help them answer their research questions?

3. What qualitative data did the authors of each article use to help them answer their research questions?

4. How does using two research methods provide information beyond what a single method could provide?

Check Your Understanding

1. What is mixed methods research?
2. What are the strengths and limitations of qualitative and quantitative data?
3. How would you describe the *convergent, additional,* and *sequential* approaches to mixed methods research?

ADVANTAGES OF MIXED METHODS RESEARCH

There are some unique benefits to implementing a mixed methods research design. This section describes four main advantages of mixed methods research: expanded scope of questions that can be answered within a single study; overcoming limitations of a single method; triangulation (confirming findings across different methods); and sequencing methods so that the findings of one inform the other.

One advantage of mixed methods is that it allows researchers to examine an expanded scope of questions that can be answered with a single research project. Different methods provide different tools for gaining knowledge about a particular topic.

A second advantage of mixed methods research is that it provides opportunities for overcoming some of the limitations of using quantitative or qualitative methods alone. As noted above, quantitative approaches, such as surveys, are better for understanding broad or generalizable trends, but are limited in the depth of information about individual cases. Qualitative methods, like interviews, allow for that more in-depth understanding, but are generally not well suited for generalizing to larger populations. By combining surveys and interviews in the *same* study, researchers can enjoy the benefits of both methods, while minimizing the limitations. For example, a researcher might do a survey of fathers to answer questions about *how common* certain experiences are for these parents; they might then do follow-up interviews to answer questions about how fathers *understand* these experiences.

A third advantage of mixed methods research is that it allows researchers to confirm findings across different methods—the process of triangulation. If researchers use multiple sources of data and multiple analytic approaches, and their findings all point to the same conclusion, then they are able to be all the more confident in their findings. An example of triangulation is shown in Figure 11.5. In this research project (the case study shown in Figure 11.4), one of the key findings was that apprentices in the construction trades who were women and/or people of color had less access to on-the-job training hours than white male apprentices. Researchers found evidence for this finding in the administrative records, in interviews, and in the survey. Such similarity across these varied sources of data allow for a high level of confidence that these findings accurately represent what is happening in the construction trades.

A fourth advantage to mixed methods research can be found in the sequential approach to mixed methods, in which findings from one method inform the data collection and analysis of the second method. As noted earlier in the discussion of qual first and quant first approaches, there are a variety of reasons why it can be helpful to have the findings of one method to inform the implementation of the second method. For example, a researcher might first conduct participant observation in a community, attending events and informally talking with community members; using what they learned from these observations, the researcher would be in a better position to develop a survey that would accurately assess the concerns of that community. Without conducting the preliminary qualitative research, the researcher might not have the same level of confidence that they know what questions to ask in the survey.

FIGURE 11.5 ■ Triangulating Data on Access to Construction Apprentices' On-the-Job Training Hours

Data from survey apprentices: "Overall, we found that 57% of women of color, 58% of white Women, and 55% of men of color, compared to 76% of white men, reported that they felt that jobs were fairly assigned during their most recent apprenticeship"

Finding: Women and people of color have less access to on-the-job training hours than white men

Data from administrative apprenticeship records: "As indicated from the OAS data, women and people of color worked fewer hours than white men. Specifically, women accrued fewer completed credits at the time of termination and fewer average credit hours per month at the time of completion. Men of color also accrued fewer hous per month than white men"

Data from interviews: "Apprentices perceived that the informal hiring practices sometimes resulted in discrimination by gender and race/ethnicity. As one apprentice articulated: "It was like having two strikes: I'm a woman, and a minority woman. So yeah, I don't think that the jobs that were offered to another person would have been offered to me (Linda, African-American female, did not complete apprenticeship)"

Source: Kelly et al., 2015.

CONSIDER THIS...

Imagine that you were working as a research scientist for a health care organization, and your job was to design a study that would help identify barriers to good health. How could a mixed methods study be beneficial?

DOING SOCIOLOGY 11.2

Design a Mixed Methods Study

In this exercise, you will design a research proposal for a sequential qualitative → quantitative mixed methods project with key elements from the table below.

Choose a population, a demographic characteristic, a general topic, a qualitative method, and a quantitative method from Table 11.1.

TABLE 11.1 ■ U.S. Residents

Population	Demographic	Topic	Qualitative Method	Quantitative Method
Republicans	Men	Sexuality	Interviews	Telephone surveys
Parents				
Baristas	Low-income people	Politics	Focus groups	Email surveys
Feminists	African Americans	Work		
College students	Lesbians	Religion	Ethnography	In-person paper surveys
Chronically ill	People age 65 and older	Parenting		

Imagine that you are putting together a research proposal using your selections from Table 11.1. You will need to choose a specific subject within your general topic. For this project, the funders will give you unlimited funding and staff for this research project, but your team only has 1 year to complete it.

With this in mind, answer the following questions about your research proposal:

1. What is your research question? Why is it important to conduct this research?

2. For your first chosen method, what is the criteria for participation, how many participants do you plan to recruit, and how will you recruit those participants?

3. What are three questions you will answer through your first chosen method?

4. How do you anticipate the findings from your first method will inform your use of your second method?

Check Your Understanding

1. What are the four benefits of mixed methods research?
2. What is triangulation, and how does it help to strengthen research findings?

CHALLENGES OF MIXED METHODS RESEARCH

Although mixed methods research has some clear benefits, there are also some challenges. In this section, we will consider those challenges.

First, given that mixed methods research projects are essentially two (or more!) research projects in one, these projects tend to take more time to complete. Depending on the methods used, mixed methods research can be expensive, with costs including monetary rewards for participation, professional transcription of interviews, funds to access quantitative data sets, as well as the cost of the research team member's time.

Additionally, mixed methods research requires expertise in more than one method. Although students are usually trained in the basics of conducting both quantitative and qualitative research, most researchers spend their careers honing their skills in a single method. For this reason, mixed methods research is often conducted by teams, with one (or more) team member specializing in each method.

When researchers choose to adopt a mixed methods approach, they must be sure to have a strong justification for why they are choosing to use multiple methods (and often multiple sources of data) in the same project. The fastest way to an *unsuccessful* mixed methods project is to utilize two methods without having a clear plan for integration. Mixed methods research is not always better; you must make the case for why each mixed methods project is stronger relative to two single method projects.

You can think about a research project using a single method as contributing to a mixed methods body of research. That is, the scholarly research on any given topic is likely to consist of both quantitative and qualitative research projects, each providing unique contributions to the cumulative knowledge scholars produce about the topic. Not every individual project needs to be mixed methods!

CONSIDER THIS...

Why isn't every research study a mixed methods study?

DOING SOCIOLOGY 11.3

The General Social Survey (GSS) and Follow-Up Qualitative Interviews

In this exercise, you will review quantitative findings from the General Social Survey and then consider what additional information could be learned in a follow-up qualitative interview study, which would make this a sequential quantitative → qualitative mixed methods project.

According to the General Social Survey data explorer, in 2018, 28% of U.S. adults "strongly agree[d]" that "methods of birth control should be available to teenagers between the ages of 14 and 16 if their parents do not approve." This figure is a slight increase from 1986, when 22% of U.S. adults held this view (GSS Data Explorer, "Key Trends").

Imagine you will design a follow-up qualitative interview study to better understand these quantitative findings. Answer the following questions with this in mind:

1. What additional information could you learn about this topic from conducting follow-up qualitative interviews with U.S. adults to better understand attitudes toward teenagers and birth control?

2. What are three interview questions that you would ask participants in a qualitative interview study to help you better understand the findings from your quantitative analysis?

1. What are the challenges of mixed methods research?

CONDUCTING MIXED METHODS RESEARCH

Best Practices for Designing Mixed Methods Research

There are several essential best practices for any mixed methods project. These include establishing a clear justification for the integration of the methods; carefully planning the sequencing of methods; identifying whether one method will have priority over other(s); following best practices for each method used; and being realistic about what is possible, given time, staff, and funding limitations.

Researchers should have a strong justification for their approach to mixed methods. As noted earlier, more methods do not always result in better research! For a strong justification of the mixed methods approach, researchers must clearly articulate the integration—that is, how the findings from one method will be integrated with the findings from the other method. The approach to integration can be described as combining, as with approaches that triangulate findings, or connecting, as with approaches that adopt a sequential approach (Plano Clark & Ivankova, 2017).

Another best practice for mixed methods research is to carefully plan the sequencing or timing of data collection. For convergent and additional mixed methods research designs, data from each method is analyzed independently—that is, analysis of one type of data does not directly inform the analysis of the other type of data. For sequential approaches, the researcher must decide which method to employ first. Remember, quantitative first and qualitative first research designs each have unique strengths that are appropriate for certain types of research projects.

In some mixed methods research designs, one method has priority over the other. One method is the *core* and the other is *supplementary*. The method with priority means that the data collection was more involved for one method than another and/or the findings from one method receive more attention in the write-up of the research. In sequential approaches, the supplementary methods can come first, as a *preliminary input,* or second, as a *follow-up extension.* Morgan (2014) describes four possible sequential approaches with two methods of differing priority, shown in Table 11.2. For example, in the science attitudes study (Figure 11.3), the researchers used a preliminary quantitative input with a core qualitative method (quant → QUAL).

Some scholars believe that determining priority early is a key element of all mixed methods research design (Creswell & Plano Clark, 2011; Morgan, 2014), while others suggest priority may shift during the research process (Teddlie & Tashakkori, 2009) and that methods may have equal priority (Plano Clark & Ivankova, 2017). As a best practice, mixed methods researchers must decide at the research design phase if one method will have priority over the other(s), and if so, which method. This decision should be revisited when the researcher writes up the study for publication.

The order in which something takes place is important. The sequence of data collection dictates when different research methods are employed.

catchlights_sg/E+/Getty Images

TABLE 11.2 ■ Four Sequential Approaches to Mixed Methods Projects	
QUAL → quant	quant → QUAL
qual → QUANT	QUANT → qual

Source: Morgan, 2014.

Researchers should follow the best practices for each method they are utilizing, such as experiments (see Chapter 7), surveys (see Chapter 8), interviews (see Chapter 9), focus groups (see Chapter 9), and content analysis (see Chapter 10). These best practices should be explicit in the research proposal for a mixed methods project. When writing up mixed methods research, researchers should be transparent about how it evolved over the data collection and analysis processes. Given the researcher has to write up multiple methods, this may mean that the methods section or chapter is longer than for a single method report.

In designing the research project, researchers should be realistic about what is possible, given time, staff, and funding limitations. Researchers who are excited about an issue or a question may want to study it from every angle possible, gathering and analyzing all the data there are to generate a comprehensive analysis. This is never possible for a single study, however, even one with multiple methods. A mixed methods research project that involves preliminary interviews with a follow-up survey is likely not feasible for a project with a single researcher and a 1-year time frame. However, an analysis of existing survey data with a small follow-up interview project certainly could be achieved in this time frame, depending on the available resources and the researcher's other commitments.

Process for Conducting Mixed Methods Research

The process for conducting mixed methods research mirrors the process for single method research projects, with a few extra steps (see Table 11.3).

Like most research, your mixed methods project will most commonly start with a review of the literature to identify what is already known and the gap the new study will fill. Next, you will develop a research question and hypotheses. This is a critical step in the research process, although the research question developed at this phase and the corresponding hypotheses may be revised over the course of the project.

Recall the example of the study analyzing news coverage of welfare reform, discussed earlier in this chapter and highlighted in Figure 11.1. In this case, the researcher asked a single question: "How were the welfare reforms of the 1990s covered in television news media?" This question was answered by both the quantitative and qualitative data. In contrast, the study of race and gender in the construction trades workforce (shown in Figure 11.5) asked three questions: (1) "What are the trends in recruitment and retention of women and people of color in apprenticeships in the highway trades in Oregon?" (answered with quantitative data); (2) "What challenges do women and people of color face in completing their apprenticeships?" (answered with both quantitative and qualitative data); and (3) "What narratives do staff and apprentices use to explain the success (and failure) of apprentices?" (answered with qualitative data).

TABLE 11.3 ■ Steps for Implementing a Mixed Methods Project

1. Review the literature to identify a gap that your study will fill.

2. Develop reseach question(s).

3. Identify two (or more) methods to be used, and identify existing data sources and/or develop plans for data collection.

4. Articulate your approach to mixed methods research; ensure that you have a clear justification for why you are including multiple methods in one study.

5. Revisit the research questions to ensure that they can be answered with your methods and data.

6. Write a research proposal and obtain IRB approval.

7. Conduct data collection (if needed) and data analysis using your first method.

8. Consider how the findings from one method will influence data collection and analysis using your second method.

9. Conduct data collection (if needed) and data analysis using your second method.

10. Write up the findings of your mixed methods research.

Once your initial research questions are developed, you can identify the methods and data sources to be used. For quantitative data, you might look to already collected (secondary) data (e.g., General Social Survey), or you may plan to collect new data (e.g., surveys, experiments) based on your hypotheses. For qualitative data, you may plan to analyze publicly available texts (e.g., news articles, websites, tweets, public records). You might collect new qualitative data from interviews, focus groups, and/or ethnographic research. In some mixed methods research, the source for the quantitative and qualitative data may be the same. For example, you might conduct quantitative and qualitative analysis of the same sample of news articles. An additional example would be a survey that has both open- and closed-ended questions.

Once the methods and data have been identified, it is essential to be able to articulate your approach to mixed methods research, and explain why this approach makes sense. That is, ensure that you have a clear justification for why you are including multiple methods in one study. At this point, you should also revisit the research questions to ensure that they can be answered with your methods and data. Once you have a solid research plan (and, if needed, an approved formal research proposal), you can apply for institutional review board (IRB) approval for the project. As discussed in Chapter 4, an IRB approves the researcher's plan to ethically protect human subjects who are involved in the research.

Next, you will conduct data collection (if needed) and data analysis using your first method, adhering to the best practices for this method. After collecting and analyzing one set of data, you will need to pause to consider how the findings from one method will influence data collection and analysis using your second method. This step is most critical for sequential mixed methods approaches, in which the findings of the first method influence what data is collected and analyzed in the second method. However, for convergent and additional approaches, it is also necessary to keep the integration of the methods at the center of your process. Then you will conduct data collection (if needed) and data analysis using your second method, again adhering to the best practices for this method.

Finally, you will write up your mixed methods results and conclusions. In the discussion of methods, it is critical to include your approach and justification to mixed methods as well as all elements of research design for both methods. In the findings, be sure to address the findings from each method as well as discuss the *integrated* findings.

CONSIDER THIS...

Imagine that a social movement has erupted on your campus and you want to study it as it develops. You do not have time to implement all of these steps, but you know you want to use a combination of sociological methods. What would you do?

DOING SOCIOLOGY 11.4

Quantitative and Qualitative Data in the News

In this exercise, you will examine how news articles draw on both quantitative and qualitative data to tell news stories to readers.

Review the excerpt from the article "Despite Progress, Ingrained Racism Still Runs Deep in Construction," by Joe Bousquin, published in *Construction Dive*, a news site for the construction trades. Then, answer the questions that follow.

Construction's "FBI"

Nate McCoy, executive director of the Portland, Oregon chapter of the National Association of Minority Contractors, said the fact that many people get into construction through family members reinforces the lack of diversity in an industry that is 88% White. That compares to 78% across all industries, according to the Bureau of Labor Statistics. By contrast, just 6% of construction workers are Black or African American, half of the 12% in the general workforce.

"We call it the 'FBI,'" said McCoy, who is Black. "That's the way you get into construction: through your father, brother or in-laws."

Calvin Williams, CEO of Lansing, Illinois–based Construction Contracting Services and Midwest Region vice chair of Associated Builders and Contractors, said those statistics uncover a deeper truth about human nature.

"People hire people who look like them," said Williams, who is Black, and holds a degree in psychology. "If you don't have a lot of experience working with African Americans or Hispanics, you're not going to be comfortable with them."

To him, that aspect of systemic racism runs throughout the industry. "In the sense that people are not hiring, or are not willing to work with minorities, that's what I consider systemic racism," Williams said. "Because it's embedded into the process of both personnel and contracting opportunities."

1. Identify where the journalist has used quantitative data (i.e., statistics) and where he used qualitative data (i.e., quotes).

2. Which type of data (quantitative or qualitative) do *you* think tells readers more about the issue covered in this news story?

3. Why do you think the journalist included *both* the quantitative and qualitative data in their article?

4. In what ways is the logic of including both quantitative and qualitative similar and different for journalists and sociologists?

Source: Bousquin, 2020.

Check Your Understanding

1. What are some best practices for mixed methods research?
2. What are the key steps for implementing a mixed methods project?

SOCIOLOGISTS IN ACTION

Melissa Thompson

Melissa Thompson

Courtesy of Melissa Thompson

I am currently writing a book, *Motherhood After Incarceration,* with Summer Newell. This book focuses on relationships between mothers and children after incarceration. More specifically, we ask, how does resumption of custodial relationships affect mothers and their children? We used a combination of methods to answer this question. We conducted interviews with 39 mothers who had been released from prison or jail in Oregon. We interviewed each mother up to three times, during the first 4 years after having been returned to the community, asking them questions about their relationships with their children and their own financial, emotional, and behavioral struggles after incarceration. We also surveyed respondents about their experiences involving crime, substance use, and experience of interpersonal violence. The survey questions also included the Beck Depression Inventory (BDI), which is designed to screen for depression.

One chapter of our book illustrates the mental and emotional difficulties mothers wrestle with while they are incarcerated and during their transition back into the community. We also examine how resumption of custody affects these mental and emotional difficulties. In our interviews, we asked respondents about their emotional well-being while incarcerated and separated from their children. We also asked about their experiences after release: the obstacles they encountered as they reentered the community and struggled to find housing, employment, and resume custody of their children. We asked about how they navigated these obstacles and how these obstacles affected their emotional well-being and their relationships with their children. These interview responses, using respondents' own words and their own interpretation of emotional and mental states, form the basis of the chapter.

To speak to concerns about the need for reliable and valid indicators of mental well-being across individuals, we included the BDI as part of a survey administered each time they were interviewed. The BDI is a series of questions—previously assessed for reliability and validity—that when answered, create a composite score of the severity of depression: "minimal depression," "mild depression," "moderate depression," and "severe depression." Because we had respondents complete the BDI as part of each interview, we can assess within-person change in depression over time, along with differences between individuals over time.

Our longitudinal mixed methods study allowed us to consider how child custody shapes mothers' emotional well-being as they reenter the community after incarceration. By using both interview and survey data, we are able to address the limitations of each type of data. The closed-ended survey questions, including the BDI data, allow us to address concerns that the interviews do not reliably capture. The interviews, however, more effectively convey the individual's lived experience and their perceptions of the relationship between stressors and emotional well-being. Together, we have a fuller, more complete picture of how these mothers' emotions are impacted by their struggles with reentry, including their fraught relationships with their children and their attempts (or in some cases, decisions not to attempt) to regain custody. This combined use of surveys and interview longitudinal data allows us to better triangulate our data, using the weaknesses of one method as a rationale to consider the strength associated with the other method.

Melissa Thompson is a professor of sociology at Portland State University. Her research focuses on the intersection of mental health/illness and the criminal justice system.

Discussion Question

What does Dr. Thompson's research reveal about the benefits of combining interviews with survey data?

CONCLUSION

This chapter has provided an overview of mixed methods research, including different approaches to mixed methods, benefits and challenges of mixed methods approaches, as well as best practices and steps for conducting mixed methods research. Mixed methods research must live up to the potential for having findings that are greater than the sum of the findings of each method; when successfully implemented, there are unique benefits to including multiple methods in a single research project.

REVIEW

11.1   What is mixed methods research, and what are the different approaches to it?

Mixed methods research integrates a quantitative method and a qualitative method in the same research project. There are three approaches to mixed methods research: convergent (qualitative=quantitative), additional (qualitative + quantitative), and sequential (e.g., qualitative → quantitative).

11.2 What are the benefits of mixed methods research?

Researchers choose mixed methods for one or more of the following reasons: expanded scope of questions that can be answered within a single study; overcoming limitations of a single method; triangulation (confirming findings across different methods); and sequencing methods so that the findings of one inform the other.

11.3 What are the challenges of mixed methods research?

Mixed methods may prove challenging because of the additional time, staff, and funding required to implement two (or more) methods; necessary expertise in more than one method; the challenge of integrating methods; and providing a strong justification for mixed methods research.

11.4 What are the best practices for mixed methods research, and the steps necessary to conduct mixed methods research?

The best practices for mixed methods research include: provide clear justification for the integration of the methods; carefully plan the sequencing of methods; identify if one method will have priority over other(s); follow best practices for each method used; and be realistic about what is possible, given time, staff, and funding limitations.

The steps for conducting mixed methods research are:

1. Reviewing the literature
2. Developing research question(s)
3. Identifying the methods and data collection processes
4. Articulating your mixed methods approach
5. Revisiting your research question
6. Writing a research proposal and obtaining IRB approval
7. Conducting data collection (if needed) and analysis
8. Considering how the findings from the first method influence data collection and analysis of the second
9. Conducting second round of data collection (if needed) and analysis
10. Writing up the findings of your mixed methods research

KEY TERMS

additional (p. 201)

convergent (p. 200)

integration (p. 208)

mixed methods research (p. 208)

priority (p. 208)

qualitative methods (p. 200)

quantitative methods (p. 200)

sequencing (p. 208)

sequential (p. 201)

triangulation (p. 200)

RESUMEN REAL

1E+02

6E+01

9E+01

3.2E+01

2.1208E+02

- Auto
- Gastos médicos
- Otros
- Entretenimiento
- Artículos personales
- Comida
- Viajes
- Casa
- Suministros

12

INVESTIGATING NUMERICAL DATA: QUANTITATIVE ANALYSIS

Catherine E. Harnois

STUDENT LEARNING QUESTIONS

12.1 What motivates quantitative analysis? What are its strengths and limitations?

12.2 What is the General Social Survey? Why is it a valuable resource for sociology?

12.3 How do you construct a frequency table? How do you interpret it accurately?

12.4 How do you calculate the mean, median, and mode of a variable? How do you calculate range and interquartile range? How do you interpret each of these statistics?

12.5 How do you construct a bivariate table or "crosstab"? How do you interpret it accurately?

12.6 What is the benefit of using control variables in quantitative analyses, and of using multivariate analyses more generally?

HOW I GOT ACTIVE IN SOCIOLOGY

Catherine E. Harnois

My dad was a sociology major. After graduating from college, he spent much of his career working with adults with intellectual disabilities and then with high school students struggling to remain in school. He and my mom taught me that, as much as we talk about equal opportunity, hierarchies of race, gender, disability, sexuality, and religion benefit some people, take a toll on others, and even cut other people's lives short. They taught me that even in a democratic society, political and economic structures systematically privilege some people over others, and that that was unnecessary and also unjust. The sociological education I grew up with was intertwined with a moral education.

In college, I was an anthropology major and a women's studies minor. But I stumbled on sociology, saw its connection to what my parents had taught me, and wanted to learn more.

I decided to pursue a graduate degree in sociology and finished with a PhD. For the past decade, I've been teaching sociology at Wake Forest University. I teach courses on social statistics and courses focusing on inequality. In my research, I use statistics to learn more about the contours of social inequalities, and how they might be undone. My formal and informal education in sociology continues to set the stage for how I view myself, others, and the world.

QUANTITATIVE DATA ANALYSIS: WHAT AND WHY?

Quantitative data are data that are represented by numbers. Some examples of quantitative data include a person's height, age, and number of siblings; a city's population; a country's unemployment rate; or the square footage of a synagogue, mosque, or church. While these examples are clearly numerical, social scientists also use numbers to represent a wide range of social characteristics and processes.

Qualitative data, such as person's religious identity, their attitudes and beliefs, and even their emotions and personalities, can all be represented numerically in the context of quantitative analysis. When researchers turn qualitative data into numeric data, it is called **quantifying**.

A **dataset** is any collection of data assembled for a particular purpose. Whether compiling your own dataset or analyzing one previously collected, it is important to understand some of its basic characteristics. Most important, it is crucial to know *how* and *when* the data were collected and *who* or *what* they represent.

Recall that when sociologists collect information from *all* of the elements (e.g., individuals, groups, organizations, social artifacts, etc.) of interest to them, they describe the assembled information as reflecting the **population**. If, for example, a researcher was interested in the GPAs and majors of students at a particular college in a particular year, and the college registrar gave the researcher a list of all students enrolled, their majors, and their GPAs, then the researcher would have information about the whole population. If on the other hand, the registrar refused the researcher's request, and the researcher instead surveyed 500 students about their GPAs, and majors, the researcher would have information about a **sample**—defined as a subset of the population.

In the course of quantitative research, researchers seek to describe the data that they have, identify patterns in the data and relationships among variables, and make some claim about what the patterns they have found mean. Researchers use the term **parameter** when describing data about the whole population of interest. The average GPA provided by the registrar in the above example is a population parameter, as it describes the average GPA of the entire student body of interest to the researcher. Researchers use the term **statistic** when they use quantitative techniques to describe data generated from samples. The average GPA generated from the sample of 500 students would be an example of a statistic.

When analyzing data from samples, it is imperative for social researchers to understand how the sample was collected and what population, if any, it represents. When a sample is well designed, using principles of probability (as described more in Chapter 5), then researchers are in a good position to make larger claims about the population based on the sample. When samples are poorly designed or not representative of a broader population, researchers are unable to make generalizable claims based on their analyses. Researchers analyzing samples should always be explicit about the limitations of their sample, and up-front about the possibility that the characteristics of the sample may be far from the characteristics of the broader population. This is particularly true in the case of nonrepresentative samples.

In this chapter, you will encounter many examples of quantitative data and learn some of the basic concepts and tools for quantitative data analysis. Like all social science research methods, mastery of quantitative data takes years of schooling and even more years of practice. The process of learning any method can feel frustrating and discouraging. But, as discussed below, quantitative data are all around us. And some of the most important concepts in quantitative data analysis are ones we use in our everyday lives, if not formally, then intuitively.

In what follows, we'll examine some of the benefits and limitations of analyzing quantitative data. We'll then look at some real-world quantitative data from one of the best resources for understanding U.S. society: the General Social Survey. We'll use this survey to think through some of the fundamental concepts and skills in quantitative data analysis.

Why Do Sociologists Analyze Quantitative Data?

Now that we have established *what* quantitative data are, let's consider the question of, Why? Why do sociologists analyze quantitative data? There are many reasons. Recall from Chapter 1 that sociology is the social scientific study of society, including how individuals both *shape*, and are *shaped* by society (Korgen & Atkinson, 2020). Analyzing quantitative data is one of the main ways in which sociologists can test their hypotheses, and further develop theories. By analyzing quantitative data about income, wealth, political power, and prestige, for example, sociologists can gain a better understanding of the class structure in the United States and globally. They can use these data to test theories about social class and how inequalities change over time.

Quantitative analyses are also an important tool for evaluation research. By analyzing quantitative data, researchers can help document the effectiveness of programs and policies. They can help policy makers and leaders of organizations to assess how well they are meeting their goals. A community agency seeking to combat community hunger and homelessness, for example, could use quantitative analyses to keep track of the number of families in need, documenting the use of food or housing subsidies, and the number of people who make use of their services. Quantitative analyses can help pinpoint high-need areas and communities, and to identify and evaluate strategies to address their needs.

Social researchers collect and analyze quantitative data in order to gain a better understanding of society, organizations, policies, and individual behavior. They also analyze quantitative data to document social inequality and to promote social justice (Harnois, 2017). As explained in the United Nations' Fundamental Principles

Community agencies, such as food pantries, can benefit from quantitative analyses in determining the effectiveness of their programs.

iStockphoto.com/SDI Productions

of Official Statistics: "Official statistics provide an indispensable element in the information system of a democratic society, serving the Government, the economy and the public with data about the economic, demographic, social and environmental situation (United Nations, 2013)." The analysis of quantitative data provides a window into multiple dimensions of social and economic well-being, inequality, and mobility. Analyzing quantitative data allows us to assess how well we, as a society, are living up to our values and ideals.

CONSIDER THIS. . .

Think of a social justice issue that is important to you. How could analyzing quantitative data help you to *document* the social justice issue? How could it help you to *address* the issue?

The analysis of *qualitative* data, whether collected in the course of interviews, through participant observation, or from cultural documents like newspapers, social media websites, or movies, can provide researchers with data that are complex and nuanced. When a sociologist asks someone in the course of an open-ended interview, "How happy are you?" it might lead the respondent to reflect on what happiness means to them. They might talk about how they understand themselves in relation to their friends, family, and the world around them. They might discuss how their happiness, the meaning of happiness, and the importance of happiness have changed over the course of their lives.

The same question on a survey, "How happy are you?" would likely be followed by only a few possible response categories, such as: (1) Very happy; (2) Pretty happy; or (3) Not too happy. Respondents' answer to this question is in many ways a lot less informative than their response might be in an open-ended interview. The benefit of asking such a question on a survey, and analyzing it in combination with other quantitative data, is that if the question is asked to a large number of people, quantitative analyses can reveal patterns and test associations that qualitative analyses cannot. For example, sociologists Glass et al. (2016) analyzed data from the European Social Surveys (ESS) and International Social Survey Programme (ISSP) and compared the happiness levels of parents and nonparents across 22 countries. They found that in some countries, such as Norway, parents tend to be happier than adults without children. In other countries, such as the United States, adults without children tend to be happier than those with children. They further analyzed survey data from each country to understand the sources of these differences.

FIGURE 12.1 ■ Predicted Happiness for Parents and Nonparents in Countries With Weak Family Policies and Strong Family Policies

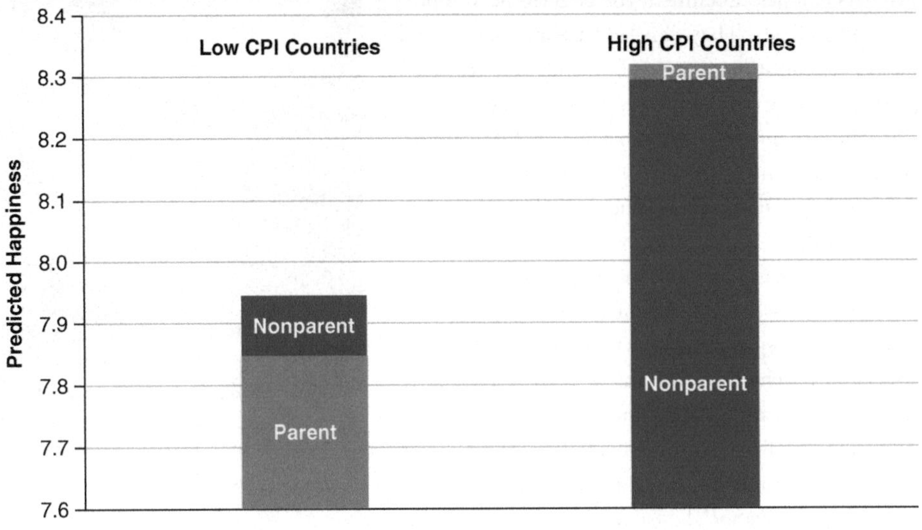

Source: Glass, Simon, and Andersson, 2017.

Figure 12.1 shows how self-reported happiness for parents and nonparents differs for parents living in countries that offer "comprehensive" social support policies for parents (high CPI countries, such as Norway) and those with more limited social support for parents (low CPI countries, such as the United States). You can see that in high CPI countries—those with comprehensive support for parents—both parents and nonparents report much higher levels of happiness compared to those living in low CPI countries. Moreover, in high CPI countries, parents and nonparents have similar levels of happiness. In low CPI countries, parents report significantly lower levels of happiness compared to nonparents.

This type of large-scale comparative study is made possible by quantitative analyses. Although qualitative data analyses could certainly add nuance to cross-national studies of parenting, the large sample (approximately 40,000 people) that the researchers use allows them to undertake analyses that smaller-scale qualitative studies could not.

How Do Sociologists Analyze Quantitative Data?

Quantitative data come from a variety of sources and take a variety of forms. Researchers can use quantitative data to test all sorts of sociological theories, on a range of topics, including crime, deviant behavior, gender, economics, health, environment, politics, emotions, and family. In some cases, researchers administer surveys that they themselves have designed, with the goal of answering a particular question. Researchers might survey members of their community about their experiences with affordable housing, accessible transportation, or available childcare. Once the surveys are collected, they could put the survey results into a spreadsheet or statistical software program, to organize and analyze the data.

In other cases, researchers analyze quantitative data that were previously collected by researchers, organizations, or governmental agencies. Governmental data, such as those collected and distributed by the U.S. Census Bureau, the Department of Labor (DOL), the U.S. Centers for Disease Control and Prevention (CDC), or even the Federal Bureau of Investigation (FBI), offer researchers a wide range of high-quality data that are available at no charge, and relevant to many of the most pressing issues facing society. Research institutes such as the Pew Research Center collect high-quality data on the opinions, attitudes, beliefs, and behaviors of people in the United States and share their data with the public as well. Global organizations, such as the World Bank and the United Nations, also offer a wealth of data for researchers from around the world to analyze.

> ## DOING SOCIOLOGY 12.1
>
> ### Quantifying Acts of Kindness?
>
> *In this exercise, you will develop quantitative measures and design research.*
>
> Imagine that you are conducting a study of kindness on your campus. You're interested in assessing the amount of kindness students show toward (1) their friends, (2) romantic partners, (3) service workers on campus, as well as (4) "random acts of kindness" directed at strangers.
>
> **1.** What research method(s) would you use to design a study of kindness on campus?
>
> **2.** Based on the method(s) you chose, what are two quantitative measures of kindness for each of the four types of kindness?
>
> **3.** What are the benefits and limitations of your measures?

Check Your Understanding

1. What are quantitative data?
2. What is the difference between a sample and a population?
3. What is the difference between a parameter and a statistic?
4. What are some reasons why sociologists would analyze quantitative data?

THE GENERAL SOCIAL SURVEY

As described on its website, the General Social Survey is a national survey of adults in the United States, which has been conducted regularly since 1972 (NORC, 2021). From 1972–1993, the survey was administered almost annually, and contained approximately 1,400 interviews each year. Since 1994, the survey has been conducted every other year and typically contains about 2,000 respondents per year. It contains numerous questions about respondents' sociodemographic characteristics; a range of questions about respondents' behaviors; and events that may have occurred in respondents' lives; as well as a range of questions about what respondents value and believe. There are also a range of questions concerning respondents' health and feelings.

Because the GSS includes such a wide range of topics and is a high-quality sample of adults in the United States, sociologists and social scientists more broadly have used it to analyze a range of different questions. Sociologists McPherson et al. (2006) analyzed data from 2 years or "waves" of the GSS, 1985 and 2004, to investigate friendship patterns in the United States. They found that, over this time period, the number of people reporting that they had no close friends—more specifically, "no one with whom they discuss important matters"—nearly tripled. More generally, they found that in 2004, people reported having significantly fewer confidants—an average of 2.08, down from 2.94 in 1985.

On a very different topic, Lawrence C. Hamilton and colleagues (2012) analyzed data from the 2006 and 2010 General Social Surveys to assess knowledge of polar regions—including ice melt, climate change, and rising sea levels. They found that knowledge about polar regions increased significantly across those 4 years, but that concerns about these issues remained relatively unchanged. Figure 12.2 shows the percentage of respondents across the 2 survey years who said they would be bothered a great deal if these consequences of global warming were actually to occur. As this chapter shows, the number of questions that can be answered with GSS data is virtually limitless.

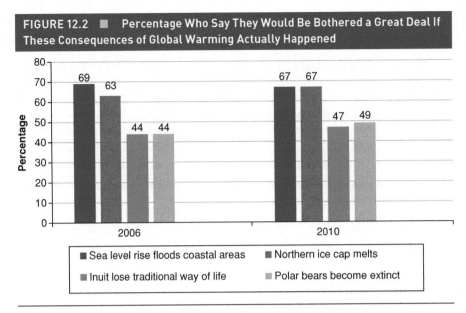

FIGURE 12.2 ■ Percentage Who Say They Would Be Bothered a Great Deal If These Consequences of Global Warming Actually Happened

Source: Hamilton et al., 2012.

CONSIDER THIS. . .

What factors do you think predict someone's level of concern about global warming?

Who Is Included in the GSS Sample?

The GSS includes respondents who are 18 years of age or older, who are living in households. It includes both citizens and noncitizens of the United States. The requirement that people are living in households means that individuals who live in institutions such as college dorms, nursing homes, prisons, or jails, and also those who are homeless, are not included in the GSS sample. From 1972–2004, the GSS included only individuals who were able to speak English. Since 2006, the GSS has been administered in Spanish as well, so now both Spanish- and English-speakers are represented in the survey.

How Are the Data Collected?

As described on its website, the GSS relies primarily on structured face-to-face interviews, though in some cases, when it is difficult to arrange an in-person interview, interviews are conducted by telephone. All interviewers undergo extensive training before conducting any interviews.

What Are Variable Weights?

For the sake of simplicity, data will be analyzed and presented in this chapter without using variable weights. In brief, variable weights are values assigned to each observation (in the GSS, each person who takes the survey can be thought of as an "observation"). By using these weights, the sample of respondents more closely matches the overall population from which the sample was drawn. For example, during the years 1975–2002, the GSS used sampling design, which gave each household in the United States an equal probability of being included in the GSS. Because only one adult per household is allowed to be interviewed, those who live in larger households had a slightly lower probability of being included in the GSS sample. Weights are used to adjust for this small discrepancy.

How Do I Access GSS Data?

There are two main ways to access data from the GSS. You can access the data for all years of the survey by using the GSS Data Explorer. Data from 1972–2018 are also available via the Survey Documentation and Analysis (SDA) program. Data can be analyzed directly online at either of these websites. Both websites also allow you to download the data into files that are compatible with software packages for statistical analyses, such as SPSS, Stata, and R.

DOING SOCIOLOGY 12.2

Keeping Track of Social Attitudes

In this exercise, you will analyze trends in some of the attitudinal questions that the General Social Survey has asked respondents over the past five decades.

Since its inception, the General Social Survey has asked respondents to indicate their level of confidence in some of the major institutions in our society. More specifically, respondents are asked, "I am going to name some institutions in this country. As far as the people running these institutions are concerned, would you say you have a great deal of confidence, only some confidence, or hardly any confidence at all in them?"

The institutions respondents are asked about include the media, science, government, and education. Figure 12.3 shows a line graph of the proportion of respondents who indicated they had "a great deal of confidence" in the Press, the Scientific Community, and Education. Examine the graph and answer the following questions.

FIGURE 12.3 ■ Level of Confidence in Social Institutions

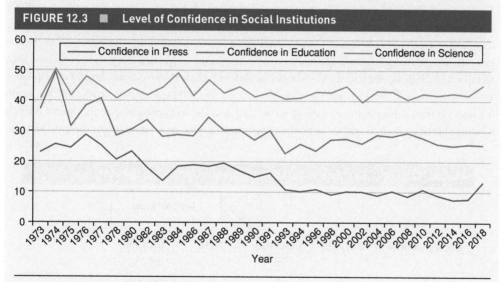

Source: General Social Surveys, 1972–2018.

1. Look at the most recent year of data in the graph, 2018. In which of the three institutions do respondents seem to have the most confidence?
   a. The Press had the highest level of confidence in 2018.
   b. Education had the highest level of confidence in 2018.
   c. The Scientific Community had the highest level of confidence in 2018.
   d. All three institutions had roughly equal levels of confidence in 2018.

2. Look at each of the lines individually. How would you describe the trend in how GSS respondents feel about the Press, Education, and the Scientific Community over time?

3. Which of the social institutions seems to have the most stable support? Which is the most volatile?

4. What factors do you think help to explain the changing attitudes about the Press, the Scientific Community, and Education since 1973?

1. What is the General Social Survey (GSS)?
2. Who is included in the GSS sample?
3. What types of questions have sociologists used the GSS to answer?

DESCRIBING QUANTITATIVE DATA

Recall that a dataset is a collection of information assembled for a particular purpose, and is often organized in some sort of spreadsheet or database. The information in the dataset might focus on individual people, organizations such as schools or corporations, or larger entities such as cities, states, or even countries. The *unit of observation* refers to the thing or person that the data describe. In the GSS, the unit of observation is an individual person. In the Annual Survey of Jails, conducted by the Bureau of Justice Statistics (BJS), the unit of observation is jails. The data collected are not focused on properties of inmates, but rather on the jails themselves, including information about the number of people jailed, the number of admissions and releases, the methods of "supervision," and the extent to which jails are overcrowded (United States Department of Justice, Office of Justice Programs, Bureau of Justice Statistics, Annual Survey of Jails, 2018).

As discussed in Chapter 6, a variable is a characteristic of interest in the dataset. Researchers assign variable names to each variable in the dataset. Sometimes these names are boring and uninformative—for example, "variable1" or "var12-b." At other times variable names hint at the meaning of the variable—"CHILDS" or "INCOME."

Even though variable names may appear straightforward, they can sometimes be misleading. Before analyzing any data, it is always important to consult the codebook for the dataset. The codebook is a document, either in print or online, that describes the dataset in detail, including information about the sampling strategy, the mode of data collection (e.g., in person, online, or by telephone), and information about all variables included in the dataset. Codebooks for surveys include the precise wording for each question, as well as the response category, and also show the order in which the questions were asked. When reporting findings from a quantitative analysis of survey data, it is always important to communicate the exact wording of the questions, as well as the possible response categories, rather than simply the variable names.

FIGURE 12.4 ■ Example of Variable Names and Cases in a Dataset

OBSERVATION	DEGREE	SIBLINGS	PETS	INCOME
1	3	1	4	35,000
2	2	1	0	38,000
3	4	2	1	65,000
4	3	0	1	27,350
5	1	1	2	10,000
6	2	1	1	55,450
7	4	2	0	78,000
8	5	4	2	127,000
9	3	2	1	42,125
10	3	1	4	76,000
11	2	1	1	32,000
12	3	0	1	5,000
13	5	0	4	145,000
14	1	5	2	19,000
15	2	1	2	21,000
16	3	1	1	40,000

Variable Name

Case

In a typical dataset, variable names are put along the top row, as in Figure 12.4, and the value of the variable for each person or observation is listed in columns. Each subsequent row in the dataset corresponds to a case: a person in the case of the GSS; a jail in the Annual Survey of Jails.

Before analyzing any variable, it is important to make note of its *level of measurement. Nominal-level variables,* also known as *categorical variables,* are variables that have no meaningful order to their categories. With nominal-level variables, it is impossible to speak of "high" or "low" values, because there is no intrinsic order to the values. The variable categories would make just as much sense if they were completely reordered. In the GSS, examples include RELIG, which corresponds to respondents' religious affiliation, and MARITAL, which corresponds to respondents' marital status (that is, whether they are currently married, widowed, divorced, never married, etc.). Variables that have only two options—typically "yes" or "no"—are called *dummy variables.*

Ordinal-level variables have a meaningful order to their response categories. Unlike interval-ratio-level variables (discussed below), however, the number associated with each category doesn't provide a meaningful indication of relative distance between each category. In other words, with ordinal-level variables, the interval between categories is undefined or nonnumeric. The size of the categories themselves is oftentimes uneven.

The variable HAPPY provides a good example. Since the first year of the survey, in 1972, the GSS has asked respondents about their self-assessed happiness: "Taken all together, how would you say things are these days—would you say that you are very happy, pretty happy, or not too happy?"

Table 12.1 shows how respondents to the 2018 survey answered this question. A **frequency distribution** is a table or chart that shows the response categories for each variable, as well as the number and/or percentage responses that fall into each category of the variable. The variable HAPPY has three possible response categories (very happy, pretty happy, and not too happy), and each response category is paired with a number (1, 2, and 3). The numbers have a meaningful order: higher numbers indicate greater unhappiness. At the same time, however, the meaning of each category is subject to interpretation and the interval between the numbers is undefined. The space between "very happy" and "pretty happy" isn't necessarily the same as the space between "pretty happy" and "not too happy." So HAPPY is an ordinal-level variable.

Like ordinal variables, *interval-ratio variables* have an underlying order to the variable response categories. Unlike ordinal variables, however, interval-ratio variables have a defined space between the categories, which is uniform throughout the range of the variable. In the GSS, variables like age (respondent's age in years), sibs (respondent's number of siblings), and NUMPETS (the number of pets the respondent's family has) are all interval-ratio variables. Not only are the categories ordered (for example, someone who scores a 4 on the variable sibs has more siblings than someone who scores a 1), but the interval between the categories is constant: Each one-unit increase in the variable sibs represents an additional sibling; each one-unit increase in the variable NUMPETS represents an additional pet.

TABLE 12.1 ■ Frequency Distribution for Self-Reported Happiness, 2018 General Social Survey

Cells contain: -Column percent -N of cases		Distribution
HAPPY	1: VERY HAPPY	**29.9** 701
	2: PRETTY HAPPY	**55.8** 1,307
	3: NOT TOO HAPPY	**14.3** 336
	COL TOTAL	*100.0* *2,344*

Source: General Social Surveys, 1972–2018.

Unpacking and Creating Frequency Tables

Let's look more closely at the frequency table for the variable HAPPY. The box in the upper left-hand corner indicates that the "cells contain" "column percent" and "N of cases." The right-most column includes a series of numbers: two in each box or "cell" of the table. The bottom number in each cell indicates the number of respondents who selected each level of happiness—that is, the *frequency* of each response. Looking again at Table 12.1, the top box in the table shows that 701 respondents indicated that, all things considered, they were "very happy." The cell below shows that 1,307 respondents indicated they were "pretty happy." Very few respondents, only 336, indicated they were "not too happy." The number in the bottom right-hand corner, 2,344, represents the total number of people who are represented in the table.

The top number in each cell, which is bolded, shows a column percent. This number is calculated by dividing the number of respondents in each category by the total number of respondents represented in the column. The top-most number in Table 12.1, 29.9, is calculated by dividing the number of people who report being very happy (701) by the total number of respondents who reported their happiness level (2,344), and then multiplying that proportion by 100:

$$(701/2,344) \times 100 = 29.9\%$$

To interpret this percentage, we'd simply say that 29.9% of respondents indicated that they were "very happy." Taken as a whole, the frequency table tells us that most respondents (55.8%) indicated that they were "pretty happy." And few indicated that they were "not too happy."

CONSIDER THIS. . .

Think about sociodemographic characteristics like age, race, gender, and educational attainment and income. Which factors do you think are associated with more or less happiness? Why?

DOING SOCIOLOGY 12.3

Constructing a Frequency Table

In this exercise, you will practice interpreting frequency tables.

The variable PRAY, from the 2018 GSS, asked respondents the following question: "About how often do you pray?" A frequency table for this variable is shown in Table 12.2. Review Table 12.2, then answer the following questions.

TABLE 12.2 ■ Frequency at Which Individuals Pray	N	%
1: SEVERAL TIMES A DAY	691	29.6
2: ONCE A DAY	674	28.9
3: SEVERAL TIMES A WEEK	215	9.2
4: ONCE A WEEK	144	6.2
5: LESS THAN ONCE A WEEK	251	10.8
6: NEVER	358	15.3
COL TOTAL	2,333	100.0

Source: General Social Surveys, 1972–2018.

1. What is the level of measurement for the variable PRAY?
2. What percentage of people say that they pray several times a day?
3. What percentage of people say that they never pray?
4. Why do you think some people pray frequently and others don't? What factors might predict whether or not someone prays often?

Check Your Understanding

1. What is a variable? What is a codebook, and why is it important for analysis?
2. What are categorical, ordinal, and interval-ratio-level variables? Give an example of each.
3. What information is displayed in a frequency table? How do you interpret that information?

UNIVARIATE STATISTICS

Univariate statistics are statistics that describe a single variable. They describe things like what values are the most typical or common for a variable. For example, we might ask, "What is the average number of small businesses per town in the state of North Carolina?" We might also be interested in the range of values that a variable takes on. We might ask, for example, "How many small businesses does the town in North Carolina with the most small businesses have, and how many small businesses does the town with the least small businesses in North Carolina have?" Perhaps we are interested in the extent to which values tend to be concentrated or dispersed. "Do most towns have between 10 and 15 small businesses, or is there much more variation, with some towns having only one or two, and others having hundreds?" If we have the right data, univariate statistics can answer each of these questions.

Measures of Central Tendency

Some univariate statistics describe what is typical for a variable. These are called measures of central tendency, and include the mode, the median, and the mean (or average). Let's examine each of these below.

The Mode

The mode of a variable refers to the value of a variable that occurs most frequently. Each variable has its own mode. In the case of survey research, the mode is the response category with the highest frequency of responses. Table 12.3 shows a frequency distribution for the variable NUMPETS from the 2018 GSS. This variable represents the number of pets the respondent's family has. As was the case with Table 12.1, the numbers in the table show the column percentages, as well as the frequency for each response category.

TABLE 12.3 ■ Frequency Distribution	
Cells contain: -Column percent -N of cases	Distribution
0: No pets	41.3 474
1	25.1 288
2	13.9 159

	Cells contain: -Column percent -N of cases	Distribution
NUMPETS	3	7.1 82
	4	3.9 45
	5	2.5 29
	6	1.2 14
	7	.7 8
	8	.4 5
	9	.4 5
	10	.3 4
	11	.6 7
	12	.4 5
	13	.3 3
	14	.1 1
	15	.3 3
	17	.1 1
	18	.1 1
	19	.1 1
	20: 20 or more pets	1.0 12
	COL TOTAL	*100.0* *1,147*

Source: General Social Surveys, 1972–2018.

Looking at the Column Total at the bottom of the table, we see that 1,147 people are represented in the table. To determine the mode for the variable, simply read down the right-hand column and find the largest percentage, or the largest frequency. In this case, the response of 0 occurs most often. Four hundred seventy-four respondents—41.3% of the 1,147 responses provided—answered that they had no pets.

The Median

The median of a variable is the value of the middle observation, when observations are ordered from least to greatest, or greatest to least. To find the median for a particular variable, the individual responses first are arranged from greatest to smallest, or smallest to greatest. Once arranged, the median is simply the value of the middle observation. More specifically, in situations where there is an odd number of observations, the

Which measure would you use when looking at the number of pets individuals have?

iStockphoto.com/Raphael Angeli

median is the value of the middle-most observation. When there is an even number of cases, and thus no single middle observation, the median is found by taking the average of the two most middle observations. The median also corresponds to the 50th percentile.

Imagine lining up the 1,147 people who answered the question about the number of pets they have. We ask the 474 people who have no pets to go to the far left, followed by the 288 respondents with one pet, followed by the 159 people with two pets, and they all agree. This goes on and on, until we get to the 12 people who report having 20 or more pets. They are now at the end of the line, on the far right. The middle person in this line, person number 574, has 573 people to their right, and another 573 people standing to their left. How many pets does this person have? The answer is one pet, so the median for the variable NUMPET is one.

The Mean

The mean of a variable is the arithmetic average, calculated by adding up all of the values for each observation and dividing it by the number of observations. In the case of the variable NUMPETS, the number of observations is 1,147. As shown in Table 12.3, 474 respondents reported having no pets, another 288 reported having one pet, 159 reported having two pets, etc. To calculate the mean, we would add up the number of pets reported by all 1,147 people, and divide that number by 1,147. The resulting number is 1.72. This means that, on average, respondents reported having 1.72 pets in their families.

Two things are of note. First, note that the mean, median, and mode for the variable NUMPETS are all different numbers. This is quite common. When doing quantitative analyses, researchers have to think through which measure of central tendency—the mode, median, or mean—makes most sense for the variables they are analyzing. Second, because an underlying order to the response categories is necessary to identify the median and mean, it is not possible to calculate a meaningful median or mean for categorical-level data. For categorical data, the best measure of central tendency is the mode. Typically, researchers report the median for ordinal-level data and for interval-ratio variables that are highly skewed.

Measures of Variation

Measures of variation are univariate statistics that describe how the values for a particular variable are distributed. Common measures of variation include the range, the interquartile range (IQR), the variance, and the standard deviation. Here we will focus on the range and the IQR.

The range of a variable is calculated by subtracting the smallest value for a variable from the largest value. In the case of NUMPETS, the smallest value is 0 pets, and the largest value of the variable is 20, which corresponds to responses of "20 or more pets." The range is calculated by the following: 20 – 0 = 20. Researchers would typically report this measure of variation by saying: "Values range from 0 through 20."

Note that very few people indicated that they had eight or more pets. The range is influenced by outlying observations; values on the variable are far beyond what is typical—such as the 12 people reporting 20 or more family pets. The interquartile range (IQR) is another measure of variation and is less affected by outlying observations—also called "outliers."

A quartile refers to the first, second, third, or fourth quarter of the distribution. Let's imagine again those 1,147 people lined up according to the number of pets they have (if any). The *lower quartile* is equal to the 25th percentile. In this case, the first 25% equals approximately 287 people (1147/4 = 286.75). There are a total of 474 people in the sample who report owning no pets, so we know everyone in the lowest quarter of the distribution has no pets. The value for the 25th percentile is thus 0. The upper quartile is equal to the 75th percentile, which in this case is equal to two, as 75% of respondents have two pets or fewer.

The IQR represents the range of values between the 25th and 75th percentiles. If we were to ignore the bottom quarter of the observations, and also ignore the top quarter of observations, we are left with the middle 50% of observations. The IQR tells us the range of values within this middle 50%. The value of the IQR is the difference between these two values, which is equal to two. (2 – 0 = 2). Researchers would typically report this by saying: "The IQR ranges from 0 through two." As you can see, this is quite a bit different from the range, which included the values from 0 to 20.

CONSIDER THIS. . .

How many pets do you and your family own? If you were a respondent in this sample of 1,147 people, would you fall above or below the median? Into which quartile would you fall?

Bar Charts and Pie Charts

Researchers frequently use graphs to visualize how a variable is distributed. Figures 12.1 and 12.2 showed bar charts of happiness and concern about global warming. Figure 12.5 shows a bar chart

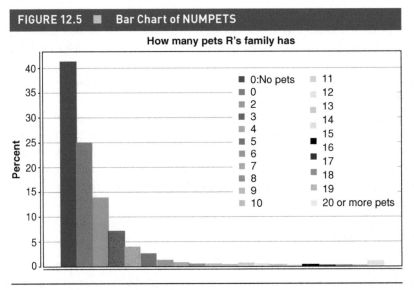

FIGURE 12.5 ■ Bar Chart of NUMPETS

How many pets R's family has

Legend: 0:No pets, 0, 2, 3, 4, 5, 6, 7, 8, 9, 10, 11, 12, 13, 14, 15, 16, 17, 18, 19, 20 or more pets

Source: General Social Surveys, 1972–2018.

of the variable NUMPETS. As you can see, the horizontal axis (also called *X*-axis) corresponds to the different values that NUMPETS can take on—in this case, ranging from 0 to 20. The vertical axis (also called *Y*-axis) corresponds to the percentage of observations that fall within each category of the variable. Looking at the left-most bar, we can see that more than 40% of respondents indicated they had no family pets. The bar chart also tells us that the variable is highly skewed. Observations are concentrated at one end of the variable—in this case, the low end—with tiny numbers of people reporting eight or more pets.

Pie charts. Most of us have encountered a pie chart before. In pie charts, data are represented in a circle—the shape of a pie—and each piece of the pie represents a different value of the variable. The bigger the piece of the pie, the larger the number of observations associated with a value. Consider the question, "How often do you consider your pet to be a member of your family?" This is an ordinal-level variable with four response categories: almost always, often, sometimes, and never. This question is included in the 2018 GSS, and asked to all respondents who, in a previous question, indicated that they owned at least one family pet. Figure 12.6 displays the distribution of responses for all respondents who provided a valid answer to the question.

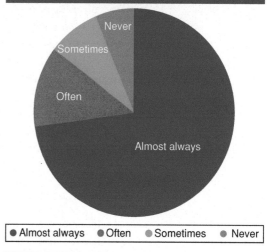

FIGURE 12.6 ■ Pie Chart of How Often Pet-Owning Respondents Consider Their Pet to Be a Member of the Family, 2018 General Social Survey, N = 671

● Almost always ● Often ● Sometimes ● Never

Source: General Social Surveys, 1972–2018.

When the number of values a variable can take on is small, a pie chart can show immediately and with great clarity the overall distribution of responses. In Figure 12.6, for example, we can see that pet owners overwhelmingly report that they "almost always" consider the pet to be a member of the family. Another sizable chunk of respondents "often" consider their pet to be part of the family. Only a small minority of respondents report that they "never" consider their pets to be part of the family. Good news for pets!

DOING SOCIOLOGY 12.4

Calculating and Comparing Measures of Central Tendency

In this exercise, you will practice identifying and interpreting the measures of central tendency.

A small survey was given to your community, which asked, "What do you think is the ideal number of pets for a family to have?" Nine people provided the following answers: 0, 0,1 1, 1, 2, 2, 2, 10.

1. What is the mode for this variable? What is the median?

2. Calculate the mean for this variable.

3. Do any of the responses seem like outlying observations? Explain.

4. Which measure of central tendency (the mode, median, or mean), do you think best captures the central tendency of this variable?

Check Your Understanding

1. How do you calculate the mode, median, and mean for a particular variable? How do you interpret each of these numbers?
2. What do measures of variation tell us about a variable?
3. How do you calculate and interpret the range and the interquartile range for an ordinal or interval-ratio-level variable?
4. How do you construct and interpret a bar chart?

BIVARIATE RELATIONSHIPS

Now that we have the tools for describing individual variables, let's focus on a few tools for examining the relationship between two variables. That is, bivariate relationships.

Bivariate tables, also known as "cross-tabulations" or "cross-tabs" for short, are used to examine the relationship between two variables. If we were interested in knowing whether people in cities and rural areas reported similar or different levels of happiness, for example, we could make a bivariate table using data from the GSS. We could examine the happiness levels (with the variable HAPPY) of people living in cities, suburbs, towns, or more rural areas (with the variable XNORCSIZ).

Before creating a bivariate table, it is useful to consider whether you believe the relationship you are investigating is a causal relationship. In a causal relationship, the variable doing the causing is termed the *independent variable* and the variable that is affected is the *dependent variable*. In other words, the dependent variable is thought to depend upon the independent variable.

CONSIDER THIS. . .

Questions about bivariate relationships are in the news nearly every day. Can you think of a recent news story that focuses on the relationship between two variables?

In an analysis of happiness and community size, we would probably argue that community size is the independent variable, and happiness is the dependent variable. To the extent that there is a correlation between happiness levels and living environment, it is probably living environment that influences happiness level, rather than the other way around. Although there is no strict rule, researchers typically present dependent variables in the rows of bivariate tables, and independent variables typically are presented in the columns.

Table 12.4 shows the relationship between community size and happiness levels, using data from the 2016–2018 General Social Surveys. As in the univariate frequency table, each cell contains two numbers: a column percentage, as well as the number of cases in the cell.

Each column tells us the distribution of happiness in communities of a particular size. For example, 116 people who report living in the "open country" report being "very happy," 195 people living in open country report being "pretty happy," and 66 people living in open country report being "not too happy."

The column totals in the bottom row of the table tell us the overall distribution of the variable in the column (XNORCSIZ). Looking at the last row of the table, we see that 377 people report living in open country. On the other side of the table, you can see that 945 respondents report living in cities of greater than 250,000 people, and more than 1,000 people report living in the suburbs of large cities.

The column percentages in each cell are calculated by dividing the number of cases in a given cell *by the total number of cases in each column*, and then multiplying the resulting proportion by 100. So, focusing on the people who live in "open country," we can see that 30.8% of those living in open country report being very happy:

$$(116/377) \times 100 = 30.8\%$$

The row totals at the far right-hand side of the table tell us the overall distribution of the row variable—in this case, HAPPY. Taken on the whole, including people who live in all types of communities, 1,507 respondents reported being very happy. And almost twice as many—2,908, 55.9% of the sample—responded "pretty happy." For respondents represented in this table, the modal category is "pretty happy."

The bottom right-hand corner of the table shows a percentage of 100, and an *N* of approximately 5,203. This number corresponds to the total number of respondents represented in the table.

TABLE 12.4 ■ Bivariate Relationship Between Community Size and Respondents' Happiness, 2016–2018 GSS

Cells contain: -Column percent -N of cases	XNORCSIZ 1 CITY greater than 250000	2 CITY, 50–250000	3 Suburb of a large city	4 Suburb of a medium city	5 Unincorporated Large city CITY	6 Unincorporated Medium City	7 CITY,10–49999	8 TOWN greater than 2500	9 SMALLER AREAS	10 OPEN COUNTRY	ROW TOTAL
1: VERY HAPPY	26.8 / 253	26.4 / 224	31.5 / 349	30.5 / 178	31.0 / 161	30.5 / 137	23.1 / 33	24.7 / 42	24.6 / 14	30.8 / 116	29.0 / 1,507
2: PRETTY HAPPY	54.7 / 517	57.2 / 486	56.0 / 621	55.2 / 322	56.7 / 295	58.1 / 261	59.4 / 85	56.5 / 96	52.6 / 30	51.7 / 195	55.9 / 2,908
3: NOT TOO HAPPY	18.5 / 175	16.5 / 140	12.5 / 139	14.2 / 83	12.3 / 64	11.4 / 51	17.5 / 25	18.8 / 32	22.8 / 13	17.5 / 66	15.1 / 788
COL TOTAL	100.0 / 945	100.0 / 850	100.0 / 1,109	100.0 / 583	100.0 / 520	100.0 / 449	100.0 / 143	100.0 / 170	100.0 / 57	100.0 / 377	100.0 / 5,203

HAPPY

Source: General Social Surveys, 1972–2018.

By comparing the percentages in the top row of the crosstab, we can see some interesting patterns. First, regardless of community type, "pretty happy" is the modal category. Most people, regardless of their living environment, report being pretty happy. But there are some differences too. While 26.8% of respondents who live in cities greater than 250,000 people report being happy, a higher percentage (31.5%) of those living in the suburbs of large cities report being very happy. People who live in the suburbs of medium and large cities (categories 3 and 4) less frequently report being "not too happy" compared to those who live in cities with populations of 50,000 and greater.

When drawing comparisons between groups (such as those living in different community types), it is important to rely on percentages with the independent variable, rather than percentages within the dependent variable or simply frequencies. Recall that Table 12.4 represents 945 people who report living in cities of greater than 250,000 people, and only 377 who report living in "open areas." Because the categories for the independent variable have vastly different numbers of people represented, it could be misleading to compare the 116 very happy people living in open areas to the 253 people living in cities greater than 250,000. Even though the table shows twice as many very happy people living in cities greater than 250,000, as compared to the number of very happy people living in open areas, the percentage of people living in these areas who are very happy is quite similar. In fact, a higher percentage of those living in open areas (30.8%) report being very happy, as compared to only 26.8% of those living in cities greater than 250,000.

Visualizing Bivariate Relationships With Graphs

A bivariate relationship can be visualized using pie charts, bar charts, and other types of graphs. In fact, Figure 12.2—the bar chart describing concern about global warming—is one example. It shows the relationship between two variables: level of concern, and year of survey (2006 or 2010). Figure 12.1—the bar chart describing happiness of parents and nonparents in different types of countries— effectively illustrates the relationship among three variables!

Let's consider another example: pet owners' feelings toward pets and political party affiliation. Do you think that pet-owning Republicans, Independents, and Democrats vary in their feelings toward their family pets? In every survey year, the GSS asks respondents about their political party affiliation: "Generally speaking, do you usually think of yourself as a Republican, Democrat, Independent, or what?" This variable is called PARTYID and has the following response categories: strong Democrat;

TABLE 12.5 ■ How Often Do You Think of the Pet as Being Part of the Family, by Political Party, 2018 General Social Survey				
Cells contain: -Column percent -N of cases	**PARTYID**			*ROW TOTAL*
	Democrats	Independents	Republicans	
PETFAM 1: Almost always	**78.2** 140	**76.8** 208	**79.3** 149	*77.9* *497*
2: Often	**15.6** 28	**11.4** 31	**10.1** 19	*12.2* *78*
3: Sometimes	**3.9** 7	**7.4** 20	**4.3** 8	*5.5* *35*
4: Never	**2.2** 4	**4.4** 12	**6.4** 12	*4.4* *28*
COL TOTAL	*100.0* *179*	*100.0* *271*	*100.0* *188*	*100.0* *638*

Source: General Social Surveys, 1972–2018.

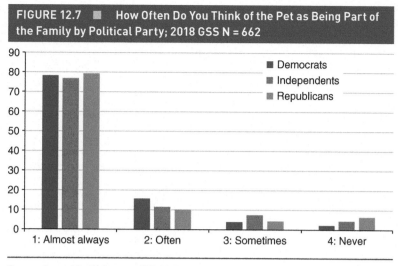

FIGURE 12.7 ■ How Often Do You Think of the Pet as Being Part of the Family by Political Party; 2018 GSS N = 662

Source: *General Social Surveys, 1972–2018.*

not strong Democrat; Independent near Democrat; Independent; Independent near Republican; a not strong Republican; a strong Republican; or "other." To simplify the presentation of the information, the analyses below collapse these eight categories into three: Democrats, Independents (including those who lean Democrat as well as those who lean Republican), and omits the small number of respondents with "other" party affiliations. This information is first presented in a crosstab (Table 12.5) and then in a comparative bar graph (Figure 12.6).

The horizontal axis (X-axis) shows the possible values for the dependent variable, in this case feelings about pets. The vertical axis (Y-axis) shows the percentage of observations falling into each category. And in this case, different-colored bars represent each category of the independent variable. The colors of the bars represent Democrats, Independents, and Republicans.

Depending on your own political party affiliation and your own feelings about pets, your eyes might be drawn to one part of the graph or another. You might focus in on the fact that the percentage of pet-owning Democrats who "almost always" consider the pet to be part of the family (78.2) is *slightly* lower than the corresponding percentage of Republicans (79.3). Or you might hone in on the fact that a higher percentage of pet-owning Republicans (6.4) "never" consider their pet part of the family compared to the corresponding percentage of Democrats (2.2%). But one thing is very clear: The overwhelming majority of pet-owning respondents, across all three political groups, "almost always" consider their pets to be part of the family. Democrats, Independents, and Republicans may differ in how they approach family issues, but pet-owners are united across political parties on their views about family pets.

When analyzing and visualizing the relationship between two variables, it is important to keep in mind the level of analysis for each of the variables, as well as the number of categories each variable has. Consider the variable AGE, for example, which ranges from 18–89. Unless the variable was recoded into a smaller number of categories, the pie chart would have more than 60 categories and would be incredibly difficult to read, as many—if not all—of the slices would likely be tiny.

In cases where you have two interval-ratio variables with a high number of categories, a scatterplot can be a useful way to visualize the relationship between two variables. In a scatterplot, also called a dot plot, the independent variable is represented on the horizontal axis, and the dependent variable on the vertical axis. Although there are variations, each dot typically represents one or more observations. Below are two sample scatterplots, the first of which (Figure 12.8) shows the relationship between respondents' education and the number of pets they own. The second (Figure 12.9) shows the relationship between respondents' educational attainment and the educational attainment of respondents' spouses. Note that educational attainment is measured in years of formal schooling that the respondents have completed, and that Figure 12.9 only includes respondents who are currently married.

FIGURE 12.8 ■ Respondents' Educational Attainment and the Number of Pets They Own

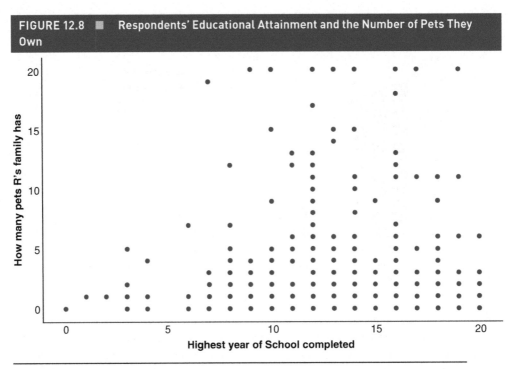

Source: *General Social Surveys, 1972–2018.*

FIGURE 12.9 ■ Respondents' Educational Attainment and Respondents' Spouses' Educational Attainment

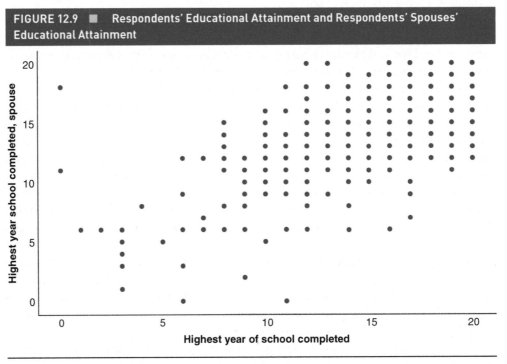

Source: *General Social Surveys, 1972–2018.*

What does Figure 12.8 tell you about respondents' educational attainment, pet ownership, and the relationship between the two? Because the dots are concentrated toward the bottom of the graph, we can say that most respondents indicate owning zero, one, or two pets. Education is more highly dispersed, with values concentrated at 12 (corresponding to high school graduate), and 16 (corresponding to college graduate). But it is hard to say much about the relationship between the two variables.

The relationship between respondents' educational attainment and that of their spouse is more clear. As respondents' own educational attainment increases (moving left to right on the graph), the educational attainment of respondents' spouse also tends to increase (moving from bottom to top).

DOING SOCIOLOGY 12.5

Age and Feelings About the Family Pet

In this exercise, you will practice describing the relationship between two variables by interpreting crosstabs.

Table 12.6 shows a crosstab of respondents' age by their feelings about pets. The table is based on the 2018 General Social Survey and is limited to respondents who say they own at least one pet. The variable "PETFAM" corresponds to the question, "How often do you consider your pet to be a member of your family?" Answer the following questions based on the table.

TABLE 12.6 ■ Bivariate Frequency Distribution for Respondents' Age by Feelings About Pets and Family, 2018 GSS

Cells contain: -Column percent -N of cases		AGE				
		1 18–30	2 31–50	3 51–70	4 71+	*ROW* *TOTAL*
PETFAM	1: Almost always	**84.7** 100	**75.7** 184	**78.4** 185	**70.8** 51	*77.7* *520*
	2: Often	**5.9** 7	**13.2** 32	**13.6** 32	**12.5** 9	*12.0* *80*
	3: Sometimes	**5.1** 6	**5.8** 14	**5.1** 12	**8.3** 6	*5.7* *38*
	4: Never	**4.2** 5	**5.3** 13	**3.0** 7	**8.3** 6	*4.6* *31*
	COL TOTAL	*100.0* *118*	*100.0* *243*	*100.0* *236*	*100.0* *72*	*100.0* *669*

Source: General Social Surveys, 1972–2018.

1. How many respondents are represented in the table?
2. What is the level of measurement for the variable PETFAM?
3. What is the mode for the variable PETFAM?
4. What can you say about the relationship between pet owners' age and feelings about the family pet, based on this table?

Check Your Understanding

1. How do you construct a bivariate table?
2. How do you interpret the information in a bivariate table?
3. What is a scatterplot?

CORRELATIONS AND CONTROLS

Correlation describes the extent to which two variables are related to each other. If an increase in one variable is associated with an increase in another, we can say there is a positive correlation between the two. Think again about the relationship between respondents' education level and that of their spouses. Individuals with high levels of education tend to be partnered with individuals with higher levels of education, and *vice versa*, indicating a positive correlation between the two variables. If an increase in one variable is associated with a decrease in another variable, then there is a negative correlation between the two. Here we might think about the relationship between education and dental problems. In the United States, individuals with higher educational attainment have greater incomes, on average indicating a negative correlation between the two.

Statistical analyses are invaluable for assessing not only the direction of a correlation, but also the strength of a correlation—the extent to which the relationship between two variables is strong or weak. A perfect positive relationship—the strongest positive relationship has a correlation of 1.0, and a perfect negative relationship—the strongest negative relationship has a correlation of –1.0. In the case of a perfect relationship—either positive or negative—the value on one variable is a perfect predictor of the other. A correlation of 0 means there is no relationship between the variables. The relationship between the number of pets one has and their educational attainment is a very weak relationship, with a correlation of –0.058. The correlation between respondents' own education level and that of their spouses is much stronger: 0.596.

CONSIDER THIS. . .

What other factors do you think are positively correlated with educational attainment? What other factors do you think are negatively correlated with educational attainment?

Thus far, we have examined univariate statistics and bivariate relationships. Multivariate analyses are those that include more than two variables—as most quantitative analyses do. A control variable is an independent variable that is included in the analysis in order to determine whether a relationship between two variables holds true when variation in a third variable (that is, the control variable) is held constant. In complex quantitative analyses researchers include multiple control variables, in order to "control for" factors that might also affect the dependent variable.

You may have heard in the news about the wage gap in men's and women's earnings—the fact that, compared with men in the United States who work full-time and year-round, women working full-time and year-round earn approximately 82% of what men earn (https://www.bls.gov/opub/ted/2017/womens-median-earnings-82-percent-of-mens-in-2016.htm). Gender (the independent variable) affects wages (the dependent variable). But, of course, the social world is complex and many things affect the wages of both men and women, including: educational attainment, type of job, work experience, family responsibilities, and inequalities of race and ethnicity. All of these factors could be included in a quantitative analysis to help researchers disentangle how much gender influences wages, "controlling for" these other factors.

Table 12.7 shows a figure from the Institute for Women's Policy Research, which draws on data from the U.S. Census Bureau. There are three variables in the analysis: wages, gender, and racial/ethnic background. Year and race/ethnicity can both be thought of as "control variables." Examining differences in the wage gap by race/ethnicity tells us that non-Hispanic white women earn approximately 81.5% of what non-Hispanic white men earn, but Black and Hispanic women earn considerably less—65.3 and 61.6% respectively. Women of all racial–ethnic backgrounds, on average, earn less than non-Hispanic white men. By controlling for race and ethnicity, we can see that there is considerable variation in women's earnings relative to men's.

TABLE 12.7 ■ **Median Weekly Earnings and Gender Earnings Ratio for Full-Time Workers, 16 Years and Older by Race/Ethnic Background, 2018**

Racial/Ethnic Background	2018			
	Women	Men	Female Earnings as % of Male Earnings of Same Group	Female Earnings as % of White Male Earnings
All Races/Ethnicities	$789	$973	81.1%	N/A
White	$817	$1,002	81.5%	81.5%
Black	$654	$735	89.0%	65.3%
Hispanic	$617	$720	85.7%	61.6%
Asian	$937	$1,241	75.5%	93.5%

Source: General Social Surveys, 1972–2018.

DOING SOCIOLOGY 12.6

Factors Associated With Llife Satisfaction

In this exercise, you will think about correlations: positive and negative, weak and strong.

The social world is complicated, with a number of factors working together to structure what we do and how we feel. Consider the issue of life satisfaction—how satisfied someone is with their life. Imagine you have created a table with the factors that you think are positively/negatively, and strongly/weakly correlated with life satisfaction.

Strong Negative Correlation

1.

2.

Strong Positive Correlation

1.

2.

Weak Negative Correlation

1.

2.

Weak Positive Correlation

1.

2.

1. What are two factors you would list as having a strong negative correlation with life satisfaction?

2. What are two factors you would list as having a strong positive correlation with life satisfaction?

3. What are two factors you would list as having a weak negative correlation with life satisfaction?

4. What are two factors you would list as having a weak positive correlation with life satisfaction?

Check Your Understanding

1. What is a positive correlation?
2. What is a negative correlation?
3. What is a multivariate statistical analysis?
4. What is the benefit of multivariate statistical analyses, relative to bivariate statistical analyses?

SOCIOLOGISTS IN ACTION
Brittany Hearne

Brittany Hearne
Courtesy of Brittany Hearne

Social science methods are powerful tools for uncovering and addressing social inequality or social injustices. My aim in teaching methods and using quantitative methods in my own research is to create an informed public and avenues for social justice. I am guided by three understandings: (1) an informed research question is necessary; (2) the power of theory; and (3) how to pick a research method.

What is an informed research question? You can only know whether you have an informed research question by understanding what kinds of questions have been asked previously. This requires reviewing the literature. In my work, I begin with a systematic search of existing research focusing on the work of scholars who use statistics and a critical lens to investigate race/ethnicity, gender, and intersectional inequalities in health. In this way, I am confident that through my research I am speaking to people who are interested in highlighting health inequalities.

Why is theory powerful? Theories are based on evidence-based research studies. Importantly, theory allows the researcher to move beyond their own projects to speak about patterns across society. Instead of summarizing thousands of studies about health disparities across social divides like race/ethnicity, researchers can speak about one theory, or a few theories, that will straight-forwardly provide a picture of the health disparities facing our society. For people social justice oriented, especially those with a passion for community or grassroots activism, I teach that it is critical to stay close to academic theory while also encouraging people in communities to speak for themselves about problems and solutions.

How to pick a research method? The research question determines the method. In my own work, I typically ask questions that require an examination of how population health outcomes differ at the intersections of race/ethnicity, gender, and education. Thus, I commonly couple an intersectionality lens and large nationally representative datasets to answer my questions. I use statistical methods because they allow me to make comparisons across social groups with a calculable level of confidence that the patterns exist in the larger population. For large-scale solutions aimed at reducing health disparities, broad patterns must be highlighted to convince policy makers that solutions are needed.

Sometimes social justice solutions are best applied locally. I recently studied mental health among Black people in a small town at the beginning of the COVID-19 pandemic. I used in-depth interviews and surveys because both methods served the research question. One stressor mentioned by some interviewees was a lack of friends in the town and the survey data showed elevated psychological distress. Using these findings and my understanding of health disparities negatively impacting Black communities, I volunteered to meet with a group of Black women in the town via teleconferencing to create a community among the women and share solutions to reduce stress.

Brittany N. Hearne is assistant professor of sociology at the University of Arkansas.

Discussion Question

How can quantitative analyses help to shed light on health disparities?

CONCLUSION

The methodological toolkit for quantitative data analysis is enormous, and in this chapter we have just scratched the surface. Social researchers use a variety of sophisticated statistical techniques to analyze the relationships among variables and to advance their understanding of how the world works. In the next chapter, you will learn some of the tools and approaches researchers use to analyze qualitative work.

REVIEW

12.1   What motivates quantitative analysis? What are its strengths and limitations?

Sociologists conduct quantitative research for a number of reasons: to test their hypotheses and further develop theories, to evaluate policies and programs, and to document social inequalities. The strengths of quantitative data analysis are that researchers can analyze large datasets and if analyzing data from a well-designed sample, can generalize their findings to a broader population. A limitation is that quantitative data are often less nuanced compared to qualitative data.

12.2   What is the General Social Survey? Why is it a valuable resource for sociology?

General Social Survey is a national survey of adults in the United States, which has been conducted regularly since 1972. It is one of the most frequently used and highest-quality surveys of people in the United States.

12.3   How do you construct a frequency table? How do you interpret it accurately?

Frequency tables present information about a variable in tabular form. Typically, they list the possible response categories in the left-most column, followed by a column showing the percentage of observations falling into each category, as well as the number of observations (i.e., the frequency of each response).

12.4   How do you calculate the mean, median, and mode of a variable? How do you calculate range and interquartile range? How do you interpret each of these statistics?

The mean of a variable is its arithmetic average. The median is the value of the variable for the middle-most observation, when the observations are ordered from greatest to least or least to greatest on that variable. The mode is the value of the response category that contains the largest number of observations. The range is the distance between the value of the largest and smallest observation. The interquartile range is the distance between the 25th and 75th percentile on a particular variable.

12.5   How do you construct a bivariate table or "crosstab"? How do you interpret it accurately?

Bivariate tables show the relationship between two variables. Each cell in the table typically contains a frequency, a percentage, or both. Column percentages tell you the percentage of each column category that fall into each row.

12.6 What is the benefit of using control variables in quantitative analyses, and of using multivariate analyses more generally?

Multivariate analyses can assess how many independent variables work together to shape a dependent variable. By using control variables, a researcher can see whether the relationship between two variables remains when the value of a third (the control variable) stays the same.

KEY TERMS

bivariate tables (p. 230)

codebook (p. 222)

column percent (p. 224)

control variable (p. 236)

correlation (p. 236)

dataset (p. 216)

frequency distribution (p. 223)

interquartile range (p. 227)

mean (p. 227)

measures of central tendency (p. 225)

measures of variation (p. 227)

median (p. 227)

mode (p. 225)

multivariate analyses (p. 236)

negative correlation (p. 236)

outlying observations (p. 228)

parameter (p. 216)

population (p. 216)

positive correlation (p. 236)

quantifying (p. 216)

quartile (p. 228)

range (p. 227)

sample (p. 216)

scatterplot (p. 233)

statistic (p. 216)

univariate statistic (p. 225)

variables (p. 222)

13 CODING QUALITATIVE DATA: REVEALING PATTERNS IN WORDS AND IMAGES

Krista McQueeney

STUDENT LEARNING QUESTIONS

13.1 How do researchers use coding and memoing to develop analyses?

13.2 How can descriptive coding be used to trace similarities and differences related to gender, race, class, and other social categories?

13.3 How do researchers develop topic codes, and how does social position influence the topic codes that researchers create?

13.4 What are some hands-on techniques researchers can use for analytic coding?

13.5 How can Computer-Assisted Qualitative Data Analysis Software (CAQDAS) programs help qualitative researchers store, organize, and code their data?

As we have seen in previous chapters, a primary goal of qualitative researchers is to identify patterns and themes in social life. But qualitative analysis is not just about searching for patterns in the data—it is also about forming explanations for what those patterns mean and why they are there in the first place. This can be a daunting task! Qualitative researchers often spend hundreds of hours collecting data in a field setting and/or searching for documents, visual images, or video in archives or online. Now, what do we do with all this messy, open-ended data?

Rather than using data to systematically test a hypothesis or theory, as a quantitative researcher might do, qualitative researchers start with the raw data and develop generalizations through repeated examination and comparison. This is called inductive reasoning, or thinking from the ground up. Of course, the type of data you are analyzing depends on the methods and sources you use. As discussed in Chapter 9, qualitative data typically consist of open-ended text and/or visual images that capture participants' views and experiences of the social world. Interview transcripts, observational field notes, documents, open-ended survey responses, cultural artifacts, photographs, video, websites, and fiction are some examples of the raw data that qualitative researchers analyze.

So how do researchers analyze the often voluminous amounts of open-ended text and/or visual images they collect? Most qualitative researchers use a technique called coding. Coding is the practice of identifying a word or phrase (a label, or "code") to summarize and capture the meaning of chunks of data. Chunks of data can be anything from a word to a sentence to an entire page of text; they can also take the form of visual images and streams of video. When you capture the essence of your data in codes, you can begin to identify patterns in the data. It is at this point in the research process when you start to more systematically map out routines, rituals, rules, roles, and relationships. These are known in qualitative research as the five "Rs" of social life. Qualitative researchers strive to tell the larger "story" of patterned social life that emerges from the individual narratives, images, and other data points they have collected. It can be really exciting to see these larger stories emerge as you organize and transform your raw data into "findings" or "results."

This chapter will introduce the basics of coding qualitative data. First, we will define and discuss coding as a method of building analysis from raw data. Second, we will explore the three types of coding that are most useful for beginning researchers: descriptive coding, topic coding, and analytic coding. Using examples from qualitative studies, we will consider which data to code, how to refine codes, how to group similarly coded data into categories, and how to ascertain conceptual themes from the data. We will also examine how researchers use memoing to build analysis. Third, we will conclude with some considerations for how to find a Computer-Assisted Qualitative Data Analysis (CAQDAS) program that best meets your needs.

HOW I GOT ACTIVE IN SOCIOLOGY

Krista McQueeney

Growing up, all I wanted to do was play basketball. But I wasn't just a student of the game; I was also a student of society's *construction* of the game. From a young age, I noticed that girls were given less desirable gym times, received far less media coverage, and didn't get the expensive uniforms and team sneakers the boys did—even though my high school team was no. 1 in the state and the boys were dead last in the league! When I discovered sociology in college, I was finally able to put names and explanations to the inequalities I had seen and intuitively known were there. This gave me a deep appreciation for the power of naming and framing—it is only when we can *name* a problem that we can see it and solve it. This is how I became a social constructionist of gender.

CODING

Regardless of their perspective and method, most qualitative researchers use a technique called coding to analyze their data. Coding—the practice of capturing the meaning of data-passages through a label (or "code")—allows researchers to summarize textual or visual data in order to identify broader themes and patterns. Let's start with a hypothetical example. A social psychologist has collected narrative accounts from 80 of the nation's richest people on the "Forbes 400" list. The researcher is interested in which personality traits are associated with financial success. As the researcher begins to read through the interview transcripts, they are immediately struck by how many times respondents describe themselves as "competitive," "winners," and "driven." The researcher codes data-passages like these as "competitive."

Once the researcher applies codes to the interview data, the next step is to merge similar codes into broader categories. Categories are groupings that you impose on the coded segments in order to reduce the number of different pieces of data and develop a broader sense of the data. The categories you develop are often guided by your research questions. For example, our social psychologist might decide to incorporate the code "competitive" into a broader category like "personality styles," which might include other codes such as "resilient," "risk-taking," "collaborative," and "extroverted," as well as the original code "competitive." Finally, themes are a higher level of analysis in which the researcher moves from an explicit description of the data—e.g., a code such as "competitive," which is derived from participants' own words—to a more implicit meaning or theme within the data. Themes are more general and abstract than categories, and they depend on the interpretation of the researcher rather than actual language used in the data themselves. They are a *result* of coding, categorization, and analytic reflection, not a code themselves. For example, our social psychologist might begin to note personality style differences among different groups of professionals on the Forbes 400 list, such as public servants versus corporate leaders. As a result, the researcher moves from a code ("competitive") to a category ("personality styles") to a theme, i.e., "personality style differences between financially successful public servants and business leaders."

The method wherein researchers develop codes, categories, and themes from qualitative data is called grounded theory (Glaser & Strauss, 1999). Through the use of grounded theory, researchers like the social psychologist in the example utilize ground-up thinking, or inductive reasoning, to move from raw data points to more general analytic categories and themes. This is called thinking up. To "think up" from the data to a more abstract level of analysis, you can ask yourself questions like, "What words, behaviors, images, or themes keep coming up, and what do they mean? What larger theme or social pattern might this be an example of? What purpose do these words, actions, and/or images serve? What role do they play within the larger cultural context or narrative they are a part of?" By asking these questions, you can "think up" from the concrete textual or visual data to analyze what the data symbolize about the social world.

CONSIDER THIS...

Your flight on a low-cost airline has been delayed for four hours. As you walk around the airport, you notice that twelve other flights on low-cost airlines are delayed as well. Thinking inductively from these observations, what conclusion might you draw? How reliable are conclusions based on inductive reasoning?

Coding is the engine that moves qualitative researchers from data collection to analysis. In his pioneering work on qualitative analysis for social scientists, Anselm Strauss, one of the founders of grounded theory, stresses the importance of coding: "Any researcher who wishes to become proficient at doing qualitative analysis must learn to code well and easily. The excellence of the research rests in large part on the excellence of the coding" (1987, p. 27). Coding is much more than simply labeling; it is linking data to codes, linking codes to categories, and linking categories to other categories. Coding allows researchers not just to reveal patterns in words and images, but to generate theoretical explanations for those patterns. In Sections A2, A3, and A4 of this chapter, we will explore the three coding techniques that are most useful for beginning researchers: descriptive coding, topic coding, and analytic coding.

Memoing

However, before we take a deeper dive into the three types of coding, it's important to mention the practice of freewriting, or memoing, on your data. Memoing is the practice of writing reflective notes or memos about what you are learning from your data. (The term *freewriting* is also used to emphasize the informal, spontaneous nature of memoing. Freewriting reminds us not to get caught up in grammar or sentence structure and just let our thoughts flow freely.) Especially for beginning researchers, it's crucial to start unpacking meanings and searching for emerging themes from the start of your research—even before you begin formal coding. Memos give you space to explore what your data mean, to formulate hypotheses about what you are seeing, and to examine connections between the codes, categories, and/or themes you have developed in order to begin generating theoretical explanations for them (Glaser & Holton, 2004).

Memoing requires consistent and disciplined practice. Every time you collect additional data, step back and ask yourself, "What am I seeing? What words, phrases, behaviors, and images are coming up again and again? What purposes do they serve for those enacting them?" This sort of reflection can be done as an in-the-moment spot check or by writing memos about whatever strikes you as interesting or surprising (e.g., Lofland & Lofland, 1995). Memos enhance the credibility of qualitative research and provide a record of the meanings you have gleaned from your data as they continue to evolve and crystallize throughout your project.

In practice, memoing can be as simple as jotting words and ideas in the margins of data transcripts. As you dig deeper into your analysis, memos often may

Memoing is a practice that allows researchers to reflect on what they have learned so far.

iStock.com/Mixmike

start to look like multipage reflection papers where you develop hypotheses and flesh out concepts and patterns you are noticing. Memos do the footwork for analysis and can sometimes even be used in the Results section of your write-up.

In addition, carefully reading through and memoing on your data early in the research process allows you to go back and collect additional data to fill in any gaps. Although it may not make sense to begin computer-assisted analysis until you have collected all of the data, writing memos regularly—i.e., whenever you have reactions or ideas—is incredibly beneficial for identifying emerging themes and patterns.

DOING SOCIOLOGY 13.1

Memoing on Field Notes From Two Church Services

In this exercise, you will practice memoing on hypothetical observational field notes.

You spent all day observing worship services for your study of evangelical churches. After taking detailed field notes of the sayings and doings in two worship services, you notice that at the predominantly Black Baptist church, there is more joyful singing, physical touch (e.g., hugging), and interaction between the pastors and parishioners (e.g., call-and-response style, laypeople sharing personal testimonies). At the predominantly white Episcopal church, there is a more quiet and contemplative tone, little to no hugging, and a more formal and predictable role of music—for example, the music cues parishioners when to kneel, when to stand, and when to line up. There is less interaction between the priest and parishioners (e.g., the priest delivers the sermon without much if any participation or response by laypeople).

1. Write a brief memo about these observations.

2. What ideas do you have about these observations? What questions do they spark?

3. If you don't know much about these differences between predominantly Black and white churches, how could you find out more?

To sum up, coding is an active process that requires disciplined thinking and writing. It is both iterative and recursive: iterative, involving multiple steps of asking questions, reflecting, and memoing; and recursive, involving back-and-forth cycles of coding, recoding, deleting or fine-tuning categories, creating new ones, and previewing or trying out ideas for upcoming phases of analysis. Qualitative researchers go back and forth between coding and memoing—and then go back and do it again—to build an analysis of the patterns and themes in the data.

Check Your Understanding

1. How do qualitative researchers analyze open-ended textual and/or visual data?
2. What is coding? How does a researcher create codes?
3. How does a qualitative analyst "think up" from their data to identify codes, categories, and themes?
4. What is memoing? Why is it important to start memoing early in the data collection process?

DESCRIPTIVE CODING

The first coding technique that is particularly useful for beginning researchers is descriptive coding (Richards & Morse, 2007). Descriptive coding is a technique where the researcher labels the data with descriptive (e.g., demographic) information in order to track group similarities and differences. For example, sociologists are often interested in how gender, race, class, age, and other social categories shape people's beliefs, experiences, and opportunities. Depending on their research questions, a

TABLE 13.1 ■ Aiello and McQueeney's Descriptive Coding Spreadsheet							
Pseudonym	Race/ Ehnicity	Length of Sentence	# Times Incarcerated	# of Children	Caregiver	Perception of Caregiver Relationship	Contact Visits With Kids?
Becky	Latina	2 years	2	1	Aunt	Good	Regularly
Lilly	Black	6 months	1	2	Mother	Good	Regularly
Miranda	White	2 years	1	8	Kids' father	Bad	Regularly

sociologist might tabulate participants' demographic information (e.g., gender, age, race/ethnicity, education, religion) in order to examine similarities and differences among social groups in their dataset.

There are several ways you can do this. Although it is recommended that beginners learn to code manually (i.e., coding in the margins with pen and paper) before diving into the world of coding software, basic word processing and spreadsheet programs can be very helpful for organizing your data. For example, in Microsoft Word you can assign brief descriptive information to each interview transcript in a header or footer. In an Excel spreadsheet, you can create columns of identifying information about each participant, image, or research event.

An example of descriptive coding can be found in the work of Aiello and McQueeney (2021), who conducted interviews with 83 incarcerated mothers in a county jail in the Northeast. They were interested in how family caregivers shaped incarcerated mothers' bonds with their children while the mothers were locked up. Prior research had found that incarcerated mothers who maintain bonds with their children are less likely to be re-incarcerated than mothers who don't. Yet researchers had not yet examined the role of the caregivers who parent the incarcerated mothers' children while they do time.

To begin descriptive coding, Aiello and McQueeney created an Excel spreadsheet to record descriptive information about each of the 83 incarcerated mothers and the caregivers of their children (e.g., race/ethnicity, length of sentence, number of times incarcerated, number of children, identity of children's caregiver, mom's perception of the caregiver relationship, mom's frequency of contact visits with children, etc.). Table 13.1 is a snippet of Aiello and McQueeney's Excel spreadsheet.

Using a spreadsheet for descriptive coding was useful not just to organize the data, but to ask questions of them. The researchers could easily search for similarities and differences among the 83 incarcerated mothers. They could ask questions like: "Did women with fewer children feel closer to their caregivers?" "Did mothers' relationships with their caregivers differ by race/ethnicity?" And, "did mothers who felt close to their caregivers have more regular visits with their children?" Once the researchers traced initial patterns, they could more carefully test relationships between factors such as closeness with caregivers (an independent variable) and visits with children (a dependent variable).

DOING SOCIOLOGY 13.2

Descriptive Coding: Men's Versus Women's Athletics

In this exercise, you will consider how to use descriptive coding to analyze images of men's and women's athletics.

Envision media images you have seen of NCAA men's and women's athletics and/or professional sports. Consider what sports are highlighted most, what types of athletes are featured (e.g., gender, sport), and what merchandise and programs or teams are heavily promoted and showcased (e.g., Notre Dame Hockey or the Los Angeles Lakers).

1. If you were to create a spreadsheet to code for how men's and women's athletics are portrayed in the media, for what descriptive information would you code?

2. Do you think counting instances within these descriptive categories would provide more valid information than if you analyzed text and images without counting them? Why or why not?

Whether you decide to print hard copies of your data and code the margins with pens, highlighters, and Post-It notes; use a word processing document or spreadsheet; or upload the data into a computer-assisted qualitative analysis program, it is vital to immerse yourself in the data. Read them all the way through multiple times, jot down ideas for codes and themes, reword your codes to better fit the data, and continually step back to ask yourself what you are seeing. It is important to note that a lack of memoing can have very negative effects on the final outcome of a project. One of the pitfalls of software programs is that they can create a false illusion that the computer will analyze your data for you. For better or worse, it is *you* who must do the mental work. Thus, although coding is an essential part of your qualitative toolkit, beware of coding fetishism (Richards & Morse, 2007), where a researcher codes or counts compulsively rather than reflecting on and memoing about their data. Nevertheless, if you do use a qualitative analysis program, an additional benefit is that you can write and associate memos to your data and use the advanced analysis tools to compile your insights and conclusions all within the program.

CONSIDER THIS...

Imagine that you've compiled hundreds of pages of text and images in the field. Which of the techniques discussed in this section would you choose to help make sense of these data?

Check Your Understanding

1. What is descriptive coding?
2. How do researchers use descriptive coding to trace group differences based on gender, race, class, and other social categories?
3. How do qualitative researchers decide what descriptive information or demographic characteristics for which to code? How can spreadsheets be used to tally demographic characteristics?
4. How can software like Word, Excel, and computer-assisted qualitative analysis software such as NVivo, ATLAS.ti, and MAXQDA help with descriptive coding?
5. What are some disadvantages of using Computer-Assisted Qualitative Data Analysis Software for coding?

TOPIC CODING

Topic coding, the most common and straightforward form of coding, involves labeling data with a salient word or phrase that grabs the reader. Topic codes are like a good title for a book in that the researcher pithily captures the meaning of salient bits of data. Topic codes can emerge from language in the data themselves (i.e., quoting the actual words people use, which is called in vivo coding). They may also come from terms used in the theoretical and research literature. With the help of topic codes, researchers can begin to develop categories that are more conceptual in nature. Importantly, topic coding is a cyclical or iterative process where you develop an initial list of codes and then refine them as you gain a firmer grasp of what's happening in the data. As you continue to unpack the meanings of your data, you will cycle back through the transcripts, rename your codes, create new ones, combine some codes with other codes, and drop some codes altogether. Abbott (2004, p. 215) uses the metaphor of decorating a room: "[Y]ou try it, step back, move a few things, step back again, try a serious reorganization, and so on." Given that topic codes are likely to change, it is a good idea to keep them short, simple, and spontaneous.

For a look at how researchers develop topic codes, let's consider a study by sociologist Matt Ezzell (2009), who conducted participant observation and interviews with women's college rugby players. His research question was, "How do female ruggers construct identities in a hypermasculine sport?" Table 13.2 is an example of one of Ezzell's coded interview transcripts. Note that Ezzell's interview text is in the left column and the codes he developed are on the right.

In this excerpt, Ezzell focused on coding data that were most relevant to his research question. Often, your research questions will point you toward the data of primary interest and importance. Table 13.3 offers several questions to help you determine which data are *sociologically* meaningful. It is not necessary to code each and every word or line of data. With experience, you will develop a sense of how to zero in on the data that reflect important social patterns in your sample. Also note that Ezzell's code for "reasserting" is a gerund, or action word. Glaser (1978), one of the founders of grounded theory, advises coding with gerunds rather than nouns. This helps to reveal *processes* and capture the fluidity of social life, whereas nouns tend to portray participants' views and experiences as static.

Topic codes like those Ezzell created in his study of female rugby players can spark analytic ideas about the data right out of the gate. However, it is fairly unusual for the codes a researcher develops in the first review of their data to stick through multiple cycles of review, reflection, and analysis. As you immerse yourself in the data, you will **recode**, or fine-tune your codes and develop new ones. The "Sociologist in Action" for this chapter, Kristen Lavelle, shares an example of how her topic codes evolved into analysis. It was her initial bafflement about white respondents' resistance to answering her questions about race that kept her returning to these data—and that ultimately sparked her analytic

TABLE 13.2 ■ Matt Ezzell's Interview With Tammie, a Female Rugby Player	
Interview Text	**Topic Codes**
I'm not this kind of person that thinks, "Oh, girls should be able to play with the boys if they want to. No. Like, I would never step on that field and play full contact rugby with the boys. They're much stronger than me I would get killed, you know?... Cause I mean, yeah, there is that level of difference there and nobody can do anything about it... I'm just happy I can play exactly what they play, just on my level.	(RE)ASSERTING MALE SUPERIORITY AS ATHLETES "NATURAL" DIFFERENCES/ INEQUALITIES; BIOLOGY AS DESTINY

Source: Ezzell, 2009.

TABLE 13.3 ■ Questions to Point You Toward Coding the Data That Are Sociologically Meaningful
What are people doing? What are they trying to accomplish?
How are they doing this? What specific meanings, cultural practices, and actions are they using? What rules and norms are they following?
What roles (teacher, daughter, athlete, church member, etc.) and social types (bully, jock, geek) can be seen in the setting or sample?
What words, themes, or actions seem to be coming up repeatedly?
What theories or concepts does this remind me of?
What do participants explicitly say is important?
What surprises me?
What disturbs me?

Adapted from Saldaña, 2016,

insight about how participants' rhetorical "maneuvers" served a larger purpose of propping up their moral identities as "good white people" (Lavelle, 2014).

SOCIOLOGISTS IN ACTION

Kristen Lavelle

From Befuddlement to Analytic Insight: The Recoding Process

I'm working on an article based on my research in which I interviewed 44 elder white southerners about their memories of the racial past, including Jim Crow/legal segregation and the Civil Rights era. I interviewed "Ava," a working-class woman in her 60s, about how she had experienced the legal segregation era during childhood. One question was intended to ascertain the level and types of interracial interactions she'd had in her formative years.

Kristen: Did you ever have any playmates or friends that weren't white when you were growing up?

Ava: Well, we never did know there was a difference. We never did see color. One of my daddy's best friends was a little Black boy, and they used to play together all the time. And the fact that somebody was Black—we never knew about slavery and that kind of stuff and felt like that somebody Black was any lower class than we were... you know, one of my best friends right now is a Black lady, and she's a lady that used to come and clean my house and... we still go out to eat and we've made plans right now to [get together].

Sitting in Ava's living room, I felt confusion: Why was she changing the subject, especially on such a simple question? I transcribed Ava's interview, read it over, and started coding. The code I ultimately applied to this section was *diversion maneuver*. Contemplating her answer in its full context, I reasoned that the most straightforward answer she could have given likely would have been "no." If she'd had Black playmates, she probably would have shared that rather than recalling her father in his youth and her current friendship. Instead, she jumped back in time to talk about her father's childhood and then forward to her adult self. In other interviews, I found several similar instances of respondents jumping abruptly to different time periods. To these excerpts, I added the code *time warp*.

I later realized that, amidst her time warps that indirectly answered my question, Ava also asserted that she had "never seen color" or viewed African Americans as inferior. Overall, based on *what* she said, *when* and *how* she shared it, and what she *didn't* say, Ava appeared to be crafting a persona as someone who had lived her entire life devoid of any racial prejudice. Other respondents gave off the same impression in their diversion maneuvers. Thus, I concluded this type of time-hopping maneuver served a larger purpose. The concept of moral identity applies well to what I was seeing in my data—how people work to craft a positive sense of self despite the existence of contradictory evidence.

Kristen Lavelle is an associate professor of sociology at University of Wisconsin–Whitewater.

Discussion Question

1. How did Dr. Lavelle use coding to "think up" from the data to a more conceptual analysis?
2. What other words and phrases can you think of to code Dr. Lavelle's data?

Topic coding is a vital tool for identifying patterns in your data. As Lavelle shows, once you start to see repeated words and themes, code for more categories, and think through their meanings and social purposes, topic coding becomes more analytic. Often, topic codes become "the bones of your analysis.... [I]ntegration will assemble those bones into a working skeleton" (Charmaz, 2014, p. 113). Yet it is typically not until you begin analytic coding, as discussed later in this chapter, that you start developing this sort of theoretical integration.

Social Position and Coding

As researchers, our life experiences, social position, and perspectives affect how we code. As you may have noted in the discussion of Ezzell's research on female rugby players, his perspective as a critical feminist symbolic interactionist informed his codes. Feminist symbolic interactionism is a theoretical perspective that critically analyzes how gender roles and inequalities—as they intersect with racism, heterosexism, and class inequality—are produced, challenged, and reproduced in social interaction (Kleinman & Cabaniss, 2019). Feminist symbolic interactionism, like any theoretical perspective, offers conceptual lenses for analyzing data. Some conceptual lenses from feminist symbolic interactionism include *ideology, power, privilege, inequality,* and *oppression*. As seen in Table 13.1, the focus on power and inequality can be seen in Ezzell's codes for *male superiority, differences/inequalities,* and his critique of *biology as destiny*. Again, decisions about what to code and how to code it—and, ultimately, the findings and conclusions of a study—are shaped by the researcher's perspective. Although qualitative researchers try to be as careful and consistent as possible, deciding which conceptual lenses best fit your data is part of what makes qualitative analysis creative, spontaneous, and fun.

It's worth repeating that in any study, codes are influenced by the researcher's perspective. For example, an ethnographer, a qualitative researcher who provides vivid and precise descriptions of the social world, would have coded the same data quite differently. An ethnographer would likely stay close to participants' own words or phrases, using in vivo codes such as "I would get killed," "there is that level of difference," and "nobody can do anything about it." In contrast, Ezzell's critical approach might be called values coding (Saldaña, 2016), where a researcher examines and unpacks the subjective values underlying the data. That is, rather than taking participants' assumptions about male superiority at face value, Ezzell critiqued the underlying values and assumptions behind their worldviews, as well as the social consequences of these values and assumptions for reinforcing or challenging inequalities. Ezzell's coding offers a great example of how to both honor participants' accounts and maintain analytic distance from them.

In addition, it is important for qualitative researchers to reflect on how their own identities—e.g., their gender, race/ethnicity, level of education, sexuality, etc.—may be shaping both the data they collect and their analysis of them. As a researcher, your social identities and positionality may shape how people interact with you in the field, your level of access to the community and/or the kind of observations to which you are privy, and the lenses through which you view your data and the world. We can never fully eliminate researcher bias in qualitative research; nevertheless, it is vital for the researcher to memo about how their own beliefs and background may be influencing the research so that we can minimize the bias.

CONSIDER THIS...

How might a researcher's race, gender, or religion affect how they code? For example, if researchers of different religious backgrounds studied laws that encourage public schools to teach the Bible, how might each approach the research differently?

As you begin coding your data, keep in mind that there is no universal guideline for how many codes you should have—some researchers limit their coding list to as few as five to six provisional codes, while others generate hundreds of codes. It is helpful to code liberally at first to be open to new knowledge that may emerge from your participants or the visual images you are analyzing. Then, once it becomes clear that some codes are appearing more frequently or are more significant than other codes, zero in on the data that fit those codes, as well as any data that may directly contradict—or pose exceptions to—those codes. Exceptions, or negative cases, will be discussed in the next section.

DOING SOCIOLOGY 13.3

Coding Images of Teen Girls in the Media

In this exercise, you will brainstorm topic codes to analyze how teen girls are portrayed in the media.

There is a growing interest among sociologists in visual media and communications. Just as we can group textual data into categories and themes, we can analyze categories and themes in visual data. In addition, we can ask, to what extent do these visual images accurately reflect and/or stereotype real lives?

1. What are some movies, TV shows, social media celebrity profiles, and other forms of media with which you are familiar that feature teen girls?

2. What are some words or phrases that describe how girls are portrayed (and/or present themselves) in popular media (e.g., "mean," "independent," or "hypersexualized")? How would you categorize these?

3. What do these codes and categories say about how teen girls are portrayed in the media? To what extent do you feel these images reflect the realities of teen girls' lives?

4. Why did you put the data in the categories you did? Would it have changed your conclusions if you had come up with different codes or categories?

Check Your Understanding

1. What is topic coding? How is it different from descriptive coding?
2. What is recoding, and how does a researcher do it?
3. How did Ezzell use values coding in his study of female rugby players? How might an ethnographer have coded the data differently?
4. How does the researcher's own social position and perspective influence their topic codes?

ANALYTIC CODING

As you progress with topic coding, your codes will grow in number and complexity. The next step is analytic coding, where you search for conceptual or theoretical categories and themes in your data. Similar to a close reading in poetry, you take fragments of your data apart and unpack the meanings of the smaller fragments (disassembling). After you glean meanings from smaller pieces of data, you reorganize the meanings of those data fragments in new ways to form a larger analytic story (reassembling). In disassembling, finer properties or elements of the categories are identified. Then, in reassembling, you step back and look at the bigger picture, asking how your codes reflect more general, or abstract categories, as a way to rearrange the smaller pieces into a larger story. The researcher also links categories to other categories, and searches for explanations in the social context and social dynamics of the worlds that give rise to the data.

Although analytic coding may seem abstract, it's not magic. There are several hands-on ways to analyze open-ended data. Two particularly useful techniques for beginning researchers are constant comparison and analyzing exceptions or negative cases. As noted earlier, these techniques should be paired with memoing, where you freewrite to think through the meanings and significance of your data. Table 13.4 offers ideas to help jump-start your memoing. When you reach the stage of analytic coding, it is important to write longer memos that try to make sense of and make connections among all information pertaining to a particular code, category, or theme in your data. The act of writing helps to stimulate new ideas and reveal your own standpoints and assumptions, which are essential to developing a strong analysis.

Constant Comparison

One technique for analytic coding, constant comparison—which was developed by Glaser and Strauss, the founders of grounded theory—involves comparing different pieces of data against each other to test for similarities and differences. For example, a researcher may code "incident with incident" (Glaser & Strauss, 1999), where they compare chunks of similarly coded data. In doing so, they start to outline the finer properties of that category, its relationship to similar or related categories, and/or the larger social contexts or conditions within which that category exists. In constant comparison, the researcher codes and analyzes the data simultaneously rather than first coding all the data and saving analysis for

TABLE 13.4   ■   Topics to Consider in Analytic Memos
● Define each code or category by its analytic properties or component parts
● Spell out and detail processes within the codes or categories
● Freewrite on similarities and differences between chunks of data or codes
● Bring raw data into the memo and freewrite your thoughts on it
● Provide sufficient empirical evidence to support your definitions of the category and analytic claims about it
● Offer hypotheses to test in the field setting
● Sort, order, and diagram codes and categories
● Identify gaps in the data or analysis
● Interrogate a code or category by asking questions of it
● Freewrite on an exception that doesn't seem to fit a code or category

Adapted from Charmaz, 2014.

later. In this way, the researcher makes a practice of "thinking up" from the data to develop analytic explanations throughout data collection.

As an example, let's consider a sociological study of emotional labor, which refers to the process where workers summon certain socially expected feelings (and not others) in themselves, their coworkers, and their clients (Hochschild, 1983). Like other workers, qualitative researchers perform emotional labor in fieldwork and interview research that involves social interactions with participants. McQueeney and Lavelle (2017) used constant comparison to explore qualitative researchers' emotional labor by comparing their experiences conducting two different field studies. They noticed striking similarities in the emotions they felt while doing their research—in particular, they often felt guilty, frustrated, or inauthentic. Intrigued by these similarities, they used constant comparison to code their data by compiling a log of each researcher's "incidents" (chunks of data coded as "frustration," "guilt," or "inauthenticity") side by side in a Word document.

Both researchers had been trained to listen to their respondents and make them feel like equals. However, they began to see that their feelings of frustration, guilt, and inauthenticity—which threatened their self-concepts as good researchers—arose when participants asserted power *over them* by making racist, sexist, and/or heterosexist comments; not taking them seriously; treating them like objects; or preaching at them. Using constant comparison, McQueeney and Lavelle identified three conditions under which they, as researchers, experienced these negative emotions in their fieldwork. Comparing incident with incident revealed that their negative and conflicted emotions were not personal failings, but a product of doing critical research. This is an example of how constant comparison can be used to "think up" from specific codes or incidents to develop theoretical arguments and analyses of why those actions, events, and feelings are happening in the first place.

Analyzing Exceptions

The second technique for analytic coding, which also comes from grounded theory, is where the researcher analyzes exceptions, or negative cases, that do not fit the pattern they have identified. When exceptions appear, they do not necessarily invalidate the pattern: They can actually help you develop a more nuanced explanation for that pattern. Exceptions inspire the researcher to refine their analysis until it can explain or account for a majority of cases. Additionally, since social life is both

Flight attendants frequently engage in emotional labor, ensuring passengers are comfortable during their flight.

iStock.com/RUBEN RAMOS

patterned and changing, exceptions or negative cases can serve as test cases to ensure that you haven't injected your personal bias or **reified** a pattern, which is when you erroneously reduce humanly created—and thus changeable—social forms to natural, universal, and fixed "things." Often the patterns you identify in your data are contingent on the larger social and historical context or the situation at hand; they are not fixed or universal. Negative cases can help you to identify the conditions under which a given pattern is likely to occur.

Let's consider Emily Cabaniss's research (2018) on undocumented student activists, or "Dreamers." Cabaniss memoed throughout the research process, and one of her memos is reproduced in Figure 13.1. Here she memos about a negative case of a female undocumented youth activist ("Cynthia") who gave an "angry" speech, similar to those typically given by men in the movement, and was urged to "tone it down." After giving the speech, Cynthia was pulled aside by a male ally and told to "watch that." The male ally told Cabaniss that Cynthia said she would, and later told a less angry and more tearful story at another public event.

Memoing on this negative case led Cabaniss to a stronger analysis. Earlier in her coding, Cabaniss noted a pattern of women activists "softening" their speeches by breaking into tears. Negative cases like Cynthia's alerted her to the resistance some women felt to presenting themselves as victims, and their desire to express anger about their legal exclusion from U.S. society. Thus, she began to ask herself, how do women deal with the double bind in which they didn't want to come off as victims, but they can't appear too angry without being perceived negatively as women? Cabaniss (2018) came to the conclusion that expressive storytelling in social movement activism may serve the interests of men better than women. Had she not examined negative cases like Cynthia's, she may not have understood the complexity of the women's dilemma, their responses to it, and its consequences for reproducing gender inequality.

FIGURE 13.1 ■ Emily Cabaniss's Memo on Negative Cases

Most of the time, when women in the DREAM Act Movement express their anger, they do so in the "backstage," as they rant to each other and to men in the movement about their frustrations with their lives, with immigration policies, and even other undocumented youth who seem politically naïve or gullible. Sometimes, though, this anger from women does creep into more public spaces (although this is rare). One notable time was when Cynthia—a woman who, usually among trusted members of the movement, denounces US culture and its policies as racist and exploitative and routinely says she thinks this country is a pretty shitty place—was invited to speak at a rally organized by a student group (all "allies" to the movement) to help fundraise for Cynthia's group. After being introduced, Cynthia started by saying her name and declaring herself undocumented. She proceeded to describe briefly her experiences feeling like she didn't fit in in the small, rural town in the US south where her family had migrated from Mexico. But then, she began talking in very pointed language about the expectations she had of allies in the movement. Her speech implied that members of the audience should work on living up to her expectations if they were going to be useful as allies. The rally was called "Giving up your dreams for the DREAM:"

> Latinos and Latinas in school, minorities in school, like, wake up, dude *[I'm feeling twinges of discomfort and confusion about her message and it seems like she's starting to direct her criticisms at this audience].* Wake up because our communities are under attack. You think SB-1070 is in Arizona? That shit is here *[A white ally begins to snap—he's the only one. It is deathly quiet otherwise as people watch and listen to her].* Does 287-g ring a bell? Does Secure Communities ring a bell? If it doesn't, then you need to go do some homework. You need to go do some research. Because our community is under attack.

> You, Latino, Latina, you think that because you're in college, oh, you're doing something? No, *mijo* [sweetheart]. Get out into the streets. Then you will do something. Then we can talk.... The time is now to get out of class, and take it into the streets, take it into the neighborhoods, and stand up and fight for your community.

> *[As she concludes, people clap briefly for her as she waves around the mic and laughs and says into it, "I'm holding the mic." In the few seconds it takes for one of the rally organizers to step forward and take it from her, the applause has stopped entirely, several people have left, and the remaining crowd is looking silently around at each other. I've never seen this kind of reaction to Cynthia's speeches. People seem uncomfortable and disengaged and like they don't want to be there—rather than fired up, which is almost always how they react to her.]*

Source: Cabaniss, 2018.

CONSIDER THIS...

Sherryl Kleinman encourages qualitative researchers to tune into their "twingeometers," a gut-level awareness that we are in a situation of coercion, cruelty, injustice, or danger—or simply that something feels contradictory or "not right" (Kleinman, 2003). These feelings can be sources of data that help us to formulate hypotheses, which we must then test against the data. Can you think of a time when you paid attention to your "twingeometer"? What did you learn from it?

At this point in analytic coding, many qualitative researchers wonder, when am I done coding? After coding incidents for the same category a number of times, you will likely have sufficient data to support the categories you have identified. To discern what constitutes sufficient data, most qualitative researchers use the yardstick of theoretical saturation. In general, you have reached theoretical saturation when nothing new seems to be happening in the data. For instance, you may be hearing the same stories or seeing the same patterns again and again. Unlike quantitative research, where the goal is to generalize to a larger population, the goal of qualitative research is to develop precise conceptual categories or new hypotheses. Sample size is not the measure of how much data are necessary to do this—instead, the goal is to develop categories that have conceptual richness. When asking questions of the data yields nothing new, a concept is "saturated" and you have likely collected enough data to build a theory.

Given the rapid advances in social media technologies, which have dramatically expanded the realm of publicly accessible visual images and platforms for self-expression, visual images have become an increasingly valuable sociological tool. Using a sociological lens, the researcher can analyze visual images—just as we analyze words—as shaped by their larger social contexts. Using this lens, we can construct categories, describe properties, and generate theoretical hypotheses from visual data.

DOING SOCIOLOGY 13.4

Coding Visual Images: Tattoos

In this exercise, you will code the meanings and attitudes that tattoos, as a visual image, communicate about a person's identity.

Visual images, including tattoos, aren't just nice to look at. Some communicate with words, others with images or symbols, and still others with both. Coding can help to analyze the meanings and messages that tattoos communicate.

Man_Half-tube/DigitalVision Vectors/Getty Images

Man_Half-tube/DigitalVision Vectors/Getty Images

Use the tattoos pictured here to respond the following questions:

1. What are some words or phrases you would use to code the *meanings* of these tattoos? For example, an American flag might be used to signify patriotism, or an *ankh* to symbolize the key of life. Colors can also be used as symbols (e.g., a rainbow to symbolize LGBTQ+ pride).

2. How would you code for the *attitude* the tattoos project? For example, are the tattoos humorous, sarcastic, stylish, self-reflective, or socially conscious?

3. How are your codes shaped by your identities, beliefs, and life experiences?

4. How might someone of a different age, gender, race/ethnic background, or educational background code the same tattoos differently? Why does this matter?

Quantitizing the Qualitative

When presenting your data, it can be helpful to present them in quantitative (numbers) as well as qualitative, forms. For example, imagine you want to show how satisfied the members of the women's basketball team on your campus are with their locker room or weight room. By quantifying your findings, you can provide representative quotes from your sample *and* reveal the percentage of your sample that gave similar responses. This can give readers a more comprehensive understanding of your findings than if you presented them in qualitative form only (e.g., by giving a quote from a team member to illustrate a category or theme).

As you might imagine, "quantitizing" qualitative findings enhances the validity and credibility of qualitative research. However, it has its pitfalls. It typically requires coding *all* the data relevant to a specific code, and it restricts the researcher's flexibility to recode if a code or category that better fits the data is revealed as you further immerse yourself in the data. For example, if the researcher discovers a new or better-fitting code halfway through coding hundreds of pages of observations, interviews, and/or visual data, it would take substantial time and effort to start over and recode all the data using the revised code or category. "Quantitizing" the qualitative is most appropriate when a researcher is interested in provisionally testing a hypothesis. In these cases, all the data should be analyzed from start to finish and assembled in a way that constitutes convincing "proof" for the hypothesis. Alternatively, if the researcher's goal is to generate new theoretical ideas, categories, or hypotheses, "quantitizing" the qualitative is not necessary. What's more, it may undermine the researcher's goal of generating new insights if they feel bound to code all the way through for a concept that ultimately proves to be insignificant or irrelevant. As such, it is important to use the right tool for the job.

Check Your Understanding

1. What is analytic coding? How is it different from descriptive and topic coding?
2. What is constant comparison? How did McQueeney and Lavelle use it in their study of qualitative researchers' emotional labor?
3. How did Emily Cabaniss analyze negative cases to unpack gendered patterns in her study of undocumented student activists?
4. What is a "twingeometer"? How can qualitative researchers use it to analyze their data?
5. What does it mean to "quantitize" the qualitative? What are some advantages and disadvantages of doing this?

CODING WITH COMPUTER-ASSISTED QUALITATIVE DATA ANALYSIS SOFTWARE (CAQDAS)

At its most basic level, qualitative analysis is about organizing and summarizing textual and/or visual data. Computer Assisted Qualitative Data Analysis Software (CAQDAS, pronounced *cactus*), a term that refers to the wide range of software that supports a variety of analytic approaches in qualitative research, can be tremendously helpful for storing, organizing, reorganizing, and retrieving data. It is indispensable when managing a large collection of interviews, field notes, documents, digital files, memos, videos, and/or other materials. Software programs can help you code easily and quickly, search and retrieve data by code or category, create and save memos, graph and diagram relationships between codes and categories, and—with many programs—import and analyze audio and video data from social media platforms such as Twitter, Instagram, and YouTube. Software programs allow you to store images, text, and audio in one virtual environment. Most interfaces provide a document pane to retrieve the text or image and an adjacent pane that displays your codes. Drop-down menus provided across the tool bar allow you easy access to all your documents, images, videos, quotes, codes, and/or memos in one place.

When beginning a qualitative project, online forums such as the CAQDAS Networking Project are helpful sources of information about trainings and comparisons of different software programs. In addition, Lewins and Silver's (2007) book *Using Software in Qualitative Research: A Step-by-Step Guide* provides step-by-step instructions on how to use selected CAQDAS packages. Table 13.5 contains a list of major CAQDAS websites that provide online tutorials and/or downloads of their most current versions (some are free and others for purchase). Currently, the most popular and user-friendly programs are Atlas.ti, NVivo, and MAXQDA.

Compiling your data files requires considerable time and careful attention. Most CAQDAS programs require you to save your data files in separate records known as "Hermeneutic Units" (in Atlas.ti) or "Documents" (in NVivo). For example, you might have 35 interviews, 25 sets of observational field notes, and 20 organizational documents and images, for a total of 80 records or cases in your dataset. As noted, a growing number of CAQDAS programs accept audio and video files, which can be easily

---

TABLE 13.5 ■ CAQDAS Programs

- AnSWR
- AQUAD
- ATLAS.ti
- CAT (Coding Analysis Toolkit)
- Dedoose
- DiscoverText
- HyperRESEARCH
- INTERACT
- MAXQDA
- NVivo
- QDA Miner
- Qualrus
- Quirkos
- Transana (for audio and video data)
- V-Note (for audio and video data)
- Weft QDA
- WordStat

uploaded from social media and websites. Which CAQDAS program you choose will depend on your situation and preferences (e.g., type of data, price, user-friendliness, transportability needs). One thing that bears repeating is that the computer will not do the analytic work for you. Unlike quantitative analysis programs where the researcher provides input data and the computer generates a result using the proper formula, you must give CAQDAS step-by-step instructions to carry out each analytic procedure. Even then, you will have to rely on your own critical abilities to develop an analysis—this means coding, memoing, recoding, experimenting with different relationships among codes and concepts by drawing arrays and matrices, and often starting the process all over again. This stage of analysis can take several months depending on the nature and scope of your data.

In addition to easy compilation, coding, retrieval, and reorganization of data, software programs are especially helpful when you reach the stage of analytic coding, where you think up from codes to develop conceptual or theoretical categories or themes. One analytic technique for which software programs are especially useful is arraying the data, or creating graphical representations of codes and concepts. Two common ways to build theory using graphics or diagrams are arraying data in hierarchical or matrix forms. Almost all CAQDAS programs allow you to create hierarchies and matrices.

Hierarchical Array

A hierarchical array, called an "array" or "tree" in many CAQDAS programs, consists of codes or categories grouped into different levels or hierarchies. The idea is that some themes or concepts are more general than others, and those below are subsets of the more general concepts at the top. Each level of the hierarchy groups related items together, ordering the codes vertically and potentially revealing "classes" or "typologies" (Yin, 2011). As seen in the hierarchical array in Figure 13.2, the more general category of fruit has many specific types falling under it (e.g., apples, oranges, etc.). Then, apples can be further subdivided into Granny Smith, McIntosh, Delicious, Honeycrisp, etc. If we had space, we could also subdivide oranges into Naval, Clementine, Tangelo, and so on.

Hierarchical arrays are helpful for unpacking the properties and dimensions of your codes and categories, which is one way to build a theoretical analysis.

Matrices

A matrix is a rectangular array organized in rows and columns. In its simplest form, a matrix is a 2 x 2 table with data entered in each cell. According to Miles and Huberman (1994), the most common matrices in qualitative analysis are time-ordered (e.g., chronological), role-ordered (e.g., according to people's roles), and conceptually ordered (e.g., a set of categories arrayed against another set). In the earlier stages of analysis, each cell of the matrix should contain your actual data, not your opinions or conclusions. Keep in mind that you may have to abbreviate your data to capture their essence so that the matrix doesn't become too crowded or unwieldy. The goal is to create a graphical representation

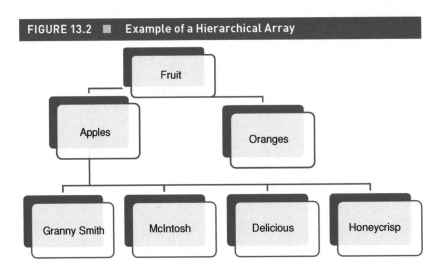

FIGURE 13.2 ■ Example of a Hierarchical Array

FIGURE 13.3 ■ Matrix Analysis of Teacher Roles in Dealing With High School Dropouts

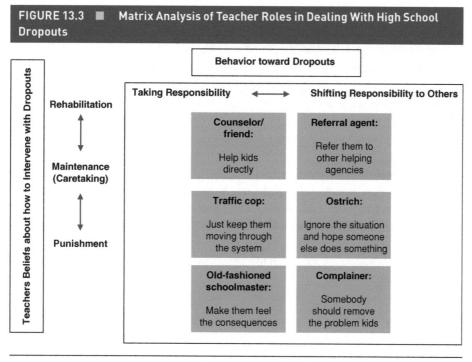

Source: Patton, 2002.

that will help you detect patterns in your data, so packing your matrix with long quotes or other data will be counterproductive. However, as your analytic findings become clearer, your matrix might illustrate complex and multilayered relationships between categories, themes, or concepts.

CONSIDER THIS...

What are some of the benefits of using software to perform coding and analysis? What are some of the drawbacks?

An interesting use of matrices can be seen in Patton's (1990) study of how teachers deal with high school dropouts. As seen in Figure 13.3, Patton initially identified two separate dimensions to explain the variation in teachers' responses to dropouts: (1) teachers' beliefs about how much responsibility they should take (tote the scale "Taking Responsibility ⇔ Shifting Responsibility to Others" on the top *X*-axis); and (2) teachers' views about effective intervention strategies (note the scale "Rehabilitation ⇔ Maintenance (Caretaking) ⇔ Punishment" on the *Y*-axis). Then, he combined these dimensions to create a 2x3 matrix (or table). The matrix shows the relationship between the two dimensions. In the cells, Patton identified six different roles that teachers adopt, each representing a combination of the two dimensions. Note the vivid descriptors he used to capture the teachers' roles (e.g., "traffic cop," "ostrich," and "old-fashioned schoolmaster").

DOING SOCIOLOGY 13.5

Using Social Media Infographics to Diagram Data

In this exercise, you will consider how social media infographics are used to diagram textual and/or numerical data.

Social media has radically changed the ways news is disseminated by journalists and accessed by the public. More and more, relational diagrams and models known as "infographics" or "hashtag infographics" are used to communicate news and other social and political messages.

Consider the infographic presented in Figure 13.4; then answer the following questions.

1. What messages does this infographic communicate?

2. How could you use this or other types of infographics to "quantitize" qualitative data?

3. How could you use this or other types of infographics to diagram the hypothesized relations between or among concepts?

Check Your Understanding

1. What is Computer-Assisted Qualitative Analysis Software (CAQDAS)?
2. How can CAQDAS facilitate the analytic process?
3. What are some of the more user-friendly CAQDAS programs, and where can researchers access them?
4. How can researchers use CAQDAS programs to create graphical representations such as arrays and matrices?

CONCLUSION

This chapter has discussed coding as a way of analyzing qualitative data. It has introduced three key techniques that can be used to reveal patterns in words and images: descriptive coding, topic coding, and analytic coding. These types of coding are practical devices to assist you in unpacking layers of meaning, identifying patterns in your data, and envisioning how these patterns fit into a bigger analytic picture or story. Used one at a time or simultaneously, descriptive, topic, and analytic coding can help you "make the leap from concrete events and descriptions of them to theoretical insight and theoretical possibilities" (Charmaz, 2014, p. 137). Regardless of whether your goal is to construct theory, provisionally test a hypothesis, closely describe social phenomena and social dynamics, or generate new hypotheses and categories that describe human experiences, these techniques can help you gain a deeper analytic understanding of the social patterns your empirical data reveal and reflect.

The biggest joys and challenges of qualitative analysis flow from the process of creative interpretation. By empathizing with the human experience and unpacking cultural meanings, qualitative researchers become attuned to patterns in social relations and social contexts. There is no formula that will reveal these patterns or auto-generate results. Instead, "the best approach to coding is to relax and let your mind and intuition work for you" (Corbin & Strauss, 2015, p. 219). This "intuition" will grow with practice, willingness to take risks, and trial and error. The more you can lean into the analytic process and work through the feelings of uncertainty and discomfort that will inevitably come up—for

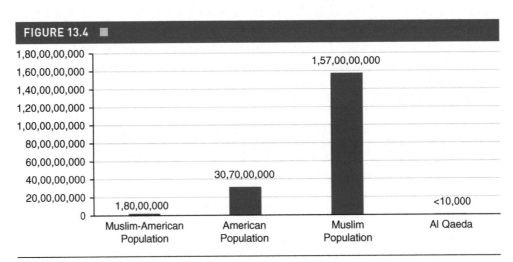

FIGURE 13.4 ■

Source: https://www.bryanbraun.com/2011/01/10/the-power-of-infographics/

novice and experienced researchers alike—the more you will learn to trust your instincts and become a skilled qualitative analyst.

REVIEW

13.1 What are coding and memoing? How do researchers go back and forth between them to build analysis?

Coding, the process of identifying a word or phrase (a label, or "code") to summarize and capture the meaning of small chunks of data, is a key tool in analyzing qualitative data. Used in combination with memoing—the act of writing reflective notes about what patterns and themes you are seeing in your data—coding helps researchers to identify patterns in the data and explanations for what those patterns mean and why they exist.

13.2 What is descriptive coding? How can it be used to trace similarities and differences related to gender, race, class, and other social categories?

Descriptive coding is a technique where the researcher labels the data with descriptive (e.g., demographic) information, typically for the purpose of tabulating group similarities and differences based on gender, race, class, age, and other demographic and social categories.

13.3 What is topic coding? How do researchers develop topic codes? How does social position influence the topic codes that researchers create?

Topic coding is a technique in which the researcher labels data with a salient word or phrase that grabs the reader. Topic codes can emerge from language in the data themselves (i.e., quoting the actual words people use, called in vivo coding), or from terms used in the theoretical and research literature. In critical research, topic codes are often derived from values coding, where the researcher critiques the meanings, causes, and social consequences of the subjective values underlying the data. As researchers, our beliefs, social positions, and perspective affect how we code. The theoretical perspective and methodology with which we approach the research affect the data we collect and the way we analyze them. Therefore, it is vital for researchers to reflect on how their own identities—e.g., their gender, race/ethnicity, level of education, sexuality, etc.— may be shaping both their data and analysis. While we can never guarantee perfect reliability in qualitative research, memoing about how our own beliefs, identities, and backgrounds may be influencing the research can help researchers minimize these biases.

13.4 What is analytic coding? What are some hands-on techniques researchers use for analytic coding?

Analytic coding is a technique in which the researcher searches for conceptual or theoretical categories and themes in the data. Similar to a close reading in poetry, researchers take fragments of the data apart and unpack the meanings of the smaller fragments (disassembling). Then, after they glean meanings from smaller pieces of data, they reorganize the meanings of those data fragments in new ways to form a larger analytic story (reassembling). In addition, through the techniques of constant comparison and analyzing exceptions, or negative cases, the researcher searches for explanations for what these patterns mean and why they exist.

13.5 How can Computer-Assisted Qualitative Data Analysis Software (CAQDAS) programs help qualitative researchers store, organize, and code their data?

Computer-Assisted Qualitative Data Analysis Software (CAQDAS) refers to the wide range of software programs that support a variety of analytic approaches in qualitative research, Software programs can help you code easily and quickly, search and retrieve data by code or category, create and save memos, graph and diagram relationships between codes and categories, and—with many programs—import and analyze audio and video data from social media platforms such as Twitter, Instagram, and YouTube. One of the main advantages of CAQDAS programs is the ability to store text, images, audio, and video files in one virtual environment.

analytic coding (p. 252)

analyzing exceptions, or negative cases (p. 261)

arraying data (p. 258)

categories (p. 244)

coding (p. 243)

coding fetishism (p. 248)

Computer-Assisted Qualitative Analysis Software (CAQDAS) (p. 257)

constant comparison (p. 252)

descriptive coding (p. 246)

disassembling (p. 252)

emotional labor (p. 253)

ethnographer (p. 251)

feminist symbolic interactionism (p. 250)

grounded theory (p. 244)

hierarchical array (p. 258)

in vivo coding (p. 248)

inductive reasoning (p. 243)

iterative (p. 246)

matrix (p. 258)

memoing (p. 245)

reassembling (p. 252)

recursive (p. 246)

themes (p. 244)

theoretical saturation (p. 255)

thinking up (p. 244)

topic coding (p. 248)

values coding (p. 251)

14 EVALUATION RESEARCH: APPLYING DATA TO PROBLEMS

Sara Haviland and Heather McKay

STUDENT LEARNING QUESTIONS

14.1 What is evaluation research? How does it relate to academic research?

14.2 What are the benefits of evaluation research for the evaluand, implementation teams, and society at large?

14.3 What are formative, process, outcomes or impact evaluations, and transformative evaluations? What methods do evaluators use to carry out these evaluations?

14.4 What major ethical considerations do evaluators need to take into account? What are the guiding principles that evaluators must follow?

AN INTRODUCTION TO EVALUATION RESEARCH

Imagine you want to help teenagers in your community develop their knowledge of math, improving their quantitative literacy as well their scores on college entrance exams. You do some research, design a tutoring program, find a local foundation willing to provide you with resources to support your work, assemble a team of tutors and support staff, and get to work. You pour your heart and soul into the project, enjoy working with the teens, and are excited to have a chance to make a difference.

Like many programs, you may have limited resources, and your future resources depend upon your success. Your funder will want to know that your tutoring is having a positive impact. If no impact is evident, they may grow impatient and withdraw their support. But how will you know if you've succeeded? How will you demonstrate the value of your program? How will you know which aspects of the program are the most successful, and which could be improved? How might you determine whether your resources could have an even greater impact?

For many programs, engaging in evaluation research is the key to answering these important questions. Evaluation is a research process used to monitor and measure changes that individuals, communities, and organizations make. According to the American Evaluation Association (AEA), evaluation involves "assessing the strengths and weaknesses of programs, policies, personnel, products, and organizations." The information collected during an evaluation helps to inform learning, decision making, and quality improvement (W. K. Kellogg Foundation, 2004). Ultimately, this process can help programs to improve, and funders and reformers to know which programs are the most effective use of their resources.

Evaluation research is an important application of social science. It can help us to understand why some programs succeed and why some fail. It can help to determine which organizational practices are most effective, and thus inform the development of new programs and improve programs already established. Evaluation research can help identify the best ways to deploy valuable resources to improve the lives of people in need. Researchers can use the tools of evaluation research in their work with nonprofit programs, governmental programs, for-profit businesses, and more. Basically, researchers can apply the principles of evaluation research to any effort to make change in people's lives or in how organizations or policies function.

HOW I GOT ACTIVE IN SOCIOLOGY
SARA HAVILAND

I started college with the intention of becoming a newspaper journalist. I took courses in sociology, political science, philosophy, and loved them all, but the sociology classes were what stuck with me the most. I appreciated how sociology took a different lens to every issue, offering new ideas and insights that connected individual actions to broader contexts. I was so enthusiastic that I entered an MA/PhD program directly after my undergraduate program, deciding that maybe the world of research was a better path for me (with hindsight, I can't believe I made such a big decision then!). As a field, I have always appreciated the breadth of topics we cover—sociology can be applied to almost anything. My sociological training has given me a strong background in research methods and social theory, which I have been able to apply to topics that interest me. Rather than seeking jobs as a professor, I opted for the world of academic research, where I apply sociological methods and theories to study the social, policy, organizational, and individual factors that affect work and careers. I am particularly interested in how educational interventions and career development can improve individuals' opportunities for movement into higher socioeconomic statuses. I also examine issues of educational access and training for adult learners, and the policy implications of workforce development programs.

HOW I GOT ACTIVE IN SOCIOLOGY
HEATHER MCKAY

As an undergraduate, I had my mind set on a career in politics. I majored in political science thinking that would help me get a job in Washington, D.C. My journey took an unexpected turn, though, when I was offered a job at a university research center. I thought this job would just be a steppingstone to something else, but I found that I enjoyed doing research and particularly liked the subject matter in which I was working—workforce development and education. I found myself drawn to the idea that doing research in this area could help to shape policy and improve the lives of Americans. I became excited by the notion that one pathway out of poverty for people could be getting a postsecondary degree and a good job. I decided to stick with it. and as I moved forward, I kept bumping into sociologists, working with them, and learning from them. While I do not have a degree in sociology, my own research is infused with sociological thinking because of the mentoring I have received throughout my career from sociologists. I really grew to love the way sociologists viewed the world, culture, and people. As my career progressed, I got the opportunity to start my own university-based research center. In this position, I find myself hiring lots of sociologists. I like the way the sociologists think, and I find that my work is better with the influence of a sociological viewpoint.

Evaluation and Sociological Research

Given that this book has focused on sociological research methods up to this point, you may be wondering about how sociological research and evaluation research are related, and how they might be different. In fact, they are not all that different. They both use the same kinds of methods, including qualitative and quantitative approaches. Concepts like samples and populations, measurement, validity, and precision are important for both, and both are guided by principles of research ethics. The difference lies in the orientation of the research.

Like academic sociological research, evaluation research is systematic, empirical, verifiable, replicable, and transparent. The key difference is that evaluation is a form of applied social science research. Its principal concern is not confirming a set of hypotheses or developing new theories, but rather applying existing theories and research methods to "real world" programs and policies. Program evaluation is defined as a "social science activity directed at collecting, analyzing, interpreting, and communicating information about the workings and effectiveness of social programs" (Rossi et al., 2004). You can think of academic sociological research as being used to create new knowledge and develop theory, whereas evaluation research is used to support decision making (Mertens & Wilson, 2019). Although there is a great deal of overlap between the two, most scholars agree that evaluation research is different because it is conducted within specific organizational and political contexts, which themselves are the object of study (Greene, 2000; Mertens, 2009; Mertens & Wilson, 2019; Trochim, 2001). Furthermore, in academic sociological research, researchers often anonymize results and offer minimal feedback to research subjects; in evaluation research, giving specific and extensive feedback to the research subjects is the whole point of the work!

CONSIDER THIS...

How might organizational leaders respond if a program evaluation showed they were meeting their goals? How might they respond if the evaluation showed the opposite?

When conducting evaluation research, evaluators use a form of inquiry called evaluative thinking (Vo & Archibald, 2018). Evaluative thinking is defined as "critical thinking applied in the context of evaluation, motivated by an attitude of inquisitiveness and a belief in the value of evidence, that involves identifying assumptions, posing thoughtful questions, pursuing deeper understanding through reflection and perspective taking, and informing decisions in preparation for action" (Buckley et al., 2015, p. 378). Evaluative thinking is essential in high-quality evaluation practices, and must be learned and practiced; it takes time to develop and hone this skill (Brookfield, 2012).

Evaluative thinking can be challenging, as people often have natural preferences for their existing beliefs and value systems. When our own beliefs and values exert influence over how we interpret evidence it can lead to confirmation bias, putting us at risk of interpreting the world in a way that confirms what we already believe to be true, rather than following the facts. In many cases, people's beliefs and values are unacknowledged and can result in bias and blind spots. Evaluative thinking requires that we be aware of our own beliefs and values so that we can carefully and critically consider how they may be shaping our work, and then make efforts to minimize their impact. Some strategies may include following systemic methods for collecting and coding data, involving multiple people in data collection and coding, verifying information with multiple sources, and checking for alternative explanations. A great deal of introspection may be necessary at times, particularly when we are examining a program or issue about which we are excited or concerned, and may be prone to blind spots regarding program weaknesses.

DOING SOCIOLOGY 14.1

Preparing for Evaluative Thinking by Addressing Confirmation Bias

In this activity, you will learn to identify your own biases and ways to manage them to encourage evaluative thinking.

Most of us have strong opinions about a variety of issues, which can influence how we perceive the world. One way we increase our confirmation bias is by engaging regularly with sources that confirm our worldview, of which we are less critical because we are prone to agree; we can reduce this bias by examining our own views and understanding why others may think differently.

Write down your answers to the following questions, and be ready to discuss your answers with your classmates.

1. Do you have many friends with whom you disagree regularly about important issues? Why do you think this is the case?

2. Do you follow any news sources that regularly surprise you with new ideas, new ways to look at the issues, or even challenge your way of thinking? Why do you think this is the case?

3. What is a current issue that you think is important? Do you have any stake in the outcome? Could that stake influence how you view the issue?

4. What would someone who disagreed with you say about this issue? Do you find any of these arguments compelling, or understand why others might hold these views? Do you see any weaknesses in your own arguments about the matter based on these other views?

Key Players in Evaluation Research

The subject of the evaluation—the program, idea, policy, or product—is called the evaluand (Mertens & Wilson, 2019). The group that makes the program, idea, policy, or product happen is the implementation team. In the example used at the beginning of the chapter, your math tutoring program is the evaluand, and you are a member of the implementation team.

Evaluations can occur in two ways. In the first approach, called internal evaluation, the researchers conducting the evaluation are members of the organization under study. In the second approach, called external evaluation or third party evaluation, the researchers conducting the evaluation are not part of the organization under study (Nevo, 2001; Scriven, 1991). For example, consider an evaluation of a program in a school setting. If the evaluation were internal it might be performed by faculty or staff of the school, including teachers, professional personnel, or administrators such as the principal or superintendent. An external evaluation, on the other hand, would be performed by someone outside of the school. This could be someone affiliated with the school, like the school district, or someone more removed from the school, like the state department of education. It could even be a third party altogether, such as an external evaluation consultant or evaluation firm (Nevo, 2001).

Evaluations involve stakeholders. Stakeholders are people who have a stake, or interest, in the thing that is being evaluated—the outcome of the evaluation is meaningful and important to them, and often affects them directly. A client who hires a researcher to conduct an evaluation is one example of a stakeholder, but they are not the only stakeholder to consider. Other stakeholders include people who run the program, people who might be affected by the program, policy makers, and/or administrators. Stakeholders may have different ideas about the goals of a project and/or how to get there. Thinking back to the tutoring-program example at the beginning of the chapter, stakeholders include students, their parents, the local schools, tutors in the program, and teachers in the students' schools, as they all might be affected by or invested in the success of the program.

Check Your Understanding

1. How are evaluation research and academic sociological research similar? How are they different?
2. What is the difference between internal and external evaluation?
3. Who are the parties involved in an evaluation?

BENEFITS OF EVALUATION RESEARCH

In ensuring that programs run effectively, research evaluation plays an important role in the programs they serve, and in society more generally. There is always a limited pool of resources available for supporting social programs (e.g., funding from governments or foundations; employee or volunteer hours; physical space to house programs), and evaluations can help to ensure that resources are directed to the best programs, and that those programs operate as effectively as possible. There is no greater frustration for an evaluator than to see resources go into dysfunctional programs that are not helpful, or that actually harm those they serve. In offering constructive feedback for programs, funders, and policy makers, the evaluator can effect change.

A good evaluation can improve the efficacy of an evaluand, increasing its likelihood of success. Evaluators help implementation teams and stakeholders to clarify the program objectives and plan, ensuring everyone understands what they want to accomplish from their project, and how they will reach their goals. One instrument that evaluators use to organize evaluation work and help stakeholders come to a shared understanding of a program's flow and purpose is a logic model. Logic models are visual road maps that ensure everyone is on the same page about the destination (the desired change) and the steps along the way. Evaluators often develop logic models in collaboration with the implementation team. Typically, they include five key components. To better illustrate these components, we consider the examples of a new job training program developed to help increase the number of nursing assistants in a community (Figure 14.1).

FIGURE 14.1 ■ Logic Model for a Nursing Assistant Training Program

INPUTS	ACTIVITIES	OUTPUTS	OUTCOMES	IMPACTS
– Federal grant funding – Matching funds from local foundation – Support of existing community college faculty – Guidance from local nursing group	– Develop new curriculum to train nursing assistants – Hire new faculty to teach the program – Hire new advisor – Recruit students through program and offer support – Develop clinical rotations with local nursing homes	– New training program is launched. – 200 students complete the program within the first year – 200 students are hired in nursing assistant positions within 6 months after graduation	**Short term** – Trainees retained in the jobs they have trained for or advancing in the medical field, with increasing wages. **Long term** – Trainees continue in employment and experience wage increases – Trainees return to education for further upskilling and promotion.	– Area unemployment reduced – Improved economic conditions – Improved quality of care for nursing home residents.

1. **Inputs.** These are the resources that will be used to make the program work. They include program funding, staffing, organizational resources, community resources, and any other resources that a program can bring to bear on the issue they are working to address. In the nursing assistant training program, this would be funding from a federal grant, matching funds from a local foundation, faculty from a community college, and guidance from a local nursing group.

2. **Activities.** These are the steps that the programs will take to put those resources to work. The training program will begin by developing a new curriculum, hiring new faculty to teach the curriculum, hiring a new adviser to recruit and help students through the program, and developing a clinical rotation for students with local nursing homes.

3. **Outputs.** Outputs are products that will directly result from program implementation. In our example, this includes the actual program itself, 200 student graduates, and placement of these graduates in nursing assistant jobs.

4. *Outcomes.* Outcomes are the specific changes you will see in program participants and can be broken down into short-term outcomes (typically within 1–3 years of program completion) and long-term outcomes (perhaps 4–8 years after program completion). For short-term outcomes, the goal is to have trainees retained in the jobs for which they have trained or advancing in the medical field, with increasing wages. For long-term outcomes, the goal would be to have trainees continue in employment and wage increases and return to education for further upskilling and promotion.

5. **Impacts.** These are the long-term results of the program implementation, typically after the program has concluded. Even though the evaluation team will likely be long gone before the impacts can be measured, it is helpful to have everyone understand the broader goal toward which they are working. In the training example, the goal might be to reduce unemployment in the area, improve economic conditions, and improve the quality of care for nursing home residents.

Logic models are living documents, subject to revision, and are typically revisited on a yearly basis for multiyear programs. This way, if the program does not receive all of the resources it had anticipated, or has difficulties rolling out specific activities in the implementation, or even if someone just comes up with an idea for how to do something better, the evaluators and the implementation team can talk together and make informed decisions about what that means for the desired program goals. Regular dialogue among stakeholders and revisiting the logic model can help everyone determine what adjustments should be made to support the program. This process of regular reflection and model refinement is very helpful for **continuous quality improvement**, where programs refine their implementation over time to offer improved performance or outcomes.

CONSIDER THIS...

Have you ever participated in a community, school, or national organization and noticed that the organization didn't seem to be living up to its goals? How might evaluation research help that organization to better meet its goals?

DOING SOCIOLOGY 14.2

Working With Logic Models

In this activity, you will work with a logic model to develop a road map between a project's implementation and its desired outcomes and impacts.

Logic models are important tools for programs and for the evaluators that work with them. For the following exercise, refer back to the Logic Model for a Nursing Assistant Training Program in Figure 14.1.

1. Look at the inputs column. Imagine the program cannot get guidance from a local nursing home. How will this affect your activities or outputs? Will the program still be able to achieve its outcomes and impacts?

2. If the local nursing group is unable to provide guidance, are there other ways to achieve those activities and outputs that might be affected?

3. Does the logic model help you understand how the program works in a different way? How so?

4. How might working with a logic model help a program to have greater success?

SOCIOLOGISTS IN ACTION
KIMBERLY MANTURUK

Early in graduate school, I was selected for a research assistantship position at the Center for Community Capital, an interdisciplinary research center focused on poverty reduction and access to capital in underserved communities. Until that point, I'd always worked as a teaching assistant, and I was looking for some experience on the research side of academic life.

A few months after I started, my supervisor came by my work area and asked, "Do you have any interest in banking regulations?" While I certainly didn't—I actually had a hard time imagining anyone being interested in banking laws—I diplomatically said, "I don't yet, but I could." That answer would become my introduction to program evaluation and the start of my career. My supervisor and I did an evaluation of the impact of banking law changes related to payday lending, and our work informed laws that protected low-income borrowers in several states.

Kimberly Manturuk
Photo courtesy of Kimberly Manturuk

I finished my PhD in sociology and continued to focus on program evaluation—using the theories and methods from social science to assess the impacts of programs and policies. One of the most gratifying aspects of my work is being able to see the impacts of my research on the lived experiences of the people I work with. I've led evaluation projects that have demonstrated the benefits of mortgage programs in disadvantaged urban neighborhoods, the impacts of college access programs, and how new technologies can create opportunities for entrepreneurs in Native American communities.

Program evaluation is an exciting career for sociologists because we get to see the impacts our work can have in the communities where we work. Being an evaluator also means that I get to help program leaders create effective interventions from the ground up. There are some challenges in being an evaluator too; I have to be the one who tells the people in charge when a project they've put a lot of time and money toward just isn't working. For that reason, program evaluation requires good communication and negotiation skills in addition to being well-versed in a wide range of research methods. But even when I'm delivering disappointing results, I make recommendations for how program staff can make changes to improve their outcomes. Program evaluation has been an extremely rewarding career for me, and one I encourage all sociologists to consider.

Kimberly Manturuk is the associate director of Research, Evaluation, and Development at Duke University Learning Innovation.

Discussion Question

How does Dr. Manturuk use sociological research skills in her program evaluation work?

Check Your Understanding

1. How does evaluation research benefit society?
2. How does evaluation research benefit evaluands and implementation teams?
3. What is a logic model, and how is it used?

EVALUATION TYPES AND METHODS

When designing an evaluation, evaluators must make two separate, but related, decisions: which evaluation type to use, and which research methods to use. Evaluation type determines what part of the program evaluators will examine, and also which research methods will be the most appropriate way to accomplish their goals.

Evaluation Types

Some evaluations have the goal of understanding the bigger picture around a program. Others seek to understand how a program works and how it can be improved. Some evaluations are more specifically geared toward assessing program effects, and still others are interested primarily in evaluating programs that address human rights and social justice. In the following sections, we outline a selection of evaluation approaches as well as the factors evaluators typically consider when deciding which approach is best. We have organized these evaluations into four types: formative evaluations, process evaluations, outcomes and impact evaluations, and transformative evaluations. Although this is not an exhaustive list of evaluation types, it represents some of the more common forms.

Formative Evaluations

Researchers conducting formative evaluations seek to understand how a program is implemented, and in the process, to improve the evaluand, fine-tune models, fix problems, determine efficacy and effectiveness, and prepare for a summative evaluation (Patton, 2012). Formative evaluations occur early in the design of a new program or policy, and are often concerned with identifying problems that can be solved by the new program or policy, or understanding the feasibility of a proposed solution. These are excellent tools for planning programs. One example is the context evaluation, an evaluative study that aims to clarify a program or policy's position in the "big picture" (Mertens & Wilson, 2019), perhaps as part of a broader system, region, or even society at large (e.g., an elementary school can be understood

Context evaluation entails seeing the big picture, or the larger environment in which a program is situated.

iStockphoto.com/guvendemir

in the context of a K–12 district, or as a part of a rural area, or as a part of the U.S. educational system). It is a research project designed to assess the needs, assets, and resources of a community or organization (Stufflebeam, 2001). Context evaluations approach programs not as individual siloes, but rather as integrated organizations in larger systems that benefit from the programs (e.g., a strong K–12 educational system may set a new college program up for success), or can challenge them (a weak K–12 educational system may make it difficult to successfully launch a new college program). They can help implementation teams better understand the intended beneficiaries of a program or policy, revise goals, and understand how a community's assets can be used to support the program being implemented (and how community challenges can also impact program success). Context evaluations are used to assess the effectiveness in meeting the beneficiaries' needs.

Another formative evaluation that can help in the design phase for a program is input evaluation. This is a process of collecting information about a project, and analyzing competing strategies, work plans, and budgets (Program evaluation theory and practice). This might include gathering information on different parts of the organization like institutional mission, goals, staff, those the organization serves, and progress being made. It could also mean looking at other programs that could serve as a model, examining different strategies and approaches that might work to determine their feasibility and viability. Input evaluations can be used for securing financial support for a project, for accountability, or even to defend the approach taken.

Process Evaluations

Most evaluation research focuses on how programs are implemented, in order to identify areas in need of improvement or to change organizational or program practices. Process evaluation (sometimes referred to as **implementation evaluation**) looks at the how a project is being executed and the quality of that implementation. It is often an organizational analysis, as it examines the functions of the implementation team and how effectively they put their theories of change into practice. When conducting a process evaluation the evaluator monitors, documents, and assesses program activities (Mertens & Wilson, 2018).

Developmental evaluation is a type of process evaluation where the evaluator intentionally interacts with the implementation teams of the evaluand to improve program outcomes, to support continuous quality improvement (Patton, 2012). Developmental evaluation can be used to support the development of innovations in complex systems or environments, with evaluator feedback being offered continuously throughout the implementation of a program rather than simply at the beginning or end. It can lead to learning, evolution, and development—if one is paying attention and knows how to observe and capture the important and emergent patterns. For example, the evaluator may meet biweekly with the implementation team to stay in touch with key players in the program and share insights in real time. This allows evaluators to nudge implementation teams toward more effective practices at the moments when improvement is most beneficial. Frequent presentations of results, both formal and informal, help the implementation team understand where things are going well, and where the course may need to be adjusted.

Outcome and Impact Evaluations

Another very common form of evaluation is research to gauge the effectiveness of programs. Two common types include outcome evaluation, which examines the concrete results of a program, typically directly upon completion, and often in statistical terms (e.g., number of people served). This helps implementation teams and funders to reach a judgment on the value or significance of the program. An impact evaluation is used to assess a program's effectiveness in the bigger picture, typically zooming out from the program to include intended and unintended outcomes of a project and at different levels like beneficiaries, staff, organization, and community. For example, if a school system introduces free universal preschool, an outcomes evaluation might examine the number of students who participate and how they perform in kindergarten the next year. An impact evaluation may look at the benefit for parents' wages, or the performance of those children years later in high school.

In determining whether a program was successful or not, we can consider whether a program has value, whether it has merit, and whether it has worth. According to Patton, "Merit refers to the intrinsic value of a program, for example, how effective it is in meeting the needs of the people it is intended to help. Worth refers to extrinsic value to those outside the program, for example, to the larger community or society" (Patton, 2002, p. 113). This may include whether the program is fulfilling its purpose. In the universal preschool example provided earlier, the program may have value if it improves student performance, or even parents' wages. It may have worth to society if it improves family incomes in the community and boosts the economy of a local area.

Transformative Evaluation

The evaluations we have outlined to this point examine programs, focusing on their designs and how well they are executed, or how big of an impact they have. However, some evaluations look to improve social justice. Transformative evaluations, also referred to as the social justice branch of evaluation, are evaluation models rooted in issues of equality and human rights (Mertens & Wilson, 2018). Rather than specifically looking at program performance or program outcomes, these evaluations look at programs through the lens of promoting social justice, often with respect to marginalized groups. There are a variety of different approaches to this kind of evaluation, including deliberative democratic evaluation, country-led evaluation, Indigenous evaluation, culturally responsive evaluation, disability- and deaf-rights-based evaluation, and feminist evaluation, among others. These evaluations all seek to incorporate marginalized groups in the evaluative work and require that the evaluator both understand and acknowledge their privilege and the power they hold in their position as evaluator. They can be very useful when the evaluator is a participant in social change activities and ensure that the evaluator is bringing the right people to the table to effect change.

Having considered common types of evaluation research, we turn to methods.

Qualitative Methods in Evaluation Research

Evaluation research often uses a variety of methods, both quantitative and qualitative. And, as you may imagine, the research methods best suited for an evaluation research project depend upon the goals of the evaluation. Researchers conducting formative or process evaluations tend to rely on qualitative methods, which are important in an evaluation because they help tell stories of both the program and the people involved. Qualitative data gathered from key project stakeholders and participants give researchers information about implementation and help them to understand context, adaptations that might occur throughout the project, and areas in need of change. Given the emphasis on gathering firsthand experiences of a program or policy from those most affected by it, qualitative methods are also particularly well-suited to transformative evaluations.

Qualitative methods are less often used by researchers conducting outcome and impact evaluations, which typically focus on quantitative methods (discussed later) to determine if a program met its objectives in terms of numbers served. However, qualitative methods are sometimes used by evaluators conducting outcomes or impact evaluations to follow up with participants or stakeholders to gather further insight into the effects of programs.

Evaluation researchers draw on a range of qualitative methods to achieve their goals, such as interviews or focus groups, observation, or document review. Where possible, using multiple methods of qualitative data collection and analysis (triangulating) can help researchers to build a comprehensive assessment. When researchers see repetitive themes from different qualitative sources, the results are stronger. Like other social science researchers, evaluators engaging in qualitative methods must monitor and report their analytical procedures and processes to maintain rigor (Patton, 2002); the process should be transparent and allow for replication.

Think of random assignments as slot machines: Every participant has the same probability of being assigned to the treatment or control group in the experiment.

Matthias Tunger/Getty Images

Quantitative Methods in Evaluation Research

Evaluation researchers use quantitative methods for a variety of reasons. In a process evaluation, researchers might survey many participants and stakeholders to understand their experiences of a program, and then analyze the resulting data using quantitative methods to assess patterns in their experiences. This can help programs to make mid-course corrections if they learn that certain elements of the program are too cumbersome or not being received well.

Quantitative methods are especially useful in outcomes evaluation, where researchers assess and then quantify the impact of a program. Ideally, these evaluations are coupled with experimental or quasi-experimental studies. As described in Chapter 7, *experimental studies* involve *random assignment,* which means that par-

ticipants are randomly assigned to either a treatment or control group. As a result, each participant or group has the same probability of being assigned to a particular condition (treatment or control) in the experiment. This is the gold standard in social science research, and an excellent way to evaluate whether the program or policy being evaluated (i.e., the "treatment") yields improved results for the population served.

Random assignment is not always possible, however, and sometimes it is inappropriate for an evaluation. For example, one cannot randomly assign individuals to long-term career training programs—that would involve the researcher selecting a career path for the respondents!

In cases where random assignment is not possible, quasi-experimental studies help to create experimental conditions for two groups that are not equivalent. In quasi-experimental studies, statistical methods are used to match similar participants after the fact to simulate an experiment. Propensity score matching is one popular statistical method that estimates the effects of a treatment (i.e., whether an intervention makes a difference in the desired outcomes) by accounting for covariates (other factors that may influence the outcomes). Evaluators typically use propensity score matching to pair demographically similar students within the sample. This allows the researcher to determine whether the new program yielded better outcomes for similar students than other programs they may have been considering.

One example of this in practice can be found in a recent evaluation of the Colorado Community College System's developmental education programs. The system decided to implement a full redesign of developmental education at all colleges. Major change was happening for all students at all colleges, which meant that there were no students who could serve as a control group. As a result, the evaluation followed a quasi-experimental design using a historic group of students: those who had taken developmental education courses in the years prior to the new program. The evaluators used propensity score matching to match current students to demographically similar former students, creating like groups and then examining academic outcomes to see what the results of the redesign were for students.

DOING SOCIOLOGY 14.3

Engaging With Evaluation Research

In this exercise, you will read an evaluation and learn about and document the methods that were used.

Read the following case study of a program evaluation and respond to the questions.

A community college received a grant to study a new approach to help students who need to improve their basic math skills. The proposed model was an accelerated course that gave students extra instruction and supplemental lessons over the course of a semester.

A study conducted by third party evaluators examined the implementation and outcomes of this model. The evaluators worked independently from the designers of the new course. A group of students were asked to participate in the study; when they consented, they were asked to pick an envelope prior to enrollment in the course. Some envelopes contained an invitation to join the new course, and some did not. Those who did not receive an invitation to enroll in the new course were enrolled in an existing class at the college. The goal of this envelope process was to create randomly assigned comparison and treatment groups. The evaluators then looked at final grades for students in both courses, as well as their performance in courses in the following semesters. At the end, the evaluators reported their findings to the course designers.

1. What kind of evaluation was used to assess the program—formative? Process? Outcomes or impact?

2. What research methodology was used—qualitative or quantitative? If quantitative, was it a randomized control trial or a quasi-experimental design? How do you know?

Mixed Methods in Evaluation Research

Many evaluations today are mixed methods evaluations, meaning they include both quantitative and qualitative methods. As described previously, researchers might collect and analyze qualitative data in the initial stages of the project to determine how well a program is being implemented, and later in the process collect and analyze quantitative data to assess outcomes, such as numbers served. As discussed in Chapter 11, researchers often collect varied types of data, and analyze them with a range of techniques, to gain a more comprehensive answer to the research question they posed.

The case study approach represents a mixed methods approach to evaluation. Case studies focus on a particular unit (e.g., a person, a site, a project), which serves as a case. The researchers conducting the evaluation try to learn as much as possible about the case, using a variety of methods to create a complete picture (Yin, 2003). Case study methods can be used in a variety of situations for different purposes; as they are very labor- and time-intensive, they are typically used in scenarios in which depth is more important than breadth. For example, a researcher may wish to study how different schools implement new policies; each school would serve as a case.

Check Your Understanding

1. What is a formative evaluation? A process evaluation? An outcomes or impact evaluation? A transformative evaluation? In what situations might an evaluator select these evaluation types?

2. What qualitative methods do evaluators use?

3. What quantitative methods do evaluators use?

4. How can evaluators conduct mixed methods evaluations?

ETHICAL CONSIDERATIONS FOR EVALUATION RESEARCH

Evaluation is a *human subjects research* endeavor. As you read about in Chapter 4, any human subjects research, whether academic or evaluation, must consider the ethical implications of the research being conducted. Researchers must ensure the research process protects the well-being of subjects by carefully considering risks to subjects, weighing the benefits against the potential risks, and ensuring that subjects are fully aware of both. Furthermore, participation in research of any form requires the time and efforts of research subjects, and the researcher must always respect and honor that fact. Researchers must ensure that their research methods are sound and have as little bias as possible, to ensure that the time and effort they request of subjects are worthwhile.

Institutional review boards ensure the protection for human subjects. They review research designs and consider whether or not they meet the ethical standards codified by the Common Rule. Evaluators have a different relationship with the people who participate in their research, however, which merits additional ethical considerations. Although academic researchers often operate at a distance from their subjects to reduce bias and influence, the researchers conducting evaluations are often closely connected to their subjects and may be in dialogue with them throughout the evaluation process. Moreover, the evaluator is often a powerful player in the dynamics of programs and funding. The results of an evaluation can alter the future of a program or policy and can improve or reduce the likelihood of an organization's future funding. This power dynamic has major ethical implications of which the evaluator must always be mindful.

On Neutrality in Evaluation Research

Academic sociologists try to be neutral observers. They often remain at arm's length throughout the study and avoid interacting with their subjects in ways that might influence whatever it is that they are studying. In evaluation, influencing the results of the phenomenon being studied is often a major goal of the research. This is particularly true of process and transformative evaluations, especially developmental evaluations as described previously. In both process and transformative evaluations, the evaluator is part of the project or program team working to explore possibilities for addressing challenges, developing innovations, supporting adaptation, documenting actions and their consequences, identifying emergent processes, and supporting ongoing development as conditions change. There is a spectrum of neutrality in the evaluation world, depending on the desired effect of the evaluation. If the purpose is strictly to see if a specific intervention succeeds or fails, a more hands-off, neutral approach makes sense. If the purpose is to understand and facilitate success, the evaluators sometimes have to roll up their sleeves and engage with implementation teams.

Different Stakes

Evaluation research is often a high-stakes endeavor. Most evaluation research takes place at the behest of funding agencies, who seek to determine how well a program performed and whether certain program goals were achieved. Funders often use evaluations to help determine whether programs are worthy of continued funding and whether a particular implementation team (that is, the group that makes the program happen) is capable of delivering the results it promised in its grant applications. A positive evaluation can increase funders' confidence in a program or implementation team. A negative evaluation can threaten a program or implementation team's survival. Funding agencies depend on evaluators to develop fair and rigorous evaluations; program implementors depend on evaluators to accurately represent their success, and to generate constructive feedback for future improvements. Research ethics require evaluators to report their findings in a way that is comprehensive, honest, and fair to both parties.

For evaluations that are tied to grant funding, there are two different models that also have different benefits and drawbacks. First, a funder may directly provide an evaluator to the implementation team. In this case, the funder is the evaluator's primary client; we refer to this as the funder client model. This means that the evaluator is expected to report results directly to the funder, and the implementation team may or may not see the actual evaluation reports. In this model, sometimes implementation teams may be cautious in their interactions with evaluators, or limit evaluators' access in an effort to protect their programs from external scrutiny.

In an alternate model, a funder may require an implementation team to hire their own evaluator, using a portion of the overall grant budget (often around 10%); we refer to this as the program client model. The implementation team then seeks and hires its own evaluator, often with approval from the funder, but the implementation team is the evaluator's primary client in this scenario. In this model, the implementation team is often more cooperative with the evaluation process, having selected an evaluator who meets their own approval and with whom they are comfortable. However, if an evaluator sees evidence of incompetence or misconduct in implementation, they are often not able to directly communicate that with the funder due to the fact that they work for the implementation team. Reports are delivered to the implementation team directly, which may withhold portions of their reports when sharing with funders. Whether evaluators are chosen by the funding agency or the implementation team, it is imperative for the evaluator to produce results that are accurate and scientifically rigorous.

Another ethical consideration that is amplified in evaluation work relative to general academic research work is the influence of the research on public perception of programs or organizations. Evaluators' work is often incorporated into reports for program funders, for the general public, or for both. As a result, these reports can influence future decisions about which programs are funded, or how generously programs are funded.

For example, federal grant programs typically make their evaluation reports available to the general public. These reports may only be read by implementation leaders—or they may be read by policy makers, watchdog groups, and reporters. The public nature of these findings, which are tied directly to the programs themselves, adds a layer of complexity to the power dynamics of evaluation research. A bad evaluation can create bad press for a program or organization and erode public confidence in the implementation team. A good evaluation, by contrast, can generate good press for a program, build good-will toward the program, and improve public confidence for an implementation team.

Risks for Subjects

Anonymity is a major concern in evaluation research. When social scientists publish their research findings and share them with other people, they often anonymize their subjects. When presenting and publishing their findings, researchers change the names of participants and remove any identifying information to ensure that whatever information the researcher collected from a subject is not traceable back to them. Researchers often apply the same principles to the organizations they study. Rather than naming an organization specifically, they might refer to it as "a medium-sized research university in the midwestern United States," or "a small technology business in the western U.S." Especially when researchers have promised confidentiality to their research subjects or when data collected involve sensitive or personal information, anonymizing data is of the utmost importance.

An evaluator's work is typically out in the open, however. Evaluation businesses often post lists of their clients on their websites. Although evaluation researchers do their best to protect anonymity, they cannot always offer full anonymity to the organizations or individuals involved in their research. In the cases where they cannot, it is critical to be up-front with subjects about this fact. Generally speaking, the rarer the position, the more difficult anonymity is to protect. Program directors, organizational leadership, and individuals in new positions are often very difficult to present with full anonymity.

Another threat to anonymity stems from familiarity and access. When we consider the typical academic research program, there is often little interpersonal linkage between the researcher and their subjects (participant observation is an important exception). Evaluation researchers typically engage with programs for extended periods of time—months or even years. They make regular site visits and conduct additional rounds of data collection, and while doing so, can develop meaningful relationships with members of the organization. Evaluators share meals with those whom they evaluate, travel with them, and even collaborate with them. This increases the researchers' knowledge of organizational policies and procedures and builds trust between evaluators and organizational members. By the end of an evaluation, evaluators often know a lot about the key players in the implementation, their interpersonal dynamics, and their concerns about their program or employer. It is imperative to be mindful of this familiarity in the process of writing about the studies, for the evaluator easily knows enough about many subjects to unintentionally disclose their identities.

Ensuring participant anonymity in research reports is essential to protecting their privacy.

iStockphoto.com/Christopher Ames

Anonymity is particularly important when evaluations take place in work environments. When evaluators report facts that make people look incompetent or unprofessional, these people might lose their jobs. Similarly, evaluators who report sensitive conversations or unpopular opinions that their respondents have shared with them are putting the respondents' well-being and livelihood at risk. Unlike other forms of sociological research, the results of evaluation research are often shared with the leadership of the organization under study. An employee who shares negative feedback about a program administrator might be passed over for a promotion, suffer a demotion, or even lose their job if the administrator suspects them of casting them in a negative light. Evaluators must always exercise great caution to minimize this risk of harm to research participants.

Strategies for maintaining anonymity include reporting results only in the aggregate, and summarizing findings across individuals rather than reporting directly what individuals shared with the evaluators. Evaluators must be especially careful when sharing quotations, as word choice, phrasing, and even the discussion of particular issues might be traced back to particular individuals. Occasionally an evaluator may need to discard a quotation, even if it is particularly vivid or illustrative, because it is too risky for the subjects involved.

Voluntary Participation

The voluntary nature of research participation is another area that requires careful consideration by evaluators. Funding agencies often require those who receive funds to cooperate with an evaluation. Individuals within the organization may be reluctant to participate and view the evaluation as an involuntary process. They may feel obligated to participate in all facets of the research, whether they are comfortable or not. As researchers, our obligation to human subjects requires voluntary participation. How do we reconcile these competing imperatives?

The first line of defense is a good consent process. At the beginning of evaluation projects, researchers should carefully discuss the voluntary nature of the survey or interview process and work with employers, supervisors, or administrators to ensure that there is no penalty for anyone who chooses not to participate. The structure of the interview itself can offer an extra safeguard for vulnerable participants. For example, if a participant has made their way to a conference room for an interview with an evaluator, their employer should see them as cooperating with the evaluation. If, in the conference room, they then decide not to participate, the evaluator must not disclose that fact to the employer. Researchers can and should also make it very clear that participants can skip any question for any reason, without penalty.

In some cases, there are elements of evaluations that are not optional. The voluntary components typically are those that may disclose their own personal information (e.g., interviews, focus groups, surveys), but employers can compel workers to work with evaluation researchers on the mechanics of the evaluation. Implementation teams are often required by their funders to cooperate with the evaluation work; they must do the legwork to help acquire data sets, distribute surveys, line up interview subjects from related organizations, and so on, as a condition of funding. In these cases, researchers should work with participants to ensure that the burden of participation is as minimal as possible and that their contributions to the project are acknowledged.

When conducting human subjects research, sociologists must consider the ethical implications of the research being conducted. This includes ensuring the safety of participants and their voluntary participation.

ZUMA Press Inc/Alamy Stock Photo

Representation and Voice

An additional ethical consideration for evaluation research concerns the issue of representation and voice. Evaluators look at programs from every angle, and as such, it is important to ensure that we involve all key stakeholders. By bringing in the proper stakeholders, evaluators give voice to groups that can influence the interpretation of program success. When thinking about stakeholders in evaluation, it is important to include underrepresented and structurally disadvantaged groups. The Kellogg Foundation prioritizes this as a focus in its *Handbook on Evaluation*, noting that evaluators should actively solicit the perspectives of marginalized people and groups, who may in some cases be the groups most knowledgeable about the intricacies of particular policies and programs, and may also be the most affected by the results of the evaluation (W. K. Kellogg Foundation, 2017).

When it comes to program evaluation, both internal representation (within the program) and external representation (outside of the program) are critical for understanding how a program truly works and what difference it may be making in its environment. Consider, for example, the nursing assistant program we described in our discussion of logic models. These programs are often run by a community college, where the program is designed to help unemployed people find careers in health care. The stakeholders in this project might include groups internal to the community college: program students, the allied health department, the career services department, the non-credit department, public relations, and university leadership. Evaluators might speak with faculty, staff, students, and leaders. They might also speak with the local workforce development board, a publicly funded entity charged with delivering services to unemployed and underemployed workers, and local workforce advocates. In addition, evaluators might collect information from employers, including those who served on the board of the university, or hosted internships and co-ops, or planned to hire graduates of the program. They may even collect data from patients and patient caregivers. There are many groups from which to choose!

Risk for partnerships is another factor the evaluator must consider when an evaluation reaches out to the broader community. Participating in an evaluation involves time and effort on the part of respondents. When those respondents have weak ties to the program being evaluated, or are in a new relationship with the program, it can be detrimental to the relationship for an evaluator to call and start asking for interviews on the program's behalf. In evaluation, it is important to observe the relationships that are developing and avoid any actions that may harm the work the implementation team is doing.

Finally, every group an evaluator adds to a study increases the cost and effort of an evaluation, and therefore it is not always possible to include every stakeholder in the study. Choosing who gets a say, and how to incorporate that say into the findings, must be done carefully to honor the field of stakeholders around a program.

Guiding Principles for Evaluation

Given some of the different ethical considerations outlined in this section, it can be difficult to understand how general research ethics apply to evaluation research. In fact, the principles are largely the same. The American Evaluation Association is a leader in professional evaluation and has developed a thoughtful set of guiding principles to ensure that evaluations are rigorous and ethical (American Evaluation Association, 2018). They require evaluations to include:

- *Systematic Inquiry:* Evaluators conduct data-based inquiries that are thorough, methodical, and contextually relevant.
- *Competence:* Evaluators provide skilled professional services to stakeholders.
- *Integrity:* Evaluators behave with honesty and transparency in order to ensure the integrity of the evaluation.
- *Respect for People:* Evaluators honor the dignity, well-being, and self-worth of individuals and acknowledge the influence of culture within and across groups.
- *Common Good and Equity:* Evaluators strive to contribute to the common good and advancement of an equitable and just society.

In following these principles, evaluators can ensure that their work honors the time and efforts of participants, represents the work of implementation teams fairly and constructively, and contributes to the improvement of society.

CONSIDER THIS. . .

What constitutes the common good and equity, when people have such different worldviews? How can evaluators contribute to the common good and equity in their work?

DOING SOCIOLOGY 14.4

Considering Ethics in Evaluation

In this exercise, you will discuss why it is important to consider ethics in evaluation work, and examine the American Evaluation Association's Guiding Principles for Evaluation *(2018).*

The American Evaluation Association's *Guiding Principles for Evaluation* (2018) outlines five principles for integrity: systematic inquiry, competence, integrity, respect for people, and common good and equity (see discussion above). Write your answers to the following questions, and be prepared to discuss with your classmates or your instructor.

1. What are some key ethical considerations in evaluation research that differ from those for academic research?

2. Consider the principles of systematic inquiry, competence, and integrity. Why are these factors such important parts of an ethical evaluation? How would their absence affect the subjects who participate in an evaluation?

3. What are some ways that evaluators can design their evaluations to maximize respect for people and the advancement of the common good and equity?

Check Your Understanding

1. How does power factor into evaluation research?
2. What unique challenges and risks do evaluations pose for their subjects? How can the researcher minimize these risks?
3. What are the five guiding principles for evaluation, according to the AEA?

CONCLUSION

Evaluation is an applied form of social science research. As such, it brings the rigor of science to bear on real-world problems. It can help programs function more effectively, foundations and policy makers to determine where to place their support, and improve the lives of those served by different programs and reforms. In your daily life, you likely encounter many programs that have been evaluated, from education to government and social programs. Our society depends on rigorous, methodical, and ethical evaluation research to help it run smoothly and apply innovative solutions to problems in an effective way. A strong evaluation represents a variety of stakeholder viewpoints to provide a holistic view of programs and policies in practice. In the next chapter, you will learn about community-based research, which also seeks to give voice to those who are most directly affected by a research project.

REVIEW

14.1. What is evaluation research? What features do evaluation and academic research share? How do they differ?

Evaluation is a form of research related to academic research, but applied directly to new programs or policies. Like academic sociological research, evaluation research is systematic, empirical, verifiable, replicable, and transparent. The key difference is that evaluation is a form of applied social science research. Its principal concern is not confirming a set of hypotheses or developing new theory, but rather applying existing theories and research methods to "real-world" programs and policies.

14.2. Why do we do evaluation research? What are the benefits of evaluation research for the programs that are being evaluated? What are the benefits for society at large?

Evaluation research helps us to understand how programs work, whether they are successful, and how society can best invest limited resources to address important challenges. Some forms of evaluation help programs to make real-time changes in strategies or practice to increase the likelihood that they will succeed.

Evaluation can help programs clarify their goals, and ensure that all players are communicating well and have a shared understanding of necessary steps and their desired effects. Evaluators will often work with programs to develop theories of action or logic models, visual representations of the program that ensure all participants are "on the same page" with regard to what the program will accomplish, and how.

Many evaluations help us to understand what works and what doesn't, allowing leaders and communities to make evidence-based decisions about their programs and policies. Evaluations are important tools to ensure that the limited resources are applied to addressing key challenges in the most effective manner, so that programs can have the best results.

14.3. What are formative, process, outcomes or impact evaluations, and transformative evaluations? What methods do evaluators use to carry out these evaluations?

There are multiple types of evaluation. Four important types include formative evaluation (conducted early in the design or implementation of a new program or policy, or a major redesign of an existing program or policy); process evaluation (conducted during the evaluation, often as part of a process of continuous quality improvement); and outcomes or impact evaluations (evaluations focused on program outputs, and whether programs have achieved their goals). Evaluations can also be transformative, aimed at creating social justice and giving voice to traditionally marginalized groups. The evaluator can select qualitative or quantitative methods, and in many cases, evaluators will select mixed methods to study these issues.

14.4. What major ethical considerations do evaluators need to take into account? What are the guiding principles that evaluators must follow?

Evaluators have special ethical considerations, as their work is typically more engaged with stakeholders in ways that can threaten neutrality and raise different questions about risks for subjects, how to maintain voluntary participation, and whether all stakeholders are fairly represented in the research. One way to address these issues is to follow the American Evaluation Association's guiding principles for evaluation, which outline best practices tailored to the evaluation context of research. Specifically, the AEA requires that evaluations include systemic inquiry, competence, integrity, respect for people, and common good or equity.

KEY TERMS

activities (p. 269)

case study approach (p. 275)

confirmation bias (p. 267)

context evaluation (p. 271)

continuous quality improvement (p. 270)

Developmental evaluation (p. 272)

evaluand (p. 268)

evaluation research (p. 265)

evaluative thinking (p. 267)

external evaluation or third party evaluation (p. 268)

formative evaluation (p. 271)

funder client model (p. 276)

impact evaluation (p. 272)

impacts (p. 269)

implementation team (p. 276)

inputs (p. 269)

input evaluation (p. 272)

internal evaluation (p. 268)

logic models (p. 268)

outcome evaluation (p. 272)

outcomes (p. 269)

outputs (p. 269)

process evaluation (p. 272)

program client model (p. 276)

program evaluation (p. 266)

propensity score matching (p. 274)

quasi-experimental studies (p. 274)

stakeholders (p. 268)

transformative evaluation (p. 273)

15 TELLING THE STORY: INTERACTING WITH THE COMMUNITIES YOU STUDY

Heather Parrott

STUDENT LEARNING QUESTIONS
15.1 What is community-based research?
15.2 What are the main steps in community-based research?
15.3 What are the unique ethical considerations of community-based research?
15.4 What are the challenges and opportunities that researchers face when conducting community-based research?

Imagine a group of sociology students studying clients at a local soup kitchen. They descend on the soup kitchen at mealtime, interview people about their life experiences, and then leave to write about it for their class. The students may have broadened their understanding of hunger, poverty, and/or inequality through this experience, but the lives of the study participants have remained unchanged.

The communities near colleges and universities sometimes become social laboratories for sociology professors and students. Their close distance from the university, coupled with their familiarity to students and professors, makes them relatively easy communities to study. In cases where researchers study nearby groups and communities that are socially or financially disadvantaged, the discrepancy between the college or university on the one hand, and the community on the other, can become a source of tension. This is sometimes referred to as the "town–gown divide." In these cases, sociologists may find themselves examining underprivileged populations as privileged outsiders, even as they seek to understand the problems that these communities face and work toward solutions.

The power dynamics in social research have historically been skewed, with the researcher setting the agenda and often benefiting disproportionally from the research (in publications, professional advancement, or even course credit). This chapter explores how researchers can work *with* communities and community organizations on social research so that the process and products can be mutually beneficial.

HOW I GOT ACTIVE IN SOCIOLOGY
HEATHER PARROTT

I was drawn to sociology as an undergraduate because it gave me the tools to better understand social problems. I also respected my undergraduate sociology professors who used their academic expertise to address the problems about which they taught; these teachers were actively involved in community agencies as volunteers, board members, and researchers. I followed their examples as activists by working at social services agencies throughout my undergraduate and graduate education, working at a rape crisis center, a group home for abused children, and a domestic violence shelter. When I got to graduate school, I struggled with whether to become an academic or a social worker. I loved sociological teaching and research, but also loved doing hands-on work to help people within the community. My academic path as a public sociologist has ultimately allowed me to merge these passions—I teach a wide range of sociology classes (social problems, race and ethnicity, immigration, gendered violence, research methods) and work with social service providers on community-based research, helping them better achieve their missions. Like my undergraduate professors, I incorporate my community work experiences into my teaching to clarify sociological concepts and, I hope, similarly inspire my students to positively impact their communities.

WHAT IS COMMUNITY-BASED RESEARCH?

The process of working with community partners on research can be broadly termed community-based research (CBR), and it shares many similarities with what others term *action research, participatory research, participatory action research,* and *feminist action research.* Researchers engaged in community-based research are often called public sociologists, a term meant to encompass sociologists who engage with topics of public concern and disseminate findings to a wider, nonacademic audience. Community research can start with a group of community members and academics coming together because of a shared social concern such as water quality, climate change, or affordable housing. In other cases, community research can start as a collaboration between researchers and community agencies, like nonprofit organizations, schools, churches, law enforcement agencies, or even businesses. Community agencies or groups sometimes want to assess the success of their programs or strategies, but do not have adequate resources to collect, analyze, and compile all of the data they believe are necessary. Agencies also often need to collect and analyze data to demonstrate the need for their services and the effectiveness of their programming to potential funders. Sociologists possess the broad methodological toolkit necessary for rigorous and comprehensive evaluations of community organizations and programming. Often, sociologists partnering with community groups offer their services at no or low cost to community groups or agencies.

As a category of sociological research, CBR has three major tenets (Strand et al., 2003):

- The research is a collaboration between academic researchers and community partners; the process is open and democratic.

- The research recognizes multiple sources of knowledge, methods of discovery, and forms of dissemination.

- The research has a goal of social change; this could include larger policy changes or relative minor changes, like changes in how a program operates.

As outlined in Table 15.1, traditional research and CBR differ on many fronts, including goals, roles of the participants, primary beneficiaries, and the means of dissemination. Traditional research revolves around academic expertise and interests, assumes the researcher is the outside expert, community members are subjects, publications are the goal, and results are disseminated in academic publications. CBR, in contrast, stresses collaboration, community needs, and social change. The researchers work with the community to create products that are mutually beneficial.

CONSIDER THIS. . .

Do you know what are the major challenges facing communities near you? Do you know what organizations are tackling these challenges? If not, how would you find out?

Examples of CBR

Jennifer Cossyleon's research on the interplay between community organizing and family life for Black and Latina women provides an excellent example of CBR. As a sociology graduate student working

TABLE 15.1 ■ A Comparison of Traditional Academic Research and Community-Based Research

	Traditional Academic Research	Community-Based Research
Primary goal of the research	Advance knowledge within a discipline	Community betterment; social change, social justice
Role of researcher	Outside expert	Collaborator, partner, learner
Role of community	Object to be studied ("community as laboratory")	Collaborator and partner
Role of students	None, or limited to research assistants	Collaborators, partners, learners
Relationship between researcher and participants	Short-term, task-oriented, detached	Long-term, multifaceted, connected
Measure of value of research	Acceptance by academic peers (ex: publications)	Usefulness for community partners, contribution for social change
Primary beneficiaries of the research	Academic researcher	Academic researcher, student, community
Means of dissemination	Written report, academic article, or book	Any and all forms that may have impact

Source: Adapted from Exhibit 1.1 in *Community-Based Research and Higher Education,* by Strand, Marullo, Cutforth, Stoecker, and Donohue, 2003.

with the Center for Urban Research and Learning in Chicago, Cossyleon connected with Community Organizing and Family Issues (COFI), a grassroots organization that mobilizes marginalized communities for social change. Cossyleon became actively involved in the agency and focused her dissertation research on women's family-focused community organizing, a "political model that recognizes the inseparability of private and public lives" (Cossyleon, 2018a, 2018b). The community organizing activities were intentionally family-friendly, such as providing free childcare and shared food, and sought to address the daily struggles of these low-income families.

Participating in 90 organizing events totaling over 250 hours, Cossyleon gained the trust of her research participants because she "showed up," became "part of the family," and openly shared her own experiences with them. Using the trust she had built up as a foundation, she interviewed 47 organiza-

tion participants who, because of her continued participation with the organization, felt more confident that she would accurately relay their stories. Although members of the organization did not contribute directly to Cossyleon's academic writing, she continually discussed research progress with her interviewees, shared drafts with those who were interested, and incorporated participants' feedback. Cossyleon viewed community members as collaborators and respected the valuable insights they provided based on their lived experience and their shared goals of community empowerment.

In Cossyleon's study, and in other community-based research projects, community members have a voice in the research process, they have an ally in their activities, and data collected can be used to further the goals of the organization. This research approach is much different from traditional research that stresses detachment and the expertise of academic researchers.

Community organizing, such as that conducted by COFI, can support social change in underserved communities.

SDI Productions/E+/Getty Images

Another example of CBR is Michelle Ronda and Robin Isserles's (2018) collaborative project with researchers at the Borough of Manhattan Community College (BMCC) and the Battery Park City Authority (BPCA). The BCPA wanted to better understand the users and types of use of the 36 acres of public parks in Battery Park City. Like many CBR studies, Ronda and Isserles actively incorporated students as research partners in their work. They hired and trained a total of 43 undergraduate student researchers for their year-long project. In addition to training all students on methodology and data collection, Ronda and Isserles trained 18 students to enter data into SPSS, a social science statistical software program.

In total, the research team surveyed 549 randomly selected park visitors; made direct contact with another 2,836 randomly selected visitors; systematically counted over 32,000 visitors in BPC parks; and held seven focus groups with BPC stakeholders in supplemental resources at the end of the chapter). Although the Battery Park City Authority could have hired a marketing firm, which may have completed the work more quickly, the Borough of Manhattan Community College was chosen for this project in part due to the educational component it offered to students. The project resulted in rigorous research and the development of a positive, ongoing university–community collaboration.

DOING SOCIOLOGY 15.1

Developing Questions for Community-Based Research

In this exercise, you will think through sociological research questions that can be addressed though community collaborations.

1. What is a sociological topic you could research using community collaborations?

2. With what community groups, organizations, or agencies could you collaborate to examine this issue?

3. What are two specific research questions you would use for this issue?

4. How might the interests of academic researchers and community organizations affect the research questions they select?

Heather Parrott and Colby Valentine's (2021) research on human trafficking is an additional example of CBR. In 2016, Parrott and Valentine started helping a new community organization—the Empowerment Collaborative of Long Island (ECLI)—collect data about the services they provide to victims of human trafficking. This information was necessary for their fund-raising and grant-writing efforts and, thus, the growth of their agency. More recently, in 2018, Parrott and Valentine helped ECLI and the Suffolk County Police Department secure a 3-year federal grant to start the Suffolk County Trafficking Initiative (SCATI), an anti–human trafficking task force that includes ECLI, the Suffolk County Police Department, the Federal Bureau of Investigations (FBI), Homeland Security, the sherriff's office, and a number of agencies that work with victims of human trafficking. The researchers run the task force meetings and, as research partners on the grant, are tasked with helping gather information about human trafficking victims and traffickers across agencies. The goals are to better understand and better address the problem of trafficking. While the research is ongoing, the results will be presented in multiple forms to satisfy different audiences, including presentations to the task force, descriptive reports, and academic articles.

Check Your Understanding

1. What is community-based research (CBR)?
2. What are public sociologists?
3. How does CBR differ from traditional research?

WHAT ARE THE MAIN STEPS IN CBR?

CBR stresses both participation and action. As noted earlier, the researcher works in *partnership* with community partners to answer research questions while bringing about positive social change. Next, we'll discuss essential steps in the CBR process. Although many of these steps mirror the research approach outlined in earlier chapters, CBR requires researchers to consider an additional collaborative layer when designing a project.

Identify the Social Issue or Community Concern

The general research topic for community-based research may come from a variety of sources—a class assignment, a proposed independent study topic, or general interest. In some cases, an agency or community group might reach out directly to explore potential partnerships.

One avenue to starting a CBR project is to see what activities are occurring in the community on a given topic. Researchers can attend public forums, meetings, protests, or other community activities to see with what issues people are engaged, and to identify the main participants. By doing so, researchers can start developing alliances with community members and/or organizations. As these relationships develop, community groups may start discussing their needs with the researcher, and the researcher might discuss their own ideas with community members. Whether the research is researcher-initiated or community-initiated, organizational leaders and other potential gatekeepers should be included in discussions early in the process, as they can provide valuable insight on potential restrictions, needed data, organizational history, and community context.

Identify Stakeholders

Once the research topic is identified, researchers should make a list of stakeholders. Stakeholders are individuals, agencies, or community groups that are either affected directly by a social issue and/or have an interest in developing a solution. The researchers often identify a "key group" of stakeholders as well as an "extended group" of stakeholders. Key stakeholders are those who deal with the issue most directly and, perhaps, in ways that are most interesting to the researchers. If the researcher is interested in farmworker rights, for example, he or she may want to begin by talking to farmworkers and leaders from farmworker rights groups, before bringing in farmers, law enforcement officials, and politicians. If research discussions start with this smaller key group, development of the research problem will be easier and the direction of the research will likely be better aligned with the interests of the researchers.

The extended group of stakeholders is more tangentially associated with the problem; they have an interest in the problem, but it is not a central concern in their lives or work. For example, a group established around the topic of educational equality would certainly include teachers and parents as key stakeholders, while police officers, employers, and religious leaders may be part of an extended group of stakeholders. The roles of the researchers, key stakeholders, and perhaps even extended stakeholders (depending on their level of involvement) should be clearly laid out in a memorandum of understanding (MOU), as discussed further in the section on ethical considerations later in this chapter.

CONSIDER THIS...

Imagine you were studying the topic of homelessness. Who would you consider key stakeholders? Who would you consider extended stakeholders? Why?

Community Advisory Boards

One unique element of CBR is the potential inclusion of community advisory boards (CAB), or community advisory groups, which are comprised of community members, key stakeholders, and academic researchers (sometimes including students too!). These boards are most prevalent in

A community advisory board, such as the one seen here, should represent the concerns of the community.

iStock.com/JohnnyGreig

health-related research (Nyirenda et al., 2018, Strauss et al., 2001) and are established to ensure that research is mutually beneficial, a variety of community voices are heard, diverse constituencies are adequately represented, community members are adequately protected, and there is an ongoing dialogue between researchers and the community. Developing a community advisory board may serve to strengthen community support and trust, especially in communities that have become wary of continually being research "subjects" (Quinn, 2004).

To set up a community advisory board, the researchers must first define who is included in the "community." Is the community the neighborhood, town, or city? Is it more centered around an organization and its client base? The goal is to have a diverse cross-section of the community, however it is defined; thus, it is important to develop procedures for recruiting a representative board and then sharing power across its diverse members. These boards can take on a number of roles, including acting as a liaison between researchers and community, representing community concerns, helping develop research materials (e.g., informed consent forms, interview questions), and providing recommendations for study recruitment (Quinn, 2004, Strauss et al., 2001).

Identify a Collective Problem

In traditional research, the academic researcher sets the research agenda, establishing the research topic, question to be answered, and method for data collection and analysis. In CBR, these are developed collectively. The researcher meets with a core group of stakeholders to determine the most pressing research needs. When researchers really listen to the stakeholders, the research question, and even the topic can sometimes be unexpectedly transformed. The research can take a different direction than the researcher had initially expected, and might also require adjustments to the research team or the stakeholders. For example, a research project on incarceration could unexpectedly end up focusing on inmate literacy, thus benefiting from the inclusion of education researchers and the expansion of community stakeholders to include educators.

Community partners bring valuable information and perspectives, but so do sociologists. Social science researchers can review and summarize existing scholarly research on a topic to determine what is already known, what remains unclear, and what questions have yet to be asked. By compiling this information, sociologists can help community partners understand the work that has already been done on the topic and can give all members of the academic-community team ideas for research. They can also provide a more removed perspective, sometimes allowing them to notice larger trends, ask seemingly naive (but often important!) questions, and uncover unspoken assumptions. Community members can add their expertise by relaying their knowledge of the communities in which they live and work. Their nuanced understandings of the problems facing their communities—as well as community successes—are crucial for asking the correct questions.

Data Collection

The scope of data collection needs for CBR can be very targeted (e.g., evaluating the effectiveness of a specific program) or quite expansive (e.g., assessing food insecurity in a city). There are often multiple research questions to pursue simultaneously, some asked by community partners and some by researchers. The specific methods chosen for CBR should be those that are best able to answer the research question or questions that the collaborators have agreed to investigate. Thus, CBR research is often "mixed methods" research, drawing from multiple methods like surveys and qualitative interviews, in the course of a single project.

Researchers and community partners should be sure that the research goals of all partners are met without making the research process too intense or time consuming for either the organization or those researched. This can be challenging, as Parrott and Valentine (2021) discovered in their collaborative research on the relationship between treatment and health outcomes for trauma victims. Parrott and Valentine worked to develop a survey with a nonprofit agency and a multidisciplinary academic research team, but found that the desire to satisfy all stakeholder interests resulted in a very lengthy survey. Victim advocates were interested in getting more information about such things as health, history of abuse, current substance abuse, and depression indicators, while the diverse group of academics wanted to include broader questions related to sociology, criminology, and social work. In the end, a surprisingly low proportion of respondents completed the survey, and the researchers speculated that this was at least partially due to the length of the survey. Thus, although a strength of community partnerships is that they can generate numerous questions and ideas, the process of prioritizing these questions and ideas in a way that is fair to all involved can be a challenge.

DOING SOCIOLOGY 15.2

Contemplating an on-Campus CBR Project

In this exercise, you will think through how you could conduct CBR on your campus.

Identify an issue that affects your campus community, *or* a hypothetical change that *could* affect your campus community. This could be something challenging, like campus sexual assault or binge drinking, or something more modest, like the introduction of new types of food in the campus dining hall.

1. What is an issue currently affecting or that could affect your campus community? How would you study this change using a community-based research approach?

2. Who are the stakeholders?

3. What is your research question?

4. What methods would you use to answer the research question?

Data Interpretation

Ideally, the interpretation of data is also a collaborative process. Researchers often present their initial findings to community partners through written drafts, informal presentations, or public forums. Researchers and community members may then work together to interpret the findings or give feedback on the existing interpretations. In cases where interpretations differ, the researcher and community partners may choose to collect more data, come to a consensus on how to present the interpretation of the findings, or present multiple interpretations of data within reports.

Share Results

Researchers can share their results in class presentations, conference presentations, and academic publications. Community partners can decide how they would like the results shared, such as through yearly organizational reports, grant documents, staff meetings, community presentations, websites, handouts, or films. The format depends on the scope of the research, desired outcomes for all partners, and the nature of the research question and findings. More favorable or surprising findings are likely to be more widely shared.

Muslim high school students from Detroit, seen here visiting Republican state senator Ken Horn, take part in the annual Michigan Muslim Capitol Day to discuss issues that concerned them. This is an example of a community coalition.

Jim West/Alamy Stock Photo

There are likely to be multiple ways of presenting data outcomes in CBR to satisfy the multiple interests of the diverse research team. First, the academics involved in the research are likely to want more formal academic presentations, papers, or books from the research. These products are generally geared toward an academic audience, which may include a more thorough review of the academic literature, links to theory, and more sophisticated quantitative analyses of data. Such final products may be interesting to community partners, but these products are often more detailed and take more time to come to fruition than is needed and desired.

Community partners often need more basic data that can be produced more quickly and easily disseminated. They may want basic descriptive data to show their activities, the success of their endeavors, or the extent of a social problem. These data may be required for applying for grants, completing organizational reports, fund-raising, trying to improve organizational function, or garnering community support. Many grants require organizations to submit data reports mere weeks after the completion of data collection—a much more rapid turnaround time than typical academic research. Helping agencies collect and analyze data and summarize the results in reports is part of giving back to community partners, and is an important step to bridge the divide between academia and the community.

Beyond reports, the products of CBR can be distributed in any number of forms, including public forums, informal community settings, flyers, art, and media. Some academics and organizations effectively disseminate information and findings to the larger community through websites and films. Films can let communities know about a social problem (e.g., environmental or health issues) and available services (e.g., support groups, health centers, or outreach programs), and researchers can even measure the impact of these films on the community of interest. For example, a collection of academic researchers, medical professionals, public health advocates, and community members in South Carolina worked with University of South Carolina filmmakers to create a film about (1) the problems of access to healthy food and the related rise of obesity in the Orangeburg area and (2) the formation and implementation of a farmer's market in the area. The research team used the film to disseminate information about the problem and possible solution, and then measured the effectiveness of the film (Brandt et al., 2016).

Develop an Agenda for Action

After the study is completed and the results shared, researchers work with community partners to develop an agenda for action, a plan for implementing the lessons learned from CBR. The agenda for action could entail such steps as creating new programs, changing existing programs, expanding services, partnering with other agencies, hiring additional staff members, applying for a new funding source, or starting a new research project. When developing a plan for action, researchers can collaborate with community members to translate research results into more tangible plans. Researchers can make suggestions based on the data collected, but this final stage of the CBR is more firmly in the hands of community partners and organizations. Organizations have to consider such things as resources, organizational networks, political climate, and community support when setting a data-driven agenda. Power certainly comes into play at this stage as well, as certain stakeholders may be more resistant to change than others, especially if the changes result in diminished power, less money, or increased public scrutiny.

Check Your Understanding

1. What are the steps of CBR research?
2. How does the collaborative process of CBR make this research different from typical research?
3. What are community advisory boards/committees?
4. In what ways may researchers and community partners share their research findings?

WHAT ARE THE UNIQUE ETHICAL CONSIDERATIONS OF COMMUNITY-BASED RESEARCH?

Ethical considerations are central in any research project, but community-based research has some unique considerations. First and foremost, everyone involved in the research needs to understand and respect the importance of confidentiality. If community organizations are involved in the research, researchers and collaborators must formulate a plan to protect individual research subjects as well as the organizations, including all clients, staff, and organizational records. Community organizations may also be bound by certain legal restrictions (like the Health Insurance Portability and Accountability Act, or HIPAA) and bureaucratic restrictions (e.g., non-profit or corporate bylaws), which may limit the collection and sharing of data. It is crucial to understand these ethical considerations and restrictions from the start of the project and to remember them throughout.

The Health Insurance Portability and Accountability Act (HIPAA) limits the collection and sharing of private patient data.

iStock.com/Hailshadow

Power and control are key ethical issues to consider when conducting any social research. Think back to the "town–gown divide" mentioned earlier in the chapter. Historically, social scientists often treated communities as if they were laboratories for the study of social problems. Researchers would determine which questions to ask, the best methods for answering them, how to interpret the data, and where to disseminate the results. Community members, particularly when they were economically and politically disadvantaged, had little influence over the research taking place, and even less influence on how they themselves were represented in resulting publications. In many ways, the unequal power dynamics between the researcher and the communities they were studying reproduced, rather than challenged, social inequalities.

CONSIDER THIS...

What are some sources of potential tension between academic researchers and community partners? Why?

Community-based researchers are not only attentive to unequal power relations, but address them head-on. Throughout the research process, they ask, "Who benefits? And how much?" Conducting research benefits the careers of academics, because research can yield scholarly publications, grants, and professional advancement. Community partners may have a different perspective regarding what is valuable to them. Ideally, the data collected in the course of CBR should be equally beneficial to the community partner and the researcher. For instance, the community may want to use findings to support grant applications, to include in yearly reports, or to evaluate a particular program, proposed law, or other type of intervention. Community partners often want to collect data in order to address a pressing community concern or even a crisis, so the applicability of data to their needs is of paramount importance. It is often necessary to explore and articulate the expectations of different stakeholders by writing them out.

DOING SOCIOLOGY 15.3

Considering Issues of Power in CBR

In this activity, you will think through the role of power in a CBR scenario.

A researcher is interested in better understanding what services are most effective for helping domestic violence victims. The researcher invites a diverse set of stakeholders to discuss the issue, including people from the local police department, child protective service workers, the director of the local domestic violence shelter, a couple of case managers from the domestic violence shelter, and several domestic violence survivors who used to receive services at the shelter. They come together to discuss potential research topics.

Based on this scenario, write your answers to the following questions:

1   How would you define power in this scenario?

2   How might differences in power affect this discussion and decision making?

3   How could you minimize these differences and their effects on the research process?

When working with community partners, the best strategy is to develop a memorandum of understanding (MOU) as early as possible. An MOU is a non–legally binding document that clearly lays out expectations and protections for all parties involved in the research (see example in Figure 15.1). The following questions should be addressed in the process of drawing up the MOU:

- How will data be collected and analyzed? What will be required of the community organization?

- What is the proposed time frame for the research? When should the community partners expect results to be available to them?

- How will the researchers share the data with the community or organization? Will they provide a written report or a presentation of the findings? How will the findings be shared with the wider community?

- Does the researcher anticipate using the findings for academic publications and presentations? If so, what protections (such as pseudonyms) will be in place to protect the organization, clients, staff, or respondents?

- Although it can sometimes feel awkward to talk about the academic use of data, being up-front with organizational leaders is best because it gives them an opportunity to decide whether they are comfortable with all aspects of the collaboration. To the extent that they are uncomfortable, it provides an opportunity for collaborators to discuss more suitable alternatives. Many organizations expect this arrangement when working with academics, and may even enjoy playing a role in producing scholarly knowledge.

As part of the MOU, the researcher may promise that the agency can review all materials before they are published or presented. When this occurs, the agency has a chance to make sure that all data are presented in ways that protect clients, staff, and the organization. The agency representatives can ask the researcher to alter anything that they do not feel is adequately protective. It is important to note that although this section of the MOU addresses confidentiality, it does not lay out a plan for potential differences in agreement about study findings. Tactics to address such discrepancies are discussed later in this chapter. Community advisory boards can certainly play a role in ensuring that adequate steps are taken to protect confidentiality as well, and may help craft MOUs between researchers and community members.

Check Your Understanding

1. What are some ethical considerations in CBR?
2. What is a memorandum of understanding (MOU)?
3. What questions are addressed in an MOU?
4. Why is an MOU important?

FIGURE 15.1 ■ Example of a Memorandum of Understanding

Memorandum of Understanding Between <<insert community organization>> and Dr. Heather Macpherson Parrott, Long Island University

THIS AGREEMENT constitutes a contract between <<insert community organization>> and Dr. Heather Parrott of Long Island University. The parties in this agreement have agreed to work to engage in the sharing of data for analysis purposes and reports, as well as relevant publications that further the body of scientific knowledge available to researchers and practitioners.

SECTION 1. PURPOSE

The primary basis of this agreement is to engage in the sharing of data for analysis purposes and reports, as well as relevant publications that further the body of scientific knowledge available to researchers and practitioners. This will be done through the collection and/or sharing of quantitative and qualitative data through <<insert community organization>>, which will be used to conduct research on various issues related to health, trauma, victim recovery, and/or organizational effectiveness.

SECTION II. ASSURANCES <<insert community organization>>

- <<Insert community organization>> will provide data or assist in the collection of data for mutually agreed upon topics of inquiry.

SECTION III. ASSURANCES Dr. Heather Macpherson Parrott

- Confidentiality Agreement

- Dr. Heather Parrott will keep confidential any personally identifying information about <<insert community organization>> clients, former clients, staff, or volunteers.

- No <<insert community organization>> materials, with or without personally identifying information, may be removed from <<insert community organization>> premises without explicit permission of <<insert community organization>> personnel.

- All <<insert community organization>> data will have all personally identifying information (i.e., name, address, phone number) removed from the data before it is removed from <<insert community organization>> premises.

- Data will not be shared with any other researcher prior to such other researcher having executed a confidentially agreement with <<insert community organization> and << insert community organization>> Executive Director having agreed to their participation in the research project.

- Dr. Heather Parrott will be responsible for (a) discussing the proposed inclusion of any other researchers with <<insert community organization>> Executive Director and (b) procuring a signed confidentiality agreement from each agreed upon additional researcher.

- At least fifteen (15) days prior to releasing any manuscript, report, or web site universal resource locator (URL) intended for public dissemination that contains <<insert community organization>> data, I agree to provide the Executive Director of <<insert community organization>> with a copy of the manuscript, report, or the URL. If the Executive Director of <<insert community organization>> determines that the manuscript, report, or web site violates confidentiality, I shall modify the report prior to its release to protect against such identification.

- The researcher(s) affiliated with Long Island University will produce reports for <<insert community organization>> on each agreed upon topic of inquiry.

Dr. Heather Parrott   Executive Director

Date   Date

SOCIOLOGISTS IN ACTION

CHRISTINA JACKSON

I consider myself to be a public sociologist and a scholar–activist—meaning that I bring together my academic work and organizing work to produce knowledge that is public and accessible. For me, being a public sociologist and scholar–activist is about using the disciplinary skills of sociology to promote the public good.

Courtesy of Christina Jackson

I teach sociology and anthropology students to *learn as they do* while taking into account their own story. This combined concept called for the creation of a *scholar–activist approach* to engaging in projects with the community that are *decolonial*, and which lead to uprooting structures of inequality already in place. A *decolonial* framework to community work promotes solidarity, mutual relationships, accountability, public participation, and decision making when engaging with more powerful or elite institutions. I believe in helping communities most impacted organize themselves while also placing their perspective at the forefront of the creation of academic knowledge.

As a method, ethnography is a natural fit for this kind of community work. *Ethnography* has provided a bridge between my organizing world and my academic world in ways that contribute positively in aiding communities in answering our society's most pressing questions. In the classes I teach, as well as in the ethnographic research I conduct, we use our skills to explore and document the lives of those studied, but also learn their perspectives and help them achieve community goals. In the process, my students develop communication skills, critical thinking, and perspective-taking.

In 2016, I began to develop a rapport with Black Lives Matter Atlantic City (BLMAC), who wanted to put their realities in a larger context of racial inequality, and asked for help putting on a year-long series of educational forums on a variety of topics including race, sexuality, family, health, and violence. In addition to providing academic expertise, I built coalitions within Atlantic City communities and connected like-minded organizations to form community panels. My students and I conducted interviews with BLM members in order to archive their experiences and blog about their perspectives.

In 2017, I started working with an organization called New Jersey Organizing Project (NJOP) through a connection with our university's service-learning program. The mutual goal was to collect more data about the lives of victims of Hurricane Sandy 5 years later and learn about the effect of hurricanes on the lives of residents in South Jersey. We trained sociology students in data collection methods so that they could canvas the victims and record the experiences of the recovery. Our data collection efforts culminated in a large report that helped victims in their efforts to demand more resources from the New Jersey state government. The state recently announced an addition of $100 million for disaster aid to help the families still not home yet after 6½ years.

Projects like this allow sociologists to learn as they do while contributing to the public good of the communities in which we live and work. Our sociology skills can be put to the test while reducing inequality and building community power.

Christina Jackson is an associate professor of sociology and former faculty fellow at the Stockton Center for Community Engagement at Stockton University.

Discussion Question

What elements of community-based research are evident in Professor Jackson's description of her project?

WHAT ARE THE CHALLENGES AND OPPORTUNITIES INVOLVED IN CBR?

Establishing social change–oriented research relationships with community organizations presents unique opportunities and challenges. Understanding these opportunities and challenges before the project begins, making plans to maximize the benefits, and seeking to avoid or navigate successfully through the challenges help to ensure a successful partnership.

Challenges

Sharing Power

Balancing differences in perspectives and power is a significant challenge in community-based research. Oftentimes community members will have more practical knowledge and first-hand experience with the issue, while researchers have more scholarly knowledge of the issue and greater methodological expertise. In all cases, researchers benefit when they clearly respect the knowledge, perspectives, and experiences of practitioners, victims, and other stakeholders. Researchers must also take into account differences in power within organizations (e.g., an executive director vs. an intern) as well as between organizations (e.g., a local police department vs. the Federal Bureau of Investigation [FBI]).

Ideally, all parties should feel comfortable speaking, and all should feel that their viewpoints are valued. For example, an employee at a rape crisis center may have ideas on how to better provide services to victims of sexual assault, but may feel hesitant to share these ideas in front of the executive director for fear that this will affect their employment. Researchers must consider a range of potential power structures, including race, ethnicity, language, gender, and social prestige, along with workplace hierarchies. It is important for researchers to consider how these different power structures create vulnerabilities for individuals, and may also affect the dynamics of the research process.

Ethical Considerations

When researchers start CBR, they typically do not know the exact direction of the research. This presents complications for securing appropriate institutional review board (IRB) approval. As you learned in Chapter 4, an IRB is an entity within a college or university that is tasked with providing ethical oversight on research projects, to make sure that human participants are protected from harm. IRB oversight requires extensive documentation of the research questions, protocols, consent forms, and MOUs with all organizations. Once the researcher and community partners agree on the terms of the research, securing IRB approval can significantly stall the research process. Community partners are sometimes unfamiliar with IRBs, and may not initially understand their importance. In these cases, researchers should explain the importance of institutional oversight for protecting research participants, including the community members and organizations involved in the research project.

Timeline

A significant consideration in CBR, especially when trying to arrange semester- or year-long projects, is that community organizations do not work on an academic timeline. Employees of community organizations may not have time to invest in research during the desired time frame. Alternatively, the community partner's need for research findings may be much more immediate, such as when a grant is due soon, or an upcoming public forum is scheduled. Academic researchers may find it challenging to maintain the necessary scientific rigor of their research while trying to move quickly to solve a problem or meet an external deadline. All partners should be up-front about timelines at the beginning of the research process.

CONSIDER THIS...

You partner with a local elementary school to collect data for it that can be used for your senior thesis. What are some things you should know from, or share with, your school research partners at the beginning of the research process?

Community Partner Commitment

CBR obviously requires the commitment of community partners. The knowledge, time, resources, and people-power that an organization can dedicate to a research project are referred to as organizational capacity. Community organizations often lack the capacity to carry out a full-scale research project

Your professor may have experience working with community partners, and can support you as you conduct CBR.

Klaus Vedfelt/DigitalVision/Getty Images

on their own, because they lack sufficient resources and are busy addressing community needs. Ideally, the CBR should represent a genuine collaboration between academic researchers and community partners, making the most of everyone's skills, knowledge, and perspective, without unreasonable demands of time and other resources.

If you are conducting CBR as a student, there are some best practices to keep in mind when coordinating with a community partner. First, remember that you are a representative of your class and university. Communicate professionally, attend all meetings and arrive to them on time, adhere to agreed-upon deadlines, and treat all research partners and participants with respect. Second, be respectful of the time of your community partners. The community partners are dedicating significant time and energy to working with you, so be sure that you dedicate time to the research and to creating a polished final product. If you are working as a student research team, designate one person as the liaison between community partners and student researchers. This helps to ensure that community partners are not answering the same questions multiple times to different team members. Finally, recognize that CBR can be unpredictable and that you may need help navigating those challenges. Do not be afraid to ask your professor for help if problems or questions transpire. Working through problems is part of the learning experience, and your professor can help you address issues in ways that preserve the university–community partnership.

Academic Research

Community partners may have very specific research needs that are limited in scope, such as evaluating a certain program. Although a narrowly focused study can be very useful for an organization, the limited scope may also constrain outlets for academic research. Throughout the process of CBR, academics should continually consider the suitability of the research project for academic publication and how research plans can be modified to meet the requirements of scholarly research. Such long-term planning can be challenging amidst thinking about more immediate, practical community concerns.

Opportunities

Social Change

For sociologists who are looking to make a difference in the world and to promote social justice, CBR provides an opportunity to do just that. Many researchers like to use their research skills in ways that help an organization or community to address a problem. Unlike many traditional research methods, which seek to maintain distance between the researcher and researched, CBR has the explicit goals of community engagement and social change. With CBR, researchers can use their skills to produce rigorous research and spur data-driven change.

Community Organizing Skills

Community organizing is the coordination of community members to promote community interests. Community organizers leading these efforts need to be able to mobilize diverse groups, effectively negotiate group power dynamics, and communicate well with a variety of individuals, including disenfranchised community residents, activists, and politicians. These skills can be developed through participation in CBR. Community-based researchers develop these leadership and communication skills as they partner with communities to decide what problems to explore, develop research plans, talk through results, and develop plans of action.

Résumé Building

Working with community organizations for social research is excellent experience to add to a résumé, especially as a student. Undergraduate sociology students often pursue careers in law, social work, health, education, and community organizations. The process of collaborating in social research projects with community partners gives students concrete skills and experiences like synthesizing research, designing surveys, conducting interviews, analyzing data, and communicating with diverse audiences. Not only do these skills look good on résumés, but they also set students up for success in graduate school and in their careers.

Just as translators must understand the nuances and interplay of culture and language, researchers must understand the unique qualities of the people and communities they study.

Casarsa/E+/Getty Images

Cultural Competence

Conducting social research in a community setting can also be an opportunity to develop cultural competence. Cultural competence refers to the knowledge, skills, and experiences that people or organizations have that enable them to practice culturally sensitive behaviors, attitudes, and policies. Cultural competence includes a range of social and cognitive skills, including valuing diversity, recognizing complexity in language interpretation, managing differences in power, working with the community to define and address their needs, and adapting to the cultural contexts of the communities researchers study. Cultural competence helps people to work more effectively with people from diverse life backgrounds who may have different experiences and perspectives.

An important aspect of cultural competence is that it centralizes issues of power and inequality without "othering" impoverished, minority, or foreign communities. Othering refers to seeing others as different than or less than oneself; the marginalization of these groups is implied, as they are compared to a white, middle-class, and American default standard (Pon, 2009; Sakamoto, 2007). Concern over power relationships is a common element of both cultural competence and cultural humility. Cultural humility is an approach to community work and research that emphasizes an awareness of power imbalances, self-reflection, and supportive interactions (Danso, 2018; Foronda et al., 2016). These practices demonstrate respect for the community members and tend to result in better outcomes, whether for research, social service, or public health initiatives (Nassar-McMillan, 2014; Sousa & Almeida, 2016).

Unique Data

Collecting data with community organizations generates unique data for potential academic publication or grant writing. In some cases, data can be aggregated across multiple research sites, or linked to existing national-level data. In all cases, data from CBR provide new information about the workings of a particular group, organization, or community and a window into how that group, organization, or community fits into a larger social context. Even when the findings are particular to a specific organization, group, or community, they can be used to generate insights and hypotheses for larger-scale studies. In addition, they can provide valuable information for grants, which can be valuable for community organizations and for academic researchers.

DOING SOCIOLOGY 15.4

Rethinking Research

In this exercise, you will think through a variety of ways to work with community partners on research.

Think again about the class research example discussed at the opening of the chapter:
Imagine a group of sociology students studying clients at a local soup kitchen. They descend on the soup kitchen at mealtime, interview people about their life experiences, and then leave to write about it for

their class. The students may have broadened their understanding of hunger, poverty, and/or inequality through this experience, but the lives of the study participants have remained unchanged.

How could this research be approached differently? To answer this question, write your responses to the following:

1. Outline how a class could research this population using the CBR approach discussed in this chapter.

2. Short of a comprehensive CBR approach, make a list of smaller ways this research could be done more sensitively and collaboratively.

Check Your Understanding

1. What are the challenges involved in CBR for community partners?
2. What are the challenges involved in CBR for academic researchers?
3. What are the best strategies for participating in CBR for students?
4. What opportunities does CBR offer researchers?

CONCLUSION

This chapter has outlined the main components, ethical issues, methods, challenges, and opportunities of CBR, a collaborative and social change–oriented approach to research. However, it is worth noting that there is really a continuum between traditional academic research and the CBR approach described in this chapter. A large portion of social science research falls somewhere in the middle. Researchers working in community settings can consider components of this approach even when their method generally falls outside of a CBR approach. For example, researchers can consider the extent to which they integrate community knowledge, incorporate cultural competence, work *with* community members to identify research problems, strive for social change, or help disseminate the results within the wider community. Integrating the themes of community-based research and treating community members as research partners, as opposed to simply research subjects, can result in strong university–community relationships, informed analyses of community issues, and increased potential for meaningful social change.

REVIEW

15.1 What is community-based research?

Community-based research is collaborative research between academic researchers and community partners that has the goal of social change. The researchers work with community members to develop research plans, interpret data, and disseminate results.

15.2 What are the main steps in community-based research?

The first step is to identify a community concern. The second step is to identify stakeholders. The third step is to create a community advisory board. Utilizing feedback from the stakeholders and community advisory board, the next step is to identify a collective problem. Once this problem has been identified, a plan for data collection must be put in place, followed by data interpretation. The final steps are to share the results and to develop a plan for action.

15.3 What are the unique ethical considerations of community-based research?

Researchers in CBR must consider issues of confidentiality and power, looking out for all individuals and organizations involved in the research. Memoranda of understanding can help outline all expectations and protections, negotiating potential problems early in the research process.

15.4 What are the challenges and opportunities that researchers face when conducting community-based research?

CBR can provide opportunities for contributing to social change, acquiring community organizing skills, résumé building, collecting unique data, and developing cultural competence. Some challenges to CBR are learning to share power, navigating the IRB process, negotiating time restrictions, avoiding overburdening community partners, and carving out opportunities for academic research. Researchers working in community settings can increase the extent to which they integrate community knowledge, incorporate cultural competence, work *with* community members to identify research problems, strive for social change, or help disseminate the results within the wider community.

KEY TERMS

agenda for action (p. 290)

capacity (p. 295)

community advisory boards (CAB) (p. 287)

community organizing (p. 296)

community-based research (CBR) (p. 284)

cultural competence (p. 297)

cultural humility (p. 297)

key stakeholders (p. 287)

memorandum of understanding (MOU) (p. 292)

public sociologists (p. 284)

stakeholders (p. 287)

16

CHANGING THE GAME: USING RESEARCH TO PROMOTE SOCIAL JUSTICE

Adam Saltsman

STUDENT LEARNING QUESTIONS

16.1 What are the historical roots of social justice research in sociology?

16.2 What are the main goals of social justice research?

16.3 What are the key concepts for doing social justice research?

16.4 How do sociologists use institutional ethnography, power mapping, and interpretive focus groups in social justice research?

SOCIOLOGY AND SOCIAL JUSTICE: FULFILLING OUR PROMISE

In his essay "On Knowledge and Power," the influential sociologist C. Wright Mills wrote that "the intellectual ought to be the moral conscience of society" (1963, p. 611). When Mills wrote this, he was calling for sociologists to use their abilities as researchers to investigate injustices and expose them to the public, to be vocal about advocating for change in society. Building on sociologists of earlier generations, Mills argued that the life of any individual could be understood only by first situating it within its social and historical context. Many of the troubles that people face, he argued, were better understood as stemming from social issues, rather than individual failings or bad luck. He believed sociology offered a privileged perspective on identifying these injustices, or social problems, and assessing their structural sources. This being the case, Mills argued that sociologists had a professional obligation to push for societal changes that would reduce social problems and better equip people with the resources they need to navigate and cope with the challenges they might face.––

HOW I GOT ACTIVE IN SOCIOLOGY

ADAM SALTSMAN

I took a sociology class when I was in college, but I didn't end up majoring in sociology. It wasn't until I was considering graduate school options that I thought about sociology as a good fit for me. After college, I had worked in the nonprofit sector in the United States and abroad, focusing on human rights and social justice work. I worked in Texas resettling refugees; in California, I worked as an advocate for human rights, and then traveled to Cambodia to work for a small conflict mediation organization. I was eager to gain research skills that could complement my passion for advocacy and I wasn't sure if I wanted to be a professor or an activist on the frontlines of social movements (or both). Sociology seemed like the place for me because I knew I would learn how to do research and I was attracted to the many voices within the discipline calling for an explicit commitment to social change. What became the most significant outcome of my training as a sociologist, though, was learning to see the world through the "Sociological Eye." I couldn't help but see injustices in terms of their structural or systemic nature; that is, the political, social, and economic roots of social problems. During graduate school and since, I have worked to bridge my commitment to social change with my intellectual curiosity about how the world operates. I have continued to support grassroots social justice organizations, integrating this work into my teaching and writing.

Sociology has a long-standing commitment to changing the world and using research to advocate for social justice. Looking back, one can see that sociologists were engaged in many of the fundamental struggles for equality and human rights, including movements for racial equity, women's rights, immigrant rights, economic justice, the end of mass incarceration, and the fight for rights and recognition for sexual minorities, among others. Two of the earliest and most influential scholars to use sociology for social justice were Jane Addams (1868–1935) and W. E. B. DuBois (1868–1963).

Jane Addams was a leader in early feminist struggles for equality. She cofounded Chicago's Hull-House, a residence for women intellectuals to do research and advocate for social reform. Addams conducted surveys among Chicago's largely immigrant working class and used her research to call for greater rights for laborers. Among her many other accomplishments, she was also an outspoken activist for peace during World War I, which earned her the Nobel Peace Prize in 1931.

Sociologist W. E. B. DuBois is notable for his commitment to social justice.

Keystone/Staff/Hulton Archive/Getty Images

Among the most influential sociologists of the 20th century, W. E. B. DuBois devoted his life to exposing and challenging racism. Writing in the early 1900s, his scholarship documented the severity of racial inequality in the United States, and developed concepts and theories to understand its structural roots and persistence. In addition to his scholarship and teaching, DuBois also led the Pan African Congress, founded the National Association for the Advancement of Colored People (NAACP), and helped form the Niagara Movement, a Black civil rights organization. Although the issues they addressed and the methods they used differed, both Addams and DuBois committed their lives to social justice and used sociological research to build a more socially just world.

The injustices that DuBois, Addams, and many others used their research to combat in the early 20th century have shifted rather than disappeared, and new forms of inequality have blossomed.

In the words of Mary Romero, the 2019–2020 president of the American Sociological Association, "Doing sociology at this crucial time of our history, we need to be social activists and sociology must be engaged in social justice" (Romero, 2020, p. 25). Today, there are many ways to be a social justice researcher—there is not one method that stands out as *the* social justice approach. Rather, social justice research is research designed to shed light on historic and present-day inequalities and to bring about a more equitable and just world. This chapter provides a toolkit of sociological concepts and methods that you can use to investigate injustices and advocate for change. It begins by introducing some of the main goals of social justice research. It then presents some of the key theoretical concepts and methodological tools for doing social justice research.

CONSIDER THIS...

Think of at least one injustice or social problem occurring in society that is important to you. What kind of research could help raise awareness about this problem? What would you want to know?

Identifying Key Social Justice Issues

In this activity, you will learn more about the social justice issues that sociologists address.

Each year the Society for the Study of Social Problems (SSSP) holds a meeting where members get together to discuss sociological issues and pressing social problems. Every year the SSSP showcases summaries of papers shared at its annual meeting, two of which are presented below. Read the abstracts and then answer the following questions:

1. **Jen Girgen, Salem State University, "Running While Female: Media Accounts of Aggression and Violence"**

   "Running while female" is a wry phrase that is used to describe the all-too-real phenomenon of street harassment and violence directed towards girls and women who run in public places. This research examines newspaper and television news reports of criminal aggression and violence against female runners, from comparatively minor acts of criminal harassment to more serious offenses such as attempted or completed abductions, sexual assaults, and homicides. The content of these articles and stories is scrutinized and analysis suggests that these reports are more than just newsworthy accounts of predatory crime. They may also serve as cautionary tales that share with media consumers—in particular, those female readers and viewers who are runners and would-be runners—powerful and discouraging messages about the dangers of daring to run while female.

2. **Chris Barcelos, University of Massachusetts Boston, and Gabrielle Orum Hernández, University of Wisconsin–Madison**

   Although research and policy making in the U.S. generally frames "LGBTQ" and "youth of color" as mutually exclusive groups, LGBTQ youth of color are increasingly included in discourses surrounding school safety. These discourses position youth as vulnerable, "at risk" subjects who are passive victims of interpersonal homophobia. Using the theoretical frameworks of queer of color critique and queer necropolitics, and a situational analysis mapping strategy, we analyze GLSEN's 2019 School Climate Report, breakout reports on LGBTQ youth of color, and related advocacy efforts. These frameworks help us to consider how school climate research and policy making relies on carceral logics that center and uphold whiteness. The GLSEN reports function as a form of embedded science that mobilizes individual understandings of violence and queer investments in punishment. We offer queer of color critique as a strategy for researchers and policymakers to get "unstuck" on school safety.

   1. What are some of the social justice issues that sociologists are addressing?
   2. What methods do the researchers use to investigate these issues?
   3. What other social justice issues do you think could benefit from a sociological investigation?

   Sources: Sources for the Subject of Sociology, 2019, 2021, Featured Abstracts, https/ www.ssssp1.org/index.cfm/m/569/Featured_Abstracts/

1. What is social justice research?
2. What does it mean to be the "moral conscience of society"?
3. What were some of the research topics of early sociologists working on social justice?

GOALS OF SOCIAL JUSTICE RESEARCH

Sociological research in pursuit of social justice takes a number of forms and relies on a variety of methodological approaches. Social justice researchers share a commitment to creating a more equitable and just global society. In most social justice research projects, researchers seek to analyze a social problem, connect their research to the public arena, or to build or strengthen a social movement. As you will see, social justice researchers often work toward more than one of these goals simultaneously and can do so using a creative variety of methods.

Identifying and Analyzing a Social Problem

One of the main goals of social justice research is to shed light on a social problem, with the ultimate goal of building a more just, equitable, inclusive, and democratic world. Sociologists committed to social justice know that good data are an indispensable part of any effort to effect social change. Mills et al. (1963, p. 269) echoed this sentiment when he wrote that sociologists must "recognize the value of truth in political struggle." Facts, produced by research and analysis, are at the root of any call for change. As researchers concerned with investigating the social world around us, sociologists are uniquely capable of applying their skills in data gathering and analysis to broaden awareness and understanding of social problems. Sociologists concerned with social justice will often look to the lived experiences of people in society to identify inequities that need to be addressed.

One example that involves undergraduate and graduate students comes from Worcester State University (WSU), a 4-year public university in Massachusetts. In 2017, students at WSU organized around the idea of opening a food pantry on campus. They approached a professor with a sociology background for guidance, and together decided that a good first step would be to assess whether students were experiencing food insecurity—a lack of access to sufficient quantities of affordable, nutritious food. They conducted a survey of the student population and found that a full third of students on campus had experienced food insecurity in the previous month. They presented this information to university administrators, who were shocked to realize the scope of the problem. The faculty and student researchers wrote a report based on their findings that considered student hunger in the context of students' economic conditions, including the high cost of a college education and the stagnation of wages in the United States. They offered recommendations based on their research to the university, the student government association, and the Commonwealth of Massachusetts. The research was instrumental in this group's ultimately successful efforts to open a campus food pantry—Thea's Pantry—and to petition for the establishment of a meal swipe donation program so students could support their peers struggling with food insecurity to access the dining halls on campus. In addition, the group incorporated recommendations from this report into legislative briefings at the state level and joined in lobbying efforts to pass legislation targeting college student hunger. By taking the problem of hunger and studying it to identify broader trends across the university, students and faculty researchers generated facts about a social problem that could then be used to call for social change and have a real impact.

Connecting Research to the Public Arena

Sociological research in pursuit of social justice often has the goal of connecting the knowledge we generate about social problems through data collection and analysis to the public in an effort to increase general awareness of important issues. Although there are many ways to refer to this goal, it is often referred to as public sociology. In his presidential address to the American Sociological Association, Michael Burawoy (2005) defines public sociology as sociology that is brought into conversation with the broader public—that is, the world beyond academic researchers. Burawoy described two forms of public sociology.

In some cases—what he calls traditional public sociology—sociologists conduct research about a social problem and take steps to share the research findings with a wide audience, particularly with those adversely affected by the issue and those in a position to do something about it. This sharing might be through writing research briefs and disseminating them among policy makers, writing books that reach a broad audience, publishing opinion pieces in newspapers, or even blogs and other online posts, both written or as video clips.

Organic public sociology takes a more collaborative form. Similar to community-engaged research, sociologists using this approach conduct research with communities, organizations, or social groups, particularly those that are marginalized. Researchers practicing organic public sociology position themselves as collaborators, partners, and learners, seeking to learn from their research partners as they work for a shared goal. Both approaches, traditional and organic, can help and have helped to advance social justice in the United States and around the world.

One prominent public sociologist is Matthew Desmond, a professor of sociology at Princeton University. Desmond is the author of *Evicted: Poverty and Profit in the American City* (2016), which won the 2017 Pulitzer Prize for nonfiction. For this book, he conducted research in low-income communities in Milwaukee, Wisconsin, and brought to life the experiences of people struggling to remain in their homes. Desmond's rich and detailed accounts showed readers the link among housing, poverty, and the injustice of inequality. In addition, he founded and runs the Eviction Lab at Princeton, which maintains a national database of evictions in the United States. This tool allows policy makers, activists, and other members of the public to find out about evictions in thousands of communities across the country, and generate maps, charts, and reports. The site provides high-quality and easily accessible information for those working for social justice.

Some public sociology seeks to document the severity, scope, or consequences of social inequality; researchers evaluate policies to assess their success at combating entrenched patterns of privilege and disadvantage. Still others examine social movements, communities, and organizations trying to establish alternative forms of living: families trying to live without gender, organizations without hierarchies, economies without money. Some social justice researchers employ qualitative methods, others quantitative, and still others both. Despite the diversity of methods and goals, social justice sociological research is characterized by attention to power and inequality in all stages of the research process.

Building and Strengthening Social Movements

In addition to documenting social problems and connecting their research to the public, sociologists in pursuit of social justice often participate in social justice movements. Some sociologists participate in social movements as typical social movement participants, but in other cases, sociologists put their sociological perspectives, theories, and methods to work in order to further the mission of the movement. As previously mentioned, W. E. B. DuBois was a founder of the Niagara Movement and also a founder of the NAACP. He used his knowledge of race and racism, politics and inequality to build enduring and effective social movement organizations, the cornerstone of the Civil Rights Movement of the 1960s.

Walden Bello, a Filipino sociologist, activist, and politician, is one sociologist who combined his sociological expertise with social movement participation, in pursuit of social justice. Bello was an outspoken activist against the Vietnam War and against the Marcos dictatorship in the Philippines in the 1970s. He combined research and activism to critique the policies and structures of global institutions such as the World Bank, the International Monetary Fund, and the World Trade Organization. In addition, he served for 5 years as a member of the Philippines Congress and continues to write books for academic, policy, and activist audiences that make the complex dynamics of globalization and capitalism understandable for a wide audience. He was named the Outstanding Public Scholar by the International Studies Association in 2008.

Beth Richie is another example of a sociologist whose work is intertwined with social movement activism. Richie is a feminist sociologist and antiviolence activist teaching at the University of Illinois, Chicago. Her research analyzes race, gender violence, and the criminal justice system in the United States. She has authored numerous books, including *Compelled to Crime: The Gender Entrapment of Black Battered Women* (1996) and *Arrested Justice: Black Women, Violence, and America's Prison Nation* (2012). In 2000, she cofounded INCITE!, a "network of radical feminists of color organizing to end state violence and violence in our homes and communities." INCITE! offers resources for Black survivors of sexual violence and hosts dialogues that critique the violence of mass incarceration in the United States. Richie's work and the work of INCITE! has helped communities of color that have

Filipino sociologist Walden Bello has been an active participant in social movements and an advocate for social justice.

AP Photo/Pat Roque

historically been persecuted by the police and other state authorities to address violence, including domestic and sexual violence, in ways that do not depend on the criminal justice system.

Whether translating sociological concepts about inequality for broader audiences or using data and theory to study, strengthen, or build social movements, social justice researchers rely on diverse methods and approaches to investigate social problems and help change the world.

CONSIDER THIS...

Do you think that different social problems fit with different kinds of public sociology—traditional or organic? Why or why not?

DOING SOCIOLOGY 16.2

Analyzing Eviction Rates During COVID-19

In this exercise, you will consider an analysis of how the eviction moratorium imposed by the Centers for Disease Control and Prevention (CDC) affected evictions during the COVID-19 pandemic in 2020–2021.

Matthew Desmond's Eviction Lab is a powerful tool that can allow users to see eviction data for cities throughout the United States. In March 2021, the group issued a report called "Preliminary Analysis: Six Months of the CDC Eviction Moratorium," written by Peter Hepburn and Renee Louis. Read the following excerpt from the report, then answer the questions.

On September 4, 2020, the Centers for Disease Control and Prevention (CDC) ordered a nationwide eviction moratorium. This policy limited evictions when tenants provided a declaration attesting that they qualified for protections. But housing courts interpreted the CDC's order differently across the country and, in October, the CDC clarified that the order was intended to halt the execution of eviction cases, but not any court operations—including receiving eviction filings.

Now that the CDC moratorium has been in place for six months—and given that it is set to expire at the end of March—we conducted a preliminary analysis of how effective it has been. To do so, we drew on data from the Eviction Tracking System (ETS), to compare eviction case filings since the CDC moratorium was enacted to what we would expect to see in a typical year.

We observed 163,716 eviction filings between September 4, 2020 and February 27, 2021 across all ETS sites. This is 44% as many filings as we would expect over the same period in a typical year (369,292). This number, however, is skewed downward: it includes a number of cities and states that maintained stronger local eviction moratoria for some or all of this period. For example, Minnesota's eviction moratorium has kept filings in the Twin Cities over 90% below historical average over the last six months, and filings in Boston were quite low until Massachusetts' eviction moratorium expired on October 17, 2020.

When we remove cities and states with stronger tenant protections, a slightly different picture emerges. Focusing on just those cities that had no additional protections—or just those times when no such protections were in place in a given city—we find that eviction filings were at 50.1% of historical average. This is a much smaller effect than we observed when analyzing the effectiveness of state and local eviction moratoria, even those that, like the CDC moratorium, permitted case filings. Various factors might account for this difference, including the requirement under the CDC moratorium that tenants proactively declare eligibility....

Where you live plays a major role in determining how well the CDC moratorium protects you. Since early September of last year, eviction filings in Richmond, VA have been at only 30.1% of historical average. This is followed closely by Philadelphia (34.8%), Pittsburgh (36.9%), and Kansas City, MO (37.%8). New York City had no local protections between September 4 and December 28; eviction filings were at 38.9% of average for that period. During the subsequent statewide eviction moratorium, which ran from December 28 to February 26, filings in the city dropped to 4.18% of average.

By contrast, the CDC moratorium appears to have little appreciable effect in reducing filings in any of the cities we monitor in Florida. Filings are near 90% of average in Tampa and Jacksonville, and aren't far behind in Gainesville (84.3%). In Ohio, both Columbus and Cincinnati have had filings above 69% of normal, which stands in contrast to the experience of Cleveland (44.9% of average).

Eviction Lab, https://evictionlab.org/six-months-cdc/

1. How does the Eviction Lab's report fit into the idea of social justice research?
2. Would you describe the report as an example of organic or traditional public sociology? Why?
3. Why do you think evictions varied so widely across different states and cities if the CDC moratorium on evictions was applied at the national level?

Check Your Understanding

1. How can sociological research shed light on social problems and help identify possible solutions?
2. What is organic public sociology?
3. What is traditional public sociology?
4. How have sociologists helped build and strengthen social justice movements?

KEY CONCEPTS FOR SOCIAL JUSTICE RESEARCH

Sociologists engage in social justice work in many ways, drawing on a range of theories and methods. Social justice research tends to emphasize four key themes. First, social justice research is generally focused on forms of power and oppression, including those that generate inequities in our world. Second, social justice research often explores aspects of democracy and civic engagement; that is, how members of our society work together for basic freedoms and equality while addressing issues of public concern. A third feature of social justice in sociology considers alternative ways of organizing our society that are more just— what we refer to as systemic alternatives. A fourth theme commonly found in sociology's approach to social justice is an emphasis on doing research that empowers participants and supports their struggles for rights and equality. Social justice researchers expose injustices in the world, tend to believe that a more just world is possible, and use their scholarship to advocate for alternatives.

Attention to Power and Oppression

Social justice research often sheds light on issues of power and inequality. This means research that explores unequal systems and relationships in society, including those that involve unjust social statuses based on race, social class, gender, dis/ability, age, and nationality, to name a few. Social justice researchers might investigate forms of prejudice and discrimination among individuals as well as those embedded within our system of laws and policies that lead to unequal access to resources and opportunities. Both the micro-level of how individuals relate to one another and the macro-level of institutions like our schools and government are powerful sites where we encounter inequality in our society. Sociologists often stress the connections between these levels, pointing to the ways in which the assumptions we make about others and the norms by which we as individuals live are influenced by broader society, including popular media, our political leaders, and our education system. For example, in his book *Punished* (2011), sociologist Victor Rios shows how young Black and Latino boys in Oakland, California, are growing up in a part of the city that local government and investors neglected for decades, leading to underfunded schools and a lack of access to jobs, fresh food, or the larger metro area's network of transportation. Rios documents how his participants work hard to survive despite these *institutional* barriers but must also withstand the acts of *individual* prejudice and aggression from some of their teachers and local police officers who profile them as dangerous based on the color of their skin, their attire, and the place where they grew up; stereotypes that are perpetuated in the *media*.

An important trend in sociological research is to explore the ways that forms of inequality are, in fact, produced as a consequence of our history, cultural norms, and political systems. Such a social constructivism perspective involves looking into how we use difference to create and give meaning to social status categories in ways that help maintain inequality. For example, throughout history, different societies have attributed unequal norms and expectations to men and women regarding how they ought to behave, with most emphasizing social rules that support a patriarchal social order in which men can accumulate advantage and resources. Such norms and expectations change over time, depending on the ever-shifting ways society regards its various identity groups. Although popular culture, the media, and even many of our leaders tend to portray race as a biological characteristic of individuals, racial categories change over time and vary across locations. Historian N. I. Painter (2010) notes that who belongs to the "white" category has shifted over time based on U.S. Supreme Court decisions as well as social attitudes. She, along with many other scholars, shows that the category of "white" doesn't refer to any biological group, but rather a system of power and advantage based on socially constructed categories of race.

Also crucial is the focus on how social categories like race, class, and gender, to name a few, relate to one another. This pertains to the concept of intersectionality, a theoretical framework for understanding how various forms of oppression like racism, sexism, classism, or homophobia and transphobia intersect with one another and compound one's experience of power and privilege (Crenshaw, 1991; Hill Collins & Bilge, 2016). Even if we see ourselves as infinitely complex beings, our society tends to use familiar categories of difference—or social division—like race, gender, sexual orientation, and our citizenship status, for example, to make assumptions about our identity. And individuals always fit into more than one of these categories. "When it comes to social inequality, people's lives and the organization of power in a given society are better understood as being shaped not by a single axis of social division, be it race or gender or class, but by many axes that work together and influence each other" (Hill Collins & Bilge, 2016, p. 2). For example, in a society divided by patriarchy and racism, it makes sense that we must consider how both of these impact access to opportunity and resources. Intersectionality also means that researchers must consider that an individual can experience privilege based on their status in one social category, like gender, and oppression based on their status in another, like race or class.

Each of the examples above point to important sources of power in our society; that is, the power to create and maintain unequal relationships between groups. One of the defining aspects of social justice research is a commitment to uncovering and interrogating the many ways that social structures and institutions distribute advantage and power in unequal ways.

Democratic Practice and Civic Engagement

In addition to exposing injustices, many sociologists who practice social justice research explore the dynamics of democratic participation. Studying democracy with a small "d" means paying attention to how people in society gather together to advocate for equality, human rights, and solutions to problems in their communities, as well as on a broader level. Social justice researchers demonstrate a wide range of political acts—acts that are crucial to maintaining and strengthening democratic society—that fall outside the formal political system of voting during election cycles. Neighborhood residents form mutual assistance associations, parent–teacher associations call for equitable treatment for children in schools, workers join together in unions, and communities that have faced institutional forms of discrimination mobilize to figure out solutions to their problems and to fight for access to rights and resources. Looking at how people work together toward these democratic goals reflects an important area for social justice sociology and relates to the concept of civic engagement. In brief, civic engagement refers to how people work to make our world better by focusing on issues of public concern, and there are a multitude of ways to do this.

Peter Levine describes civic engagement as "a combination of deliberation, collaboration, and civic relationships" among an engaged public (Levine, 2013, p. 3). How people gather, how they work together, the topics they discuss, their rules of participation, and the kinds of relationships they forge are crucial to study in order to know how change happens. When people connect, collectively reflect, organize, and mobilize for a specific goal, they have the potential to change the world. Times when people become civically engaged—either as individuals or as groups—are called "acts of citizenship," and can truly effect change by gathering people together in collaborative deliberation, and in harnessing the power of active citizens to transform our institutions and our national culture. In many instances, civically engaged individuals and groups have organized to push their governments to change practices they consider unjust. Think about the Fridays for Future movement, which started as a local effort by then-14-year-old Greta Thunberg in Sweden to raise awareness about climate change, and which has turned into a global effort. Think about Mari Copeny, who was 8 years old when she wrote to then-President Barack Obama about the poisoning of the water supply in Flint, Michigan, calling for a solution. Social justice research analyzes efforts like these to understand their potential for making positive change in our world. Sociologists also teach civic engagement by sending their students to work with community partners, and they practice civic engagement through the forms of public sociology mentioned earlier. One thing that unites social justice researchers is our belief that a better world is possible.

Systemic Alternatives

Hope for a better world inspires many social justice researchers to look for alternatives to our current economic, political, and social systems, which have led to so much inequality and oppression. We refer to these alternatives as systemic alternatives because we're talking about solutions that involve all of us together as a society, and not just as individuals. Doing sociology puts you in a good place to think about these because research reveals social patterns and injustices, which

Nobel laureate Malala Yousafzai is a world-renowned activist for female education.

©Star Shooter/MediaPunch/IPx

better enables you "to propose solutions to social problems based on the results your research has produced" (White & White, 2019, p. 4). Researching systemic alternatives might start with questions like, "What would a world built around human rights and equity look like?" "How would our society be organized if it was driven by well-being over profit?" "What are we as a society already doing that can be expanded to replace our system of greed and inequality with something more sustainable and democratic?" J. Schor and K. E. White delve into the last question in their book *Plenitude: The New Economics of True Wealth* (2010). They show that our society can have a more stable future if we shift to a green economy, make changes to how we consume, and distribute resources more equitably. Research like this is vital for anybody concerned with social justice because it helps provide a vision for what we can work toward. Many public sociologists like Schor and White write and speak on this topic for non-academic audiences because they know that social change can only happen with broad public support.

Research as Empowerment

Feminist poet and essayist A. Lorde (1984) famously wrote that "the master's tools will never dismantle the master's house." Sociologists using a social justice research framework recognize that to be effective, social research must think carefully about the tools and practices that they use in the course of their research. Socially just research practices are better positioned to produce more socially just outcomes.

Doing social justice research means designing methods that can have a positive impact on your research participants and their communities. To do this, we have to ask how our methods impact participants and whether we're practicing research that will benefit or harm them. This means paying attention to power throughout the design of our research projects, from how we formulate research questions, to the interview or survey questions we develop, to how we collect, analyze, and share our data. Using what are called *reflexive practices,* researchers consider and address their own social position relative to others, and within the broader social context (Denzin, 1997). Beyond just thinking about these issues, though, reflexivity means thinking about power dynamics at every step of the research process (Mauthner & Doucet, 2003). Sociologists conducting social justice research often take steps to challenge the inequalities that may be built into the research process.

One way to help make sure our research is empowering participants is by inviting them into various parts (or every step) of the research process. This means we give up some of the control that sociologists have traditionally wielded over the process of designing and implementing studies. This also means asking ourselves which communities our research will impact and finding ways to invite members of these communities to weigh in, reflecting the concept of organic public sociology mentioned above. Working interactively at the grassroots level is a great way to identify social problems and social patterns and to work toward community-level or systemic alternatives. "Checking-in" with participants throughout the research process helps ensure that your methods are supporting their struggles for rights and equality.

Some researchers have created projects where community members are coresearchers who contribute the direct knowledge they have about a social problem through their lived experience. Participatory action research and community-based research, about which you learned in Chapter 15 of this book, are common ways for social justice researchers to empower participants to have some level of control over the research process. Other researchers find ways to get feedback on their methods or their interpretation of data to see how relevant communities will perceive the analysis. For example, social justice researchers who do more macro-level work with large data sets, like the U.S. Census, often reach out to relevant communities to get feedback on their hypotheses, to see how participants perceive their initial findings, and to make an effort to share their research in public arenas that are accessible to the affected communities. Building on this last point, we can see why public sociology is such an important part of being a social justice researcher. Presenting our findings in a clear and accessible way to audiences that our research concerns is one crucial way our work can be part of broader struggles for equality.

CONSIDER THIS. . .

What do you think an alternative to a society driven by capitalism might look like? How do you think you could use research to better understand that alternative?

DOING SOCIOLOGY 16.3

Identifying Methods and Concepts for Researching Social Movements

In this exercise, you will analyze the abstracts of two research studies to better understand diverse approaches to social justice research.

#BlackLivesMatter, often represented with a hashtag to reflect the centrality of social media to the campaign, is a broad-based social movement focused on racial justice, and in particular to putting an end to police violence against Black people in the United States. Many sociologists have conducted research that examines the movement and its impact on society. Consider the two abstracts below, and then answer the following questions.

Ince, J., Rojas, F., & Davis, C. A. (2017). The social media response to Black Lives Matter: How Twitter users interact with Black Lives Matter through hashtag use. *Ethnic and Racial Studies, 40*(11), 1814–1830.

This paper focuses on the social media presence of Black Lives Matter (BLM). Specifically, we examine how social media users interact with BLM by using hashtags and thus modify the framing of the movement. We call this decentralized interaction with the movement "distributed framing." Empirically, we illustrate this idea with an analysis of 66,159 tweets that mention

#BlackLivesMatter in 2014, when #BlackLivesMatter becomes prominent on social media. We also tally the other hashtags that appear with #BlackLivesMatter in order to measure how online communities influence the framing of the movement. We find that #BlackLivesMatter is associated with five types of hashtags. These hashtags mention solidarity or approval of the movement, refer to police violence, mention movement tactics, mention Ferguson, or express counter-movement sentiments. The paper concludes with hypotheses about the development of movement framings that can be addressed in future research.

Hordge-Freeman, E., & Loblack, A. (2020). "Cops only see the brown skin, they could care less where it originated": Afro-Latinx perceptions of the #BlackLivesMatter Movement. *Sociological Perspectives*. doi: 0731121420961135

The increasing visibility of Afro-Latinxs in the United States has catalyzed interest among researchers about this group's unique experiences of racialization. However, much less attention has been given to the relationship between Afro-Latinx identity formation and perceptions and/or participation in social movements. Drawing on web-based survey data with 115 Afro-Latinxs, we examine how Afro-Latinxs view the Black Lives Matter Movement with a focus on the extent to which they perceive that this explicitly anti-racist movement is relevant to their own lives. We theoretically ground our analysis in research related to collective identity and group consciousness to explore how Afro-Latinxs' unique understanding of their ethno-racial identity and group position impacts their participation in the movement. We find that overwhelmingly Afro-Latinx respondents believe they should participate in Black Lives Matter, but how they articulate their support sheds light on the diverse ways they position themselves vis-à-vis other Black-identified groups in the racial hierarchy.

1. What is the research question for each of the articles?

2. What methods are being used for this research?

3. Do you think the methods the researchers use are appropriate for answering their research question?

4. How does each study contribute to a sociological understanding of #BlackLivesMatter?

SOCIOLOGISTS IN ACTION
CHARLOTTE RYAN

Growing up in a rusting mill town, I never knew a sociologist. For that matter, I didn't know that sociology existed. My family and neighbors drove trucks, painted and cleaned houses, made beer, and worked in offices. My friends and I watched as life ground our parents down. We were afraid for ourselves. Our classmates—every bit as smart as us—began to drink, fight, and give up. As they despaired or turned hard, we wondered how to stop this. Why did it have to be this way?

First, I looked to history, searching for times when communities like mine had changed their lot. Then, I stumbled into sociology. I loved two things immediately: First, sociology named the problems, the patterns for which I had had no words. Second, sociology showed me how I could prove that the problems I saw were not a product of my imagination. I could gather evidence. I could document and replicate how I gathered evidence. And anyone who wanted to challenge me was free to do so. I also could work with others to fix problems. We ourselves could test to see if we were having an effect. We could learn and get better.

Courtesy of Charlotte Ryan.

I settled into a pattern; I'd ask a community partner to talk about their work, the questions they wanted to answer, or the hunches they wanted to test.

- The Rhode Island Coalition for the Homeless (RICH) asked if my students and I could document how homeless people were being portrayed on YouTube. We found that home-made bum fight videos represented homeless people far more commonly than videos explaining the causes of homelessness. Homeless families, the elderly, and veterans were rarely represented. Using this and other evidence, RICH passed an antihate bill protecting Rhode Islanders who were abused for being homeless.
- The Rhode Island Coalition Against Domestic Violence (RICADV) had a hunch that its work with courts and police was changing their understanding of domestic violence. We analyzed what police were saying to mass media and found that the police spokespersons had begun to align their comments with the coalition: Domestic violence is a community problem and we need to work together to stop it. Knowing its public education was working, RICADV called a conference and shared what it had learned with 37 states.

I was not a lone crusader in any of these situations. In both cases, organizer Karen Jeffreys, who studied sociology as an undergraduate and a grad student, led the discussions that set the agenda. But she is not an outlier—in almost any community group, hospital, housing, immigration rights, or environmental group, someone has studied sociology. They form teams to search for and name social patterns that hurt communities. They are comfortable gathering evidence to show the problems' importance. And they know how to share what they learn with broader groups. If you are studying sociology, someday you could be a community's secret weapon.

Charlotte Ryan is a sociologist teaching participatory methods and environmental sociology at UMASS Lowell. She and Karen Jeffreys still collaborate.

Discussion Question

What research methods does Charlotte Ryan use in her work? How do these methods promote social justice?

Check Your Understanding

1. What are some ways that social justice researchers explore power and oppression?
2. What is the connection between social justice research and democracy and civic engagement?
3. What is a systemic alternative?
4. How might researchers design their methods to have a positive impact on research participants and their communities?

SOCIAL JUSTICE RESEARCH METHODS: TOOLS FOR THE FIELD

Thus far, we've looked at some of the goals and concepts that are central to social justice research in sociology. In this section, we'll explore some specific tools that researchers can use to (a) direct their work toward social justice outcomes and (b) include marginalized people and perspectives in the research process. As mentioned earlier, there is no single method to carry out social justice research. More important is to embed a commitment to equality and justice in every step of the research process, from the identification of a topic to the selection of methods and the output of results.

Institutional Ethnography

One way to develop an understanding of how inequality and oppression operate in our society is to "study up"; that is, to look at the organizations, relationships, and people that exercise some control over the levers of power—what Dorothy Smith (2005, p. 11) calls the "ruling relations." One way of doing this is through institutional ethnography (Smith, 1987). Institutional ethnographers explore the relationships and processes for maintaining and reproducing the systems that perpetuate injustice. When we write "institutions" here, rather than thinking about individual organizations (like a single hospital, for example), we are analyzing aspects of a broader system of which that organization might be one small part (like the health care system of which that one hospital is part, to use the same analogy). So, even if researchers focus on a case study set in one site, it is important to examine that site as part of a larger network, and as impacted by our social structures. Doing this allows researchers to identify broader social patterns that are involved in perpetuating inequalities.

In particular, researchers using institutional ethnography give attention to three key interdependent aspects of how social institutions are part of everyday life. First, we consider the official policies and texts related to these institutions. What are the official discourses, rules, or regulations that govern how members of the public interact with this institution? Which of these rules are explicit— social norms or official policies that are known and discussed—and which are present in our lives, but rarely acknowledged? What kind of social order do these rules and official texts or discourses appear to maintain? Second, it is crucial to document the actual practices associated with the institution being studied. Institutional ethnographers ask what can be learned by observing the everyday practices of doing the work associated with the institution. How do those implementing this work perform their duties? What kind of discretion do they exercise in how they allocate resources, advantage, and opportunity? What are the ways in which ideas about race, class, gender, or other social categories seem to be enacted or performed in the practices associated with this institution? Finally, researchers pay attention to the perspectives and experiences of those members/workers of the institution they're studying. How do these individuals make meaning and understand their work and the nature of their association with an institution? How do they see themselves and others in relation to this institution?

By studying how practice, experience, and discourse are intertwined, we can begin to document and better understand how power operates in ways that maintain inequalities.

Power Mapping

Although the previous two tools are particularly useful to facilitate collective understanding of power, inequality, and social problems, it is not always easy or clear how to proceed toward making change. Taking the previous two methods as an example, once we have developed a sense of how inequality is produced and maintained, how do we go about using that information to make social change? Who should our audience be? Should we target the broader public, or is there a key individual who can effect change?

Power mapping, sometimes called power analysis, is a great tool that can help researchers deepen their understanding of how different sources of power relate to one another and what it might take to change a problematic situation. It is also a method on which social scientists have relied to understand how groups see themselves in relation to others (e.g., Noy, 2008). While there are many ways to map out power relations, the method involves identifying the actors who are relevant to a particular problem and assessing how much power they have over resources and decision making, and their relationship with each other, and with the issue itself. A common version of a power map identifies who allies and opponents are in relation to the problem (see Figure 16.1). This helps a researcher or an organization strategize about who they can influence and, therefore, where they should direct their efforts.

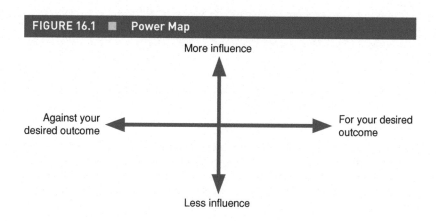

FIGURE 16.1 ■ Power Map

As a research method, doing power mapping in a participatory way with a community or an organization not only helps foster understanding of how actors see themselves amidst unjust conditions. The method can also be a first step in designing a research project; the map can identify who the audience is, the most relevant way to frame an issue to affect that audience, and the particular kinds of information or data that need to be gathered to produce an influential study or campaign. Darren Noy (2008) writes about his experience using power mapping to understand how politics in San Francisco impacted the homeless population. While he relied on complex methods to generate his map in order to produce social theory about the relationship between homelessness, ideology, and policy making, he utilized this research to offer useful power maps to organizations advocating for, and mobilizing, the homeless population in the San Francisco area. Among other insights, his maps helped organizations think about how to "more effectively use relationships, networks, and channels of information" in their social change work (Noy, 2008, p. 8).

Interpretive Focus Groups/Check-Ins

Once data have been gathered through the method of choice, a researcher is faced with the task of analyzing and interpreting their results. This involves organizing the data into variables or themes that researchers can then make sense of. In quantitative research, we have to take the raw data—sometimes hundreds or thousands of responses to survey questions—and turn them into variables that can be used to identify trends or to create measures of difference. In qualitative research, data often consist of field notes and/or transcripts from interviews. Organizing this mass of words, answers, and stories into themes and topics helps us to tease out patterns and to understand how participants make meaning of a particular situation. Traditionally, this work rested firmly under the authority and control of the researcher.

More recently, however, we have witnessed an increasing push to consider the views of those who participated in the study and those who are affected by the issue in question (e.g., Lincoln & Guba, 2000). Scholars increasingly recognize that they benefit when participants, community members, or those affected by the issue being studied are involved in the data analysis process. Interpretive focus groups (IFGs) offer a means to include relevant actors' views (Dodson et al., 2007). IFG, also called "member checking," involves presenting and discussing initial analysis with relevant actors—sometimes the folks who participated in interviews or surveys, themselves—in order to assess how accurate and significant findings are in their view. This tool has helped many researchers correct misunderstandings, fill in gaps, and often yields a whole new and rich body of data about the issue being studied.

CONSIDER THIS...

How do the specific tools outlined in this section seem to center the voices of historically underrepresented populations? How are these methods tied to possible social justice outcomes?

DOING SOCIOLOGY 16.4

Designing Your Own Power Map

In this exercise, you will create a power map based on a case study of an advocacy campaign to secure driver's licenses for undocumented immigrants.

Read the following case summary

In their effort to secure the right for undocumented immigrants to apply for driver's licenses in Massachusetts, advocates and state lawmakers are pushing for passage of the "Work and Family Mobility Act." Although the bill has widespread support among immigrant justice organizations, like the Massachusetts Immigrant and Refugee Advocacy Coalition (MIRA) and

Cosecha, and though the bill has strong cosponsorship support in the state house among state senators and representatives, it will be a tough legislative battle to win. Lawmakers in support of this bill argue that one's ability to drive has nothing to do with their legal status, that this bill is about quality of life, safety, and access to opportunity for people who are in our communities as students, workers, neighbors, family members, friends, and more. They also stress that with a federal government that has been largely inactive—or anti-immigrant, under certain administrations—when it comes to solving a broken immigration system, it falls to the states to pass such laws. Advocacy organizations stress that it is unjust to force immigrants to decide between meeting the basic needs of their families and the risk of driving without a license. Representatives of the local chapter of the SEIU (Service Employees International Union) also stood up for this bill, recognizing that many of their union members and their families are undocumented. The Massachusetts Major City Chiefs of Police Association also got behind this bill, arguing for its economic and safety benefits.

Despite this support, Massachusetts governor Charlie Baker has indicated that he would veto this bill if it came across his desk. Baker, and other opponents to the bill, argue that it is difficult to verify the identity of undocumented immigrants, and allowing them to have driver's licenses would create opportunities for fraud. Although this bill has been circulating the state legislature for 18 years, the issue has received renewed media, lawmaker, and advocate attention during the COVID-19 pandemic.

(adapted from Lisinski, 2020):

Now, considering the case, imagine you are creating a power map like that seen in Figure 16.1. Answer the following questions:

1. Where would you put "media" on your power map? Why?

2. Who else that isn't mentioned in the case study do you think could either help oppose the bill or persuade the governor to support the Work and Family Mobility Act? Where would you put them on the map?

3. Where would you put students like yourself on the power map? What kind of power do you think you have to oppose or advocate for a law like this?

4. Based on the driver's license campaign discussed, the actors involved, and their attitudes toward the campaign and the proposed bill, what are two issues or topics that would be relevant for a social justice researcher to explore to get further information?

Check Your Understanding

1. What is institutional ethnography, and how can researchers use this when pursuing social justice research?
2. What are some of the ways you could use power mapping to use research findings for advocacy?
3. In what ways does using interpretive focus groups bring greater accountability into the research process?

CONCLUSION

In this chapter, you have learned that social justice lies at the heart of the discipline of sociology. It is part of our commitment to use the "Sociological Eye" and the tools of research to make a difference in the world around us. Sociology has a long history of looking into and exposing social problems around the world, using a variety of methods for this. This chapter has introduced core concepts and terminology associated with social justice work and brought together many of the different ways that sociologists are practicing social justice work in the way they do research. We have looked historically at early 20th-century sociologists as well as scholars today who have sought to infuse their methods with principles of social justice. Such principles include inquiry into the nature of power and inequality and a commitment to social change.

Sociologists have relied on these as they carry out research that treats participants with dignity and that aims to achieve both small-scale and large-scale social change. We encourage you to think about how you might integrate these principles in your sociological research. What problems do you see out there that you would like to address? With whom can you partner in your community to tackle those issues? What research method can help you in that work, and how can you practice democracy and equality as you carry out your research? There are many ways to have an impact in the world. Being a sociologist committed to social justice can open the door to a fulfilling career at the heart of movements that are working to make society more equitable and sustainable.

REVIEW

16.1. What are the historical roots of social justice research in sociology?

Since the early years of the 20th century, sociologists have worked to identify social patterns and analyze how contemporary issues fit within their social and historical context. Sociologists like Jane Addams and W. E. B. DuBois used research to document how people of color, women, immigrants, and the working class experienced inequality in U.S. society. They started organizations to advocate for social justice and made sure their research reached the public and elected officials. These sociologists and many others can be considered foundational thinkers when it comes to using research to call for social change.

16.2. What are the main goals of social justice research?

Sociologists working toward social justice are often focused on identifying and analyzing social problems, disseminating their research to members of the wider public (public sociology), and contributing to the work of social movements. Uncovering and documenting inequalities and other forms of injustice can constitute important evidence that policy makers and members of the wider public can use to push for change. Often, when enough members of the public are mobilized and organized in their call for change, this can produce a social movement.

16.3. What are the key concepts for doing social justice research?

While social justice researchers can rely on different methods, there are some concepts that are common to this approach. Social justice research is generally focused on forms of power and oppression, including those that generate inequities in our world. This includes social constructivism, i.e., thinking about how forms of inequality are produced as a consequence of our history, cultural norms, and political systems. It also includes intersectionality; that is, how various forms of oppression intersect with one another and compound the experience of power and privilege. Social justice research also often explores aspects of how members of our society work together for basic freedoms and equality. A third feature of social justice in sociology considers alternative ways of organizing our society that are more just. A last concept commonly found in sociology's approach to social justice is an emphasis on doing research that empowers participants and supports their struggles for rights and equality.

16.4. How do sociologists use institutional ethnography, power mapping, and interpretive focus groups in social justice research?

These are three tools that social justice researchers have used to explore inequalities and use their research to advocate for change. Institutional ethnography explores the relationships and processes for maintaining and reproducing the systems that perpetuate injustice. This tool is an approach for studying those with power and how such power is reproduced and maintained. A power map identifies who allies and opponents are in relation to a social problem, and considers their relationship to each other and to those seeking to make change. Researchers often deploy the interpretive focus group discussion as a way to share and discuss initial findings from data analysis with those who are directly impacted by the topic of study. This discussion helps to assess how authentic the research is in the eyes of concerned communities.

KEY TERMS

civic engagement (p. 307)

institutional ethnography (p. 312)

interpretive focus groups (p. 314)

intersectionality (p. 308)

organic public sociology (p. 304)

power mapping (p. 313)

public sociology (p. 304)

reflexivity (p. 310)

social constructivism (p. 308)

social justice research (p. 302)

systemic alternatives (p. 307)

traditional public sociology (p. 304)

GLOSSARY

academic conference presentations: Gatherings at which sociologists present their findings to a live audience during a formal presentation.

academic journals: Publications that feature scientific articles describing their research question, hypotheses, methods, analyses, and findings.

account: Researchers doing fieldwork need to be able to provide an account, or a narrative, to other people for why they are there, and what they are doing while there, and what they plan to do afterward.

activities: The steps that programs will take as part of the implementation of a new program or policy.

additional: An approach to mixed methods research in which researchers answer different (but related) research questions paired with each method. We might symbolize this as: qualitative + quantitative.

agenda for action: A plan for implementing the lessons learned from CBR.

analysis of existing statistics: The use of quantitative data that have already been collected by someone else and applying them to study something from a sociological perspective.

analytic coding: A technique where the researcher searches for conceptual or theoretical categories in the data.

analytical sampling: Researchers use analytical sampling to systematically focus on collecting and assessing data from particular types of cases that will help them investigate a social problem from multiple vantage points (*see* critical cases, deviant cases, and typical cases).

analyzing data: Making sense of the information that has been gathered about the social world.

analyzing exceptions, or negative cases: A technique within grounded theory where the researcher analyzes data that do not support or appear to contradict patterns emerging in the data. This is used to refine an analysis until it can explain or account for a majority of cases.

anonymously: A situation in which researchers themselves do not know the names, addresses, or other identifying information of the people providing the data.

applied research: Research conducted with the goal of having practical use regarding problems and issues in society today.

applied sociologists (public sociologists): Sociologists who disseminate their findings to policy makers, community organizations, and local citizens.

arraying data: An analytic technique in which the researcher creates graphical representations of codes and concepts.

audit study: A type of field experiment where members of the research team engage in social activities outside of the laboratory in real-world settings, each performing a slight variation on otherwise identical roles, in order to detect different responses.

ballot-stuffing: When a single respondent completes multiple surveys. More common in online surveys that do not use an individualized link.

Belmont Report: Published in 1979, this extensive report serves as the blueprint for the ways in which scientists conduct social and biomedical research today.

beneficence: Ethical principle detailed in *Belmont Report* that specifies that research does not harm the individual, and that it maximizes possible benefits and minimizes possible harms.

bivariate tables: Also known as "cross-tabulations" or "crosstabs," these are tables showing the relationship between two variables. Typically, they present frequencies within each cell, along with a column or row percent.

blinding: The condition where participants do not know whether they are included in the treatment or control group.

bourgeoisie: Wealthy capitalists who own the technology and resources to make things.

capacity: The knowledge, time, resources, and people-power that an organization can dedicate to a research project.

case study approach: A method that focuses on a particular unit, called a case—this can be a person, a site, a project, etc. The researchers try to learn as much as possible about the case, via a variety of methods with a variety of participants.

cases: The specific people, groups, or objects from which data are collected for a specific research study.

categories: Groupings that you impose on the coded segments in order to reduce the number of different pieces of data and develop a broader sense of the data.

civic engagement: Individual and group efforts to advocate for democratic principles and to address issues of public concern.

class position: One's economic situation.

climate surveys: A type of survey designed to measure feelings of support and belonging. Often used in workplaces, schools, and other institutions.

closed-ended questions: Questions that specify answer choices; the researcher provides a set of answers from which the respondent chooses.

codebook: A document, either in print or online, that describes the dataset in detail, including information about the sampling strategy, the mode of data collection (e.g., in person, online, or by telephone), and information about how to code all variables included in the dataset.

coding fetishism: A pitfall of coding in which a researcher codes or counts compulsively rather than reflecting on and memoing on their data.

coding sheet: A sheet of paper or electronic document that is a matrix in which you code data for content analysis. Each row of data on the coding sheet is all of the information for one variable. Each column of data includes the data for one variable.

coding: The process of identifying a word or phrase (a label, or "code") to summarize and capture the meaning of small chunks of data.

cohort data: A type of longitudinal data that involves collecting the same information from different generations (or age-cohorts) over multiple points in time; the data collection must be timed so that each later generation/cohort is contacted at the same age as the earlier ones were when they participated in the study.

collecting data: Gathering information about the social world.

collective risk: The possibility that a research project might cause harm for groups, organizations, and society as a whole.

column percent: In a frequency table, the percent of observations in a column that falls into a particular row.

community advisory boards (CAB): Also called community advisory groups, these are comprised of community members, key stakeholders, and academics; established to ensure that research is mutually beneficial, a variety of community voices are heard, diverse constituencies are adequately represented, community members are adequately protected, and there is an ongoing dialogue between researchers and the community.

community organizing: The coordination of community members to promote community interests.

community-based research (CBR)/community action research: A type of applied research where sociologists work in collaboration with community members to address problems or issues facing that community.

complete observer: As a complete observer during fieldwork, you want to have as little effect on what is happening as possible, since you are just hanging out as an audience member witnessing the activity or setting being studied.

computer-assisted qualitative analysis software (CAQDAS): A term that refers to the wide range of software that supports a variety of analytic styles in qualitative research.

conceptualization: To think carefully about the meaning of each of the concepts in the research question and hypotheses, and to specify precisely what each one means.

confidential: A situation in which researchers know the identities of the people involved in a research project, but do not disclose the names and other identifying information of the participants.

confirmation bias: Focusing on our own beliefs and values, rather than evidence.

conflict theory: A theoretical perspective that focuses on the strife that institutions and social patterns create in society.

conflicts of interest: Failure to report any financial relationship (or sponsorship) researcher(s) share with the individuals or organizations they are studying.

constant comparison: A technique within grounded theory where the researcher compares different pieces of data against each other to test for similarities and differences.

construct validity: A concept describing how well a measure (e.g., survey questions) captures the phenomenon for which they are designed.

construct: The concept for which a measure (e.g., survey questions) is designed, such as attitudes, personal characteristics, or experiences.

content analysis: The systematic analysis of cultural products—print, visual, and electronic.

context evaluation: An evaluative study that aims to clarify a program or policy's position in the larger social context, with attention to the needs, assets, and resources of a community or organization.

continuous quality improvement: Programs working to refine their implementation as they go to offer improved performance or outcomes.

control group: The experimental group that receives a placebo.

control variable: An independent variable that is included in the analysis in order to determine whether a relationship between two variables holds true when variation in a third variable (that is, the control variable) is held constant.

convenience sampling: Researchers build their samples through a process of convenience sampling when they recruit research participants that they can access efficiently. The focus is on recruiting a sample that is sufficient to address the research questions, but it is not necessarily systematic or representative of the target population.

convergent: An approach to mixed methods research in which researchers use the same research question for both quantitative and qualitative research. We might symbolize this as qualitative = quantitative.

correlation: A measure describing the extent to which two variables are related to each other. If an increase in one variable is associated with an increase in another, we can say there is a positive correlation between the two. If an increase in one variable is associated with a decrease in another variable, then there is a negative correlation.

coverage error: Error introduced into surveys when the sampling frame used for the survey does not include all relevant or eligible individuals.

covert participant: Researchers doing fieldwork may choose not to disclose their identities as researchers but instead operate covertly as a participant. Those with whom they interact may not know that they are being observed for the purposes of research because the researcher is actively involved in the activity or setting being studied.

critical cases: Critical cases are unusually rich in information pertaining to the research question. They are selected for their uniqueness when using analytical sampling.

cross-sectional: Data where information has been collected from research subjects at only one point in time.

cues: Words in survey questions that may trigger memories relevant to the question.

cultural competence: The knowledge, skills, and experiences that people or organizations have that enable them to practice culturally sensitive behaviors, attitudes, and policies.

cultural competency: The knowledge, skills, and experiences that people or organizations have that enable them to practice culturally sensitive behaviors, attitudes, and policies.

cultural humility: An approach to community work and research that emphasizes an awareness of power imbalances, self-reflection, and supportive interactions.

cycle of research: The process of conducting sociological research, in which descriptive research is used to develop an understanding of social life, theories are developed based on that description, and the theories are then tested through explanatory research.

dataset: A collection of data assembled for a particular purpose. Datasets usually take the form of spreadsheets or databases.

deductive questions: Questions that start with a theoretical premise that a researcher hopes to verify by examining specific observations in the social world.

dependent variables: Variables that sociologists expect to be changed by something else.

descriptive coding: A technique where the researcher labels the data with descriptive demographic information in order to identify group similarities and differences.

descriptive research: Research conducted with the goal of documenting and describing a social phenomenon.

Developmental evaluation: a type of process evaluation where the evaluator intentionally interacts with the implementation teams of the evaluand to improve program outcomes and to support continuous quality improvement.

deviant cases: Deviant cases stick out in contrast to typical cases. These types of cases are not the focus of the research; rather, the case is used as a critical comparison when using analytical sampling.

direct probes: Direct probes focus on clarifying what an interviewee said by asking the participant to directly expand on an answer they provided during an interview.

disassembling: The act of taking fragments of the data apart and unpacking the meanings of the smaller fragments; similar to doing a close reading in poetry.

disproportionate stratified sample: A type of probability sample in which the proportions of the sample in each designated strata are not equal to those that appear in the larger population.

double-blind: The condition where the specific researchers who measure the outcomes do not know whether participants have received the treatment or placebo. This prevents them from biased outcomes based on their desire for the treatment to have an effect. Other researchers on the team will have kept the necessary data about which participants received the treatment in order to allow for the necessary group comparison to be made.

double-barreled questions: Survey questions that unintentionally include more than one construct. These types of questions make it difficult to determine which construct is being measured.

emotional labor: The process in which workers summon socially expected feelings (and not others) in themselves, their coworkers, and their clients.

empirical data: Observations about the social world that are made using our five senses.

empirical questions: Questions you can answer with scientific data; you can use the steps of the research process to arrive at an answer to the question.

error: The difference between the true information we intend to collect and the actual information gathered.

ethnographer: A qualitative researcher who provides vivid and precise descriptions of the social world.

ethnographic research, or ethnography: The study of people within the context of their social setting. Researchers immerse themselves in a specific group, organization, or community for an extended period of time to collect detailed, accurate, holistic data on all that they observe.

eugenics: The study of how to arrange reproduction within a human population to increase the occurrence of heritable characteristics regarded as desirable.

evaluand: The subject of an evaluation (i.e., the person, program, policy, or product being evaluated).

evaluation research: An application of social science; the process used to monitor and measure changes that individuals, communities, and organizations make. Information collected during an evaluation helps to inform learning, decision making, and quality improvement. Conducted within specific organizational and political contexts, which themselves are the object of study.

evaluative thinking: Critical thinking used in the process of evaluation research motivated by an attitude of inquisitiveness and a belief in the value of evidence.

exhaustive: When *every* respondent can find a category that describes their answer to a closed-ended question.

exhaustive coding categories: Cover all of the possible cases that apply to that variable.

experiment: A way of designing research that allows us to answer a question by detecting causal relationships.

experimental studies: a research design in which two or more groups are assigned to either placebo or experimental conditions of an independent variable. A pottest is used to compare the outcomes of the groups.

explanatory research: The goal of explanatory research is to demonstrate a relationship between two or more variables, asking whether or not variation in one variable explains changes in another variable.

exploratory research: The goal of exploratory research is to do preliminary data collection and analysis in an area where very little previous research exists because the topic is new, unstudied, or understudied.

extended case method: Researchers adopting the extended case method typically use ethnographic data to test hypotheses formulated in other research. Existing social theory drives not only the research question but also the case selection, data collection, and analysis.

external, or third-party, evaluation: An evaluation conducted by an outsider to the organization implementing a program or policy.

face validity: This is a type of validity that asks, "On the face of it, does this variable seem to be measuring what it proposed to measure?"

Feminist Symbolic Interactionism: A theoretical perspective that critically analyzes how gender roles and inequalities—as they intersect with racism, heterosexism, and class inequality—are produced, challenged, and reproduced in social interaction.

field experiment: When experimental designs are applied outside of the laboratory to analyze real-world social processes.

field notes: Written or recorded descriptions systematically capturing what the researcher hears, observes, and otherwise experiences during fieldwork.

Final Disposition Code: A code assigned to each respondent indicating the outcome of the survey. These often designate whether the survey was completed, refused, or if the contacted respondent was ineligible to participate.

focus groups: Group interviews with a facilitator leading multiple participants in a discussion of a particular issue, object, or phenomenon.

forced response: When a survey question does not have the option for respondents to select "don't know" or "no opinion," and, instead, forces them to state a directional opinion. Another type of forced response is when a respondent does not have the option to skip a question in an online survey.

formative evaluation: An evaluation that occurs early in the design or implementation of a new program or policy. It can be used to define the problem the program addresses, and/or assess the feasibility of the proposed solution.

frequency distribution: A table or chart that shows the response categories for each variable, as well as the number and/or percentage responses that fall into each category of the variable.

FRUGGING: Fund-raising Under the Guise of conducting a survey. This occurs when fund-raising attempts are portrayed as survey research in order to gain people's trust and influence them to donate.

functionalism: A theoretical perspective that argues that society is composed of interrelated systems that shape and constrain individuals, and in so doing, help create, maintain, and stabilize that society.

funder client model: An evaluation where the evaluator is hired directly by the organization funding the project.

gatekeeper: Someone who can help the researcher gain access to a field site that requires permission, either formal or informal, to enter; a key participant who is known and respected in a community and can provide information about the community, identify potential participants, and build trust between participants and researchers.

generalizability: The ability to apply (or generalize) findings from the sample to the larger population from which they were selected.

grand tour questions: Interviewers use broad sweeping grand tour questions to elicit lengthy narratives from interviewees in order to engage them in the topic of interest.

Grounded Theory: The researcher works inductively, starting with observations, moves to empirical generalizations, and finally creates a theoretical explanation for patterns in the data. Researchers try to bracket their theoretical guide and enter into their fieldwork with the goal of understanding participants on their own terms.

group level: The group-level perspective in focus groups is when researchers assess viewpoints among the group, and it provides an opportunity to unearth points of consensus or tension among all the participants as a collective.

Hawthorne effect: This refers to the fact that people may change aspects of their behavior simply because they know they are being observed.

hierarchical array: An analytic technique in which the researcher maps codes or categories into arrays organized in different levels or hierarchies, with data from more general categories at the top to more specific categories or subsets at the bottom.

history: The set of common events experienced by participants of both the treatment and control group during the experiment. Except for receipt of the treatment or placebo, this should be the same for both groups.

human subject: A living individual about whom an investigator (whether professional or student) is conducting research.

Human Subjects Research: Obtaining identifiable private information through intervention or interaction with an individual.

hypothesis: An unverified but testable statement that a researcher believes represents a potential answer to their research question.

impact evaluation: An evaluation that examines the program's effectiveness in the bigger picture, typically including the intended and unintended consequences of the project in the long term.

impacts: The long-term results of the program implementation, typically after the program has concluded.

implementation team: The person or group of people putting a program into action.

in vivo coding: A type of coding where the researcher utilizes the actual words of people or images themselves.

inconvenient sample: A sample designed to specifically challenge prevailing theories or dominant beliefs about the topic being studied.

independent variables: Variables that sociologists believe will impact some aspect of the social world; things expected to cause a change in something else.

index: When several different measures are *added* together to create a combined score for a particular concept.

indirect probes: Probes that focus on clarifying what an interviewee said by using neutral utterances such as "uh-huh," "mm-hmm," or "interesting" to indicate the interviewer is listening without steering the conversation in one direction or another.

individual level: The individual-level perspective in focus groups is when researchers assess distinct viewpoints held by each participant within a group conversation to understand how individuals articulate their thoughts in a group setting.

inductive questions: Questions that result from specific observations of facts that a researcher thinks might point to a general tendency.

inductive reasoning: An approach where a researcher begins with specific observations or raw data and develops generalizations that help explain the observed data through repeated examination and comparison.

inference: Describing the characteristics of a population by using a representative sample of that population.

informed consent forms: Documents that provide details of the research study—all aspects of the research design, risks and benefits of participation, and possible compensation.

informed consent: A situation wherein research subjects are made aware of procedures for and potential risks and benefits associated with a research study.

inputs: The resources that implementation teams can draw upon to make their programs work.

input evaluation: the process of collecting information about a project, and analyzing competing strategies, work plans, and budgets.

institutional ethnography: A method that uses observation and interviews to explore the relationships and processes within institutions for maintaining and reproducing the systems that perpetuate injustice.

institutional review board: A unit within a university or other research organization that reviews all research proposals and determines whether they provide sufficient informed consent, pose a risk to research subjects (and if the project minimizes such risks), and if they adhere to all existing ethical standards.

integration: How the findings from one method will be integrated with the findings from the other method.

interactive level: The interactive-level perspective in focus groups is when researchers narrow in on participant dynamics that emerge throughout the conversation—what unexpected interactions occur among the participants when a particular question is raised or a topic comes up.

intercoder reliability: The main way of reporting the reliability of measurements in content analysis. Two or more coders double-code the same set of cases, then calculate the number of times they agreed/the number of cases they double-coded x 100. This yields a percentage score of intercoder reliability.

internal evaluation: An evaluation conducted by members of the organization that is implementing a program or policy. This contrasts with external evaluation, where a neutral third party conducts the evaluation.

interpretative questions: Interpretative interview questions encourage the interviewee to assess a scenario or informational statement related to the interview topic.

interpretive focus groups: The practice of taking a study's results back to those with direct experience with the issue/problem being investigated so that they can discuss the accuracy and relevance of the findings

interquartile range: The distance between the 25th and 75th percentile on a particular variable. Also called IQR.

intersectionality: A theoretical framework for understanding how various forms of oppression intersect with one another and compound the experience of power and privilege.

intersubjectivity: When many researchers look at the social world and compare and contrast their findings in order to ascertain the consistencies and inconsistencies across their findings.

interview guide: A written list of questions and potential probes in a particular order; researchers often use them when conducting semistructured interviews.

interviewer effects: When responses to surveys are influenced by the characteristics or behaviors of interviewers.

introductory questions: Interview questions that are easy to answer for the respondent and often focus on gathering descriptive information about the interviewee.

item nonresponse error: An inaccuracy in survey results caused by differences between respondents who skip a given question in the survey and those who do not.

iterative: An iterative process is when researchers move back and forth between data collection and data analysis to refine their theory and hypotheses. In qualitative work, a process involving multiple steps of asking questions, reflection, and memoing.

justice: Ethical principle detailed in *Belmont Report* that specifies that benefits and burdens should be shared equally, and carefully scrutinized in instances when they are not (e.g., when benefits accrue to the wealthy but burdens are borne by the poor).

key informant: A person in the field who can provide "behind the scenes" insight into the interactions and other elements of social life that a researcher is observing.

key stakeholders: Those who deal with the issue most directly and, perhaps, in ways that are most interesting to the researchers.

latent content: Underlying meaning and content that require interpretation.

literature review: a section of writing, usually found at the beginning of a research article, that outlines theoretical perspectives and findings from previously published literature

logic model: A visual map of the inputs and activities in a program, and how they will lead to outputs, outcomes, and impacts that the implementation team desires.

longitudinal: Data where information is collected over multiple points in time.

macro approach: A perspective that focuses on large-scale entities and institutions, like the economy, politics, law, and education.

manifest content: Content that is on the surface—obvious and clear, and that does not require much interpretation to code.

margin of error: A measure of uncertainty in estimates generated from a sample.

matrix: An analytic technique in which the researcher creates rectangular arrays in rows and columns, such as a 2 x 2 table, with data entered in each cell.

mean: The arithmetic average for a particular variable.

measurement error: Inaccuracies in survey responses caused by question wording or response options.

measurement validity: A type of measurement quality that focuses on accuracy.

measurement: The process of assessing social phenomena through survey construction.

measures of central tendency: Measures that describe what is typical or central for a variable.

measures of variation: Measures describing the distribution and variability of a variable.

mechanism: The theorized relationship between the independent and dependent variables.

media literate: Being able to understand the ways in which various media operate so that one is not misled by claims made in mediated communication,

median: The value of the variable for the middle-most observation, when the observations are ordered from greatest to least or least to greatest on that variable.

memoing: The act of writing reflective notes about what patterns and themes you are seeing in your data.

memorandum of understanding (MOU): A non-legally binding document that clearly lays out expectations and protections for all parties involved in the research.

micro approach: A perspective that emphasizes individual-level and group-level interaction.

mixed methods research: An approach to research that integrates quantitative methods (e.g., surveys) and qualitative methods (e.g., interviews) in the same research project.

mode effects: Survey error arising from the way in which the survey is conducted, such as face-to-face, computer-assisted personal interviews, or mail surveys.

mode: The value of the response category that contains the largest number of observations.

multistage cluster sampling: A type of probability sample in which cluster sampling occurs at two or more stages rather than just the first stage.

multivariate analyses: Analyses that include multiple independent variables in addition to the dependent variable.

mutually exclusive: When a respondent is able to classify themselves into *one* category only in a closed-ended question.

mutually exclusive coding categories: Coding categories that do not overlap.

necessary conditions: Conditions or states of being that must exist in order for the dependent outcome to occur. For example, completing coursework is a necessary condition for earning a degree. Not everyone who completes coursework receives a degree, but if someone doesn't complete any courses they can't earn one.

negative correlation: A relationship between two variables where an increase in one variable is associated with an increase in the other.

nonempirical questions: Questions that cannot be answered scientifically and tend to be more opinion-based.

nonprobability sample: A sampling technique in which the probability of inclusion for any particular case is unknown. Sampling techniques are not grounded in mathematical principles of probability.

nonresponse bias: Error that occurs when not all selected respondents participate in the survey or answer all questions in a survey.

nonspuriousness: The condition where there are no additional, external variables that can explain the observed relationship between the independent and dependent variables.

objective: Being able to see the social world without relying on one's emotions, values, or beliefs.

open-ended questions: Questions that do not have any pre-specified response categories; the person answering the questions come up with their own answers, rather than picking from a list of answers.

operational definitions: Definitions that specify precisely how each abstract concept is measured; researchers specify exactly how each concept in their study is represented in their data.

operationalization: The process of creating a definition that specifies precisely how an abstract concept is measured.

optimizers: The opposite of satisfiers. Optimizers are respondents who read each question thoroughly, deeply consider their answers, and do their best to provide the most accurate responses possible.

Organic Public Sociology: Research conducted through collaboration with concerned groups and communities to address social injustice, and published in ways that are accessible to the public.

outcome evaluation: An evaluation that examines the concrete results of a program, typically upon completion, and often in statistical terms (e.g., number of people served).

outcomes: The specific benefits that program participants experience, both short- and long-term, by participating in the program.

outlying observations: Observations that are far beyond the typical values a variable takes on.

outputs: Products that will directly result from program implementation; the specific changes you will see in program participants, and can be broken down into short-term outcomes (typically within 1–3 years of program completion) and long-term outcomes (4–8 years after program completion).

overt participant: Researchers doing fieldwork may choose to be known to the participants as researchers in order to explicitly ask questions and check whether they have correctly interpreted what is being said, expressed, or done in a setting.

panel data: A type of longitudinal data that involves collecting data from the same research subjects over multiple time points.

parameter: A specific measure used to describe the population, such as the population mean.

participant observation: A type of ethnographic research designed to gain a close and intimate familiarity with a given group of individuals and their practices. Researchers both participate and observe.

party position: One's access to special interest groups, such as unions, lobbies, and political associations.

peer review: A process that academic journal articles go through before publication, in which they are evaluated by experts on the topic. Sociologists scrutinize another author's research methods and findings, point out weaknesses, and make suggestions for improvements.

periodicity: A characteristic or property that repeats in some sort of interval pattern. It is a concern associated with systematic random sampling.

placebo: The nontreatment (e.g., pill with no drug) given to the control group.

placebo effect: The effect on the outcome that results from participants thinking that they might have received the treatment, regardless of whether they actually did.

plagiarism: Presenting the words or ideas of another person without giving them credit.

population: All of the elements (e.g., individuals, groups, organizations, social artifacts, etc.) that could be included in a study depending on what the research is about.

positive correlation: A relationship between two variables where an increase in one variable is associated with an increase in the other.

power mapping: An analytical tool often used for advocacy that plots actors that are relevant to a particular problem and assesses how they relate to each other and how much power they have over resources and decision making.

priority: The method that is more important or central, as used in some mixed method research designs.

probabilistic causality: The condition where an independent variable affects the likelihood or level of a dependent outcome but can produce varied results.

probability sample: A sampling technique in which the elements of the sample (people, objects, schools, newspaper articles, etc.) are chosen based on principles grounded in mathematical chance.

probability sampling: A type of sampling procedure where every member in the target population has a known and nonzero probability of being selected for the survey. Probability sampling can be used to generate representative samples and the results of surveys based on probability samples can be generalized to the population as a whole.

probes: Additional questions used during an interview to further explore an interviewee's answers.

process evaluation: An evaluation that monitors, documents, and assesses program activities during the program's implementation.

processing error: Error caused by mistakes made by respondents or interviewers in the collection of surveys, such as through checking the wrong response to a survey question or when multiple researchers inconsistently code survey responses.

program client model: An evaluation where the program hires its own evaluator.

Program evaluation: The application of evaluation research to studying social programs.

proletariat: The workers who do not own the means of production under capitalism.

propensity score matching: A popular statistical method that pairs demographically similar participants and nonparticipants to determine whether a program yields better outcomes for those who participate.

proportional stratified sample: A type of probability sample in which the proportions of the sample in each designated strata are the same as those that appear in the larger population.

public sociologist: A sociologist who engages with topics of public concern and disseminates findings to a wider, nonacademic audience.

push polls: "Survey-like" contacts typically with a large number of people that are designed to change public opinion rather than to measure it. They are often designed to expose respondents to information or narratives that would sway their opinion.

qualitative content analysis: A research tool that focuses on interpreting and describing the text and visual images in media and communications. Using content analysis, we can group the data into categories and themes and ask, to what extent do these media images accurately reflect and/or stereotype social realities?

qualitative methods: Research methods that use thematic analysis and present data in the form of text, observations, and/or quotes. Examples of qualitative methods include interviews; focus groups; content analysis or discourse analysis; and ethnography, observation, or fieldwork.

qualitative: Data used by sociologists that consist of language, such as descriptions or narratives.

quantifying: The process of turning qualitative data into numerical data.

quantitative content analysis: Refers to analyses that turn the results into numbers.

quantitative methods: Research methods that include statistical analysis of numeric data (generally performed using statistical software) with results typically presented in the form of tables and figures. Examples of qualitative methods include surveys, experiments, and quantitative content analysis.

quantitative: Data used by sociologists that consist of numbers and categories.

quartile: The first, second, third, or fourth quarter of the distribution of a variable.

quasi-experimental studies: A form of quantitative study often used when random assignment is not possible, which uses statistical methods to match similar groups of people to simulate an experiment.

random assignment: A procedure by which participants in an experiment are placed into either the placebo condition or the experimental condition by chance

range: The distance between the value of the largest and smallest observation.

rapport: A feeling of good-will and trust that is created when the person being interviewed feels comfortable with the process and the interviewer.

reassembling: The act of reassembling the smaller data fragments in new ways to form a larger analytic story.

recoding: The act of fine-tuning your codes and developing new ones.

recruitment: The process of soliciting participants for an experiment.

recursive: A process that involves back-and-forth cycles of coding, recoding, deleting or fine-tuning categories, creating new ones, and previewing or trying out ideas for upcoming phases of analysis.

referendum: A vote by a group of constituents about a single political issue.

reflexivity: When researchers reflect upon their own position in the field. This process helps others determine how a researcher's perspective may influence their reporting of how and what they did in the field. Researchers may consider and address their own social position relative to others, and within the broader social context, and use this to consider power and inequality in the research process.

reify: The process of coming to believe that humanly created, changing social forms are natural, universal, or fixed "things."

replicable: When studies that make observations about the social world are able to be reproduced, with largely the same conclusions.

representation: The degree to which a sample reflects characteristics of its respective population.

research subjects: The people being studied.

Respect for Persons: Ethical principle detailed in *Belmont Report* that specifies that researchers must protect the freedom of individuals to choose to participate in a study, and details the steps that must be taken to protect vulnerable populations, or those who are vulnerable or perhaps unable to freely choose to participate in a study (e.g., children or prisoners).

respondent-driven sampling: A nonprobability sample based in snowball sampling in which a researcher selects at least 5–10 sample participants, who then recruit additional study participants through their own personal networks.

response rate: The proportion of eligible cases that resulted in completed surveys.

retract: The process whereby journal editors issue formal notifications for potential readers that a study was deeply flawed and should be disregarded.

sample size: The overall number of respondents or artifacts to include in a sample.

sample: A subset of a given population.

sampling error: The discrepancy (or error) that exists between the characteristics of a sample and a population. Error is always involved when a sample is used instead of the entire population of interest. Uncertainty stemming from the sample is usually described through a margin of error that provides an estimated range within which the true population estimates will fall.

sampling frame: A list of all members of the population from which respondents are recruited (or artifacts are selected) and a sample is generated. Used typically in probability sampling.

sampling: The process used to identify and contact members of a population to be included in a survey.

satisficing: The tendency for some respondents to go through the process of answering questions quickly, incompletely, and with minimal effort in order to finish a survey as fast as possible.

saturation: The point in the data collection process that occurs when additional data collection yields little new information.

scales: When several different measures are first weighted, and then added together to create a combined score for a particular concept.

scatterplot: A graph representing the relationship between two (or sometimes more) variables, where each observation is represented by a dot or similar symbol. The independent variable is on the horizontal axis and the dependent variable is represented on the Y-axis.

scientific method: An empirical approach to gathering data about the world around us that relies on testing hypotheses using systematically collected data, resulting in potential theories that explain observed patterns.

self-plagiarism: When a researcher reproduces what they published previously, but present it as new, original research—without citing their previous work.

semi-structured interviews: Interviews that consist of a series of planned questions that are open-ended and allow the respondent to answer in their own words.

sequencing: The timing of data collection; in other words, which method will be used first.

sequential: An approach to mixed methods research in which the results of the first method inform the use of the second method. We might symbolize this approach as qualitative → quantitative or quantitative → qualitative.

Social Constructivism: A theory and methodological approach for looking into how our current social reality—including social hierarchies and social problems—is produced as a consequence of our history, cultural norms, and political systems.

social desirability bias: The tendency for respondents to answer survey questions in ways that portray themselves in a positive light, but are not entirely accurate.

social facts: Societal influences that shape individuals' behaviors.

social justice research: Research designed to shed light on historic and present-day inequalities and to bring about a more equitable and just world.

sociological questions: Questions that seek to understand the complex relationships between people and society.

sociological theory: Represents a set of background perspectives about how the social world operates.

sociology: The scientific study of society, including how society shapes individual people and groups, as well as how individual people and groups shape society.

stakeholders: Individuals, agencies, or community groups who have a stake, or interest, in the thing that is being evaluated—the outcome of the evaluation is meaningful and important to them, and often affects them directly. They may be interested in developing a solution.

standardized: The practice of conducting a survey as consistently as possible across respondents (e.g., question wording, order, presentation of response categories, etc.).

Stanford prison experiment: A study conducted by Philip Zimbardo in which he recruited and randomly assigned student volunteers to serve as "guards" and "inmates" to determine the impact of prison life.

Stanley Milgram: Social psychologist who, while at Yale University, conducted experiments to gauge subjects' obedience to authority.

statistic: A specific measure used to describe the sample, such as the sample mean.

status position: One's access to prestige and social honor.

structured interviews: Interviews comprised of standardized questions presented in a fixed order, along with a range of possible response options in a questionnaire format.

sufficient cause: An independent condition that always produced the outcome. For example, dropping out of school prevents earning a degree. Everyone who drops out will have this experience, though people can fail to earn degrees for other reasons, too.

SUGGING: Selling Under the Guise of conducting a survey. This occurs when attempts to sell something are portrayed as survey research in order to gain people's trust and influence them to purchase a product or service.

survey: A method of data collection in which research subjects are asked to respond to a series of questions that are purposely designed to elicit information about the researcher's topic of interest.

Symbolic Interactionism: A theoretical perspective in which repeated social interactions produce the meanings and hierarchies associated with socially constructed characteristics, events, and identities.

systematic data collection: Gathering observations about social life in a strategic and playful way.

systemic alternatives: Alternatives on a society-wide level to our current economic, political, and social system that have led to so much inequality and oppression.

tacit knowledge: Knowledge that comes from insights gained from observing unspoken practices by participants—sometimes so taken for granted by those who are doing it that they do not recognize it. It is a form of knowledge that requires close observation by researchers in order to capture.

temporal priority: The occurrence of the independent variable being studied prior in time to the dependent variable being studied.

themes: Higher levels of analysis, in which the researcher moves from an explicit description of the data to more implicit meanings or themes within those data. Themes are more general and abstract than categories, and they depend on the interpretation of the researcher rather than words explicitly used in the data.

theoretical saturation: A yardstick in grounded theory that indicates that sampling more data will not lead to more information related to the research questions. Typically, researchers see similar instances over and over again, which makes them empirically confident that their categories are accurate and data collection should be ended.

theory: Refers to the general or abstract principles associated with a particular discipline.

thick description: When ethnographic researchers describe the site and its participants with close attention to detail. The goal is to holistically understand the individuals or groups within one particular field site.

thinking up: A technique used in grounded theory where the researcher uses inductive reasoning to make generalizations from specific raw data points to build a more conceptual analysis of what the data symbolize about the social world.

topic coding: A technique where the researcher labels data with a salient word or phrase that grabs the reader.

Total Survey Error Framework: A framework used by researchers to evaluate all known sources of error in survey estimates from all possible causes, including survey design, data collection, and data analysis.

Traditional Public Sociology: The practice, in sociology, of doing research and writing up findings in ways that are accessible to a wider audience, including those adversely affected by an issue or those in a position to effect change.

transformative evaluation: A form of evaluation oriented toward social justice for marginalized peoples.

treatment: The term used to describe the independent variable being studied in an experiment.

treatment group: The experimental group that receives the treatment.

trend data: A type of longitudinal data that involves collecting the same information from the same population over multiple time points; however, different research subjects who are members of that population are contacted each time.

triangulation: The process of confirming findings by using different research methods.

Tuskegee study: A study that ran from 1932–1972 involving the recruitment of African American men from 1930–1970 from impoverished and rural Macon County, Alabama, for assessment of health impacts of untreated syphilis (sometimes referred to as the Tuskegee syphilis study).

typical cases: Typical cases are standard. These types of cases are the focus of the research when using analytical sampling.

Unit Nonresponse Error: Inaccuracies in survey results occurring when respondents who participate in the survey are different from those who do not.

unit of analysis: The type of thing that data are being collected about in sociological research, such as individuals, groups, or objects.

univariate statistic: A statistic that describes a single variable.

unobtrusive methods: Refers to when data are collected in a way that does not involve direct contact and/or interaction with human subjects.

unstructured interviews: Unstructured interviews consist of loosely planned questions. The goal is to allow respondents more room to open up and develop the conversation in their own words and at their own pace. They are often used during ethnographic fieldwork.

values coding: A type of coding where a researcher examines and unpacks the subjective values that underlie the data.

variables: Elements of the social world that can have more than one value.

vulnerable population: Individuals who may not be able to fully or freely give consent for their participation in a research study and for whom participation may create an elevated risk of harm.

REFERENCES

CHAPTER 1

Artiga, S., Orgera, K., Pham, O., & Corallo, B. (2020, April 21). *Growing data underscore that communities of color are being harder hit by COVID-19.* https://www.kff.org/coronavirus-policy-watch/growing-data-underscore-communities-color-harder-hit-covid-19/

Barker, R. T., Knisely, J. S., Barker, S. B., Cobb, R. K., & Schubert, C. M. (2012). Preliminary investigation of employee's dog presence on stress and organizational perceptions. *International Journal of Workplace Health Management, 5,* 15–30.

Benefits.gov. (n.d.). *Head start and early head start.* https://www.benefits.gov/benefit/616

Chambliss, D. F., & Schutt, R. K. (2019). *Making sense of the social world: Methods of investigation.* SAGE.

Congressional Budget Office. (2018). *Eliminate head start.* https://www.cbo.gov/budget-options/2018/54778

Federal Bureau of Investigation. (n.d.). *Services: Uniform crime reporting.* https://www.fbi.gov/services/cjis/ucr

Heckman, J. J. (2017, March 6). *Early education packs a high return on investment.* https://www.ced.org/blog/entry/comprehensive-birth-to-age-five-early-childhood-education-has-the-highest-r

Korgen, K. O., & Atkinson, M. P. (2019). *Sociology in action.* SAGE.

Lee, M. Y. H. (2015, July 8). *Donald Trump's false comments connecting Mexican immigrants and crime.* https://www.washingtonpost.com/news/fact-checker/wp/2015/07/08/donald-trumps-false-comments-connecting-mexican-immigrants-and-crime/

Mills, C. W. (1959). *The sociological imagination.* Oxford University Press.

National Academies of Science. (2016). *The integration of immigrants into American society. Issue Brief: Crime.* https://www.nap.edu/resource/21746/issue_brief_crime.pdf

Puma, M., Bell, S., Cook, R., & Heid, C. (2010). *Head Start impact study: Final report.* https://www.acf.hhs.gov/sites/default/files/opre/hs_impact_study_final.pdf

Ro, C. (2020, April 20). *Coronavirus: Why some racial groups are more vulnerable.* https://www.bbc.com/future/article/20200420-coronavirus-why-some-racial-groups-are-more-vulnerable

Stieg, C. (2020). *Science says pets can buffer stress, boost productivity and help keep you healthy while you WFH.* https://www.cnbc.com/2020/03/20/pets-make-you-less-stressed-more-productive-and-healthy-amid-covid-19.html

CHAPTER 2

Durkheim, E. (1984). *The Division of labor in society* (W. D. Halls, Trans.). The Free Press. (Original work published 1893)

Holtzman, M. (2020). Bystander intervention training: Does it increase perceptions of blame for non-intervention. *Sociological Inquiry.* https://doi.org/10.1111/soin.12391 (online first version)

Holtzman, M., & Menning, C. (2015). A New model for sexual assault protection: Creation and initial testing of elemental. *Journal of Applied Social Science, 9,* 139–155.

Holtzman, M., & Menning, C. (2019). Developments in sexual assault resistance education: Combining risk reduction and primary prevention. *Journal of Applied Social Science, 13,* 7–25.

Marx, K. (1977). *Capital* (B. Fowkes, Trans.). Vintage Books. (Original work published 1867)

Mead, G. H. (1962). In C. W. Morris (Ed.), *Mind, self, and society.* The University of Chicago Press.

Menning, C., & Holtzman, M. (2015). Combining primary prevention and risk reduction approaches in sexual assault programming. *Journal of American College Health, 63,* 513–522.

Menning, C., & Holtzman, M. (2020). Predicting successful self-protection to attempted sexual assault: Factors, tactics, and outcomes. *Sociological Focus, 53,* 89–109.

Pampel, F. (2007). *Sociological lives and ideas: An introduction to the classical theorists.* Worth Publishers.

Weber, M. (1978). *Economy and society* (E. Fischoff, H. Gerth, A. M. Henderson, F. Kolegar, C. W. Mills, T. Parsons, M. Rheinstein, G. Roth, E. Shils, & C. Wittich, Trans., Vol. 2). The University of California Press.

CHAPTER 3

Harris, K. M., Halpern, C. T., Whitsel, E. A., Hussey, J., Tabor, J. W., Entzel, P. P., & Udry, J. R. (2009). *The National longitudinal study of adolescent to adult health: Research design.* https://addhealth.cpc.unc.edu/documentation/study-design/

Ovink, S. M. (2014). 'They always called me an investment': Gendered Familism and Latino/a College Pathways. *Gender and Society, 28*(2), 265–288.

Sáenz, V. B., & Ponjuán, L. (2012). Latino males: Improving college access and degree completion completion – A new national imperative. *Perspectivas: Issues in Higher Education Policy and Practice, 1*(Spring), 1–12.

Smith, T. W., Davern, M., Freese, J., & Morgan, S. L. (2019). *General social surveys, 1972-2018: Cumulative codebook* (National Data Program for the Social Sciences Series, no. 25). NORC.

Stewart, A. J., Lal, J., & McGuire, K.. (2011). Expanding the archives of global feminisms: narratives of feminism and Activism. *Signs: Journal of Women in Culture and Society, 36*(4), 889–914.

CHAPTER 4

Allen, C. (1997). Spies like us: When sociologists deceive their subjects. *Lingua Franca, 7*(9), 30–39. http://linguafranca.mirror.theinfo.org/9711/9711.allen.html

American Sociological Association. (2018). Code of ethics. *ASA.* https://www.asanet.org/sites/default/files/asa_code_of_ethics-june2018.pdf

Banks, S., Armstrong, A., Carter, K., Graham, H., Hayward, P., Henry, A., Holland, T., Holmes, C., Lee, A., McNulty, A., Moore, N., Nayling, N., Stokoe, A., & Strachan, A. (2013). Everyday ethics in community-based participatory research. *Contemporary Social Science, 8*(3), 263–277.

Beauchamp, Z. (2018). The controversy around hoax studies in critical theory explained. *Vox.* https://www.vox.com/2018/10/15/17951492/grievance-studies-sokal-squared-hoax

Boissonault, L. (2017). A Spoonful of sugar helps the radioactive oatmeal go down when MIT and Quaker Oats paired up to conduct experiments on unsuspecting young boys. *Smithsonian Magazine.* https://www.smithsonianmag.com/history/spoonful-sugar-helps-radioactive-oatmeal-go-down-180962424/

Brown, S., Esbensen, F.-A., & Geis, G. (2019). *Criminology: Explaining crime and its context.* Routledge.

Buck v. Bell, 274 U.S. 200. (1927).

Burton, L. M. (2010). Uncovering hidden facts that matter in interpreting individuals' behaviors: An ethnographic lens. In B. Risman & V. Rutter (Eds.), *Families as they really are* (pp. 20–23). W.W. Norton.

Centers for Disease Control and Prevention. (2020). *The Tuskegee timeline.* https://www.cdc.gov/tuskegee/timeline.htm

Desmond, M. (2015). *Unaffordable America: Poverty, housing, and eviction.* Institute for Research on Poverty Fast Focus No. 22.

Desmond, M. (2016). *Evicted: Poverty and profit in the American City.* Crown Publishers.

Desmond, M., & Gershenson, C. (2016). Housing and employment insecurity among the working poor. *Social Problems, 63*(1), 46–67.

Desmond, M., & Gershenson, C. (2017). Who gets evicted? Assessing individual, neighborhood, and network factors. *Social Science Research, 62,* 362–377.

DuBois, J. (2020). The Tearoom trade study. *Ethics in Mental Health Research.* https://sites.google.com/a/narrativebioethics.com/emhr/contact/the-tearoom-trade-study-1

DuBois, W. E. B. (1899 [1996]). *"Preface", The Philadelphia Negro. From Robert Williams Note #1.* http://www.webdubois.org/wdb-phila.html

Dworkin, E., & Allen, N. (2017). For the good of the group? Balancing individual and collective risks and benefits in community psychology research. *American Journal of Community Psychology, 60,* 391–397.

Fowler, K. A., Gladden, R. M., Vagi, K. J., Barnes, J., & Frazier, L. (2015). Increase in suicides associated with home eviction and foreclosure during the US housing crisis: Findings from 16 national violent death reporting system states, 2005–2010. *American Journal of Public Health, 105*(2), 311–316.

Geis, G., Mobley, A., & Schichor, D. (1999). Private prisons, criminological research, and conflict of interest: A case study. *Crime and Delinquency, 45,* 372–388.

Gold, A. E. (2016). No home for justice: How eviction perpetuates health inequity among low-income and minority tenants. *Georgetown Journal on Poverty Law and Policy, 24,* 59.

Grisham, J. (2006). *The Innocent Man: Murder and injustice in a small town.* Doubleday.

National Institutes of Health. (2020). *Definition of human subjects research.* https://grants.nih.gov/policy/humansubjects/research.htm

Pager, D. (2003). The Mark of a criminal record. *American Journal of Sociology, 108*(5), 937–975.

Pfohl, S. (1994). *Images of deviance and social control: A sociological history* (2nd ed.). McGraw-Hill.

Picou, J. S. (1996). Compelled disclosure of scholarly research: Some comments on 'High Stakes Litigation'. *Law and Contemporary Problems: Court-Ordered Disclosure of Academic Research: A Clash of. Values of Science and Law, 59*(3), 149–157.

Public Broadcasting Service. (2018). *American experience: The Eugenics crusade: What's wrong with perfect?* WGBH.

Reynolds, G. (2003). The stuttering doctor's 'Monster study'. *New York Times Magazine.* https://www.nytimes.com/2003/03/16/magazine/the-stuttering-doctor-s-monster-study.html?auth=login-email

Skloot, R. (2011). *The Immortal life of Henrietta lacks.* Crown.

Tucker, T. (2006). *The Great Starvation Experiment: The Heroic Men who starved so that millions could live.* Free Press.

United States Code. (2014). Title 42 The Public Health and Welfare, Chapter 6A, Public Health Service, Subchapter III, National Research Institutes; Part H, General Provisions; Sec. 289, Institutional review boards.

United States Department of Health & Human Services. (2019). *Informed consent FAU.* https://www.hhs.gov/ohrp/regulations-and-policy/guidance/faq/informed-consent/index.html#4142

United States Department of Health, Education, and Welfare. (1979). *The Belmont Report: Ethical principles and guidelines for the protection of human subjects of research.* The National Commission for the Protection of Human Subjects of Biomedical and Behavioral Research.

Weber, M. (1904 [1949]). *'Objectivity' in social science and social policy* (pp. 50–112).

Zimbardo, P. (2020). Shocking 'Prison' Study 40 years later: What happened at Stanford?. *CBS News and Philip Zimbardo, Inc.* https://www.cbsnews.com/pictures/shocking-prison-study-40-years-later-what-happened-at-stanford/24/

Zinn, H. (2018). *You can't be neutral on a moving train: A personal history*. Beacon Press.

CHAPTER 5

Bacchus, L. J., Buller, A. M., Ferrari, G., Brzank, P., & Feder, G. (2018). Its always good to ask': A mixed methods study on the perceived role of sexual health practitioners asking gay and bisexual men about experiences of domestic violence and abuse. *Journal of Mixed Methods Research, 21*(12), 221–243.

Cohen, C. J. (1997). Punks, bulldaggers, and welfare queens: The radical potential of queer politics? *GLQ: A Journal of Lesbian and Gay Studies, 3*(4), 437–465.

Compton, D. R., & Baumle, A. K. (2012). Beyond the Castro: The role of demographics in the selection of gay and lesbian enclaves. *Journal of Homosexuality, 59*(10), 1327–1355.

Connell, C. (2018). Thank you for coming out today: The queer discomforts of in-depth interviewing. In D. Compton, T. Meadown, & K. Schilt (Eds.), *Other, Please Specify* (pp. 126–139). University of California Press.

De Pedro, K. T., Lynch, R. J., & Esqueda, M. C. (2018). Understanding safety, victimization and school climate among rural lesbian, gay, bisexual, transgender, and questioning (LGBTQ) youth. *Journal of LGBT Youth, 15*(4), 265–279.

Dreby, J. (2015). *Everyday illegal: When politics undermine immigrant families*. Temple University Press.

Feldman, L., Maibach, E. W., Roser-Renouf, C., & Leiserowitz, A. (2012). Climate on cable: The nature and impact of global warming coverage on Fox News, CNN, and MSNBC. *The International Journal of Press/Politics, 17*(1), 3–31.

Ghaziani, A. (2014). *There Goes the Gayborhood?* Princeton University Press.

Ghaziani, A. (2018). Queer spatial analysis. In D. Compton, T. Meadown, & K. Schilt (Eds.), *Other, please specify* (pp. 201–215). University of California Press.

Haj-Yahia, M. M., Wilson, R. M., & Naqvi, S. A. M. (2012). Justification, perception of severity and harm, and criminalization of wife abuse in the Palestinian society. *Journal of Interpresonal Violence, 27*(10), 1932–1958.

Jones, S. R., Torres, V., & Arminio, J. (2014). *Negotiating the complexities of qualitative research in higher education*. Routledge.

Kincaid, J. D. (2016). The rational basis of irrational politics: Examining the great Texas political shift to the right. *Politics and Society, 44*(4), 525–550.

Laus, V. (2013). An exploratory study of social connections and drug usage among Filipino Americans. *Journal of Immigrant Minority Health, 15*, 1096–1106.

Malcolm, L. E., & Dowd, A. C. (2012). The impact of undergraduate debt on the graduate school enrollment of STEM baccalaureates. *The Review of Higher Education, 35*(2), 265–305.

Ocampo, A. (2016). *The Latinos of Asia: How Filipino Americans break the rules of race*. Stanford University Press.

Parrado, E. A., McQuiston, C., & Flippen, C. A. (2005). Integrating community collaboration and quantitative methods for the study of Gende and HIV risks among Hispanic migrants. *Sociological Methods and Research, 34*(2), 204–239.

Strangfeld, J. (2019). I just don't want to be judged: Cultural capital's impact on student plagiarism. *Sage Open, 9*(1), 1–14. https://doi.org/10.1177/2158244018822382

Thomson-Deveau, A. (2016, October 17). Cosmopolitan.com readers think Hillary Clinton should – and will – win the election. *Cosmopolitan*. https://www.cosmopolitan.com/politics/a6434488/election-poll-survey-hillary-clinton-win/

Vlack, S., Foster, R., Menzies, R., Williams, G., Shannon, C., & Riley, I. (2007). Immunisation coverage of Queensland indigenous two-year-old children by cluster sampling and by register. *Australian and New Zealand Journal of Public Health, 31*(1), 67–72.

Zandee, G. L., Bossenbroek, D., Slager, D., & Gordon, B. (2013). Teams of community health workers and nursing students effect health promotion and underserved urban neighborhoods. *Public Health Nursing, 30*(5), 439–447.

CHAPTER 6

Dahl, R. A. (1971). *Polyarchy: Participation and opposition*. Yale University Press.

Furstenberg, F. F. (2000). The sociology of adolescence and youth in the 1990s: A critical commentary. *Journal of Marriage and Family, 62*(4), 896–910.

Harnois, C. E. (2015). Race, ethnicity, sexuality, and women's political consciousness of gender. *Social Psychology Quarterly, 78*(4), 365–386.

Harris, D. R., & Sim, J. J. (2002). Who is multiracial? Assessing the complexity of lived race. *American Sociological Review, 67*, 614–627.

Parker, R. (2001). Sexuality, culture, and power in HIV/AIDS research. *Annual Review of Anthropology, 30*, 163–179.

Risman, B. J. (2018). *Where the millennials will take us: A new generation wrestles with the gender structure*. Oxford University Press.

Simon, R. W. (2008). The joys of parenthood, reconsidered. *Contexts, 7*(2), 40–45.

Thorne, B. (1993). *Gender play: Girls and boys in school*. Rutgers University Press.

United States Department of Agriculture. (2020). *Food security in the US*. https://www.ers.usda.gov/topics/food-nutrition-assistance/food-security-in-the-us/

CHAPTER 7

Correll, S. (2004). Constraints into preferences: Gender, status, and emerging career aspirations. *American Sociological Review, 69*, 93–113.

Pager, D. (2003). The mark of a criminal record. *The American Journal of Sociology, 108*(5), 937–975.

CHAPTER 8

American Association for Public Opinion Research. (2016). *Standard definitions: Final dispositions of case codes and outcome rates for surveys.* American Association for Public Opinion Research. https://www.aapor.org/AAPOR_Main/media/publications/Standard-Definitions20169theditionfinal.pdf.

Baker, R., Brick, J. M., Keeter, S., Biemer, P., Kennedy, C., Kreuter, F., Mercer, A., & Terhanian, G. (2016). *Evaluation survey quality in today's complex environment.* American Association for Public Opinion Research.

Biemer, P., de Leeuw, E., Eckman, S., Edwards, B., Kreuter, F., Lyberg, L., Tucker, C., & West, B. T. (2017). *Total survey error in practice.* John Wiley & Sons.

Cain-Miller, C. (2018). Americans value equality at work more than equality at home. *New York Times.* https://www.nytimes.com/2018/12/03/upshot/americans-value-equality-at-work-more-than-equality-at-home.html.

Groves, R. M. (1989). *Survey errors and survey costs.* Wiley.

Groves, R. M., Fowler, F. J., Couper, M. P., Lepkowski, J. M., Singer, E., & Tourangeau, R. (2009). *Survey methodology* (2nd ed.). Wiley.

Groves, R. M., & Lyberg, L. (2010). Total survey error: Past, present, and future. *Public Opinion Quarterly, 74*(5), 849–879.

Kane, E. W., & Macaulay, L. J. (1993). Interviewer gender and gender attitudes. *Public Opinion Quarterly, 57*, 1–28.

Krosnick, J. A. (1991). Response strategies for coping with the cognitive demands of attitude measures in surveys. *Applied Cognitive Psychology, 5*(3), 213–236.

Schaeffer, N. C. (1980). Evaluating race-of-interviewer effects in a national survey. *Sociological Methods & Research, 8*(4), 400–419.

Tourangeau, R., Conrad, F. G., & Couper, M. P. (2013). *The science of web surveys.* Oxford University Press.

Tourangeau, R., Rips, L. J., & Rasinski, K. (2000). *The psychology of survey response.* Cambridge University Press.

CHAPTER 9

Bernard, H. R. (2018). *Research methods in anthropology* (5th ed.). Rowan & Littlefield.

Burawoy, M. (1979). *Manufacturing consent: Changes in the labor process under monopoly capitalism.* The University of Chicago Press.

Burawoy, M. (1998). The extended case method. *Sociological Theory, 16*(1), 4–33.

Connell, C. (2018). Thank you for coming out today: The Queer discomforts of in-depth interviewing. In D. Compton, T. Meadow, & K. Schilt (Eds.), *Other, please specify: Queer methods in sociology* (pp. 126–139). University of California Press.

Cyr, J. (2015). The pitfalls and promise of focus groups as a data collection method. *Sociological Methods & Research, 45*, 231–259.

DeWalt, K. M., & DeWalt, B. R. (2011). *Participant observation: A guide for fieldworkers.* Altamira Press.

Duneier, M. (2011). How not to lie with ethnography. *Sociological Methodology, 41*, 1–11.

Geertz, C. (1973). *The interpretation of cultures* (Vol. 5019). Basic Books.

Glaser, B. G., & Strauss, A. L. (1967). *The discovery of grounded theory: Strategies for qualitative research.* Aldine Transaction.

Guest, G., Namey, E., & McKenna, K. (2016). How many focus groups are enough? Building an evidence base for nonprobability sample sizes. *Field Methods, 29*, 3–22.

Herrman, A. R. (2017). Focus groups. In M. Allen (Ed.), *The SAGE encyclopedia of communication research methods.* SAGE. https://doi.org/10.4135/9781483381411

Jerolmack, C., & Khan, S. (Eds.). (2018). *Approaches to ethnography: Analysis and representation in participant observation.* Oxford University Press.

McDonnell, T. E. (2010). Cultural objects and objects: Materiality, urban space, and the interpretation of AIDS campaigns in Accra, Ghana. *American Journal of Sociology, 115*, 1800–1852.

Spradley, J. P. (2016 [1979]). *The ethnographic interview.* Waveland Press, Inc.

Tavory, I., & Timmermans, S. (2014). *Abductive analysis: Theorizing qualitative research.* The University of Chicago Press.

Wilkinson, B. C. (2015). *Partners or rivals? Power and Latino, Black and white relations in the twenty-first century.* University of Virginia Press.

CHAPTER 10

Frank, D. J., Camp, B. J., & Boutcher, S. A. (2010). Worldwide trends in the criminal regulation of sex, 1945 to 2005. *American Sociological Review, 75*, 867–893.

Gerding, A., & Signorielli, N. (2014). Gender roles in Tween television programming: A content analysis of two genres. *Sex Roles, 70*, 43–56.

Ghaziani, A., & Baldassarri, D. (2011). Cultural anchors and the organization of differences: A multi-method analysis of LGBT marches on Washington. *American Sociological Review, 76*, 179–206.

Hilliard, D. C. (1984). Media images of male and female professional athletes: An interpretive analysis of magazine articles. *Sociology of Sport Journal, 1*, 251–262.

Kain, E. L. (2018). Using content analysis to study the sociology curriculum in the United States. In *SAGE research methods cases: A peer-reviewed online library resource.* SAGE.

Kain, E. L., Contreras, L., Hendley, A. O., & Wyatt-Baxter, K. K. (2007). Sociology in two-year institutions. *Teaching Sociology, 35*, 350–359.

McCabe, J., Fairchild, E., Grauerholz, L., Pescosolido, B. A., & Tope, D. (2011). Gender in twentieth-century children's books: Patterns of disparity in titles and central characters. *Gender and Society, 25*, 197–226.

Messner, M. A., Duncan, M. C., & Jensen, K. (1993). Separating the men from the girls: The gendered language of televised sports. *Gender and Society, 7*, 121–137.

Morestin, F. (2012). *A framework for analyzing public policies: Practical guide*. National Collaborating Centre for Healthy Public Policy. http://www.ncchpp.ca/docs/Guide_framework_analyzing _policies_En.pdf

Pescosolido, B. A., Grauerholz, E., & Milkie, M. A. (1997). Culture and conflict: The portrayal of Blacks in U.S. children's picture books through the mid- and late-twentieth century. *American Sociological Review, 62*, 443–464.

Rowell, K. R., & This, C. (2013). Exploring the sociology curriculum at community colleges in the United States. *The American Sociologist, 44*, 329–340.

Schmidt, H. C. (2018). Forgotten athletes and token reporters: Analyzing the gender bias in sports journalism. *Atlantic Journal of Communication, 26*(1), 59–74.

Shor, E., van de Rijt, A., Miltsov, A., Kulkarni, V., & Skiena, S. (2015). A paper ceiling: Explaining the persistent underrepresentation of women in printed news. *American Sociological Review, 80*, 960–984.

Taylor, J. K., Lewis, D. C., & Haider-Markel, D. P. (2018). Education policy. In J. K. Taylor, D. C. Lewis, & D. P Haider-Markel (Eds.), *The remarkable rise of transgender rights* (pp. 260–281). University of Michigan Press.

Vasi, I. B., Walker, E. T., Johnson, J. S., & Tan, H. F. (2015). "No fracking way!" Documentary film, discursive opportunity, and local opposition against hydraulic fracturing in the United States, 2010 to 2013. *American Sociological Review, 80*, 934–959.

Webb, E. J., Campbell, D. T., Schwartz, R. D., & Sechrest, L. (1966). *Unobtrusive measures: Nonreactive research in the social sciences*. Rand McNally.

Zingraff, R. (2002). *Final report of the task force on the articulation of sociology in two-year and four-year sociology programs*. American Sociological Association.

CHAPTER 11

Armstrong, E. A., England, P., & Fogarty, A. C. K. (2012). Accounting for women's orgasm and sexual enjoyment in college hookups and relationships. *American Sociological Review, 77*(3), 435–462. https://doi.org/10.1177/0003122412445802

Bousquin, J. (2020, October 21). Despite progress, ingrained racism still runs deep in construction. *Construction Dive*. https://www .constructiondive.com/news/despite-progress-ingrained-racism -still-runs-deep-in-construction/587391/

Creswell, J. W., & Plano Clark, V. L. (2011). *Designing and conducting mixed methods research*. SAGE.

Desmond, M. (2012). Eviction and the reproduction of urban poverty. *American Journal of Sociology, 118*(1), 88–133. https://doi. org/10.1086/666082

Kelly, M. (2010). Control over the reproduction and mothering of poor women: An analysis of television news coverage of welfare reform. *Journal of Poverty, 14*(1), 76–96.

Kelly, M., Gauchat, G., Acosta, K., Withers, E., & McNair, J. (Forthcoming). Does science do more harm than good? A mixed methods analysis of African American women's attitudes towards science. In M. Kelly & B. Gurr (Eds.), *Feminist research in practice*. Rowman and Littlefield.

Kelly, M., & Gurr, B. (2019). *Feminist research in practice*. Rowman and Littlefield.

Kelly, M., Wilkinson, L., Pisciotta, M., & Williams, L. S. (2015). When working hard is not enough for female and racial/ethnic minority apprentices in the highway trades. *Sociological Forum, 30*(2), 415–438. https://doi.org/10.1111/socf.12169

Morgan, D. L. (2014). *Integrating qualitative and quantitative methods: A pragmatic approach*. SAGE.

Plano Clark, V. L., & Ivankova, N. V. (2017). *Mixed methods research: A guide to the field*. SAGE.

Teddlie, C., & Tashakkori, A. (2009). The inference process in mixed methods research. In C. Teddlie & A. Tashakkori, *Foundations of mixed methods research: Integrating quantitative and qualitative approaches in the social and behavioral sciences* (pp. 285–314). SAGE.

Waller, M. R., & Emory, A. D. (2018). Visitation orders, family courts, and fragile families. *Journal of Marriage and Family, 80*(3), 653–670. https://doi.org/10.1111/jomf.12480

CHAPTER 12

General Social Surveys, 1972–2018. (2019). National Science Foundation.

Glass, J., Simon, R. W., & Andersson, M. A. (2016). Parenthood and happiness: Effects of work–family reconciliation policies in 22 OECD countries. *American Journal of Sociology, 122*(3), 886–929.

Hamilton, L. C., Cutler, M. J., & Schaefer, A. (2012). *Public knowledge about polar regions increases while concerns remain unchanged*. Carsey Institute: Issue Brief 42.

Harnois, C. E. (2017). *Analyzing inequalities: An introduction to race, class, gender, and sexuality using the general social survey*. SAGE.

Korgen, K. O.., & Atkinson, M. P. (Eds.). (2020). *Sociology in Action*. SAGE.

McPherson, M., Smith-Lovin, L., & Brashears, M. E. (2006). Social isolation in America: Changes in core discussion networks over two decades. *American Sociological Review, 71*(3), 353–375.

NORC. (2021). http://www3.norc.org/GSS+Website/

United Nations. (2013, July 24). *Economic and social council, fundamental principles of official statistics (E/RES/2013/21)*. https:// unstats.un.org/unsd/dnss/gp/FP-Rev2013-E.pdf

United States Department of Justice, Office of Justice Programs, Bureau of Justice Statistics, Annual Survey of Jails. (2018). *Inter-university consortium for political and social research [distributor], 2020-04-23*. https://doi.org/10.3886/ICPSR37392.v1

CHAPTER 13

Abbott, A. (2004). *Methods of discovery: Heuristics for the social sciences*. W. W. Norton.

Aiello, B., & McQueeney, K. (2021, February). "Grandma is the next best thing to mommy": Incarcerated motherhood, caregiver relationships, and maternal identity. *International Journal of Care and Caregiving, 5*(1), 105–128.

Cabaniss, E. (2018). Pulling back the curtain: Examining the backstage gendered dynamics of storytelling in the undocumented youth movement. *Journal of Contemporary Ethnography, 47*(2), 199–225.

Charmaz, K. (2014). *Constructing grounded theory: A practical guide through qualitative analysis* (2nd ed.). SAGE.

Corbin, J., & Strauss, A. (2015). *Basics of qualitative research* (4th ed.). SAGE.

Ezzell, M. (2009). "Barbie dolls" on the pitch: Identity work, defensive othering, and women's rugby. *Social Problems, 56*(1), 111–131.

Glaser, B. (1978). *Theoretical sensitivity.* Sociology Press.

Glaser, B. G., & Holton, J. (2004). Remodeling grounded theory. *Forum Qualitative Sozialforschung/Forum: Qualitative Social Research, 5*(2). https://doi.org/10.17169/fqs-5.2.607

Glaser, B., & Strauss, A. (1999). *The discovery of grounded theory: Strategies for qualitative research.* Aldine de Gruyter.

Hochschild, A. R. (1983). *The managed heart: Commercialization of human feeling.* University of California Press.

Kleinman, S. (2003). Feminist fieldworker: Connecting research, teaching and memoir. In B. Glassner & R. Hertz (Eds.), *Our studies, ourselves: Sociologists' lives and work* (pp. 215–232). Oxford University Press.

Kleinman, S., & Cabaniss, E. R. (2019). Towards a feminist symbolic interactionism. In M. H. Jacobsen (Ed.), *Critical and classical interactionism: Insights from sociology and criminology* (pp. 119–137). Routledge.

Lavelle, K. (2014). *Whitewashing the South: White memories of segregation and civil rights.* Roman & Littlefield.

Lewins, A., & Silver, C. (2007). *Using software in qualitative research: A step-by-step guide.* SAGE.

Lofland, J., & Lofland, L. (1995). *Analyzing social settings: A guide to qualitative observation and analysis.* Wadsworth.

McQueeney, K., & Lavelle, K. (2017). Emotional labor in critical ethnographic work: In the field and behind the desk. *Journal of Contemporary Ethnography, 46*(1), 81–107.

Miles, M., & Huberman, A. M. (1994). *Qualitative data analysis: An expanded sourcebook* (2nd ed.). SAGE.

Patton, M. Q. (1990). *Qualitative evaluation and research methods.* SAGE.

Richards, L., & Morse, J. (2007). *Readme first for a user's guide to qualitative methods* (2nd ed.). SAGE.

Saldaña, J. (2016). *The coding manual for qualitative researchers* (3rd ed.). SAGE.

Strauss, A. L. (1987). *Qualitative analysis for social scientists.* Cambridge University Press.

Yin, R. (2011). *Qualitative research from start to finish.* Guilford Press.

CHAPTER 14

American Evaluation Association. (2018). *Guiding principles for evaluators.* https://www.eval.org/p/cm/ld/fid=51.

Brookfield, S. (2012). *Teaching for critical thinking: Tools and techniques to help students question their assumptions* (1st ed.). Jossey-Bass.

Buckley, J., Archibald, T., Hargraves, M., & Trochim, W. M. (2015). Defining and teaching evaluative thinking: Insights from research on critical thinking. *American Journal of Evaluation, 36*(3), 375–388.

Greene, J. C. (2000). Challenges in practicing deliberative democratic evaluation. *New Directions for Evaluation, 2000*(85), 13–26. https://doi.org/10.1002/ev.1158

Mertens, D. (2009). *Transformative research and evaluation.* The Guilford Press.

Mertens, D. M.., & Wilson, A. T.. (2018). *Progam evaluation theory and practice.* Guilford Publications.

Mertens, D., & Wilson, A. (2019). *Program evaluation theory and practice: A comprehensive guide* (2nd ed.). The Guilford Press.

Nevo, D. (2001). School evaluation: Internal or external? *Studies in Educational Evaluation, 27*(2), 95–106.

Patton, M. (2002). *Qualitative research and evaluation methods* (3rd ed.). SAGE.

Patton, M. (2012). *Essentials of utilization-focused evaluation.* SAGE.

Rossi, P., Lipsey, M. W., & Freeman, H. E. (2004). *Evaluation: A systematic approach* (7th ed.). SAGE.

Scriven, M. (1991). *Evaluation thesaurus* (4th ed.). SAGE.

Stufflebeam, D. (2001). Evaluation models. *New Directions for Evaluation, 2001*(89), 7–98. https://doi.org/10.1002/ev.3

Trochim, W. (2001). *The Research methods knowledge base* (2nd ed.). Atomic Dog Publishing.

Vo, A. T., & Archibald, T. (2018). New directions for evaluative thinking. *New Directions for Evaluation (Online), 2018*(158), 139–147.

W. K. Kellogg Foundation. (2004). *Logic model development guide.* https://www.wkkf.org/resource-directory/resource/2006/02/wk-kellogg-foundation-logic-model-development-guide

W. K. Kellogg Foundation. (2017). *The Step-by-Step guide to evaluating how to become savvy evaluation consumers.* https://www.wkkf.org/resource-directory/resource/2006/02/wk-kellogg-foundation-logic-model-development-guide

Yin, R. (2003). *Case study research: Design and methods* (3rd ed.). SAGE.

CHAPTER 15

Brandt, H. M., Freedman, D. A., Friedman, D. B., Choi, S. K., Seel, J. S., Guest, M. A., & Khang, L. (2016). Planting healthy roots: Using documentary film to evaluate and disseminate community-based participatory research. *Family and Community Health, 39*(4), 242–250.

Cossyleon, J. E. (2018a). *"Hear Us, See Us!": How mothers of color transform family and community relationships through grassroots collective action.* Dissertation from Loyola University Chicago. https://ecommons.luc.edu/luc_diss/2949/

Cossyleon, J. E. (2018b). °Coming out of my shell": Motherleaders contesting fear, vulnerability, and despair through family-focused community organizing. *Socius, 4,* 1–13.

Danso, R. (2018). Cultural competence and cultural humility: A critical reflection on key cultural diversity concepts. *Journal of Social Work, 18*(4), 410–430.

Foronda, C., Reinholdt, M. M., & Ousman, K. (2016). Cultural humility: A concept analysis. *Journal of Transcultural Nursing, 27*(3), 210–217.

Nassar-McMillan, S. C. (2014). A framework for cultural competence, advocacy, and social justice: Applications for global multiculturalism and diversity. *International Journal for Educational and Vocational Guidance, 14*, 103–118.

Nyirenda, D., Sariola, S., Gooding, K., Phiri, M., Sambakunsi, R., Moyo, E., Bandawa, C., Squire, B., & Desmond, N. (2018). "We are the eyes and ears of researchers and community": Understanding the role of community advisory groups in representing researchers and communities in Malawi. *Developing World Bioethics, 18*(4), 420–428.

Parrott, Heather Macpherson., & Valentine, Colby. (2021). Where Scholar-Activism and Ethnography Meet: Contributing to the Conversation and Documenting Social Life. In Leslie. Hossfeld, E. Brooke. Kelly, & Cassius. Hossfeld (Eds.), *Routledge International Handbook on Public Sociology*. Routledge.

Pon, G. (2009). Cultural competency as new racism: An ontology of forgetting. *Journal of Progressive Human Services, 20*, 59–71.

Quinn, S. C. (2004). Ethics in public health research: Protecting human subjects: The role of community advisory boards. *American Journal of Public Health, 94*(6), 918–922.

Ronda, M., Isserles, R., & Borough of Manhattan Community College. (2018). *Battery Park City Authority parks user count and study 2017-2018*. Report created for the Battery Park City Authority.

Sakamoto, I. (2007). An anti-oppressive approach to cultural competence. *Canadian Social Work Review, 24*(1), 105–118.

Sousa, P., & Almeida, J. L. (2016). Culturally sensitive social work: Promoting cultural competence. *European Journal of Social Work, 19*, 537–555.

Strand, K., Marullo, S., Cutforth, N., Stoecker, R., & Donohue, P. (2003). *Community-based research and higher education: Principles and practices*. Jossey-Bass.

Strauss, R. P., Sengupta, S., Quinn, S. C., Goeppinger, J., Spaulding, C., Kegeles, S. M., & Millett, G. (2001). The role of community advisory boards: Involving communities in the informed consent process. *American Journal of Public Health, 91*(12), 1938–1943.

CHAPTER 16

Burawoy, M. (2005). The critical turn to public sociology. *Critical Sociology, 31*(3), 314–326.

Crenshaw, K. (1991). Mapping the margins: Intersectionality, identity politics, and violence against women of color. *Stanford Law Review, 43*, 1241–1296.

Denzin, N. K. (1997). *Interpretive ethnography: Ethnographic practices for the 21st century*. SAGE.

Desmond, M. (2016). *Evicted: Poverty and profit in the American city*. Penguin.

Dodson, L., Piatelli, D., & Schmalzbauer, L. (2007). Researching inequality through interpretive collaborations: A discussion of methodological efforts to include the interpretive voices of participants in research findings. *Qualitative Inquiry, 13*(6), 821–843.

Hepburn, P., & Louis, R. (2021). *Preliminary analysis: Six months of the CDC eviction moratorium*. https://evictionlab.org/six-months-cdc/

Hill Collins, P., & Bilge, S. (2016). *Intersectionality*. Polity Press.

Levine, P. (2013). *We are the ones we have been waiting for: The promise of civic renewal in America*. Oxford University Press.

Lincoln, Y. S., & Guba, E. G. (2000). Paradigmatic controversies, contradictions, and emerging confluences. In N. K. Denzin & Y. S. Lincoln (Eds.), *The handbook of qualitative research* (2nd ed., pp. 163–188). SAGE.

Lisinski, C. (2020, July 28). Immigrant driver's license bill stalls. *Telegram & Gazette*.

Lorde, A.(1984). *Sister outsider*. Berkeley.

Mauthner, N. S., & Doucet, A. (2003). Reflexive accounts and accounts of reflexivity in qualitative data analysis. *Sociology, 37*(3), 413–431.

Mills, C. W., Mills, C. W., & Horowitz, I. L. (1963). *Power, politics and people: The Collected essays of C. Wright Mills*. Ballantine.

Noy, D. (2008). Power mapping: Enhancing sociological knowledge by developing generalizable analytical public tools. *The American Sociologist, 39*(1), 3–18.

Painter, N. I.. (2010). *The history of white people*. W. W. Norton & Company.

Richie, B. (1996). *Compelled to crime: The gender entrapment of Black battered women*. Routledge.

Richie, B. (2012). *Arrested justice: Black women, violence, and America's prison nation*. NYU Press.

Rios, V. (2011). *Punished: Policing the lives of Black and Latino boys*. NYU Press.

Romero, M. (2020). Sociology engaged in social justice. *American Sociological Review, 85*(1), 1–30.

Schor, J.., & White, K. E.. (2010). *Plenitude: The new economics of true wealth*. Penguin Press.

Smith, D. E. (1987). *The everyday world as problematic: A feminist sociology*. University of Toronto Press.

Smith, D. E. (2005). *Institutional ethnography: A sociology for people*. AltaMira Press.

Sources for the Subject of Sociology (Ed.).

White, J. M., & White, S. K. (2019). *The engaged sociologist: Connecting the classroom to the community* (6th ed.). SAGE.

INDEX

academic research, 265–66, 280, 290, 296, 299

advantage, 146, 205, 308, 313

AEA. *See* American Evaluation Association

African American, 60–61, 87, 114, 132, 202, 206, 210–11

age groups, 5, 49–50, 81, 87, 131, 183

agencies, 52, 259, 284–87, 290, 292

American Evaluation Association (AEA), 265, 279–81

American National Election Study (ANES), 102, 104

American Sociological Association. *See* ASA

American Sociological Review, 51, 203

analytic approaches in qualitative research, 257, 261

analytic coding, 243–45, 250, 252–53, 255–56, 258, 260–62

analyzing data, 28, 34, 102, 112, 159, 168, 181, 185, 216, 239, 251

ANES (American National Election Study), 102, 104

Anne's Answer, 105

Annual Survey, 222–23

anonymity, 72, 76, 277–78

answer choices, 104, 108–9, 115

answer questions, 40, 42, 49, 131, 145, 150, 205

answers

    complex, 105

    respondent, 109, 154

answer survey questions, 89, 144–45

applied research, 41–42, 55, 72, 74

apprentices, 199, 202, 205, 209

approaches, 5, 62, 84–86, 90–91, 93–95, 141–42, 146–47, 151–54, 161–62, 167–69, 171, 175, 199–202, 204, 208–10, 212, 271–73, 297–98, 316

ASA (American Sociological Association), 65–66, 68–73, 76, 302, 304

athletes, 182, 188, 247, 249

audiences, 30–31, 37–38, 51–53, 55, 112, 168, 254, 286, 304–5, 310, 313–14

bachelor's degree, 14–15, 53, 110, 133

BDI (Beck Depression Inventory), 212

Beck Depression Inventory (BDI), 212

behavioral research, 63–64

beliefs, people's, 246, 267

Belmont Report, 63–65, 67, 77

best practices, 54, 199, 208–13, 281, 296

biomedical research, 63

bivariate relationships, 230–32, 236

bivariate tables, 215, 230, 235, 239–40

Black Lives Matter (BLM), 82, 294, 310–11

BLM. *See* Black Lives Matter

broader population, 129, 131, 133, 139, 158, 216, 239

budget, 138, 142, 152, 158, 272

businesses, 12, 130, 162, 164, 225, 284

CAPI (computer-assisted personal interviewing), 148

CAQDAS (Computer-Assisted Qualitative Data Analysis Software), 243–44, 248, 257, 260–62

CAQDAS programs, 257–58, 260–61

Carolina Population Center (CPC), 51

catalog, 80, 186, 188–89

CATI (computer-assisted telephone interviews), 148–49, 158

causality, 117–33

causal relationships, 117, 119, 121, 129, 133, 230

CBR (community-based research), 42–43, 57, 72, 74–76, 280, 283–92, 294–99, 310

CDC, 13–14, 60–61, 218, 306

Census Bureau, 14–16, 140–41, 200, 218, 236

Center for Survey Research (CSR), 54

children, 15–16, 25–28, 45, 58–60, 63–64, 73, 75, 87, 103–4, 165, 171, 181, 211–12, 217, 247

cities, 29, 49, 80–81, 86, 120, 140–41, 157, 222, 230–32, 288, 306–7

civic engagement, 154, 307–9, 312, 317

class position, 23, 34

climate change, 4–5, 59, 80, 92, 219, 284, 309

climate surveys, 140, 153, 159

closed-ended questions, 104–6, 108–9, 115, 203, 210

cluster sampling, 86–87, 95

codebook, 186, 188, 190–91, 196–97, 222, 225, 240

code data in content analysis, 179, 196

coding, 156, 158, 188, 190–91, 243–51, 254–62, 267

Coding Qualitative Data, 243–61

coding sheet, 189–90, 192–93, 196–97

cohort data, 49–50, 55

collecting data, 28, 34, 45, 48, 83, 86, 112, 115, 154, 156, 159, 163

collective risks, 66–67, 72–73, 75–77

college students, 29, 32, 38, 86–87, 129, 139, 153–54, 206

    first-generation, 82–83, 93

community-based research. *See* CBR

community groups, 52, 284, 286–87, 312

community organizations, 31, 283–84, 286, 291–92, 294–95, 297

community partners, 42, 51–53, 55, 132–33, 284–85, 287–92, 295–98, 309, 312

community research, 284

community types, 232

community work, 294, 297

composite measures, 97, 106–8, 112, 115

computer-assisted personal interviewing (CAPI), 148

Computer-Assisted Qualitative Data Analysis Software. *See* CAQDAS

computer-assisted telephone interviews. *See* CATI

concepts, 26, 28, 94, 97–100, 102–4, 106–8, 110–12, 114–15, 249–50, 255–56, 258–60, 308, 310, 312, 316

conceptual definition, 98, 100, 103, 111–12, 115

confidence, 41, 54, 84, 172, 186, 205, 221, 238, 276

conflicts of interest, 70–72, 75, 77

conflict theory, 22–25, 27, 34, 73

content analysis, 84, 88, 179–93, 195–97, 200, 209

control, 60, 88, 122, 125–28, 130–31, 149, 155, 201, 310, 312, 314

convenience sampling, 88, 92, 153, 162, 167, 177

correlation, 107, 119, 121, 133–34, 182, 230, 236–37, 240

counterfeit research, 70, 72

covert participant, 165, 177

CPC (Carolina Population Center), 51